Richard C. Anderson
University of Illinois at Urbana-Champaign

Gerald W. Faust
Brigham Young University

EDUCATIONAL PSYCHOLOGY

The Science of Instruction and Learning

DODD, MEAD & COMPANY
New York 1974 Toronto

LIBRARY OF CONGRESS CATALOG CARD NUMBER: 79–184191
ISBN NO. 0–396–06545–7

SECOND PRINTING

PRINTED IN THE UNITED STATES OF AMERICA

To Jenny and Merrily

Contents

PART II TEACHING AND THE SCIENCE OF LEARNING

Editors' Introduction

All of us try to teach. Parents, friends, relatives, workers, bosses, school teachers, and students are all busily teaching each other, trying to arrange conditions calculated to modify in some way the beliefs, values, attitudes, expectations, skills, and behaviors of those around them. We are frequently not aware that we are engaged in this activity, and frequently fail to approach it in a systematic and effective way. The classroom is not immune to these deficiencies; and in such instances we are particularly likely to wonder why, and to attempt to discover what kinds of arrangements have a greater probability of success. This is what texts in educational psychology are about.

This book differs from many other texts in educational psychology in that it focuses not so much on the factors that determine learning as upon the conditions of effective teaching. The two approaches have much in common with respect to content, organization, and goals, yet the difference is important. The authors of this book are concerned with the problems of teaching, and with the explication of reasons why teaching in certain ways is more likely to be successful than teaching in other ways.

Appropriately, the first half of the book deals with the technology of teaching. Teaching is treated as a skill—a complex skill, to be sure, but one that is eminently learnable. The second half of the book deals with the science of learning; that is, with the principles and laws of learning adduced from a wide range of investigations, both experimental and naturalistic. Thus the authors follow the precept of one of their own chapters—namely, that the formulation of a conceptual framework broadens the range of situations in which the technology of teaching can be applied. The implications of the studies cited are examined with a congenial but careful eye. We suspect, for instance, that the authors' conclusions about the inadequacies of many conventional grading procedures will be happily endorsed by most students and a substantial number of teachers, if not by a majority of college registrars.

There is a widespread if somewhat inarticulate belief that the skills comprising good teaching can be learned but not taught. If this view be true, we are wasting a huge amount of money, to say nothing of teachers' and students' time and effort, in our attempts to arrange effective teaching-learning conditions in our schools. The authors of this text do not accept this view. They believe that people can be taught to be more effective teachers, and that more is known about the techniques and principles of effective teaching than is customarily put into practice. We agree with them. This book describes and explains many of these techniques and principles, and what is perhaps even more important, encourages, by precept and example, their practical use.

I. E. FARBER
LINDLEY J. STILES

Preface

We believe that learning and instruction lie at the heart of the teacher's and school's task. Our conviction is reflected in this book, which gives selective emphasis—from among the vast array of topics that psychologists have considered and the mountains of facts that psychological research has accumulated—to those topics and facts that bear directly on learning and instruction. This means that a number of issues traditionally given space in educational psychology texts are not treated at all or are mentioned only in passing. But it also means that we have been able to present the field of learning and instruction in enough depth and detail so that the book will be of functional value to the prospective teacher. No other educational psychology text that we know of contains as comprehensive a treatment of such topics, for instance, as task analysis, active student responding, reinforcement, stimulus control, or concept and principle learning.

A practical strategy for instructional development is taught in the first section of the book. It consists of (1) formulating educational goals as behavioral objectives, (2) analyzing the task implied in each objective into component skills and concepts, (3) devising instruction to teach the components and integrate them, (4) teaching, (5) evaluating student performance, and then (6) revising the instruction and reteaching the students who failed to reach every objective the first time. This strategy is, in our opinion, the major achievement of the educational technology movement of the past two decades. Valuable in its own right, it also provides a framework within which the prospective teacher can understand and appreciate psychological research and theory.

Whereas the first section of the book is concerned with a strategy for instructional development, the second deals with the techniques of teaching and design of instructional materials. The three "moves" a teacher or teaching materials can make—presentation, provision for student response, and reinforcement or corrective feedback contingent upon student response—are extensively analyzed.

Throughout the book, our language is behavioral; but we also encourage the prospective teacher to formulate inferences about unobservable, internal processes in the belief that such inferences are not only permissible, but necessary. We insist only that these inferences be anchored in the reality of observable events.

Because there is a great deal of truth in the observation that teachers teach as they were taught, we feel it is especially important for education courses and textbooks to practice what they preach. This we attempt to do by incorporating a variety of instructional techniques within the book itself. These include the following:

Each chapter is introduced by statements of behavioral objectives to guide student study.

Questions are inserted throughout the text to help maintain attention and to facilitate the learning and remembering of important points.

Every chapter contains a test, usually requiring the application of concepts and principles to cases different from those used earlier as illustrations.

Scoring keys for these tests are included within the text to provide immediate feedback and to illustrate systematic procedures for evaluating student performance.

Every chapter ends with a summary which recapitulates the major points.

Two self-instructional programs are bound into the text.

Most concepts are profusely illustrated with research results and segments from model lessons.

In short, we believe that the probability of good teaching will be substantially increased if the prospective teachers who use this book do as it does, as well as do as it says.

RICHARD C. ANDERSON
GERALD W. FAUST

PART

I

THE TECHNOLOGY OF INSTRUCTION

Introduction: A Technology of Instruction Based on a Science of Learning

The aim of educational psychology is to apply psychological concepts and principles to improve educational practice. Psychology is not a unified discipline. Rather, it contains a number of more or less distinct areas dealing with such matters as human development from infancy to old age; differences among individuals in aptitude and temperament; psychophysiology; psycholinguistics; sensation and perception; motivation; thinking; problem-solving; psychopathology; the dynamics of personality; and group processes. Areas in psychology can also be classified according to theoretical schools and preferred research techniques. Psychologists of all kinds are producing mountains of facts and theories. In 1971 alone the *Psychological Abstracts* listed over 22,000 separate books and articles.

Almost all areas represented within psychology as a whole are also represented within educational psychology; and, indeed, there are a great many psychological facts and concepts that have potential relevance for education. This book, however, will give selective emphasis to certain aspects of psychology and ignore or give little attention to others. Working on the assumption that the chief function of the schools is to get students to learn, we will describe the fundamental processes of learning and some of the conditions under which learning is maximized. Our hope is to be able to shed light on those teaching techniques that will be most effective for a given purpose with given students.

There is wide agreement that psychology is the science which ought to underlie educational practice. Perhaps it is for this reason that psychologists generally enjoy high status in educational circles, even though it is sometimes difficult to point to specific instances in which psychology has made an important contribution to instructional practice. Generally, there have been two strategies for applying psychology to education. The first, a tradition of educational research dating back to the turn of the century, has involved direct, experimental investigations of learning in school settings. The second has been to distill from basic psychological research outside the school a set of general propositions about learning and human nature. These propositions have been taught to teachers who, it was hoped, could apply them in the classroom. Neither strategy has worked very well.

Research on Learning in Classroom Settings

The research completed in classrooms has appealed to psychological theory and the findings of basic research to some extent, though the connection has usually been a vague one. Most educational investigators in other words, have been trying to apply the methods of science to obtain dependable answers to practical questions about school learning. Unfortunately, research attempting to answer the practical questions—e.g., whether small classes are better than large classes, whether the discovery method is better than the expository method, whether televised lectures are superior to live lectures, etc.—has been almost uniformly inconclusive. For instance, a review of forty studies comparing "learner-centered" with "teacher-centered" instruction (Anderson, 1959) found that some studies favored learner-centered instruction, some favored teacher-centered instruction, and most showed no difference.

In retrospect, it is clear that practical experiments of this sort were asking unmanageable and sometimes unanswerable questions (Cronbach, 1963; Lumsdaine, 1965). In the abstract and without qualifications, it is very difficult to prove that one *method* of instruction is better than another. About all a single experiment can show is that one particular *lesson* (or set of lessons) is more effective than a comparison lesson. Suppose that a hypothetical experiment shows that students learn more from a series of lectures than from several textbook chapters covering the same material. Obviously one should not conclude from this study that all lectures are better than all textbooks. Nor should one conclude that the difference in achievement is due to the superiority of the spoken word over the printed word. It may have been the case, for example, that the lecturer expressed concepts more clearly or used more informative examples than the textbook, or that the percentage of students who attended class and listened to the lectures was greater than the percentage that actually read the textbook.

Nevertheless, the prevailing assumption has been that it would be possible to demonstrate the general superiority of a method, if not in one experiment, then in several similar experiments. The lessons employed in these experiments therefore were of little interest for their own sake. They were merely the vehicles for evaluating a method of instruction that would supposedly apply broadly to many lessons. Of course, theoretically it was possible that one method of instruction would prove consistently better than others under various conditions, with various subject matters, and with various kinds of students. Unfortunately, though, educators have been unable to discover such a general method. Neither the *discovery method,* the *learner-centered method,* the *Socratic method,* the *project method,* the *laboratory method,* or the *tutorial method* has proved consistently more effective than alternative methods with which they have been compared.

There are many possible explanations for the inconclusive results of studies of teaching methods (Wallen & Travers, 1963). First, there is the obvious point that different methods may work best for different students, different purposes, and under different conditions.

Second, there has been confusion about what is meant by a given method. Various investigators, for example, have defined methods differently. Naturally, variations in method could lead to variable results with students. Furthermore, although most researchers give at least a brief description of what a method is supposed to involve, few of them state specifically what the teachers actually did. Often the same teachers are asked to teach according to two methods; however, it is not certain whether teachers can readily modify their teaching practices to conform to the demands of a method. Perhaps the typical study has shown no difference because teachers were actually teaching about the same way regardless of the methods they were supposed to be using. Indeed, since there has almost always been ambiguity about what teachers in "methods" experiments were actually doing, even the occasional striking result has not been very valuable because of the difficulty of recreating in other classrooms the conditions that produced the result.

Third, each method emphasizes a few processes and features of instruction, but ignores others. In most methods studies important factors have been overlooked.

Finally—and, we believe, most important in the majority of the studies—the teaching methods under consideration have not been very good. Few investigators have taken pains to develop a method until it was demonstrably effective. Frequently, comparisons among methods have been premature. Practically speaking, first it is best to develop a set of techniques and instructional materials that do a good job of teaching specific concepts and skills to a particular kind of student. Later, one may wish to determine whether this set of techniques and materials is better or worse than another set designed for the same purpose. Such a determination would be useful to school administrators, teachers, and students who had to choose among alternative lessons (Anderson, 1969). Still later, one might wish to determine whether similar techniques are effective for teaching different concepts and skills. If this is proved to be true in many cases, one might eventually be in a position to claim that he has a good method.

Application of the Findings of Basic Psychological Research to Learning

The second strategy for applying psychology to education has been to distill a set of general propositions about learning and human nature—Laws of Human Nature—from the papers of theorists and the reports of basic research. According to this strategy, the purpose of educational psychology courses is to explain to prospective teachers the significant general propositions about learning, thinking, problem-solving, personality, behavior, etc. The teacher, in turn, is supposed to apply these principles in the classroom. While we think it desirable that teachers keep abreast of developments in psychology, we doubt very much whether this strategy alone can have much impact on instructional practice.

To be sure, most teachers are perfectly capable of understanding psychology and are eager to take any steps necessary to improve instruction. The difficulties lie in the undeveloped state of psychological knowledge and, more generally, in the uncertain manner in which sciences influence practical fields.

It is often said that there is nothing more practical than a good theory. In our view, a better maxim for the educator would be that there is nothing more theoretically interesting than good practice. One of the obstacles to improving instructional practice has been the overemphasis on very general propositions about learning and teaching. This is reflected, for instance, in the research comparing teaching methods. Consider the statement, "People learn best when they are actively engaged." This has been a recurrent theme in the educational literature of the past thirty years. While the statement is undoubtedly true in some sense, it is so broad that it is empty of functional meaning. A great variety of instructional practices, some effective and many ineffective, could be (and have been) justified with an appeal to this principle. Active responding, for instance, is one of the most prominent features of programmed instruction. To everyone's dismay, however, most of the early programmed instruction studies seemed to show that students who responded actively learned no better than students who were allowed to be passive and merely read the program with blanks filled in. Some argue that this proved that the principle of active engagement was wrong. Others persisted in their faith in active participation. Now, after over a decade of research, we know that under certain specifiable conditions active student responding facilitates learning. And we know that under other conditions active responding makes no difference or may even interfere with learning. (Chapter 6 discusses in detail the conditions under which active student responding promotes learning.)

The main problem in applying psychological principles to education, we believe, is one of engineering. Engineering plays a critical role in the application of scientific principles in any field. Take the development of rockets, for example. One cannot make a rocket or even a blueprint of a rocket solely on the basis of the principles of physics and chemistry. Of course, physical laws serve as guidelines in the design and construction of rockets, but countless decisions must be made for which scientific principles are of little or no help. A rocket, in other words, cannot be built without the use of rule-of-thumb and a good deal of trial-and-error. Good engineering is crucial for the practical application of physical laws.

Engineering is probably of even greater importance in applying psychology to teaching than in applying physics to the design and construction of rockets. There is a high degree of empiricism (Conant, 1952) in the social sciences. This means that psychology and other social sciences have relatively little capacity to generalize to new situations. In practical terms, psychology provides only modest power to predict which teaching procedures and arrangements of instructional materials will maximize student learning. The important word here is "predict." We do not now know enough to have much confidence *before* a lesson is tried that it will work well. The only sure way to determine whether a lesson is effective is to try it.

The difficulty is not that behavioral science has failed to discover anything of general import about processes of learning. The problem is, rather, that processes work somewhat differently in each new situation. Translating general conceptions about learning into workable instructional techniques is difficult for even the most thoroughly trained person. We must hasten to add that these remarks are limited to systematic, "formal" application of psychological principles. Every experienced teacher, of course, has insights into the processes of learning.

Basic educational and psychological research should gradually increase our capacity to specify in advance of tryout the features of instruction which are most likely to facilitate student learning. Gradual progress is being made. However, it would be unrealistic to expect that we shall ever be able to predict effective modes of instruction with more than modest confidence. We have no doubt that instructional development will always depend to some extent on rule-of-thumb, and that a considerable amount of trial-and-error will always be an ingredient of successful instruction.

A Practical Strategy for Developing Effective Instruction

A realistic picture of the status of "hard," research-based knowledge about instructional procedures suggests that a practical strategy for developing effective instruction is needed. What follows is the outline of such a strategy. *(The first section of this book explains the steps in the strategy in more detail and describes the techniques for implementing the strategy.)*

1. The first requirement of a successful instructional strategy is the preparation of a very clear, detailed statement of objectives. A goal that has been expressed thus precisely is called a "behavioral objective." Statements of educational goals should avoid such vague words as *understand, know,* and *appreciate.* Instructional decisions must be based on what students say and do—in other words, their behavior. One can't see a person understand. Therefore, to make appropriate decisions about instruction it is necessary to define the observable student performance which will be taken as evidence for abstract and unobservable states such as understanding. (Chapter 1 considers this topic of behavioral objectives.)
2. Next, analyze the skills and knowledge a student will need to attain the objectives. (This process, called "task analysis," is detailed in Chapter 2.)
3. Another step is to determine the skills and knowledge students already possess. The information, capacities, skills, etc., a student has attained before attempting a given lesson are called "entering behaviors." (They are considered in Chapter 3.)
4. Devise or select instructional materials and techniques to teach the concepts and skills identified in the task analysis.

5. Teach. *(The second section of this book is devoted to a consideration of the techniques and arrangements of materials that are likely to be successful for teaching specific kinds of knowledge, skills, and attitudes.)*
6. After teaching has begun, systematically evaluate student performance to determine whether all students have attained each objective. Evaluation is a pervasive theme in this book. (Chapter 4 is entirely devoted to this topic, and it is considered in several other places as well.)
7. If students fail to master objectives on the first try, re-teach them, reviewing the foregoing steps and revising the instruction so that it will teach better when next used. (This topic is discussed in Chapter 5.)

Almost everyone seriously involved in teaching or producing instructional materials will use a strategy that approximates the one described above. Unfortunately, though, many teachers do not apply the strategy in a thorough and consistent manner. The most important thing that can be said about the strategy is that it works (Glaser, 1964). A process that includes specifying objectives clearly, then trying and revising materials and techniques, usually results in effective instruction (Anderson, 1967, 1969; Tiemann, Paden, & McIntyre, 1966).

The key feature of the strategy is that every aspect of materials and technique and every step in teaching is judged in terms of the results it produces with students. If the strategy is to work well, actual evidence of effectiveness must be obtained. Instructional decisions made on faith or based on impressions are likely to be unreliable. There are no experts whose acumen in judging lesson effectiveness has been established (Ryans, 1960).

Effectiveness cannot be judged in the abstract. The question is: effective for what? Effectiveness is usually equated, and rightly so, with amount learned. But, again, the question is: effectiveness in promoting the learning of what? The answer is in the kinds of skill, knowledge, or attitude named in the objectives. Herein lies the importance of a precise formulation of objectives. Effectiveness cannot be judged unless there is a clear standard against which to compare student performance.

Lessons, units, and curricula must be judged by the extent to which they reach their goals, but effectiveness cannot be the only criterion. Other criteria include the cost of the instruction in student and teacher time, cost in money for materials and equipment, consistency with which results are achieved, attitudes of students and teachers toward the instruction, and any side effects. Stake (1967) has presented a comprehensive discussion of the criteria for evaluating instruction, and we consider the matter further in Chapter 4. The accuracy, up-to-dateness, and "elegance" of the subject matter have been the important criteria for the major curriculum reform projects, such as the Physical Science Study Committee and the Biological Sciences Curriculum Study. Another most important criterion is the worthiness of the goals the instruction aims to reach. As Scriven (1967, p. 52) has noted, "it is obvious that if the goals aren't worth achieving then it is uninteresting how well they were achieved." On the other hand, Anderson (1969, p. 6) has made the point that "a complementary assertion is also true: no matter how worthy the goals, a lesson cannot be valued highly if it is ineffective in reaching these goals."

The Psychology of Learning and the Technology of Instructional Planning and Teaching

The strategy of clearly defining objectives, analyzing the component skills and knowledge implied by the objectives, arranging instruction to teach the components not already possessed by the students, and then trying and revising the instruction until objectives are attained is the backbone of an emerging technology of instruction. Despite our earlier expressions of doubt about previous approaches, there is reason for optimism that the technological strategy here described holds far greater promise for education than older strategies that have been tried and found wanting.

The first reason that the proposed technological strategy warrants more optimism about prospects for effective instruction is its requirement that one keep trying out procedures until one finds what actually proves effective. The second reason is that the technological strategy provides a framework for specific application of psychological principles to instructional practice. Kendler (1966, pp. 174–175) has made this point in the following way:

> As a psychologist, I think I can say with some degree of confidence, that our discipline has been successful in controlling behavior only when we know the kind of behavior we want to encourage. To put it in terms of specific examples, when we train people to be effective pilots or efficient radio code operators, we can develop effective techniques to select and train them. When we try to train people to be adjusted, we run into difficulty because we are uncertain what adjusted behavior is. Psychology often seems ineffective only because we are uncertain about what kind of behavior we want to encourage. Once we are sure what behavior we want to encourage, the chances of developing tech-

niques to get people to behave in this way improve tremendously. The effectiveness of psychology in solving educational problems will be proportional to the precision with which our educational goals are stated.

The approach to instruction that we are calling the "technological strategy" leads one to ask questions about learning and teaching that are manageable. Indeed, competent psychologists and educational researchers are quite sophisticated at discovering limited, conditional generalizations. In brief, we now possess an increasing number of small-scale propositions that have functional utility for the design and implementation of instruction.

In the past, instruction has depended on intuition, common sense, and trial-and-error. The technological strategy makes an important improvement in this process. It represents the change from hit-and-miss trial-and-error to systematic trial-and-error. One need not be a psychologist to use the technological strategy. Whatever insights a person has about learning and instruction, he is bound to teach more effectively if he specifies objectives clearly and does not rest until student performance matches these objectives. Today we possess a few fairly general propositions about learning and, related to these propositions, quite a number of specific techniques that are demonstrably effective under certain conditions. However, there is much more to be learned about learning.

In 1954, in a paper entitled "The Science of Learning and the Art of Teaching," B. F. Skinner, a famous psychologist and perhaps the single most influential figure in the educational technology movement, concluded:

> We are on the threshold of an exciting and revolutionary period, in which the scientific study of man will be put to work in man's best interests. Education must play its part. It must accept the fact that a sweeping revision of educational practices is possible and inevitable. When it has done this, we may look forward with confidence to a school system which is aware of the nature of its tasks, secure in its methods, and generously supported by the informed and effective citizens whom education itself will create (p. 97).

We are not so sure that the millennium is just around the corner. Nonetheless, there has been enough progress in the years since Skinner wrote these words to show that a technology of instruction based on a science of learning can lead to much more effective education than we have today.

Selected Readings

Anderson, R. C., "The Comparative Field Experiment: An Illustration from High School Biology," *Proceedings of the 1968 Invitational Conference on Testing Problems.* Princeton, N.J.: Educational Testing Service, 1969. A practical strategy for instructional development described and illustrated.

Anderson, R. C., Faust, G. W., Roderick, M. C., Cunningham, D. J., & Andre, T., eds., "Section I. Approaches to Instructional Research and Development," *Current Research on Instruction.* Englewood Cliffs, N.J.: Prentice-Hall, 1969. Reprints of four papers containing contrasting views on educational research and development.

Kuhlen, R. G., ed., Section 2. "The Psychology of Learning and Educational Practice." *Studies in Educational Psychology.* Waltham, Mass.: Blaisdell, 1968. Reprints of three papers on the relationship between psychology and education.

Skinner, B. F., *The Technology of Teaching.* New York: Appleton-Century-Croft, 1968. An influential psychologist presents his views on education.

CHAPTER

1

Behavioral Objectives

The identification and proper statement of the educational objectives of a lesson can be the most important step in instructional planning. The teacher preparing a lesson is like a traveler preparing for a long journey. To insure an easy, interesting, and profitable journey the traveler must be sure to decide upon the purposes of his trip before he leaves. He must decide what he wants to see and do or where he wants to go before he is ready to consider other aspects of his trip, such as how he is going to travel or how long he will be gone. Likewise, the teacher must decide where he is going before he attempts to design a lesson. Only after he has decided exactly where he is going is the teacher ready to begin considering how he will get there. Getting a clear statement of educational objectives is the first step in the systematic application of psychology to education.

Understanding the Terms "Understanding" and "Knowing"

The terms "understanding" and "knowing" are key ones in many educational objectives. However, these words are subject to many interpretations. Consider the following statements of objectives. Pay special attention to the underlined words.

> The student should develop a thorough knowledge of American history.
>
> The student should understand the process of mitosis.
>
> The student teacher should recognize the importance of promoting mental health.

Now ask yourself: what is meant by a thorough knowledge of American history, or an understanding of the process of mitosis, or recognizing the importance of promoting mental health? Before you get lost, let us assert that the answer in each case is indeed complex and that the purpose of this entire chapter is to help you interpret and clarify statements such as these. In more precise terms, the objectives of this chapter are to enable you to:

1. list the three characteristics of properly stated objectives.
2. differentiate between properly stated and improperly stated objectives.
3. express educational goals in terms of behaviorally stated objectives.

Let us begin to approach these objectives by considering some apparently simple problems.

Suppose you hear a baby say "Da-Da." How can you tell whether the baby knows the meaning of the word he speaks? One cannot ask a baby what he has on his mind when he says a word. The only way that we have a chance of figuring out whether the baby is referring to his father is by observing carefully the circumstances in which he utters "Da-Da." When the baby first says something like "Da-Da" in his father's presence, for instance, father probably responds with exclamations of pleasure and may fondle the child. As a consequence, the baby says "Da-Da" more frequently in his father's presence. If the child could talk, however, he might say, "Smile at me and tickle my tummy" instead of "Da-Da." Saying "Da-Da" in the father's presence can be taken as a favorable sign, but not as proof that the baby "knows" the meaning of what he says.

Suppose—in a related problem—you want to find out whether a second grader "understands" the concept of addition, so you ask him. Maybe he replies, "It's like two plus two equals four" or "When you add things, you have more." These are not bad answers, and are probably about what could be expected from a second grader. Perhaps you would have been more satisfied with the answer, however, if it closely resembled a definition that a textbook might contain. If so, you will be interested in an experience John Dewey is said to have had (Bloom, et al., 1956, p. 29). Dewey asked a class, "What would you find if you dug a hole in the earth?" Getting no response, he repeated the question; again he got nothing but silence. The teacher chided Dewey, "You're asking the wrong question." Turning to the class, she asked, "What is the state of the center of the earth?" The class replied in unison, "Igneous fusion." The teacher was easily able to elicit the "textbook" response by asking the textbook question; however we seriously doubt whether Dewey or you would be entirely convinced of the students' understanding of the geological composition of the earth.

If a person gives what is taken to be an ideal answer, this may indicate "real understanding" and "depth of knowledge" or only that the person has learned to say certain prescribed words when asked the question. Information about the background of the person is needed to tell which. Spontaneous answers provide a better test of understanding than rehearsed answers. This is not to say that prescribed answers should be avoided in teaching. On the contrary. Getting students to say words in prescribed ways is often an important part of teaching.

Returning again to the concept of addition, suppose that a second grader has given an appropriate verbal explanation of addition. Suppose, further, that he writes the correct sum when presented with any pair of one- or two-digit numbers in the following form:

$$\begin{array}{r} 12 \\ +\ 9 \\ \hline \end{array} \qquad \begin{array}{r} 11 \\ +47 \\ \hline \end{array} \qquad \begin{array}{r} 8 \\ +64 \\ \hline \end{array}$$

Are you now willing to say that the child understands the concept of addition? Your answer depends partly on whether you believe being able to add is the same as understanding the concept of addition. It may happen that a child who can add columns of numbers is unable to write the correct sums when presented with numbers in rows like this:

$$9 + 12 = \underline{\qquad}, \qquad 47 + 11 = \underline{\qquad}.$$

Would you then say the child understands the concept of addition?

Suppose the child were presented with several word problems such as this one: "John went to the candy store and bought three lollypops for $.05 and a bag of candy corn for $.19. How much money did John spend on candy?" It would not be surprising to find that a child could not solve such word problems even though he could tell you that "When you add, you have more" and could write the correct sums when presented with numbers in rows or columns.

Jean Piaget (1965, pp. 406–14), the famous Swiss psychologist, has conducted some important investigations of children's understanding of mathematical concepts. A child of five or six, for instance, can easily be taught to say the numbers from one to ten. If ten objects are laid out in a row he can usually count them correctly. But if the objects are rearranged in a haphazard manner, he can no longer count them with consistent accuracy. Piaget concludes that "Although the child knows the names of the numbers, he has not yet grasped the essential idea of number; namely, that the number of objects in a group remains the same, is 'conserved,' no matter how they are shuffled or arranged." In a similar experiment, a child is given two boxes that are the same size and shape. He is asked to put beads into the two boxes using both hands. Each time he puts a red bead into one box with his right hand, he is, at the same time, to put a blue bead in the other box with his left hand. When the boxes are more or less filled, the child is asked how they compare. Usually, he is sure that both boxes contain the same number of beads. Then the child is asked to pour the blue beads into a container of a different size and shape. "Here again," Piaget states, "we see differences in understanding according to age. The smallest children think that the number has changed: if, for instance, the beads fill the new receptacle to a higher level, they think there are more beads in it than in the original one; if to a lower level, they think there are fewer. But children near the age of seven know that the transfer has not changed the number of beads." Another series of experiments shows that young children do not grasp that the whole is the sum of its parts. Show a child of five or six fifteen flowers, ten marigolds and five snapdragons. He may be able to tell you that there are more marigolds than snapdragons. But ask him if there are more flowers or more marigolds and he very likely will say that there are more marigolds! It seems that the typical child of this age does not understand that flowers includes marigolds and that, therefore, there must be more flowers.

By seven years of age, the age of the average second grader, most children perform successfully on conservation of number problems and part-whole problems. Still, it would be possible for a second grader—or a first grader or even a younger child, for that matter—to perform correctly the so-called addition facts while not knowing that the number of objects in a collection is the same regardless of the spatial arrangement of the objects.

Like trying to figure out whether a baby knows the meaning of "Da-Da," the question of whether a second grader understands the concept of addition can be answered only by seeing whether the child behaves appropriately in a range of circumstances that involve, or can involve, addition concepts. We can confront the child with questions, test situations, and problems. We cannot look into his head to see what he is thinking. As in the case of the baby saying "Da-Da," the more one knows about the previous experience of the child the better able one is to evaluate what one sees and hears. While spontaneous answers and performance on novel problems should be given greater weight, it is not possible to tell whether an answer is spontaneous or a problem is novel without knowing whether the child has been presented with the identical problem previously.

The safest course is to regard the different kinds of understanding of a concept as relatively independent of one another. About half a dozen tests for an understanding of the concept of addition were mentioned in the above discussion, for example. As was emphasized, the fact that a child can give a passable verbal explanation of addition does not guarantee that he can add columns of numbers. The demonstration that he can answer correctly questions about the relationship of a whole to its parts does not prove that he can solve word problems involving addition. Nor does the child's knowing the addition facts imply that he will believe that changes in the arrangement of a collection of objects do not change the number of objects.

People learn to generalize from a few observations. In ordinary affairs such generalization is a necessary evil, for we seldom have the time, the skill, or the opportunity for a thorough investigation. If a person believes that a doctor has successfully treated one or two illnesses, the person is inclined to believe that the doctor can successfully treat other illnesses as well. This is not an irrational belief. Predictions such as this are useful. Such implicit reasoning can, however, have harmful consequences when applied to educational objectives. For instructional purposes, a teacher may tacitly restrict addition to summing columns of numbers, with the expectation that the children will also learn other aspects of addition and related concepts. This expectation is not usually based upon a careful analysis of the skills involved. Instead it is often an implicit, unthinking generalization. If the teacher were to explain his expectation in words, he might say, "It has been my experience that when people perform successfully on one task, I can usually assume that they will do well on related tasks." This kind of assumption is unwarranted if, in fact, the new tasks entail new procedures or unfamiliar components. It is not safe to assume that other concepts will be acquired automatically through some inner necessity.

It should not be imagined that the conclusions that have been reached apply only to infants and children. They also apply to adolescents and adults. A professor of history might teach his students the pendulum theory of social change, which asserts, in part, that following a period of change there will be a period of reaction that is equal in magnitude to the magnitude of the change. Thus, a violent revolution will be followed by a violent reaction, a temperate change by a mild reaction. Suppose the professor took upon himself the job of evaluating whether his students "really understand" the pendulum theory of social change. He might begin by asking students to explain the theory. Some students might give answers that sound as though they came verbatim from lecture notes or a textbook. Do these students "really" understand? To find out, he might ask them further questions: "Why is this called the *pendulum* theory?" "What do you mean by the 'magnitude of the reaction?' " One would expect that a person who "really understands" the pendulum theory of social change would be able to apply the theory to explain and predict. If the professor asks a student to tell how the theory applies to an historical episode and the student is unable to do so even though he gave an adequate verbal explanation of the theory, the professor then knows something about the limits of the student's understanding.

Consider now another, related situation, perhaps an education course. A professor of education describes a school district that has been slow to introduce modern innovations. A new, forward-looking superintendent of schools is hired. He introduces modern curricula in mathematics, the sciences, and social studies; language laboratories; nongraded grouping; merit pay raises for teachers; and does away with report cards. The question is: "What will happen in this school district?" The pendulum theory of social change predicts a reaction—opposition from teachers or the community, or both—and students who really understand the theory should make such a prediction. Suppose they do. Is it enough that students who studied the theory simply *believe* that the superintendent will encounter opposition? Or is it required that students *explicitly apply* the theory—that is, say to themselves or out loud, that "according to the pendulum theory of social change there will be a severe reaction since the superintendent has introduced drastic changes into the school district"?

It may happen that the predictions of students who studied the pendulum theory are no different from those of other students. Shall we then say that they do not really understand the theory? It could be argued that they understand the theory all right, but that it just didn't occur to them to apply it in the case of the innovations of a school superintendent. This case is precisely like that of the second grader presented with a word problem in addition. Some persons might say that the child understands addition but that he just didn't "think of" adding the price of the lollypops to the price of the candy corn to get the total cost of John's candy. How one evaluates this argument depends upon how one interprets "understanding." Usually in education the term "understanding" is intended in a broad sense. If it is said that a person "understands" a concept, the implication is that he manifests his understanding in all—or at least a wide range of—the cases to which the concept is relevant. In the case of the second grader and the word problem, surely most people would agree that the child does not really understand addition unless he can solve problems such as the one included for illustration. Perhaps the case of the pendulum theory and the school superintendent is debatable. The general rule is, nonetheless, clearly proper.

The test for whether a person—child or adult—"knows" or "understands" a concept is whether he talks or acts appropriately. Looking into a person's head is impossible. To find out whether a person understands, one must listen to him talk or watch him act, either when confronted with questions and test situations or when circumstances arise in the natural course of events. What behavior is appropriate depends upon the concept. Understanding a concept is not a simple matter. Those concepts with which schools are concerned usually involve many aspects. In order to be sure how much a person understands, the wisest policy is to check all of the aspects of the concept.

On the Proper Statement of Educational Objectives

In deciding what is required to evaluate a person's understanding you are, in essence, identifying those tests which you want students to pass after instruction. At the same time you are pinpointing the skills and knowledge which are entailed in an understanding. Teaching these is your educational goal. All of the preceding discussion has been preparation for facing the issue of the proper form for statements of educational objectives.

The inclination is simply to say that the instructional objective is to teach the concept, or to teach an understanding of the concept. For instance, one objective of primary-school education could be phrased, "to teach an understanding of addition." An important objection to such a statement is that it is too general. The concept of addition involves many things. An understanding of addition could be broken down into an understanding of part-whole relationships, a knowledge of the sums of columns and rows of numbers, an understanding of word problems involving addition, and so on.

Breaking down the objective into more specific statements removes some of the vagueness. Nonetheless, a serious objection remains. The problem, again, is with the word "understand" itself. You can listen to a person talk. You can watch a person act. You cannot hear or see a person understand. An objective, therefore, that contains a word such as "understanding" is intrinsically vague. It is for this reason that objectives are stated behaviorally, in terms of what the student is to do or say.

A behavioral objective indicates what the student should be able to do or say when he has finished the lesson or, over the long run, when he has completed his education. The main verb in a behavioral objective is *active.* If a child knows the sum of any pair of one- or two-digit numbers, then he should be able to *compute* these sums or, better said yet, he should be able to *write* or *say* the correct sum when presented with any of the pairs of numbers. The latter expression captures a second quality of the well-formed behavioral objective. Insofar as possible, the behavioral objective specifies an action that is *observable.* The verb "compute" is active; however, the activity of computing may or may not be observable. A child could think the sums to himself. A teacher couldn't tell whether the child had computed the sums correctly unless he could observe the child say the sums or look at sums the child had written.

People often have considerable difficulty learning to state objectives behaviorally. Part of the reason for the difficulty can be found in language habits. People have a lot of practice, formal and informal, in discussing human affairs in the language of passive, unobservable mental states. Talk in behavioral terms is relatively foreign. Like Gertrude Stein who felt that ultimately all one could say is that "A rose is a rose is a rose," many persons believe there is nothing more to say than that "understanding is understanding is understanding." Teachers often feel that the heart of what they are trying to say evaporates when translated into the specifics of what the student should do or say. However, sometimes it is good that the original expression evaporates under examination, for not infrequently mental-state expressions of objectives contain little or no substance. Just about anyone can assert that "the goal is to teach a thorough understanding of the basic concepts of mathematics." Though the assertion has a profound ring, it is empty unless it can be given flesh and blood. The person who is unable to spell out "a thorough understanding" in behavioral terms must face the fact that he is probably unprepared to plan instruction, teach, or evaluate the effects of instruction.

Finally, it must be remembered that the philosophy behind behavioral objectives is student-centered. The idea is that the quality of instruction should be evaluated in terms of its effect on the learner (Popham, 1970). Objectives are stated in terms of what the *student* will be able to do after instruction rather than in terms of what the teacher will do during instruction. That is, the focus is on the student and his ability to perform rather than on the content or the technique of the teacher. Throughout the steps in instructional planning and, indeed, throughout the entire instructional process, instructional objectives are used to help the student learn (Kapfer, 1970). Behavioral objectives continually refocus the teacher's attention on his reason for being in the classroom—the student.

How to Express Educational Goals as Behavioral Objectives

This section is a program. When you complete the program you should be able to:

1. state in writing the characteristics of a well-stated behavioral objective.
2. describe the shortcomings of educational objectives presented to you.
3. rewrite in the form of behavioral objectives educational goals that are presented to you.
4. construct behavioral objectives for educational areas of interest to you.

The program consists of sentences with blanks in them. Fill in each blank in the way that you feel best completes the sentence. Then, turn the page to check your answer. Notice that you are to go all the way through the programmed section looking first only at the tops of the pages. Then return to the beginning and go through the next section, following the numbers in order until the entire program is completed.

Please *write* an answer to each item or frame before turning the page. Sometimes a single word is required, sometimes a phrase, or even a sentence or two. Optional or alternative words are indicated along with the authors' preferred answer.

PROGRAM I

1

If it is true that a person "knows how to swim" and he gets into the water, he should actually be able to swim. Likewise, when presented with a paragraph from a suitable book, a person who "knows how to read" should ______________________.

Turn to page **24**

---

ans. 20

behavioral objectives

21

"When presented with long-division problems involving whole-number divisors and no remainders, the fifth grader should correctly calculate the quotient in at least 95% of the problems."

Which phrase states the *standard* of performance?

(a) long division problems involving whole-number divisors and no remainders
(b) correctly . . . at least 95% of the problems

Turn to page **24**

---

ans. 40

There are a number of satisfactory renderings of the objective. Here is one:

The student should be able to answer correctly questions about what he reads.

41

Course descriptions should be distinguished from behavioral

______________________.

Turn to page **24**

ans. 2

does (or says)

3

Taking a philosophy examination without hidden notes or other aids is one of the *conditions* that a professor of philosophy would insist upon before agreeing that the results of the test show that a student ____________ philosophy.

Turn to page **28**

ans. 22

behavior (action)

23

". . . the child should be able to read correctly any printed material, provided its difficulty level does not exceed that of a third-grade primer."

Underline the phrase that describes a *condition* of the child's reading performance.

Turn to page **28**

ans. 42

course description

Note: It is *not* a behavioral objective since it describes what topics the course covers and not what the desired behavioral outcomes of the course are.

43

____

____

specify desired terminal behavior.

Turn to page **28**

ans. 10

definition

11

A complete behavioral definition states (a) ____________________, under specified (b) ____________, according to a certain (c) ____________________.

Turn to page **25**

ans. 30

condition (proviso, restriction)

31

The principal verb in a behavioral objective should

____________________________________.

Turn to page **25**

ans. 49

The statement tells what the teacher will do ("acquaint . . . participants") rather than what the students should be able to do. The statement is really a course description, and not a very clear one at that, since it leaves the reader in the dark about the nature of the "principles" and "theories" to be presented.

Turn to page **25**

ans. 1

In your own words:

be able to read the paragraph.

2

The test for deciding whether a person "knows" how to do something is whether under the proper conditions he ______ the appropriate something.

Turn to page **26**

ans. 21

(b)

22

The key word in a behavioral objective is the main verb, which should specify some active, observable ______________ on the part of the student.

Turn to page **26**

ans. 41

objectives

42

"This course covers topics such as atomic and molecular structure, properties and thermodynamics of gases, liquids, crystals, phase equilibria, surface chemistry, and chemical kinetics."

The preceding statement is a

______________________________.

Turn to page **26**

ans. 11

(a) **what the person is to do or say (behavior, actions)**
(b) **conditions**
(c) **(minimum) standard (of performance)**

12

When an educational objective is defined in terms of what the student should be able to ______, the statement is called a *behavioral objective.*

Turn to page **27**

ans. 31

In your own words:

specify a kind of active, observable behavior on the part of the student.

32

Typewriting performance can be described in specific numerical terms, such as words typed per minute, number of errors per page. In many other areas, such as the fluency with which a child reads out loud, it is (a) ____________ (more, less) difficult to be specific about characteristics of performance. In the preceding statement, (b) ____________ refers to reading (or speaking) at an appropriate rate of speed with an acceptably small number of hesitations and misarticulations.

Turn to page **27**

50

How do the following three objectives differ from one another?

(a) "The student should be able to solve quadratic equations."
(b) "The student should be able to solve quadratic equations containing one unknown."
(c) "The student should be able to solve quadratic equations containing one unknown, when the equations are presented in canonical form, without consulting the teacher or a reference book. The student should solve equations involving small integer roots ($X < 10$) with paper and pencil only. A slide rule or tables may be employed otherwise."

Turn to page **27**

ans. 12

do (or say)

13

A word or phrase capable of many interpretations is called "vague" or even "empty." To avoid the vagueness in such terms as "comprehending," "understanding," and "knowing," the words may be restated in a ____________________ (two words) that tells what the person who understands can do or say.

Turn to page **29**

---

ans. 32

(a) more
(b) fluency

33

It would be most elegant to define the fluency with which children read out loud in terms of number of words per minute, number and length of hesitations, and percent misarticulations. In practice, it is often necessary to set the ________________ of performance in terms of what an expert observer, like a teacher, believes is adequate fluency.

Turn to page **29**

---

ans. 50

The objectives, all of which are behavioral, are increasingly specific about the conditions of performance.

51

"The student should be able to choreograph an original dance composition that makes effective use of a variety of expressive movements."

Underline the phrase that refers to a *standard* of performance.

Turn to page **29**

ans. 3

knows (understands, comprehends)

4

If a child can balance his bicycle without training wheels or without having his father run alongside holding the seat, then you would probably be willing to say that he "knows how" to ride. The child's balancing without help is a necessary ____________ for saying that he can ride his bicycle.

Turn to page **30**

ans. 23

"provided its difficulty level does not exceed that of a third-grade primer" ("any printed material" is also part of the condition)

24

The behavioral objective states what the student *should* do. What the student *actually* does at the end of a lesson is called "terminal ____________."

Turn to page **30**

ans. 43

Behavioral objectives

44

"The student should be able to compute accurately simple descriptive statistics such as the mean, standard deviation, and the product-moment correlation coefficient without the aid of reference books or notes."

Underline phrase which specifies a *condition* of performance.

Turn to page **30**

ans. 13

behavioral definition

14

As it stands, the phrase "an understanding of citizenship in a democracy" has ______________ interpretations, and, therefore, the phrase may be called "vague" or "empty."

Turn to page **31**

---

ans. 33

standard

34

In each of the following pairs, indicate which phrase most nearly resembles a section from a well-formed behavioral objective.

(1a) knows the difference between verbs and nouns
(1b) can name the verbs and nouns in sentences presented to him

(2a) can say when asked that a noun is the name of a person, place, or thing
(2b) is aware that a noun is the name of a person, place, or thing

(3a) understands the axioms and major theorems of Euclidian geometry
(3b) can write valid proofs containing the axioms and major theorems of Euclidian geometry

Turn to page **31**

---

ans. 51

"makes effective use of a variety of expressive movements" (The word "original" also refers to a standard of performance.)

52

"When he finishes the eighth grade the student should be able to read two hundred words per minute."

Indicate the chief way in which this objective could be improved.

Turn to page **31**

ans. 4

condition (criterion, piece of evidence, step)

5

In general, to assert that a person knows something is to assert that he can ______ or say something under certain conditions.

Turn to page **32**

ans. 24

behavior

25

By comparing ________________ behavior—what the child actually can do at the end of a lesson—with the desired ________________ behavior or the behavioral objectives for the lesson, it is possible to judge the degree of success the lesson had.

Turn to page **32**

ans. 44

"without the aid of reference books or notes"

45

Describe the *principle* difficulty with the following objective:

"The third objective is to provide them [students] with criteria for judging the quality of programmed material."

Turn to page **32**

ans. 14

many

15

A ______________________ objective expresses an educational goal in terms of what the student should be able to do or say when he completes a lesson or course.

Turn to page **33**

---

ans. 34

(1b)
(2a)
(3b)

35

When presented with a list of Supreme Court cases, the student who has completed the Problems of American Democracy course should be able to identify within five minutes all the cases that involve the rights of minority groups.

Which phrase specifies a *condition* of performance?

(a) "when presented with a list . . ."
(b) "to identify within five minutes . . . minority groups"

Turn to page **33**

---

ans. 52

The objective could be improved by stating the conditions of performance, such as the difficulty level of the reading material.

53

Phrases in a behavioral objective referring to the characteristics of acceptable performance, to the accuracy, to the speed, or to the criteria by which performance will be evaluated, describe the

______________________________.

Turn to page **33**

ans. 5

do

6

One of the __________ that you probably would want to insist upon before agreeing that what a person was doing should be called swimming, is that the person propel himself through the water without hanging on to a raft, or the like.

Turn to page **34**

---

ans. 25

terminal, terminal

26

The description of the desired terminal behavior should include a statement of what the person says or does, a statement of the level or standard of performance, and a statement of the

__________________________.

Turn to page **34**

---

ans. 45

The main problem is that the statement indicates one of the things the teacher or book will do ("provide criteria . . .") rather than the things the student will be able to do. The statement is actually a course description instead of an objective.

Turn to page **34**

ans. 15

behavioral

16

Is the following statement a behavioral objective?
"The purpose of the senior-year [American history] course is to cover the period from the Civil War to the present."

Turn to page **35**

---

ans. 35

(a)

36

One can judge the degree of success a lesson has had by comparing the student's (a) ____________ behavior with the behavioral (b) ____________.

Turn to page **35**

---

ans. 53

standard of performance

54

The things a student can do and say under specified conditions at the beginning of instruction comprise his ____________.

Turn to page **35**

ans. 6

conditions (criteria)

7

In a race such as the 100-yard dash the standard of performance is the ____________ it takes the runner to cover the 100 yards.

Turn to page **36** 〉

---

ans. 26

conditions of performance

27

Behavioral objectives are actually no more than statements of desired terminal ____________________.

Turn to page **36** 〉

46

An objective can be stated in behavioral terms and still be ambiguous. A well-written behavioral objective describes the conditions under which the student is to demonstrate achievement of the objective and also indicates clearly the level or ____________________ of performance that is required.

Turn to page **36** 〉

ans. 16

No. It does not indicate what the student should be able to do when he completes the course.

17

Consider this objective.

"By the time he completes the third grade, the child should be able to read correctly any printed material, provided its difficulty level does not exceed that of a third-grade primer."

The word "correctly" refers to the ____________________ of performance.

Turn to page **37**

---

ans. 36

(a) terminal
(b) objective

37

Though you have not seen the term before, you can probably guess that *entering behavior* refers to

____

at the beginning of instruction.

Turn to page **37**

---

ans. 54

entering behavior

55

When the goal in question is a good style of writing, phrases in the objective mentioning such characteristics of good writing as "apt choice of words," "clear organization," and "varied sentence structure" refer to

______________________________.

Turn to page **37**

ans. 7

time

8

If you saw a child flailing the water ineptly you might believe that the child's performance did not deserve the name "swimming." If such were the case, you would be tacitly maintaining that a person cannot be said to swim unless what he does in the water meets a minimum __________ of performance.

Turn to page **38**

---

ans. 27

behavior

28

After a beginning course, a typing speed of 50 words per minute might be an acceptable __________ of performance.

Turn to page **38**

---

ans. 46

standard

47

Phrases such as "provided the keys are blank," "without the aid of reference books," "any printed material with a difficulty level not exceeding that of the daily newspaper" clarify an objective by specifying the __________ of performance.

Turn to page **38**

ans. 17

standard

Note: Although "correctly" refers to the *standard* of performance, it does not describe the standard.

18

Objectives often include the phrases "material to be covered" or "topics to be considered." Surely the purpose of instruction is *not* to cover the material, but rather for students to learn.

"Covering the material" is a ____________ to an end, rather than the end itself.

Turn to page **39**

---

ans. 37

In your own words:

the things the student can do or say (behavior)

38

One can think of the behavioral objective as the *desired* ____________ behavior.

Turn to page **39**

---

ans. 55

standard of performance

56

"The student teacher should recognize the importance of promoting mental health."

Describe the faults, if any, of this objective.

Turn to page **39**

ans. 8

standard (criterion)

9

If a person knows something, then under certain (a) ______________ he can (b) ______________ something that meets a (c) ______________ of performance.

Turn to page **40**

ans. 28

(minimum) standard

29

As far as accuracy is concerned, a reasonable

____

might be no more than three errors per page after an introductory typing course.

Turn to page **40**

ans. 47

conditions

48

The description "given a ring stand, clamp, Bunsen burner, and the unidentified solution" specifies the conditions of performance in ______________ (more, less) detail than the description "given the unidentified solution and the necessary equipment."

Turn to page **40**

ans. 18

means

19

A complete behavioral objective indicates not only what the student should be able to do and say but also the minimum acceptable standard of performance and

________________________________.

Turn to page **41**

ans. 38

terminal

39

"The most important goal is that the student learn to comprehend what he reads."

Is this a behavioral objective?

Turn to page **41**

ans. 56

First, "recognizing the importance" is not active, observable behavior. In fact, this expression is quite obscure, and it is difficult to decide what is intended. Second, no conditions of performance are indicated. Third, no standard or criterion of performance is suggested. In short, this goal is badly stated.

57

"We want to give the children a thorough understanding of how to tell time."

Rewrite this objective in behavioral form.

Turn to page **41**

ans. 9

(a) conditions
(b) do or say
(c) standard (minimum standard)

10

A definition is a statement that gives the meaning of a word or group of words. You may be able to guess that a "behavioral ____________" of knowing is a statement of what the person who knows can do or say.

Turn to page **23**

ans. 29

(minimum) standard (of performance)

30

A ________________ under which typing performance might be evaluated could be that the typewriter have blank keys.

Turn to page **23**

ans. 48

more

49

What is wrong with the following objective?

"It is the objective of the institute to acquaint a selected group of participants with the principles and underlying theories of modern linguistics."

Turn to page **23**

ans. 19

In your own words:

the <u>conditions</u> under which the student will act.

20

Some of the vagueness in such terms as "appreciating," "knowing," and "understanding" can be eliminated by stating educational goals in the form of

________________________________.

Turn to page **22**

---

ans. 39

No.

Note: Comprehension is not active, *observable* behavior.

40

Rewrite the following statement to make it into a behavioral objective:

"The goal is that the child learn to read with comprehension."

Turn to page **22**

---

ans. 57

There are a number of acceptable forms. Here is one:

When shown any setting of the hands on a wall clock or wrist watch, the child should always be able to report the time accurately.

END OF PROGRAM

Turn to page **42**

Putting the Behavioral Objective in Perspective

In the preceding pages you have learned how to state specific behavioral objectives. You now know that a properly stated objective contains a description of what the student must be able to do or say after instruction. It also contains a statement of the conditions under which the student will demonstrate his ability and a standard of acceptable performance. However, despite all of the attention which this chapter has given to the *form* in which educational objectives should be stated, the *content* and *completeness* of statements of educational goals are even more important.

A statement of a single behavioral objective seldom stands alone. Rather, a behaviorally stated objective is usually only one link in a long chain of objectives that describe the desired outcomes of an hour, day, unit, or course of instruction. Because objectives may be used to describe desired outcomes of variously sized units of instruction, objectives have different degrees of generality and ultimate importance. Consider the following objectives for a course in first aid.

1. Given a patient who is bleeding externally, the student will be able to stop the bleeding as quickly as possible.
2. Given instances of external bleeding, the student will correctly identify all those which are arterial.
3. The student will be able to list the characteristics of arterial bleeding as distinguished from nonarterial bleeding.

Notice that although these objectives are all stated in behavioral terms, they are not all stated at the same level. Objective 2 is what we call an *enabling objective* (or subobjective) of objective 1; that is, the behavior described in objective 2 is a component (or subtask) of the behavior described in objective 1. Likewise, objective 3 is an enabling objective for objective 2. In other words, in order to bring students to the level of performance required by objective 1, the teacher must first reach objective 3 and then objective 2. Because there often is such a hierarchy of objectives, major objectives which describe desired terminal performances (like objective 1 above) are best broken down into enabling objectives for purposes of planning instruction.

One other point should be made with respect to the three first-aid objectives just cited. You will note that objectives 1 and 2 state desired terminal performances which most likely will not be evaluated as stated.

Few first-aid instructors are going to confront students with patients actually bleeding, even though the objective is to enable students to perform under such conditions. The instructor must keep his ultimate objective (emergency medical treatment) in mind while evaluating student performance under less demanding circumstances. In other words, the instructor must translate job performance (stopping bleeding) into test performance (describing procedures, performing procedures on a dummy, etc.). This task is one with which the football coach and the shop teacher are often confronted. In cases in which desired terminal performances cannot be evaluated directly, the instructor should therefore prepare ultimate performance objectives as well as immediate instructional objectives. Of course, instructional objectives should match ultimate objectives as closely as possible.

As the scope of objectives increases the importance of breaking down the objective for purposes of educational planning also increases. Unfortunately, within most educational systems, as the amount of instruction covered by the objective increases, the generality, ambiguity, and nonbehavioral flavor of the objective also increases. General statements of goals have an established place in education. They are a primary means by which school superintendents, school boards, principals, and parents communicate their desires and expectations. However, if these goals are to be properly understood, sought, and achieved the teacher should first translate them into broad behavioral objectives and then analyze those objectives in order to identify enabling objectives.

Let us assume, for example, that your school board decides that graduates of your elementary school should "know something about geometry." This may be interpreted by the principal to mean that "students should receive some instruction in geometry," and he may even give further guidance by encouraging his teachers to develop a unit of instruction on the subject. It is at about this point that we should hope that objectives will begin to be stated in terms of student outcomes.

These student outcomes may at first be stated in nonbehavioral terms, such as "the student will develop an understanding of the concepts of circles, angles, and parallel lines." However, the educational planner at the action level (i.e., the person who is developing and presenting the instruction) should take it upon himself to identify specifically the various behaviors that will be accepted as evidence for the proposed understanding and knowledge. These behaviors will then become the instructional objectives for the lesson or unit.

The following are but a few of the possible objectives for a unit of elementary-school instruction intended to give students an "understanding of the concepts of circles."

1. Given circles with diameters between 1 and 10 inches (diameters in even inches only) and given a 12-inch ruler, the student should be able to:

    a. measure and correctly report the diameter of these circles.
    b. compute each radius correct to the nearest ½ inch.
    c. compute each circumference correct to the nearest hundredth inch.

2. The student should be able to compute exactly each of the three measures of a circle (radius, diameter, and circumference) given any of the remaining measures of that same circle. The student should use pi = 3.14 in his computation (all dimensions supplied to him will be in even inches, feet, yards or miles).

3. The student should be able to state which of any group of geometrical figures is a circle. (Ellipses presented to the student will have a ratio of height to width or width to height of no less than 1.5.)

However, to attain these objectives, some other enabling objectives must first be reached. For example, the objectives:

4. Given lines varying in even inches from 1 to 10 inches in length and given a 12-inch ruler, the student should be able to measure each line and report its length correctly.

5. The student should be able to correctly point out and label each of the three measures of a circle (radius, diameter, circumference), given a drawing of a circle which graphically indicates these three measures.

6. The student should be able to state the numerical value of pi correct to hundredths (i.e., pi = 3.14).

As we indicated, there are other objectives which could be stated for this unit on circles. You might even want to try to list some of them. However, this small sample should be sufficient to indicate that the process of interpreting broad, ambiguously stated educational goals is one of clarifying desired terminal behavior, and breaking down broad statements of objectives into hierarchies of behaviorally stated objectives.

Notice that as the instructional planner breaks down objectives into more basic objectives he will eventually come to the point at which the behavior described in the objective is already a part of the student's behavioral repertoire. It is at this point, and only at this point, that the teacher may stop analyzing the objective into component, enabling tasks.

Getting a clear picture of the educational goals for a lesson involves more than the mere use of action verbs and the specification of conditions and standards. In addition to a consideration of what it is hoped the student will be able to do after instruction, instructional planning requires the analysis of objectives into component tasks (Chapter 2), each of which involves enabling objectives and an appraisal of the skills and concepts the student already possesses (Chapter 3).

The Promise of Behavioral Objectives

Test and measurement specialists were the first to emphasize the importance of behavioral objectives, not surprisingly; for those who evaluate instruction inevitably confront the fact that you can only measure differences in observable behavior. Thus, about 1950 a group of evaluation experts held a series of conferences culminating in the publication of *The Taxonomy of Educational Objectives* (Bloom, 1956). Though the language fell short of being behavioral, this book did have the favorable effect of bringing attention to the clear statement of educational goals. In another important related trend, military psychologists —employed by the Federal government, on a fairly large scale since World War II, to develop procedures for efficiently training military personnel—took analyzing goals in behavioral language as a prominent theme (Glaser, 1964). Finally, in the mid-1950's, programmed instruction began to emerge. Persons involved in programmed instruction, a number of whom have done training research for the armed forces, have been typically very insistent upon the importance of stating objectives in behavioral terms. Test and measurement specialists, who contend that behavioral objectives are required to properly *evaluate* instruction, are joined by those in programmed instruction, who contend that behavioral objectives are also necessary to *teach* or even to *plan* instruction.

Experiments performed at the University of California, Los Angeles, have demonstrated the instructional value of behavioral objectives. In one study, for example, McNeil (1967) investigated the effects of requiring statements of behavioral objectives from student teachers.

The student teachers taught in secondary schools for a period of two days as part of an exercise in a Principles of Instruction course. All were told that their teaching performance would be evaluated by their supervising teachers in terms of:

1. success in teaching as evidenced by pupil achievement.

2. poise and personality.
3. application of principles of learning taught in the course on Principles of Instruction.

The two groups differed only in that they received different instructions on how to prepare for the two-day teaching experience. Student teachers who were randomly assigned to the experimental group were told to reach an agreement with their supervising teachers as to the objectives for each of their lessons. The supervising teachers were asked to agree that the performance of student teachers would be evaluated in terms of how well the agreed-upon objectives were attained. In contrast, student teachers in the control group were told to meet with their supervising teachers in order to "familiarize themselves with the on-going activities of the class," and to reach agreement on the contents of lesson plans to be used by the student teachers.

After instruction, significantly more of the student teachers in the experimental group were rated by their supervising teachers as having "achieved success in teaching as evidenced by pupil achievement." In addition, student teachers in the experimental group received significantly better ratings on their ability to apply principles of learning than did student teachers in the control group.

A second study by McNeil (1967) makes an even more impressive case for the educational value of behavioral objectives. In this study McNeil again compared the teaching effectiveness of two groups of student teachers. However, this time the teachers spent more time in the classroom, and teaching effectiveness was measured directly by assessing what pupils had learned from the instruction.

In the study McNeil told a random half of a group of 44 college undergraduates preparing to be elementary-school teachers that "their grade [in student teaching] would depend upon their ability to select appropriate behavioral changes to be sought in the learner" in the area of punctuation and then to produce these changes. The remaining student teachers were instructed to prepare and submit detailed lesson plans and were told that they would be judged on their ability to "follow the course of study" and their ability to "use the materials authorized for the class" in the area of punctuation.

Two tests were used to evaluate the performance of the elementary-school pupils taught by the student teachers. The first test was a standard printed composition that contained 67 errors in punctuation. The pupil's task was to identify and correct the errors. The second test was an open-ended "creative writing" exercise, in which students were read the beginning of a story and asked to supply the ending. This exercise was scored for number of punctuation errors. Pupils taught by teachers who prepared behavioral objectives performed substantially better on both tests, despite the fact that both groups of student teachers spent the same amount of time teaching punctuation. The experiment indicates that students learn more when taught by teachers who define and then try to reach behavioral objectives.

There are several reasons why behavioral objectives make teachers more effective. The teacher knows exactly where he is going and he knows the route he is taking. Moreover, when a complete set of behavioral objectives, including enabling objectives, is prepared, the teacher is less likely to overlook a component which is vital if students are to master the ultimate objective. Behavioral objectives also provide detailed criteria against which instruction, as well as terminal performance, can be evaluated. In addition, a complete statement of objectives pinpoints intermediate behaviors that the teacher can check during instruction. Behavioral objectives therefore provide the framework for an on-going system of instructional quality control. If student performance is evaluated in terms of behavioral objectives throughout a course of study, those students who are not progressing or who have not reached the desired level of performance can be given additional instruction. Similarly, on-going evaluation in terms of behavioral objectives allows teachers to make accurate decisions as to when an objective has been reached and it is desirable to move on to another.

In addition to their value to the teacher in instructional planning, evaluation, and decision making, behavioral objectives can directly assist the student. When given to mature students, clear statements of desired terminal performance serve as guides to study. They indicate to the student exactly what he is expected to get from instruction. And they provide him with criteria to evaluate his own progress.

Our belief in the practice of providing students with statements of objectives is so strong that we have prepared statements of our objectives for each chapter of this book. You will note that the objectives stated at the beginning of this and other chapters are not usually as complete as those discussed in this chapter. The reason for this will become clear as you proceed, but for the present let us affirm that to be useful to students, objectives should indicate what students will be required to say or do after instruction. They should be stated in enough detail so as to guide a student's study and provide a basis for his own evaluation of his progress. However, we feel lists of objectives provided to students (as contrasted to those a teacher prepares for his own use) should not be so long that they appear unattainable or are ignored, and they should also not be so detailed that they restrict the student's attention during instruction.

Reservations About Behavioral Objectives

Those involved in the curriculum reform movement in mathematics, the sciences, and other areas sometimes have been suspicious of heavy emphasis on behavioral objectives (Ebel, 1970). Atkin (1963) has presented some arguments that reflect the views of many of those associated with course-content improvement projects. He agrees that intangible objectives, ultimately speaking, are unsatisfactory. However, his first reservation is that an emphasis on behavioral objectives may have a very conservative effect. The tendency under such an emphasis could be to shift attention toward easily measured and observed behavior, behavior that can be shown to change during short periods of time, resulting in an emphasis on such skills as adding, typing, and spelling—to the neglect of such skills as those necessary in the "process of scientific inquiry." Atkin (1963, p. 131) has stated:

> In most of the curriculum projects, there is a suspicion that rather higher order intellectual abilities than those readily observable and measurable in terms of immediate behavioral change are achieved, or at least sought. There is the fear that a preoccupation with short-term goals may obscure the long-term ones.
>
> More profoundly, it is suspected that the ability of certain senior scientists radically to restructure their disciplines in a manner that is aesthetically as well as intellectually pleasing and potent has outdistanced the ability of many educational evaluators to understand completely the import of this restructuring for purposes of curriculum. "Define your objectives," says an evaluator, "and I will help you to determine your degree of success." But there is a real danger that the objectives are not understood even when enunciated, or at least their implications not appreciated. Clever men for centuries have been helping to build our conception of science. There is some danger of achieving less than the possible in curriculum revision if insights into science must be subordinated to the state of development of the field of educational evaluation.

Atkin has identified a problem. Note that the problem does not lie in the conception of a behavioral objective but rather in the elusive nature of the vital "higher order intellectual abilities." The solution will lie in pinning down these intellectual abilities in concrete terms.

Atkin challenges the proposition that behavioral statements of objectives should always be the *first step* in curriculum planning. He argues (p. 131) that "too early a statement of objectives may obscure potentially significant outcomes that do not become apparent until later because they are seldom anticipated." The point that instruction may have unanticipated outcomes, desirable or undesirable, is well taken. That the outcomes—that is, the terminal behavior—can *seldom* be anticipated is doubtful. It is an indictment of an approach to constructing teaching materials and techniques if the effects can *seldom* be predicted.

The main question is whether stating educational goals in behavioral terms, as the first step in curriculum development, will "obscure potentially significant outcomes." It is difficult to see why this should be the case. There is little reason to believe that stating objectives in clear form would blind a person to other, unexpected consequences. On the contrary, there is some reason to believe that an unambiguous formulation of goals might make a person more sensitive to a variety of outcomes of teaching. Dressel (1954) has edited a book describing the experiences of a group of college and university teachers who attempted to evaluate general education programs. Initially, they mainly were interested in learning how to construct achievement tests. This interest led them to recognize the need to crystallize goals in terms of clearly formulated objectives. As the teachers became skilled in defining objectives, they became increasingly sensitive to the outcomes instruction actually had and began to question the methods of teaching that were being used. Though based entirely on the testimonial of those involved, the report suggests that a concern for evaluation and clearly defined objectives led to improvement in the quality of instruction and raised student achievement.

Many educators have stressed the importance of advance formulation of objectives. Perhaps they have permitted the inference that, once enunciated, goals need not be reexamined. Such a policy is inadvisable. One does not really know what one's objectives are until one has wrestled with the problem of trying to reach them. This assertion may seem mystifying, but it is intended quite literally. Consider a man and wife who are talking with an architect, attempting to describe a house they want to build. At this early stage it may happen that neither the couple nor the architect mentions closets. Nevertheless, though the first sketch may not, the final plans for the house will include the closets. Serious omissions in any educational plan are not, unfortunately, always as obvious as missing closets in the plan for a house. If objectives are "frozen" in the form first conceived, important considerations can be overlooked.

Logically, it may seem that the formulating of objectives should always be the first step in preparing to teach. In practice, it may make better sense to elaborate objectives while making an analysis of what will be taught and while developing teaching materials and techniques. Detailed decisions about what will be taught and how, are partly determined by the objectives and, in turn, those decisions shape the objectives to some extent. The insistence therefore upon a comprehensive formulation of goals as the first step in educational planning seems artificial, and is perhaps one explanation of the functionless lists of platitudes that frequently introduce school courses-of-study with such ill grace.

Roughing out the main goals of a lesson, unit, or course first is the best plan. The completeness of this first statement of objectives will depend upon familiarity with what is to be taught and also upon preference. It can be argued, though, that spending a lot of time initially pondering objectives is likely to be unproductive and that getting into the substance of the lesson rather quickly generally seems like a good idea. Tentative decisions regarding methods and materials can be weighed against the trial versions of the objectives. Eventually—preferably as soon as possible—a full-blown statement of objectives should be elaborated. When the objectives have been clearly and precisely formulated, this formulation will become a valuable tool for selecting topics and concepts to be included in a lesson, editing irrelevant material, organizing or sequencing the lesson, and choosing the teaching techniques. Once available in satisfactory though not necessarily final form, the statement of objectives can serve as a yardstick for judging the adequacy of components of lessons.

These preliminary goals may need refinement. Details regarding the conditions or standard of performance, for instance, cannot always be elaborated until one has roughed out lesson plans and perhaps not until one has tried to teach the lesson. Obviously, in an introductory typing course it would be capricious to pick just any number as the hoped for typing rate. The decision regarding the number of words per minute that should reasonably be expected must depend upon a number of factors—characteristics of the students, demands to be made of students when they complete the course, materials and techniques to be employed, and so on. Not all of these will be known in advance. As a first step, one could say that typing speed is important, and later indicate the specific standard of performance.

Terms such as "knowledge," "understanding," and "appreciation" are capable of various interpretations and, hence, suffer from vagueness. From another perspective, the variety of meanings and shades of meaning that each possesses lends a certain richness. (Philosophers use the phrase "open texture" to refer to the quality of taking on different meanings in different contexts.) Usually writing a behavioral objective entails *translating* a term such as "understanding" into one or more definite, observable actions on the part of the student. The concept may suffer in translation, however. There may be some loss of meaning. A reexamination of behavioral objectives in the light of more generally-stated educational goals is therefore always in order. Make no mistake, though; behavioral statement of objectives has valuable consequences that outweigh the risks of distorting "real" goals.

SELF-TEST ON BEHAVIORAL OBJECTIVES

Taking the following self-test is just as much a part of completing this book as reading the text or finishing the program. Do not skip the test. Write your answers to the questions below before proceeding. While taking the test do not look back through the program nor ahead to the next section.

1. Write a paragraph explaining in detail the characteristics of a well-written behavioral objective.

2. Write a sentence or two defining entering behavior.

3. Briefly indicate the chief fault or faults, if any, of each of the following objectives:

- **a.** The candidate for a driver's license should be familiar with the rules for safe driving set forth in the official *Driver's Manual.*
- **b.** Given a list of the axioms in a logical system with which he has had no previous experience and a list of theorems to prove, the student should construct at least five valid proofs within an hour.
- **c.** The student should know how to operate an electron-microscope without the aid of a manual.
- **d.** The student should develop an awareness of the process of scientific inquiry.
- **e.** The student should be able to list and then define with Venn diagrams the four moods of the syllogism, making no mistakes and without a reference book or other help.
- **f.** The music student should be sensitive to fine differences in pitch.
- **g.** The student should be able to spell correctly.
- **h.** The purpose is a study of the problems faced by management and labor in establishing employee benefit plans for death, disability, and retirement.
- **i.** The student should be able to understand at least 85 percent of the questions asked him in German, provided the questions are stated slowly and clearly by a native German and the words used can be found in the glossary in Schmidt's *Basic German.*

- **j.** The purpose is that the student correctly identify all well-written behavioral objectives.
- **k.** When presented with pairs of complex tones between 5,000 and 20,000 cps of standard loudness and duration, the music student should always correctly identify the second tone as higher or lower than the first whenever the second tone is as much as $\frac{1}{6}$ of a musical half-step different from the first.
- **l.** During the free listening period, the student should (without being influenced by the teacher) select classical and Baroque records instead of rock-and-roll or hillbilly recordings.

4. Rewrite each of the following to form a behavioral objective.

- **a.** The student should know how to use a dictionary.
- **b.** The student should be able to deal appropriately with graphs and maps.

5. Write two behavioral objectives, different from any you have seen in this program, from an educational area of interest to you.

Summary

When used to indicate the desired outcomes of instruction, words like "understanding" and "knowing" pose serious problems for the instructional planner. These words, commonly used to indicate a conglomerate of skills and knowledge, are by their very nature ambiguous. Behavioral objectives can be used, however, to clarify the specific skills and knowledge implied by words and phrases such as these. As contrasted with statements of goals that include words like "understand," "know," and "appreciate," the behavioral objective is a tool that the teacher can use in deciding what material from lessons to include and exclude, in selecting teaching techniques, in planning and conducting the evaluation of instruction, and in communicating precisely to others the goals that a lesson has.

A behavioral objective specifies exactly what it is hoped the student will be able to do or say when he completes a lesson or series of lessons. The main verb in a behavioral objective is active. It specifies an observable or partly observable act on the part of the student. To be complete the statement of an educational objective should also include a specification of the important circumstances or conditions under which students will have to perform, and a formulation of the criteria by which terminal performance will be judged, the standard of performance.

While stating educational objectives in the proper form is important, the content and completeness of objectives are even more important. A complete list of objectives specifies the skills or knowledge that a student must possess in order to perform a task or demonstrate an understanding. Furthermore, it breaks down major objectives into component skills and knowledge so as to indicate exactly what the student must learn if he is to progress from the level of his entering behavior to terminal performance. (The following chapters on task analysis and entering behavior are designed to enable you to construct complete analyses of skills and interrelated sets of concepts and principles.)

An excess of zeal for stating educational goals in the form of behavioral objectives could have the effect of limiting attention to simple, observable behavior that can be modified in a short period of time, to the neglect of hard-to-define but important goals. On the other hand, there is no sound argument for remaining satisfied with intangibles, however grand these may sound. The way out is to continue the effort to render complex, illusive goals in behavioral terms.

Objectives cannot generally be set forth in final form upon first writing. It seems a good idea to define objectives in the context of the detailed analysis and development of what will be taught and how. When at last forged, the statement of objectives should be reviewed from the perspective of general educational goals.

Clearly formulating objectives is a step that can be recommended to anyone developing teaching materials. Teachers are busy people. It is not to be expected that they will write down behavioral objectives for every lesson taught. But whenever a teacher is going to take the trouble to spend considerable time and effort planning a lesson or unit, the careful development of objectives is probably a sound investment of energy.

Perhaps the most convincing argument for unambiguous, behavioral objectives is that these may have a direct effect on student learning (McNeil, 1967). There is some evidence (Mager & McCann, 1961) that giving students a detailed statement of instructional objectives can markedly reduce the time required for learning. It seems reasonable to suppose, though the evidence on the matter at this time is slight, that rather striking improvements in instruction could be accomplished simply by making students aware of objectives.

SCORING KEY FOR THE SELF-TEST ON BEHAVIORAL OBJECTIVES

Score your own test using the following guide.

1. *(5 points)*

(1) One point is earned if you indicated that a behavioral objective states what the student should be able to do or say.

(1) One point is earned if you said that a behavioral objective includes a statement of the conditions under which the student will demonstrate his mastery of the objective.

(1) One point is earned if you said that a behavioral objective specifies the standard of performance the student should achieve.

(1) One point is earned if you said that the behavioral objective is desired or intended *terminal* behavior (saying that the objective states behavior is not enough to earn this point—you've already said that).

(1 extra) Credit one point if you gave one or more examples of desirable phrases in objectives OR contrasted desirable with undesirable characteristics OR defined "conditions" and "standard."

2. (*1 point*)

(1) One point is earned for saying that entering behavior consists of the things a student can do or say when instruction begins.

3. (*12 points*)

a. (1) One point is earned for indicating that being "familiar with" is not behavior.

b. (1) One point is earned if you said that the objective is acceptable in its present form.

c. (1) One point is earned if you stated that "knowing how" is not doing.

d. This objective, though it may *suggest* a very important goal, is utterly vague as it stands.

(1) One point is earned if you said "awareness of" is not behavior *and* indicated the lack of either specific conditions of performance or a standard of performance.

e. (1) One point is earned if you said the objective is acceptable.

f. (1) One point is earned if you said "being sensitive to" is not active, observable behavior.

g. (1) One point is earned for noting the lack of a statement of the conditions of spelling performance.

h. (1) One point is earned for indicating that the objective is not behavioral OR saying that the statement is a course description.

i. (1) One point is earned for stating that "understanding" is not doing.

j. (1) One point is earned if you said the statement does not describe the conditions of performance.

k. (1) One point is earned if you said this objective is acceptable.

l. (1) One point is earned if you noted the lack of performance standard.

4. *(6 points)*

a. *(3 points)*

(1) One point is earned for translating "know how" into one or more words or phrases indicating active behavior.

(1) One point is earned for a phrase or phrases describing conditions of performance (whether the conditions you state are really appropriate is another matter).

(1) One point is earned for describing characteristics of acceptable performance.

b. *(3 points)*

(1) One point is earned for translating "to deal . . . with" into less ambiguous words that refer to active behavior.

(1) One point is earned for a phrase or phrases describing conditions of performance.

(1) One point is earned for specifying a standard of performance.

5. *no score*

Though creating behavioral objectives is a most important goal, no guides for scoring will be outlined because of the variety of objectives that students may invent. Anyway, if the objective of the program was reached, you should be able to judge yourself whether the statements you wrote satisfy the criteria for a behavioral objective.

The total possible score on the self-test is 24. A score of 21–24 is good performance. A score of 18–20 is passing. A score of 17 or less is unacceptable. If very many students fail to reach the minimum acceptable standard of performance (a score of 18 or more), then the program is not reaching its objectives. If you are one of those whose terminal behavior falls short of the standard, there are two courses of action open. You could set the program aside for a couple of days, then go through it again. You will undoubtedly do better the second time. Usually, if there is an alternative, it is slightly better to attempt to learn the material a different way the second time than to repeat the same series of steps. Although there is often no viable alternative to repeating the same instruction, in the present case, there is an alternative. Robert F. Mager (1962) has written an excellent book (a thin one) entitled *Preparing Objectives for Programmed Instruction* that covers the same topics as the program you completed. The recommended remedial step for those who did poorly on the program is reading Mager's book, which, incidentally, is also a program. (Notice that the person who showed substandard terminal behavior is *not* given the alternative of doing nothing. The presumption is that students should learn instead of just covering material.)

Selected Readings

Anderson, R. C., Faust, G. W., Roderick, M. C., Cunningham, D. J., & Andre, T., eds., "Section II. Instructional Objectives," *Current Research on Instruction.* Englewood Cliffs, N.J.: Prentice-Hall, 1969. Reprints of four papers containing research evidence and arguments for and against behavioral objectives.

Mager, R. F., *Developing Attitude Toward Learning.* Palo Alto, Calif.: Fearon, 1968. Mager discusses attitudinal and emotional objectives.

Mager, R. F., *Preparing Instructional Objectives.* Palo Alto, Calif.: Fearon, 1962. This programmed booklet teaches the specification of objectives in behavioral form.

CHAPTER

2

Task Analysis: The Functional Analysis of Skills and Concepts

A behavioral objective designates a *task*: a definite, definable activity which, it is hoped, the student can perform successfully when he completes a lesson or series of lessons. A companion step in planning the lesson, since in practice these steps will often be accomplished together, is the *task analysis*. In this step, the task is analyzed into the set of skills that the person must perform to accomplish the task. Human performance is usually labeled in this analysis according to what the performance accomplishes (i.e., according to the function it serves rather than according to the person's actual movements). For example, the phrase "opening the door" states what is accomplished by a particular performance. It does not tell how the person who opens a door actually goes about this task. He may exert force on the door with his hip, push the bottom of the door with his foot, lift a latch with his left hand and then pull, turn a knob in a clockwise motion with his right hand and then push, or step on a mat concealing a switch that activates a motor that moves the door. Each of these possible behaviors is an analytic account of how the task of opening a door may be accmplished. A completely developed task analysis will present a detailed description of the component behavioral skills that the accomplishment of the task entails, the relationships among those components, and the function of each component in the total task.

The expression "task analysis" was coined by applied psychologists concerned with teaching and learning. Within the field of education, there has been no special name for task analysis; the activity has been lumped together with other aspects of planning. In some measure, teachers and educators have always performed task analyses. However, the trouble with many of these task analyses is that they have been done according to common sense, in only a casual manner, so they have often been secondary to other aspects of planning.

A true task analysis specifies in order the steps the learner will be taking when he is successfully performing the task. Thus, the behavioral objective designates the task, while the task analysis identifies the series of actions required of the learner to demonstrate that he has attained the objective. Consider an example from elementary school arithmetic, which will be developed in detail later in the chapter to illustrate the process of task analysis. The objective is as follows:

> Students should be able to divide decimal fractions up to at least six digits in length. The divisors, which can also be decimal fractions, may range up to four digits in length. Students should reach 90 percent accuracy with problems presented in standard written form.

In this case the task is to divide decimal fractions of a given level of difficulty. The task analysis will identify and describe the steps involved in the division skill.

It is important to distinguish sharply between a task analysis and a lesson plan. A lesson plan, as it is ordinarily conceived, has some connection, at least by implication, with a clarification of what the student should be doing, but the emphasis is mainly on what the *teacher* wants to do. The lesson plan most commonly outlines the topics that will be covered, the assignments to be given, the things the teacher will do or say in teaching that lesson. One of the easiest and most insidious of the assumed equivalences in education is that between executions of the teacher and skills the students are supposed to learn. Task analysis, however, shifts the perspective from what the teacher is doing to what the *student* is doing. The task analysis is, in a sense, the "blueprint" of the skill that the student is expected to learn—its main purpose to provide the teacher with guidelines for the development and selection of teaching materials and techniques.

The person who reads this chapter should be able to:

1. describe the methods of task analysis.
2. list the criteria by which the adequacy of a task analysis may be judged.
3. describe the role of task analysis in the total enterprise of instructional planning.

Ideally, the authors would like to set the following goal for persons who complete the study of this chapter.

> The student should be able to analyze in written and diagrammatic form any task from an area of interest to him. The analysis should be complete, presented in the proper amount of detail, with relationships among the component skills clearly specified. The analysis should identify when and under what circumstances each component skill is to be performed. Above all, the students should be able to present evidence that the final version of a lesson based on the task analysis has accomplished its objectives, given the kind of learner for whom the lesson was intended.

More realistically, though, this chapter can teach the person who reads it to talk and write more precisely about task analysis. It cannot *directly* teach the person to *do* a task analysis. The most that we can hope is that these verbal skills—talking and writing—can constitute a beginning in the skill of task analysis itself.

The strategy for doing a task analysis is really very simple. For each objective, ask "What skills and knowledge will the student need to reach this objective?" Having identified the major components of the task, ask for each component, "What subskills and subconcepts must the student possess to master this component?" Subskills and subconcepts are analyzed in a similar fashion when necessary. You will eventually trace back to skills and knowledge that are part of the student's entering behavior. This is the point at which the analysis stops. To put the matter another way, task analysis is the process of identifying the intermediate behaviors the student must acquire to proceed from the level of his entering behavior to desired terminal behavior.

Completeness

An important requirement is that the task analysis include all of the components. It is surprisingly easy to overlook components in the complex skill required to successfully accomplish a task. A helpful procedure is to mentally "walk through" the task yourself. Try to visualize each of the steps in a given task in the order that they occur. Write the steps down in this order. Visualizing the components in a smooth, synchronized, rapidly performed skill may be difficult, but it can be done. A golf ball is hit in an instant. Yet the golf pro is able to talk about "addressing the ball," the "back swing," and the "follow-through." It is often useful to think of smoothly integrated skills in "slow motion" so as to more distinctly isolate the components.

The notions that have been set forth in the preceding paragraph can be applied to any skill required to accomplish a task. Let us work through the solving of a "typical" long-division problem, for example.

The problem given is 19.2) 3471 . The first step, if one is using the procedure most people have learned, is to set the decimal point in the proper place—in this case, moving the decimal point in the divisor and the dividend (number being divided) one place to the right, and then, marking the decimal point in the proper place in the quotient (answer), that is, in the quotient space directly above the decimal point in the divisor. After the first step has been performed, the problem looks like this:

```
                     . ←
(1)     192. ) 34710.
```

The second step is to estimate the first digit of the quotient, and then write the estimate as indicated below:

```
           →    1   .
(2)     192. ) 34710.
```

The third step is to multiply the divisor by the estimated quotient (1 × 192 = 192) and then write the product below the problem as shown here:

```
                1   .
(3)     192. ) 34710.
               192   ←
```

Fourth, subtract the product from the number being divided and write the difference in its proper place:

```
                1   .
(4)     192. ) 34710.
               192
               ---
               155  ←
```

The fifth step is to "bring down" the next digit in the number being divided:

```
                1   .
(5)     192. ) 34710.
               192   ↙
               ----
               1551
```

After step 5, the procedure will begin again with estimating a digit of the answer, multiplying the divisor by the estimated digit, and so on.

The process will continue until either a point is reached at which there is no remainder or until the desired degree of accuracy is attained.

The "typical" case that one initially uses to analyze a task may not be representative of the entire class to which the analysis is supposed to apply. It is important to apply the tentative analysis to other cases to see if the analysis fits them also. One should systematically search for exceptions and special cases. A really thorough exploration is necessary to be sure that at least all of the important cases are covered by the analysis. A thoughtful person can often devise a single, elegant analysis for a task even when to begin with it appears that there are many exceptions and special cases.

Below is a question which you should try to answer before going on. Such questions will appear throughout the remainder of the book. They are designed to help you learn and remember important concepts. Later, evidence will be presented to show that questions inserted within a text do indeed enhance student learning.

Which of the following describes a task analysis?

A. The students will read selected works of Thoreau, Hawthorne, and Emerson; consider Transcendentalism in the light of economic conditions in the middle of the nineteenth century; and examine the relationship between Transcendentalism and the abolition movement.

B. Most of the chemical energy in glucose is contained in the carbon-to-hydrogen and carbon-to-carbon bonds. When the glucose molecule breaks down the energy is released and carbon dioxide and water are produced as by-products.

C. To construct a standard expository paragraph, the student first writes a topic sentence, then a paraphrase of the topic sentence, then one or more sentences containing illustrations or details, and finally a summary sentence that either repeats or paraphrases the topic sentence.

The answer appears on p. **63.**

Amount of Detail

The question of when to stop subdividing a task into smaller and smaller components is most important. A task could be subdivided indefinitely. As shown earlier, we can go from "opening the door" to "turning the knob in a clockwise motion and pushing." We could also describe each movement required of the skeletal muscles to turn the knob; then for each muscle, the performance of fibers and tendons; for each fiber the action of cells; then the intracellular performance, and so on. What is the *right* amount of detail?

In theory, the answer to the question of how detailed a task analysis should be is simple. For each subtask or component skill, the analysis is detailed enough when the *intact skill* is part of the student's entering behavior. Gagné (1962, p. 117) has proposed a rough test for the presence of an intact component skill. When a student can perform the component skill upon simply being asked to do it, then the skill has been analyzed in sufficient detail. A doctor could get the desired performance from a nurse by asking, "Please tell me the patient's temperature." The same words would not elicit the appropriate behavior from the typical junior high school girl. Taking a temperature, then, is probably not an intact skill for most junior high school girls, whereas it is for a nurse.

To return to our long-division example. For typical pupils in the fifth and sixth grades, subtraction and multiplication are intact skills. Most fifth and sixth graders could multiply two numbers correctly if asked. When presented with the following expression

$$\begin{array}{r} 347 \\ -192 \\ \hline \end{array}$$

almost any average student of this age could tell you that the remainder is 155. Thus step 3 in the long-division analysis, which calls for multiplication, and step 4, subtraction, need not be stated in greater detail for most fifth and sixth graders since these steps can usually be regarded as intact component skills. This is not to say that prior to instruction in long division, the child will know when to multiply, what numbers to multiply, or where to write the product. (These matters will be more extensively treated in following sections.) What is true is that multiplication and subtraction are part of the typical fifth and sixth grader's entering behavior. However, these intact skills must be hooked into the sequence of activities constituting the skill of long division. Long division itself then becomes an intact skill for many, if not most, people who are junior-high-school age and older.

Neither skill in setting the decimal point in the proper place (step 1) nor skill in bringing down the next digit (step 5) can actually be said to be intact entering skills before a person learns to do long division. But teaching either of these components would probably be rather easy, so perhaps greater detail is unnecessary.

Estimating a digit of the quotient is another matter. This is not an intact entering skill. Teaching estimation might not be easy. Consequently, a detailed analysis of this subskill probably is needed. (All of the remarks regarding the analysis of a total task or skill—as in the case of the analysis of long division—apply also to the analysis of a subtask or component skill. The subtask or component skill is itself analyzed into components. For a very complex or large task, even further subdivisions may be desirable.)

One way to further analyze step 2, estimating a digit of the quotient, is to work through several cases yourself, in order to find the steps that are involved. Let us begin the process. Assume the problem is the same as before: to divide 3471 by 19.2. Having set the decimal point, the first step would seem to be to look at a series of digits in the number being divided that is equal to the number of digits in the divisor. The number being divided should be scanned from left to right. For the problem given, the first step is this:

(1) Look at 192. It is three digits long; therefore, look at the first three digits of the number being divided (3471).

As a second step, determine whether the divisor is larger or smaller than the portion in question of the number being divided.

(2) Determine whether 192 is larger or smaller than 347.

The third step, in which we confront directly the task of estimating, depends upon whether the divisor is larger or smaller. In the case being considered it is smaller,[1] so one may proceed directly to the first substep under 3. The question is:

(3a) Can I guess the largest one-digit number to multiply 192 by in order to get 347 or less? Yes? No?

If the answer is "yes," proceed directly to the fourth step. If the

[1] For the sake of completeness, imagine a case in which it is larger. Then it would be necessary to look at one more of the digits of the number being divided before going on to step 3. Suppose 6543 were to be divided by 71. Seventy-one is larger than 65. So the person should look at 654 instead of just 65.

Answer to the question on p. **61.**

Only **C** describes a task analysis. **A** describes what students will cover rather than what they must learn. **B** describes a biochemical analysis instead of a task analysis.

answer is "no," what then? Perhaps simplifying the problem would help. Round off an equal number of digits (starting from the right) in both the divisor and the portion of the number being divided such that the left-hand digit is the only non-zero digit remaining.

(3b) Round 192 to 200 and round 347 to 300. (To simplify even further, drop the zeroes, leaving 2 and 3.)

Now ask what is the largest one-digit number that can be used to multiply 200 by in order to get 300 or less.

(3c) One is the largest one-digit number with which 200 can be multiplied in order to get 300 or less.

Having obtained an estimate of the first digit of the quotient, the next step is to locate the place to write that digit. The digit is written directly above the rightmost digit of the portion of the dividend that was involved in the preceding steps. In the illustration:

(4) Write 1 above the 7 in 347:

```
          1  .
   192 ) 34710.
```

The steps (3a–4) that have been outlined represent a finer analysis of the skill of estimating the quotient, which skill in turn is a component of the skill of long division. Notice that the procedure for analyzing the component skill is the same as the one for analyzing the overall skill. It is possible that a still finer analysis of the skill of estimating the quotient may be required. The general rule is that a skill or component skill has not been specified in enough detail until the point is reached at which the subskill being identified is part of the student's entering behavior (i.e., is an intact skill). You know that a subskill is part of a student's entering behavior when he can perform the skill upon simply being asked to do so.

Relationships Among Subskills and Concepts

There is an old saw characterizing the person who gets lost in details: "He can't see the forest for the trees." Subskills and concepts cannot be put together in just any order. The smooth integration of components is the essence of highly skilled performance.

The most basic of the types of relationships that may exist among skills is the *simple chain.*

In a simple chain, one skill or response follows another. Fig. 2.1 depicts the starting routine for a late-model car with automatic transmission.

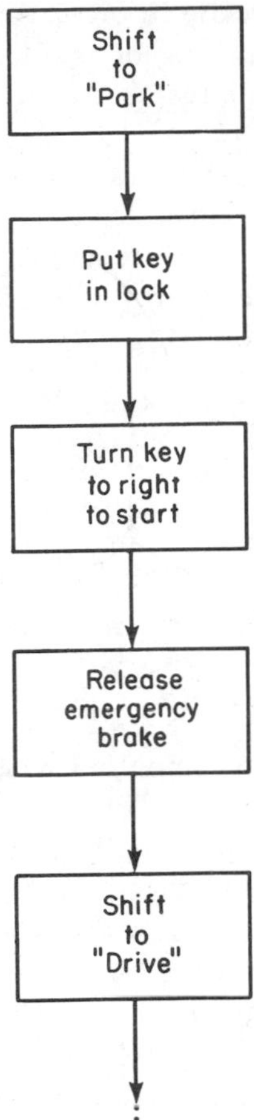

FIGURE 2.1 *A simple response chain—the starting routine for a late-model car with automatic transmission.*

An important characteristic of the simple chain is that the completion of one segment is the signal for the next to begin. All of the segments in a well-learned chain can be run off easily once the chain begins. Often, however, if the performance of a chain is interrupted in the middle for some reason, it may be difficult to continue from the point of interruption. It may even be necessary to start the chain over from the beginning.

Most of us learned to recite the alphabet as a chain. If we begin with *A*, we are able to say the twenty-six letters with extraordinary ease, impeded only by the speed with which our lips and tongue can form the letters. But try to answer these questions! What letter precedes *U*? What letter follows *J*? You may find that you have to get a running start, beginning a few letters before the letter in question (if not from *A*), and then listen to yourself recite in order to answer these questions. To convince yourself that the saying of one letter is indeed the signal for the next, try reciting the alphabet backward. You will find this a difficult task.

Often the answer to the question of what should be done next is, "it depends." When a certain subskill has been executed, one of several steps may then be appropriate depending upon circumstances involved. The generic psychological term for the decision required under such circumstances is "discrimination."

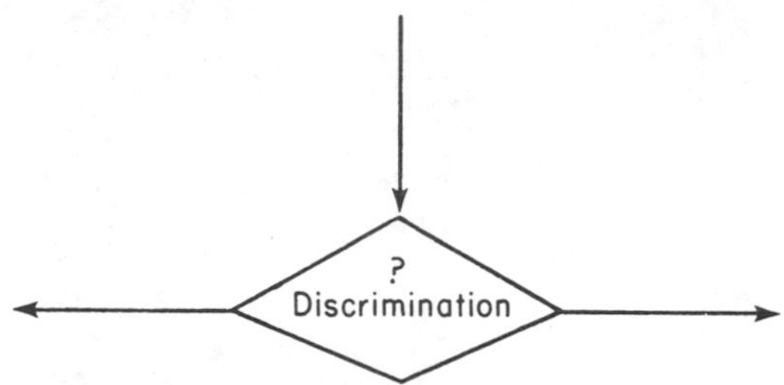

A person has learned a discrimination when he can notice a difference and act appropriately as a result. For instance, a child can discriminate between *P* and *B* when he responds differently to them, by naming, pronunciation, or the like. Some discriminations are quite complex, for example, telling the difference between verbs and nouns. Sometimes discriminations are hooked together in series. Such a case is illustrated in Fig. 2.2. If the light is green as the driver of a car approaches an intersection, he continues. If it is red he stops. When the light is yellow, a second discrimination is required. Depending upon the driver, the latter discrimination should be between "am I too close to stop?" or "can I make it?"

The relationships between components in a complex skill can be very complicated, especially when the details are specified. Nonetheless, these relationships, no matter how involved, can be conceived in terms of sets of chains and discriminations arranged in patterns. In recent years it has become popular to represent complex skills with diagrams called "flow charts." You have already seen several of these. The essence of a flow chart of an action is that it reveals in a single diagram what is to be done at every point in time, thus showing both direction and sequence. The flow chart is a visual aid, developed originally by systems analysts and computer programmers, that can be used to picture the relationships among components in a complex skill. Like reading blueprints or maps, the reading of flow charts is a skill that must be acquired.

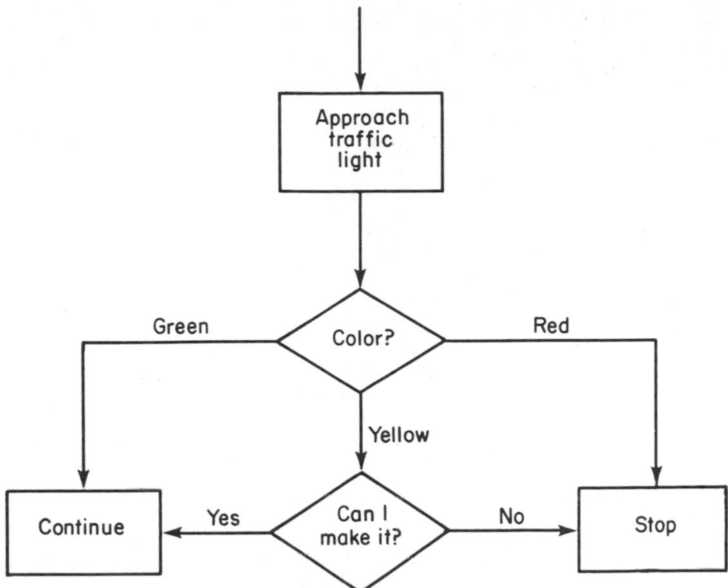

FIGURE 2.2 *Discriminations required of a driver as his car approaches a traffic light.*

A flow chart of a long-division skill appears in Fig. 2.3. This figure reveals the order in which the components of the long-division skill must be completed. The completion of one component constitutes the signal, or a part of the signal, that the next component should begin. Notice that the long-division skill has been diagrammed as a *loop* (see the long arrow up the left side of the flow chart that joins the original path under the first component). The loop signifies that the student may cycle through that path of essentially the same series of steps several times until the answer to the question, "enough accuracy?" is "yes."

The main aspect that a flow chart of a skill illustrates is the *temporal* organization of that skill; in other words, the order in which segments must be completed. Flow charts can also be employed to display what may be called *hierarchical* organization. The boxes and diamonds in flow charts may represent large chunks of behavior, such as "Approach traffic light" in Fig. 2.2; or they may depict minute subskills, such as "Bring down the next digit . . ." in Fig. 2.3. By using flow charts, the educator and the psychologist interested in complex human learning can see both the forest and the trees. Fig. 2.4., for example, contains a flow chart picturing in some detail the operations of estimating a digit,

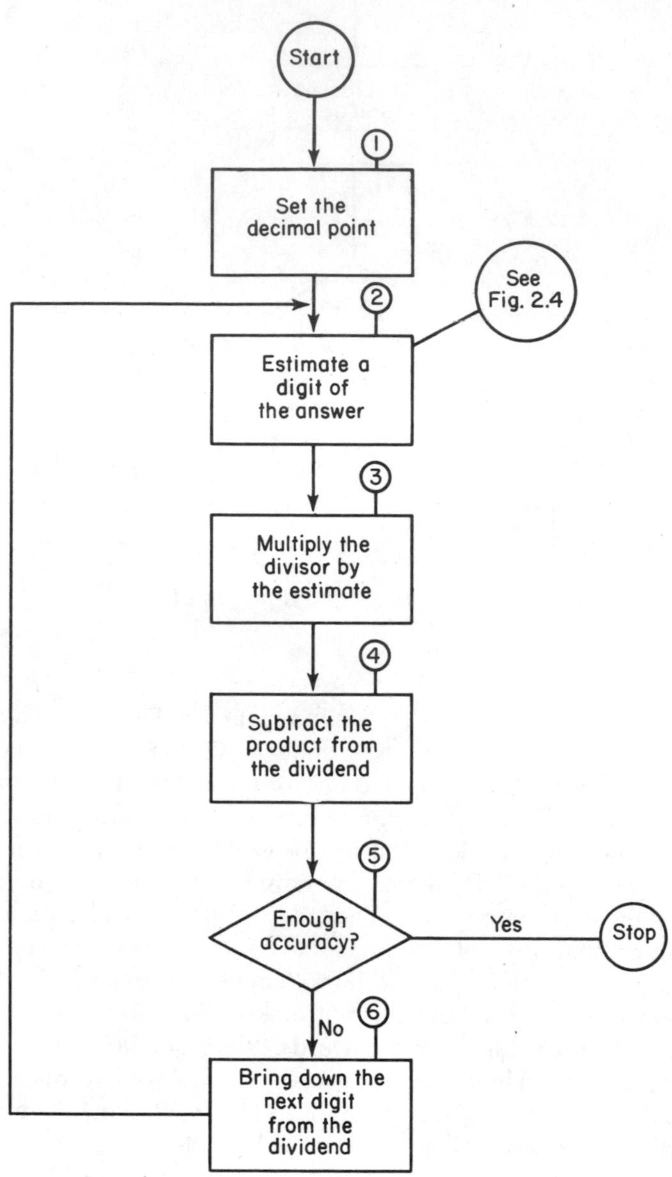

FIGURE 2.3 *Flow chart of the major components in a common long-division procedure. The numbers in the circles identify the steps.*

whereas Fig. 2.3 gives the overview. The circled numbers serve as cross-references to facilitate moving back and forth between the two figures.

Try to work through a long-division problem, let us say $36.56\overline{)2197.1}$ using the flow charts. Start with Fig. 2.3. When you get to ②, shift to Fig. 2.4. Let the flow chart direct what you will do next. Notice how the flow chart indicates a course of action for each contingency that might arise.

A convincing case may be made in support of the need for a "language of skills" that includes the essential operations that are basic to all skills —a language which places limits upon the rich irrelevancies of ordinary language. The electrical engineer, for instance, uses circuit diagrams to represent the flow and control of current. There is a written language of music. There is even a way to represent by written symbols the choreography of a dance.

Flow charting may be helpful in clarifying ordinary language descriptions and analyses of complex human skills and concepts. Flow charts highlight the critical features of complex skills within the constraint of a limited number of operations. At the same time, such representations are open to various usages and can be conveniently explained with English commentary. Flow charting, moreover, demands about as much rigor as psychology and the educational arts are currently capable of sustaining. It is most important to clarify the relationships among the components in a complex skill. Flow charts are not the only device for clarifying these relationships, but they are one potentially useful one.

Upon what grounds does one decide that a task analysis has been developed in sufficient detail? Please *write* your answer.

The answer appears on p. **71.**

When and Under What Circumstances Is a Skill to be Performed?

If a book gets misplaced, filed on the wrong shelf in a large library for instance, it is as good as lost. In a roughly parallel way, a skill is useless unless it can be called up at the appropriate times. And whether a skill will be performed at the appropriate times depends in large measure on how the skill is "referenced" and "cross-referenced" by the person who possesses it.

FIGURE 2.4 *Detailed flow chart for ② estimating a digit of the answer and ③ multiplying the divisor by the estimated digit.*

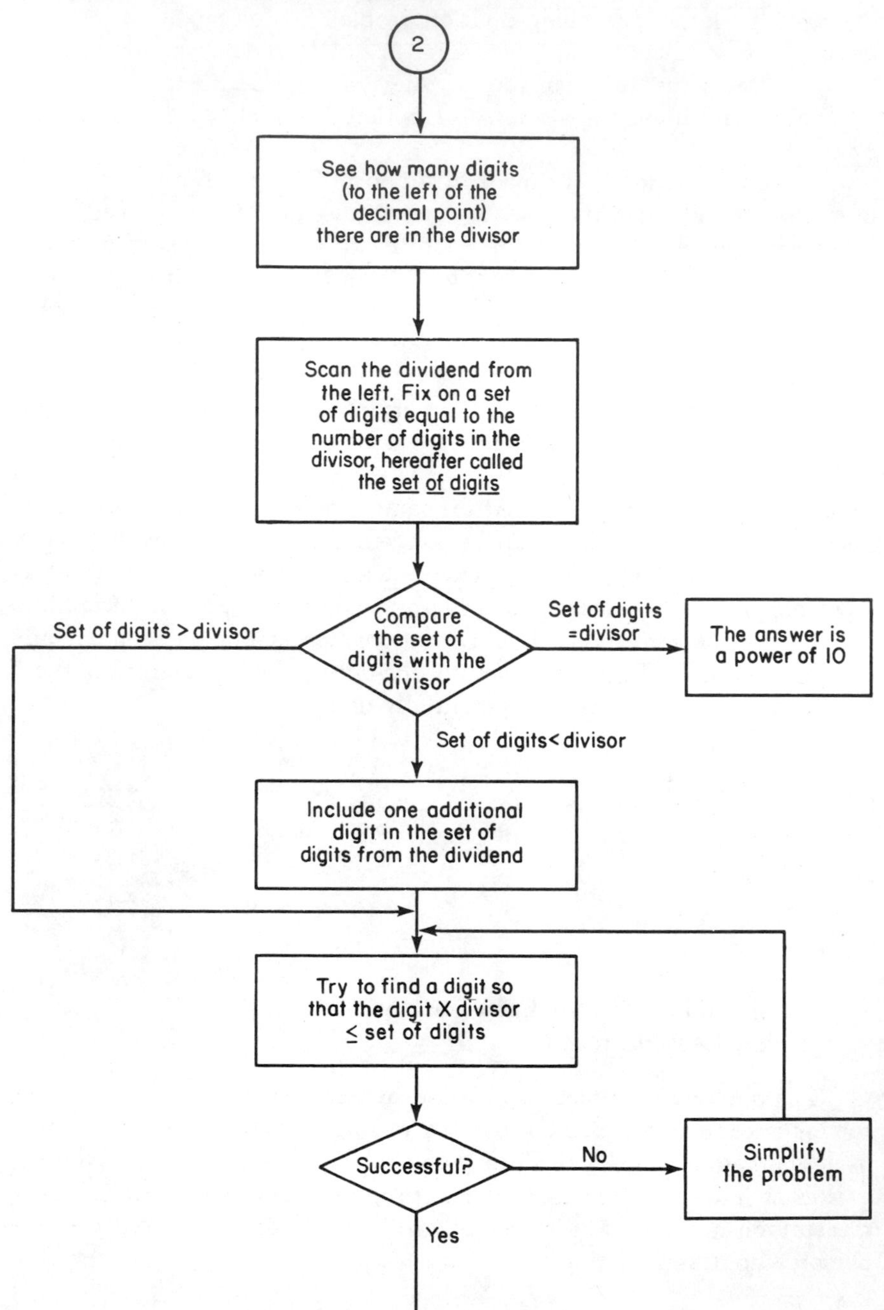

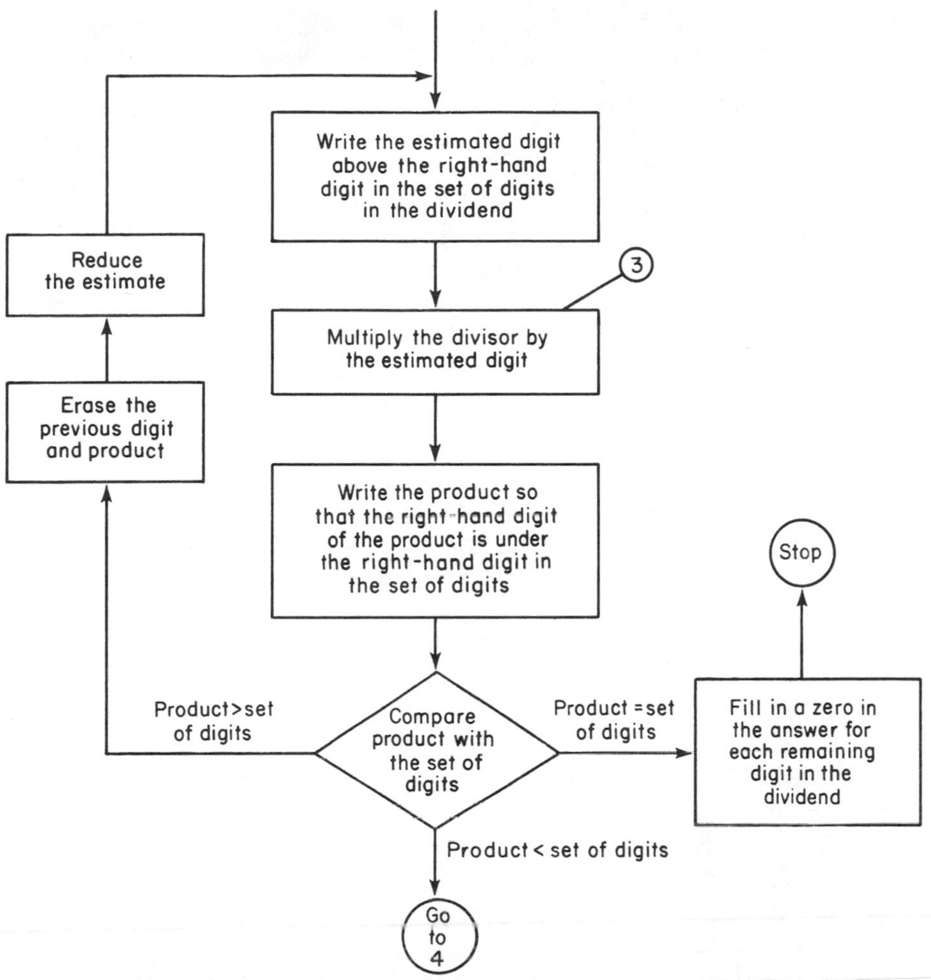

FIGURE 2.4 *Continuation of flow chart.*

Answer to the question on p. **69.**

A task analysis is detailed enough when the total task has been divided and subdivided until component skills and concepts are identified which are part of the student's entering behavior. A rough test is to ask yourself, "could the student do this upon simply being asked?"

How does a child who is capable of long-division know *when* to perform the skill? The answer is that he gets some distinctive signal from his environment that informs him of these occasions. The signal that occasions a skill is called, in technical terms, a *cue* or a *discriminative stimulus*. The discriminative stimulus is said to *control* the skill (see Chapter 9). Typically, the student will learn to divide when he sees this arrangement of symbols:

$$17\overline{)356}$$

or this one

$$356 \div 17 =$$

The student will also be prepared to divide when he hears or sees the command, "divide 356 by 17."

There are many other kinds of occasions upon which it is appropriate to divide. It is possible, however, for a person to be very proficient at a skill and yet not use the skill when it would be applicable: the student will report that he didn't "think of" employing the skill in question. Since a skill is useless unless one knows when to use it, one of the important aspects of a task analysis is to specify the cues that should occasion a skill.

Two cases were mentioned in Chapter 1 involving persons who had mastered a skill but were unable to use the skill when it was needed. There was the child who could compute the sums of numbers in columns and rows, but who didn't think of adding when presented with a word problem in addition. In the second case, it didn't "occur" to the college student to apply the pendulum theory of social change to predict the course of events in a school district. In each of these cases the concept or skill was valueless because of the lack of a discriminative stimulus to signal the skill into action.

The cues that guide a skill once the person begins to perform it are also important. It has already been mentioned that these cues are of two general kinds. First, there are the discriminative stimuli to which the situation gives rise, the cues which occasion the skill. Second, responses produce cues that may signal the next response. Together, these two kinds of cues serve to coordinate the components of a complex skill and control its "timing." For example, when a batter brings the bat forward to hit the ball the swing is partly controlled by cues resulting from the completion of the backswing and partly by the cues furnished by the batter's sight of the pitcher and his sight of the ball moving toward the plate.

For each of the components of a skill, it is important to determine cues that will guide the student in the performance of the subskill. Moreover, for the skill as a whole, the discriminative stimuli that determine when the skill should be performed must be identified by the task analyst (this means, for example, knowing when to divide). One characteristic of the person who "really understands" is that he employs the skills he has learned in a wide range of circumstances in which the skill could be used to advantage. This will not happen automatically. The student must learn when to employ a skill as well as how. In the task analysis, the range of circumstances in which the student should use the skill must be catalogued and the critical cues in each of these circumstances identified.

Consistency with Objectives

A task analysis is seldom unique. There are usually several different skills that will serve the same function as a given skill and several different procedures that will accomplish a single objective as satisfactorily as a given procedure. For example, a number of computational routines exist or could be invented for solving long-division problems. Some of these, though, may be less easy to reconcile with general educational goals than others.

The long-division skill makes a good illustration for task analysis. As a skill it is relatively complex, yet it is one that most adults have mastered. However, there is a question as to whether the particular skill outlined is consistent with the objectives held by mathematics educators. In general, regardless of what the skill or subject matter being analyzed may be, the question should be asked as to whether the task analysis is consistent with both the specific objectives for a particular lesson and those for the broader educational goals.

One objection of mathematics educators to the long-division procedure described in this chapter is that the student who follows it can learn to compute answers without knowing why the procedure gives the correct answers. (By "knowing why" we mean "giving an acceptable explanation of the complete procedure.") One standard for an acceptable explanation might consist of an informal appeal to the characteristics of the number system. A more ambitious standard to demonstrate that the student knows why a computational procedure yields the correct answer might require him to derive the procedure by employing basic mathematical principles. Whatever the standard may be, it cannot be assumed that the child who learns, for example, a certain procedure for dividing numbers will be able to show why the procedure works. "Explaining why" is also a skill. If it is important that the student learn to give explanations, then this skill should be analyzed so that it too may be taught.

In a subject such as mathematics, every application of the subject can be conceived of as a combination or recombination of a small set of fundamental principles and operations. The same is true in greater or lesser degree in other subject-matter areas. One of the chief aims of the modern curriculum reform movements is to organize instruction around basic principles; and, by any standard, this has led to enormous improvements in the quality of education being offered today. The old curricula differed from the new not only in that the material was often out of date, but also in that it was sometimes superficial, misleading, or inaccurate. Most important, the old curricula tended to consist of collections of isolated topics not integrated by overarching principles.

Should a method of long division be taught at all? This is a reasonable question raised by the curriculum reform movement. Long-division methods inevitably involve many procedural details that are difficult and tedious but hardly profound. Moreover, long division does not illustrate any mathematical principles that could not be more clearly illustrated another way. Whether a computational method for long division should be taught depends, first, upon how much of a premium is placed on people's ability to compute. This matter is one of the issues in a controversy that has raged among educators, scientists, and mathematicians (DeMott, 1964). There are those who insist that mathematics should be conceived of as entirely independent of the physical world; that is, as the subject that deals with the analysis of abstract systems and patterns. On the other hand, there are those who believe that mathematics is interesting and vital chiefly when it is applicable to some problem in the real physical world. The latter view is held not only by educators who worry about whether the next generation will be able to make change in the supermarket, but also by mathematicians and by some physicists, who are concerned that if the present trend continues, schools and colleges will not teach the mathematics skills that the physical sciences require.

Suppose that computational skill is valued highly. Is it then necessary to place a large emphasis upon computation? There are those who have argued vigorously and persuasively that when the student has learned the basic principles and operations that comprise the structure of a discipline, then he will easily acquire skill at such things as computation. In his influential book *The Process of Education* (1960, pp. 17–32) J. S. Bruner argued that students should be taught the basic structure of each subject in the curriculum. There are, he believes, a relatively few fundamental ideas in each area of knowledge which comprise its structure. The concept of natural selection in biology and the commutative, associative, and distributive laws of mathematics are examples of fundamental ideas. According to Bruner there are several important reasons why instruction should focus on fundamental concepts. He asserts that the learning of fundamental principles "makes a subject more comprehensible," improves the memory of the subject, decreases the gap between "advanced" knowledge and "elementary" knowledge, increases joy and excitement in learning, increases the chances for the development of "intuitive" thinking, and "appears to be the main road to adequate transfer of training."

An emphasis on fundamental concepts can indeed be heartily recommended. Nonetheless, not all good things will automatically flow from a knowledge of fundamental ideas. It is, for example, clearly wrong to believe that what may be called "manipulative skills" will follow naturally from an understanding of "essential structure." A child may become skilled at set theory, proofs in symbolic logic, or derivations involving field axioms, yet the same child could be completely unable to divide decimal fractions. Operations in arithmetic can be derived from set theory. But there is a world of difference between the *logical* "follow from" and the *psychological* "follow from." To expect that the child will be able to compute easily after he has learned set theory is to demand of the child that he reinvent arithmetic whenever it is needed. While no one's position is quite as radical as the one suggested in this paragraph, there is need for concern that dissatisfaction with the old curriculum and an uncritical enthusiasm over the new mathematics have led many persons to be altogether too sanguine about the effects that the learning of a "logical structure" will have on the learning of manipulative skills (Schwartz, 1965). Similar conclusions can be reached regarding other subject-matter areas.

While learning basic mathematical operations will not automatically facilitate the learning of manipulative skills, neither is there necessarily antagonism between the two kinds of learning. There is a long tradition in education which places "mere skill" in opposition to "true understanding." One of the most influential proponents of this view was Max Wertheimer, a Gestalt psychologist who coined the term "productive thinking" to characterize original problem-solving. He contrasted productive thinking with "reproductive thinking," which referred to a person's simply repeating what he had been taught to do. Wertheimer (1945, p. 189) wrote: ". . . We have found what, in contrast to other processes, we may call genuine, fine, clean, direct, productive processes. . . . Of course, there are often strong external factors working against those processes as, e.g., blind habits, certain kinds of school drill, bias, or special interests."

Our position in this book is that the frequently claimed distinction between skill and "deep understanding" is false. We believe that it is more useful and enlightening to consider that manipulative skills are at the same descriptive level as supposedly "deep" processes, such as problem-solving. These are both kinds of skills. We may properly speak of a problem-solving skill, a reasoning skill, or a theorem-proving skill just as we speak of skill at dancing or long division. To be sure, these are different skills and there is no psychological sense in which one kind of skill follows automatically from another. But, with the proper task analysis, it is often possible to reconcile objectives that call for rather different skills. Indeed, it is possible for such skills to develop simultaneously in a mutually supportive fashion.

In summary, the point is that for any one or two objectives, there are usually several and often many task analyses that will accomplish these objectives. But it cannot be assumed that other objectives will be accomplished automatically through some inner necessity once the primary objectives have been achieved. When an advance is made toward a range of objectives in a single lesson, it usually means that a really incisive analysis has been attempted, as well as painstaking attention given to the development of teaching materials and techniques.

Task Analysis and the Classroom Tryout

A task analysis cannot be regarded as satisfactory until it is demonstrated to work with students. There are very few sure things in the world of teaching. Psychological principles and reliable rules-of-thumb can carry a person only so far. Lessons are very complicated, and one cannot assume that a lesson will inevitably teach what it is supposed to, even though it may seem to be based on trustworthy principles and to incorporate sound practices.

The chief purpose of the lesson tryout is to obtain information that will be useful in revising and improving the lesson. It should be understood that the purpose of the tryout is not to find *whether* the lesson needs revision. Even the best of lessons can be improved. The purpose of the tryout is to find *which* aspects of the lesson should be modified.

The importance of the tryout is universally stressed by those whose business it is to develop lessons—whether for schools, industry, the military or some other group. Emphasis on the tryout is especially prominent in the programmed instruction movement, and it is also a part of the standard operating procedure of many of the curriculum reform projects. Zacharias and White (1964, pp. 72–73) have set forth the requirements for major curriculum revision as they saw them on the basis of their experience with the Physical Science Study Committee.

They state:

> . . . It cannot be assumed that the selection and ordering of subject-matter will flow unerringly from the decision on purpose. The test of a curriculum lies in the classroom. However ingenious the selection and ordering, they must prove their worth in practice. It must be demonstrated that the student understands and, indeed, employs those elements of the professional outlook which have been presented to him. Classroom experimentation with materials, and the provision of a system by means of which classroom experience can be evaluated and fed back into the process of revision, are basic requirements of any major program of curriculum revision. Without such a feedback system, the program wanders blindly into unknown territory, and is likely to end with a curriculum which in practice accomplishes no part of what it intended.

The more detailed and comprehensive the information obtained from the tryout, the more valuable it is. This section will not dwell on methods for trying out lessons, since Chapter 4 is entirely devoted to this topic. At this point we simply observe that if you know from the tryout how the lesson worked step by step, question by question, then you are in a much better position to pinpoint its weaknesses.

Although a tryout may reveal a weakness in a lesson, there remains the problem of diagnosing the reason for the shortcoming. The fault may lie with the task analysis or it may lie with the materials and techniques of teaching that the lesson uses. Just as an experimental airplane may fail because it is poorly designed or badly constructed, so it is with the first or second experimental versions of a lesson. It is often difficult, however, to diagnose the reason for a weakness and to make the revision that will correct it. Sometimes a radical change in the task analysis is indicated; the sensible thing to do is to start the task analysis again from scratch. For example, if one had trouble teaching the long-division skill that was outlined earlier, one might consider teaching an entirely different method for dividing. Rather frequently the difficulty can be traced to a gap in the existing task analysis, a subskill that was overlooked. Finally—not to be underestimated as the source of failure—there is the cumulative effect of many small imperfections, though each may be seemingly insignificant when considered alone.

Actually several cycles of tryout, revision, and tryout again may prove necessary. The stopping point: when the lesson demonstrably reaches its objectives.

A case study: The analysis of a beginning reading skill. Silberman (1964) and his associates have developed a lesson to begin to teach first graders of below average intelligence to read. His experience serves as an excellent illustration of the application of the techniques of task analysis.

The objective of the lesson was for the child to be able to sound out and read the letter combinations that can be formed from the initial consonants *f, r, s, m* and the word endings *an, it, at,* and *in.* When the child completed the lesson, it was hoped that he would be able to read words using those letters even though he had never seen the words before. Consequently, four words were reserved as a test of the child's ability to transfer the skill he acquired in the lesson to the novel letter combinations. The child did not see any of these test words during the lesson. The hope was that the lesson which was developed—though limited to a small number of letters, sounds, and words—could lead to an improved school reading program.

The lesson was tried with one child at a time. When a child made a large number of mistakes, the teacher attempted to discover the reason for his difficulty and then tried to help the child overcome the difficulty by trial-and-error, using one technique and then another until the child succeeded. The teacher made a note of the technique that seemed to work. These notes served as a basis for revising the lesson. The revised version of the lesson was then given to other children and so on until the lesson did accomplish its objectives.

Now for the task analysis. The initial assumption was that a capability for discovering letter-sound relationships is a part of the entering behavior of first graders with below-average intelligence. Accordingly, the early versions of the lesson presented words in a variety of contexts, with the expectation that the children would induce the correct letter-sound patterns. At first words were grouped with a common ending such as *man, ran, fan.* With this procedure, however, children responded only to the initial consonant. When later presented with a word such as *fit,* the child would say *fan.* Then the lesson was revised to hold the initial consonant constant, while varying the endings like this: *san, sit, sat, sun.* "This procedure," according to Silberman (1964, p. 2), "resulted in greatly increased error rates, accompanied by an annoying tendency of the children to avoid looking at the words."

An assortment of other devices was used in an attempt to improve the lesson. Pictures and little rhymes were used to elicit vowel sounds: for example, a picture of an Indian was used to elicit *i;* a rhyme containing the word *apple* was used to elicit *a.* Stories were designed around the words: "Mr. Ban is a man with a fan." Verbal reminders were given, such as "Remember the letter *a* goes with the *ae* sound."

Despite all of the hard work and the clever features, the lesson that had been developed to this point was a failure; it was not reaching its objectives. Clearly, a major rethinking of the assumptions in the task analysis was required. Silberman (1964, p. 3) has stated, "The assumption that children would quickly induce the phonic generalizations without explicit development of these subskills within the lesson was abandoned."

In the next analysis two subskills were identified: first, the skill of pronouncing each of the separate parts of the three-letter word, and, second, the saying of the word as a whole. The assumption was that the child could make the transition from "sounding out" or phoneticizing the word to saying the word as a whole. Instead, the letter responses and the whole-word response seemed to be separately associated with the letters. The children accurately sounded out the letters, but this did not lead them to say the whole word. The child could, for instance, say *f* and *it* without saying *fit*. Consequently, Silberman has indicated, the children had no success on the test words though they did learn to read the words used in the lesson.

A gap in the task analysis had appeared: the children were not able to blend together or amalgamate the individual sound elements so as to produce the whole word. A variety of techniques was tried before a method was discovered which worked in teaching children this blending skill. The child echoed the teacher rhythmically in a singsong fashion; first saying the separate sounds, and then the whole word in rapid succession like this:

m . . . . an . . man
m . . . . an . . man
m . . . . an . . man

The problem was to get the child to listen to himself say the separate letter sounds in such a way that these would come to serve as the signal, or *cue*, for the pronunciation of the whole word. Silberman and his associates found that it was particularly important to require the children to master the blending skill before they were allowed to continue with the rest of the lesson.

At this point the children were still unable to say the test words. Once again a gap in the task analysis was discovered. The missing subskill entailed decoding *new* letter combinations. When special practice on translating unfamiliar words was given within the lesson the children were able at last to read the test words.

Eventually, a full-scale comparison was made between the final version of the lesson and the first version. A group of fifteen first-grade children with below average intelligence was presented with the original version of the lesson. Another group of fifteen first graders with below-average intelligence, equated with the first group in terms of scores on a reading readiness test, received the final version.

It is interesting to note that upon looking through the two lessons many persons might prefer the first version since it seems to incorporate a "linguistic" approach (Fries, 1963) that has been popular among some reading specialists. The facts, however, do not support such a preference for below-average first graders. Silberman found that the children who received the final version of the lesson were afterward able to read significantly more words than the children who had received the first version, with the greatest difference found on the test words. On the average, the children who got the final version of the lesson read three out of four of the test words, whereas none of the children who received the original version could read any of the test words.

The Relationship of Task Analysis to Other Aspects of Instructional Planning

As a step in instructional planning, task analysis would seem, logically, to follow the definition of objectives. In practice, however, these steps will often overlap and be dealt with simultaneously. After the task analysis has been completed, the next logical step is the development of the lesson, a step which includes both selection and development of materials and techniques to be used in teaching the lesson. At this point also, in practice, task analysis merges with the development of the lesson.

Even for those who are quite conscious of the need for task analysis as an explicit step in educational planning, preconceptions about the desirability and practicality of various educational media may constrain both the definition of objectives and the task analysis. Very likely the person who is going to employ educational TV will develop a different task analysis than a person committed to programmed instruction or a person committed to a group discussion technique. Objectives and the task analysis do play a role in determining materials and techniques; but it is also true that an implicit or explicit commitment to an educational medium influences goals and shapes the functional analysis of the skills to accomplish these goals.

The influence of technique on goals may seem to raise a serious tail-wags-dog problem. Perhaps it does. A strong case can be made, though, for the position that planning which takes place at too high a level of abstraction will be sterile and that on the other hand making provisional practical decisions about what will be taught, and how it will be taught, is essential to successful planning. As a matter of fact, there are several different strategies for instructional planning. It is therefore a gross oversimplification to speak as though there were a single satisfactory procedure for instructional planning.

One good strategy for instructional planning consists, first, of definition of objectives; then, of task analysis; finally, of lesson development.

In a second strategy, the planner develops the test to assess terminal behavior as soon as he has defined the objectives (Markle, 1964). The argument for this strategy is that the writing of the test will *force* one to be explicit about the behavior required of students, the conditions of performance, and the standard of excellence that it is hoped students will achieve. After all, so the argument goes, the test must be developed sooner or later anyway; if it is developed before the lesson, it can serve to make explicit the goals the lesson has. This is a strategy that has much merit. It can be recommended to the teacher who finds that otherwise he does not discipline himself to make the vital, detailed analysis. And it can be recommended to the curriculum director who is having trouble in getting teachers to define objectives behaviorally and to make thorough task analyses.

Another strategy emphasizes the importance of early face-to-face experience with students. After the barest minimum of attention to objectives and task analysis, one is urged to try to teach the lesson to some students. On the basis of this trial experience, the definition of objectives can be sharpened and the task analysis refined.

In short, there are several different orders in which the various elements of instructional planning and development can be accomplished. There is no single formula that can be recommended to all. Which strategy will work the best for a given school, a given curriculum project, or a given teacher, undoubtedly depends upon a number of factors—not all of which it is possible to be very clear about.

While the order of the steps and the relative emphasis on them at different stages of lesson development may reasonably vary, certain components must be included somewhere in instructional planning and development if effectiveness in teaching is to be achieved. An incisive task analysis is one of these essential components.

SELF-TEST ON TASK ANALYSIS

This test is intended to teach as well as test. Do not look at the rest of the chapter while taking the test. Please write your answers on some scratch paper. Then grade your own test using the scoring key provided at the end of the chapter.

1. Which of the following is the best definition of task analysis?

a. A task analysis specifies the concepts, principles, and skills that scholars and educational specialists in a field believe are important.

b. A task analysis specifies in detail the material to be covered in a lesson, unit, or course.
c. A task analysis specifies in detail the activities, exercises, and assignments students will be expected to complete.
d. A task analysis specifies the skills and knowledges a student will have to acquire in order to attain an objective.

2. What is a "gap" in a task analysis?
3. Briefly, in two or three sentences, describe what is entailed in doing a task analysis.
4. List the characteristics of a satisfactory task analysis. (Our list mentions six characteristics.)

Summary

Task analysis is an important part of instructional planning. A task analysis describes the subskills and subconcepts a student must acquire in order to master a complex skill or an interrelated set of concepts and principles. Such an analysis should be complete, presented in the proper amount of detail, with relationships among component skills and concepts clearly specified. It should identify when and under what circumstances each component skill is to be performed. In short, the task analysis provides a blueprint of the things a student must master if he is to reach the objectives that have been set.

A satisfactory task analysis has at least these two important characteristics. First, the analysis is consistent with objectives, general objectives as well as the specific ones for a given task. Second, lessons based on the analysis successfully teach all or most students.

Task analysis plays two roles in instructional planning. First, it is the starting point for lesson development. Materials, activities, and teaching procedures are created or selected—then arranged into a sequence—on the basis of the task analysis. The task analysis also guides the diagnosis of poor student performance. Usually students have trouble because they have failed to master one or more of the critical subskills or subconcepts identified in the task analysis. Sometimes the fault is with the task analysis itself; there is a gap in the analysis (and in the lesson based on the analysis), a missing component which students must master before they can acquire the skill as a whole. When the cause of unsatisfactory student performance has been discovered, students who have done poorly should receive remedial instruction and the lesson should be revised so that it will teach better when next used.

SCORING KEY FOR THE SELF-TEST ON TASK ANALYSIS

Grade your own test using this guide. A satisfactory score is 8 of 11 possible points.

1. *(1 point)* d

2. *(1 point)* A "gap" is an important subskill or subconcept which was overlooked in the analysis.

3. *(2 points)*

(1) One point is earned for indicating that the task analyst determines each of the major component skills and concepts that the student will have to possess to reach an objective, perhaps by thinking through the steps involved in the task himself.

(1) Credit one point for indicating that each component is then analyzed into its constituents, and the process continues until the analysis has traced back to skills and knowledges which are part of the student's entering behavior.

4. *(7 points)*

(1) Completeness. If a lesson based on an analysis is to succeed, every important subskill and subconcept must be identified.

(1) Proper amount of detail. The analysis should continue until the total task has been reduced, through a chain of intermediate steps, to skills and knowledges already in the student's repertoire.

(1) The relationships among component skills and concepts should be specified.

(1) The cues which must signal the skill into action and guide its execution should be specified.

(1) The task analysis should be consistent with general educational goals.

(2) Most important, the lessons based on the task analysis should work effectively with students.

Selected Readings

Gagné, R. M., "The Acquisition of Knowledge," in R. C. Anderson and others, *Current Research on Instruction*. Englewood Cliffs, N.J.: Prentice-Hall, 1969. This paper contains the classic statement of the view that knowledge can be analyzed into hierarchies of component skills, concepts, and principles.

Gagné, R. M., *The Conditions of Learning*. New York: Holt, Rinehart, and Winston, 1965. Gagné presents a more complete analysis of the components of kinds of knowledge, relates these components to types or levels of learning, and attempts to describe the conditions under which the various components are most readily learned.

Gibson, E. J., "Learning to Read," *Science* (1965), *148*, 1066–1072. Described in this paper is an analysis of beginning reading skills, with emphasis on discriminations among letters and letter-sound correspondences.

Hively, W., "A Framework for the Analysis of Elementary Reading Behavior," *American Educational Research Journal* (1966), *3*, 89–104. In an award-winning paper, Hively presents another analysis of beginning reading.

Mechner, F., "Science Education and Behavioral Technology," in R. Glaser, ed., *Teaching Machines and Programed Learning, II*. Washington, D.C.: National Education Association, 1965. Mechner clarifies some of the important objectives of science education, and analyzes the skills and concepts designated in these objectives.

CHAPTER

3

Entering Behavior

The student who presents himself for instruction has much potential and many capabilities, yet he still has much to learn. He has, however, particular skills and knowledges acquired from previous instruction or incidental experience; and he also has established patterns of behavior and ways of thinking or feeling which have developed through various conditioning processes. These entry-level characteristics of students are the building blocks of new learning. They are the materials which the teacher must work with, add to, or develop in order to achieve his objectives.

In this chapter we shall discuss entering behavior and various related concepts. After reading the chapter you should be able to:

1. define entering behavior.
2. distinguish entering behavior from other characteristics which students possess prior to instruction.
3. specify in proper form the critical entering behavior for a lesson within your field of specialization.

Entering Behavior and Its Relation to Objectives

Not all of the characteristics of the student who presents himself for instruction can be classified as entering behavior. Entering behavior is comprised of the skills and knowledge, specifically related to course objectives, which the student possesses before instruction. It includes (1) prerequisite skills, skills which the student must know but which will be assumed instead of taught; and (2) preinstructional skill at enabling objectives and terminal objectives.

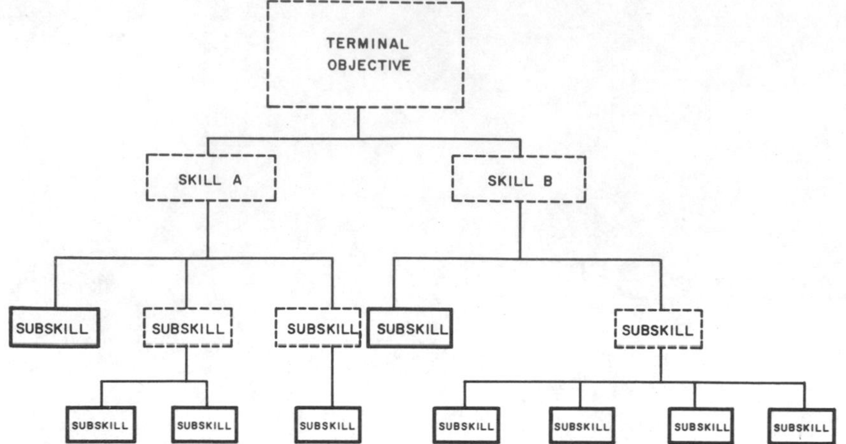

FIGURE 3.1 *A diagram representing a hypothetical lesson objective and its component skills and subskills.*

Look at Fig. 3.1. This diagram represents the objective of a lesson and the skills and subskills which the student must acquire before reaching it. The boxes with solid borders represent what the student can do prior to instruction. Since these skills are subskills of the terminal objective, they can be called entering behaviors. These entering behaviors represent the starting point of instruction, the objective represents the goal of instruction, and the boxes in between represent what must be taught. Entering behaviors and objectives therefore can be said to define the limits of the teachers' responsibility. The teacher must see to it that students move from the point of entering behavior to that of desired terminal performance.

Identifying Entering Behaviors

The job of identifying and describing entering behavior involves more than merely describing the students who walk in your door that first week in September. Many characteristics of the student are irrelevant to the attainment of lesson objectives. Some characteristics, for example, height and hair color, undoubtedly have little effect upon a student's ability to perform in most classrooms. Similarly, a student's ability to define the term "carnivore" or to read a micrometer will have little bearing upon whether or not he will be able to master the concepts of plane geometry. The instructional planner must learn to identify those characteristics of students which are critical to attainment of course objectives and to distinguish them from characteristics which, though they may make interesting items of conversation, are not related to objectives.

Entering behaviors should be identified during the task analysis. You will remember that in our discussion of task analysis we stated that for each subtask or component skill, the analysis is detailed enough when the intact skill is part of the student's entering behavior. This means that during task analysis you continue breaking down the component skills until you have reached a point where the subskills are already a part of the student's behavioral repertoire. A lesson or series of lessons is then designed to fill the gap between entering skills and the objectives.

Adapting instruction to student's entry level. But how do you know when you have broken down a task to the point of entering behavior? The answer is, first, you guess and, then, you test students to see if your guess was right. The first step is one in which you rely upon your experience. Once you have made your guess you develop a test to check your hypotheses about entering behavior. This test is then given to representative samples of students (if you are so lucky as to have them available). Of course, sample students are not always available and thus you sometimes have to develop instruction without any assurance that your estimate of entering behavior is correct. Whether or not you have tested samples of students, you should be prepared to give remedial instruction to those students who do not meet minimal standards of entering behavior.

As you are quite aware, all students entering a particular grade are not alike with respect to level of entering behavior. In Fig. 3.2 we have illustrated the entry level of knowledge of three hypothetical students. The teacher confronted by these three students has some difficult decisions to make. He may decide to begin his course at level 2, as indicated by the shaded area on the figure. If so, he will be fitting the course well to Dick's entry level. But he will probably end up losing Tom and boring Harry. If the course begins at level 3, on the other hand, two students are likely to be lost. At some point in the planning process, though, the teacher must make a decision about what level of entering behavior to assume, and must develop his instruction accordingly.

The most reasonable course of action when students do not possess essential prerequisites is to teach them. Sometimes teaching prerequisite skills and knowledges is not feasible, however, or at least is not *believed* to be feasible. A physics teacher will argue that he should not be expected to teach mathematics. A high school English teacher contemplating assignments in Hemingway, Salinger, and Camus will be dismayed by students who can't comprehend a fourth-grade basal reader. People

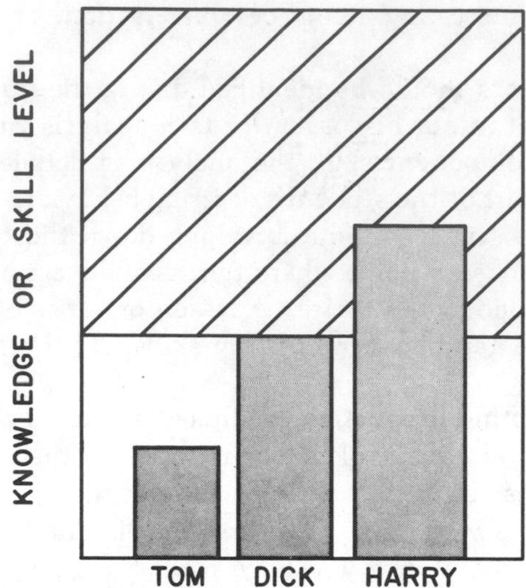

FIGURE 3.2 *A comparison of the entry level of knowledge for three hypothetical students. The diagonal shading represents the skill or knowledge level spanned by a course of instruction.*

who somehow progress through school without mastering vital skills and concepts are in deep trouble since teachers of advanced subjects often will not take the time nor bend the curriculum to reach deficient students. In our opinion, such teachers should reflect further about the purpose of education. There is a good deal of truth in an aphorism of progressive education: "School is to teach children, not subjects."

The argument on the other side is that education is reduced to its lowest common denominator when every course of study must begin with the ABC's. The student who has already mastered prerequisites is penalized when he has to mark time instead of moving on to fresh ideas. One way to maintain the integrity of a curriculum without punishing the deficient or penalizing the competent is to establish admissions criteria. Admissions criteria often include previous course work. For instance, a person may be admitted to high school physics only if he has taken algebra and earned a grade of B or better. A better procedure is to require the candidate to pass a test of prerequisites in order to be admitted.

Assessing entry level. It is common practice to gather some information about students prior to the development or presentation of instruction. Often this information is of a very general nature: the student "has passed second grade" or "is an underachiever" or "has a high IQ." But what do such statements mean to the teacher who must develop instruction?

A child who has passed first grade *may* be able to read a basic vocabulary of 300 words or possibly 1200 words. Or it may be that he can add and subtract using the numbers 1 through 10, or count up to 100, or describe the four seasons, or tell time. But really you don't know exactly what any one child who has "passed first grade" can do. Even if you know that a student has passed first grade at Edison Elementary School and has an IQ of 110 you still do not have the specific kind of information that is needed for sound educational planning.

General statements about students' entering characteristics are not enough. The first step in developing instruction which is sensitive to student differences is the construction and use of tests of specific entering behavior. You need tests which let you determine what disparity exists between what your students can do and what you want them to be able to do after instruction. That is, you need tests which will indicate to you what you need to teach in order to reach your objectives.

Because we want to measure students' ability to meet required entry standards, we should be careful to state entering behaviors in measurable terms. That is, entering behavior should be stated behaviorally. Taken on their own, statements of entering behavior and objectives should be indistinguishable. One teacher's statements of entering behavior should be another's objectives; thus, the sixth-grade teacher's statements of objectives and the seventh-grade teacher's statements of entering behaviors would be identical. Indeed, if all teachers stated their objectives behaviorally, measured them accurately, and reported pupil progress in terms of objectives attained, tests of entering behaviors would not be so necessary and teachers would lead much less troubled lives. Until that time, however, we suggest that each teacher make his own assessment of his students' entering behaviors and program his instruction accordingly.

Entering behavior is assessed using a "pretest," meaning simply a test given before instruction. The pretest should include measures of:

1. the skills named in terminal objectives.
2. the subskills and subconcepts named in enabling objectives, and
3. prerequisite skills and knowledge.

The pretest is an achievement test, covering the specific knowledge and skills which will be taught in the lesson. (The word "test" should be interpreted in a broad sense to include any evaluation of complex student performance, such as leading a discussion or adjusting a carburetor.) Specific procedures for developing achievement tests will be described in Chapter 4.

With the exception of the sections on prerequisites, the same test could be used after instruction to determine whether objectives have been attained. However, it is usually not a good idea to use exactly the same test before and after instruction. The reason is that if the student repeats an identical test, he may do better merely because he has memorized the answers to specific questions.

Pretest information is useful in two ways. First, it tells you what students already know and, therefore, what will not have to be taught. It may be that students have previously mastered some of the enabling objectives, or perhaps even the terminal objectives. If so, the lesson should be condensed or omitted. Second, the pretest serves as a check on assumptions about prerequisite skills. Prerequisite skills and knowledge are the behaviors identified in the task analysis as ones the student already possesses. These behaviors are presumably vital if the student is to learn but they are not taught within the lesson. If there has been an adequate task analysis, lessons based on the analysis probably won't teach very well unless students have mastered prerequisites.

Research completed with a self-instructional program on population genetics for high school biology students illustrates the value of information about prerequisites (Anderson, 1969). The authors of the program assumed that students taking it would be skilled at the arithmetic of proportions, capable of squaring a binomial and factoring a squared binomial. These prerequisite entering behaviors were assessed in a five-item section of the pretest. However, to the authors' dismay, a large-scale tryout of the program showed that only 40 percent of the students possessed the mathematics skills necessary to earn a passing score (four out of five problems). The importance of these entering skills is evidenced in Fig. 3.3, which plots percent correct on the posttest as a function of scores on the prerequisite section of the pretest. In the study the "no program" classes used a textbook and laboratory exercises prepared by the Biological Sciences Curriculum Study. As you can see, the program was slightly more effective at every level, but its advantage was substantial only for students who possessed the mathematics skills.

Thus, pretests which are designed to measure both prerequisite skills and already-achieved lesson objectives should be the teachers' guide to individualizing instruction. Since entering behavior tests can be used to pinpoint what needs to be taught to which students, instruction geared to entering behavior will avoid a major cause of academic failure, underpreparation, and a major cause of boredom, overpreparation.

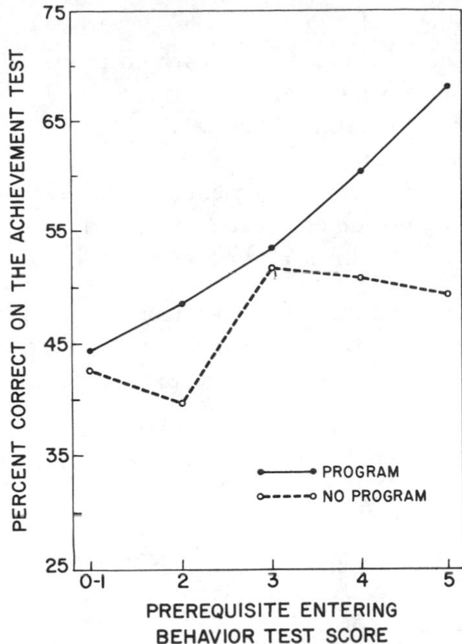

FIGURE 3.3 *Achievement as a Function of Prerequisite Entering Behavior (from Anderson, 1969).*

Measurement of Student Differences

The search for factors which affect how people differ in rate, extent, style, and quality of learning has had a time-honored place in the annals of psychology. Presumably this search has an even longer history among teachers. As psychologists record and analyze data on this subject, teachers continue evaluating and making allowances for a wide variety of student differences. Their assessments of individual differences may be either formal or informal, and the uses made of these assessments are many and varied. In the following sections we shall attempt to put various measures of individual differences in perspective, to show how they relate to entering behaviors and how they can be used by the instructional planner.

Individual differences as measured by standardized tests. There are many ways of describing students prior to the beginning of instruction. One very common one is to describe them in terms of intelligence, personality, or academic achievement. These descriptive dimensions are so popular that there are over 1200 standardized tests now available on the American market with which to measure them.

The following pages will contain a discussion of the characteristics and proper interpretation of standardized tests. We feel it is important that teachers have a general knowledge of standardized tests because they are so common a fixture in our present educational system. However, because of their limited usefulness in the day-to-day routine of most classrooms, our objectives for this section are rather limited. They are:

1. when given the requirement to select a standardized test and a statement as to the purpose the test will serve, select the standardized test best suited to that purpose.
2. when given the results of a standardized test and the test manual, interpret these results and be able to explain their meaning to others.

Standardized tests generally have three characteristics in common: (1) they have a fixed set of items; (2) they have a set of specific directions for administration and scoring; and (3) they have been tried on some representative sample(s) of individuals and a summary of this tryout accompanies the test. The standardized set of items and standard administration and scoring procedures make these tests particularly useful for comparing individual scores or groups of scores which were obtained at different times and places, while the summary data of past administrations provides the standards or norms against which to make comparisons.

To evaluate the potential value of standardized tests to the educational planner, you must first understand the types of information generated by such tests. Such an understanding requires that you have a general knowledge of the rationale behind the selection of items for standardized tests. The following sections are designed to produce such a general knowledge.

It is important to understand that the objective of standardized tests is *not* to evaluate progress through a particular course of instruction; that is, they are not designed to measure attainment of specific educational objectives. Standardized tests are designed to fulfill evaluative functions, however, and to do this consistently. What the particular evaluative function is depends upon the type of test under discussion (i.e., intelligence test, personality test, achievement test). How well the function is performed is determined by the test's validity and reliability. Validity and reliability are the two major criteria by which test developers and users judge standardized tests.

Validity. Validity is a measure of the extent to which a test measures what it is presumed to measure. If you are testing student attainment of course objectives, your test will be valid insofar as it actually measures attainment of these objectives. If, on the other hand, you are using a test to predict future job success or mental stability, validity is measured in terms of how well the test makes such predictions. A test may be valid for one purpose and invalid for another. For example, a test which validly measures English achievement generally is an invalid measure of physical stamina. The point to remember is that validity is not determined by the test alone. The specific purpose of the test must be considered.

Standardized tests are designed to assess either the general educational development (achievement); the academic potential (intelligence); or the attitudes, interests, and adjustment (personality) of students. Their validity is determined by how well they make these assessments.

Validity is often divided into two basic types: content validity and criterion validity. *Content validity* has been defined by Gronlund (1965) as "the extent to which a test measures a representative sample of the subject matter content and the behavioral changes under consideration." The content validity of an achievement test is determined by the degree to which the test measures the objectives of instruction or the degree to which the content of the test reflects the content of instruction.

Standardized achievement tests are usually designed to evaluate student performance with respect to the general educational objectives of a representative sample of educators or subject-matter experts. Content validity for this purpose is derived by having the sample of educators or experts agree upon the general educational goals or the important items of information which should be derived from a "good education," and then by developing tests which measure attainment of these goals.

Criterion validity is determined by the extent to which test performance can be used to predict a given criterion behavior. A test which allows one to predict job success perfectly, for example, would have perfect criterion validity for this purpose. Criterion validity is often measured by the statistical procedure of *correlation,* and is reported in terms of a numerical index called a "correlation coefficient." The correlation coefficient indicates the degree of relationship between two (or more) variables. When used as a measure of criterion validity, at least one of these variables is a test score and at least one other is the criterion performance. The criterion performance can take the form of another test score, a job rating, success in one's chosen profession, or any other variable or set of variables we are interested in predicting.

While the explanation of the precise mathematical meaning of the correlation coefficient must await a course in statistics, it is sufficient here to note that such coefficients will range from 0 to ±1.0; and the larger the absolute value of the coefficient, the better is the criterion validity. The sign of the correlation (+ or −) is irrelevant, so far as *degree* of relationship is concerned (i.e., coefficients of −.70 and .70 indicate a similar degree of relationship between two variables; however in both of these cases the indicated relationship is greater than one indicated by a coefficient of +.60). Minus signs (−.45, −.75, −1.0, etc.) merely indicate an inverse relationship between the variables. That is, high scores on one measure are predictive of low scores on the other. In the case of a criterion validity coefficient of −1.0, for example, prediction of one measure from another is perfect. This indicates that if an individual scores high on the test, he will score low on the criterion performance. Positive coefficients, on the other hand, indicate that high scores on one measure are predictive of high scores on the other.

Many standardized tests are used for purposes of prediction. When the college registrar uses standardized achievement or aptitude test scores in selecting students for college entrance, he is taking advantage of the ability of these tests to predict college success. He wishes to admit students who will eventually graduate. He wants a test with high criterion validity, the criterion being success in college.

When teachers use the scores of aptitude or IQ tests to group students prior to instruction they, too, are interested in the predictive power of these tests. They are using the tests to predict which students will need a particular kind of instruction, which will need extra help, or which will be able to move rapidly through a subject. They are, therefore, interested in a test with criterion validity.

Which do you think will be a better predictor of subsequent success (attainment of objectives) in a particular elementary-school lesson in mathematics?

A. a test of the required entering behaviors for that lesson
B. a standardized test of mathematics achievement
C. a standardized intelligence test

The answer appears on p. **97.**

In summary it should be emphasized that validity is the chief characteristic upon which to base the decision to use or not to use any test. Remember validity is purpose-specific. A test has validity for a specific purpose. Validity is not something inherent in the test itself. Therefore as the purpose for using a particular test changes, the validity of the test will also change. The guideline should be this: no matter how well constructed the test, if it does not fulfill your needs or is not suited to your purpose it should not be used.

Reliability. A reliable test is one which measures a given performance consistently. More precisely, it will place individuals in about the same position relative to each other if it is given twice to the same group of individuals. An unreliable test, on the other hand, cannot be "relied" on to yield such consistent results. Its results are erratic. A student may do relatively well on the test one day, but not on the next. Thus, an unreliable test is by definition low in validity. Since it cannot be *counted on* to measure anything consistently, it cannot be counted on to measure what we intend it to measure.

Although low reliability necessarily results in low validity, *it is not true* that a test with low validity must necessarily have low reliability. A test may consistently measure something we do not expect or want it to measure.

The teacher who uses a standardized mathematics test to help assign students to social science study groups may be using a reliable test, but for his purpose its validity is certainly suspect. A rule to follow in selecting a test is that, although reliability is a most desirable characteristic for a test to exhibit, it should never be purchased at the expense of validity.

In evaluating or selecting a standardized test the teacher must first consider his purpose. Reported validity figures are relevant only to the extent that the criteria used to determine the validity coefficients are the same as those the teacher is interested in. As we see it, a major danger in the use of standardized tests is that teachers use the tests without being clear as to the purposes the test will serve or how their own purposes relate to criteria used in determining the test's reported validity. The danger is so real that for most day-to-day educational decisions about entry level we recommend teacher-made tests which are direct tests of specific entry-level performance. For such teacher-made tests validity is determined by the degree to which test questions measure the specific entry-level performances, and the teacher's concern for reliability is limited to considerations about the objectivity or consistency of scoring and whether or not the test allows for an adequate sample of the to-be-tested performance.

As Gronlund (1967) states, "a logical analysis of a test will provide little evidence concerning the reliability of the scores." Reliability can only be determined through the statistical analysis of test results. Thus, though the reliability is generally determined for standardized tests, it is seldom known exactly for teacher-made tests. Teachers may attempt to build reliability into their tests but they seldom bother to check it statistically.

There are basically two ways in which reliabilities of standardized tests are reported: (1) in terms of a correlation or reliability coefficient; (2) in terms of the standard error of measurement of the test. The most common method is to report reliability as a correlation coefficient, which indicates the degree of relationship between the scores of people who have taken the same test twice or who have taken equivalent forms of the test. Reliability can also be determined by correlating scores on two halves of the test. (However, the "reliability" coefficient obtained by use of split-halves is a measure of *homogeneity,* whereas that obtained by test-retest is a measure of *stability.*) Test makers usually hope for a reliability coefficient of .90 or better.

The standard error of measurement is another way of indicating the reliability of a test. It is an estimate of the amount of variability there would be in the scores of one person if that person took the test a very large number of times. We know, for example, that if a particular student takes the same IQ test several times he will most likely not get exactly the same score each time. Such factors as practice, variability in his attention to the task, fatigue, guessing strategies, and emotional strain will cause his scores to fluctuate. The standard error of an IQ test is an estimate of how much one person's scores are likely to fluctuate if the test is administered repeatedly. That is, it is a measure of the reliability or consistency of the test.

The certainty of statements about students' aptitudes, achievement, and performance as measured by standardized tests should be tempered by what is known concerning the reliability of the measuring instrument. Less reliable tests justify less certain statements, since such tests are more prone to error than their more reliable counterparts. It is a common phenomenon to find teachers who make far-reaching decisions on the basis of test differences of only a few points when such differences cannot be reliably detected with the measuring instrument used.

Interpreting standardized tests. If standardized tests are to be of any value in the classroom, teachers must be able to interpret scores. Because of the way in which most standardized tests are developed, they can only be interpreted by comparing scores or groups of scores. To help the teacher make such comparisons, test developers provide information about how other groups of students have performed on the tests. Therefore, once the test maker has decided upon test objectives, planned the content of the test, written the test questions, tried out the questions, revised and reassembled the test, and written the test directions, he gives the test to a carefully selected sample of persons. The sample is selected so as to represent a cross section of the people who are expected to take the test, because test data gathered on the sample is used to construct the tables of norms. It is in the light of the performance of the sample that the test user evaluates the performance of his students.

The tables of norms presented in test manuals are, then, no more than summaries of the test performance of various representative groups of students. It is important that the user remember two things when using tables of norms:

First, he should remember to compare the scores of students to *appropriate* norm groups. Little is gained when the social studies achievement of high school freshmen is compared with that of second-year law students. Appropriate norm groups are those which a student is a member of, is likely to become a member of, or would like to become a member of in the near future. Thus, college freshmen generally provide an appropriate norm group with which to compare high school seniors. In determining the appropriateness of a norm group the test user should consider more than the type of the norm group. He should also consider the currency of norm groups. Contemporary high school seniors, for example, can be assumed to have different abilities and interests than the class of '29 and therefore the 1929 norms are inappropriate.

Second, the user should remember that data presented in tables of norms only indicate the performance of other groups of students. The norms do not necessarily represent standards or goals that we should

Answer to the question on p. **94.**

We believe that the most valid predictor of the attainment of the objectives of a particular elementary school lesson in mathematics would be **A,** a test of the required entering behaviors for that lesson. What little research there is on this matter supports this view (Gagné & Paradise, 1961; Gagné, Mayor, Gartens, & Paradise, 1962). We also believe that such a test would be the most valuable pre-lesson test for the teacher to give, since it provides information concerning students' readiness for the instruction which has been developed; and, if they are not ready, it can be used in prescribing the kind of instruction which will make them so.

hope to attain. Test producers do not attempt to make value judgments as to the acceptability of performance reported in tables of norms, leaving such judgments to the parents, counselors, and teachers who use the information provided by the test.

Test makers usually indicate the performance of norm groups through the use of descriptive statistics or derived scores. The descriptive statistics which are most often used in this way are measures of central tendency and variability.

Measures of central tendency. A measure of central tendency is used to describe a point around which scores tend to cluster. Such a point will lie somewhere between the extreme scores. There are three common measures of central tendency: the mean, the median, and the mode. The mean is the average score and is determined by dividing the sum of all the scores obtained on the test by the number of scores. If ten students scored 1, 3, 4, 4, 4, 5, 6, 6, 7, and 8 respectively, the mean (abbreviated $\overline{X}$) score on the quiz would be 48 ÷ 10 or 4.8. The mean is the most commonly used measure of central tendency.

The median, another measure of central tendency, indicates the middle of the score range. In other words the median is that point above and below which 50 percent of the scores fall. For the ten scores mentioned above the median would be 4.5, the point halfway between the two middle scores. If we add one more score, let's say a 7, to the list above, the median would change to 5, the middle score. Notice that the *magnitude* of the new score has no effect upon the median. The median will be 5 whether the new score is 7, 17, or 700.

The third measure of central tendency is the mode. It is defined as the most common score, that score which the largest number of people obtain. In the list of ten scores above, for example, the modal score is 4, since more people got this score than any other. The mode of a distribution is frequently neither a stable nor a reliable measure of central tendency. Sometimes the mode is indeterminate. A distribution may be bimodal (have two modes, as in the case of the scores 1, 2, 2, 2, 3, 4, 4, 4, 5), or even trimodal.

Measures of variability. Measures of variability are used to indicate how much the scores on a test are spread out. The range and the standard deviation are the most common measures of variability. The range of a test is the difference between the highest and lowest score. If the scores are 2, 5, 10, 11, 12, the range is 12–2 or 10. The range gives information about only two of the scores in a distribution (the highest and lowest) and is therefore rather unstable.

The standard deviation is generally the preferred measure of variability. It describes a score interval; the greater this interval the greater the spread of scores in the distribution. To compute a standard deviation: (1) find the mean of the scores; (2) subtract the mean from each score; (3) square each of these deviations from the mean; (4) sum the squared deviations; (5) divide this sum by the number of scores; and, finally, (6) take the square root of the answer obtained in (5). It is not essential that you know this procedure; it is described here only to give you some idea of the nature of the standard deviation (SD) and to demonstrate that, unlike the range, the SD is based on all the scores.

The meaning of the standard deviation is best explained in terms of the normal distribution curve. This curve is in actuality a family of symmetrical, bell-shaped curves which can be described by a common mathematical function. Look now at the normal curve depicted in Fig. 3.4. Notice that the mean, median, and mode coincide (all equal 100) in this distribution, as they will in any normal distribution..

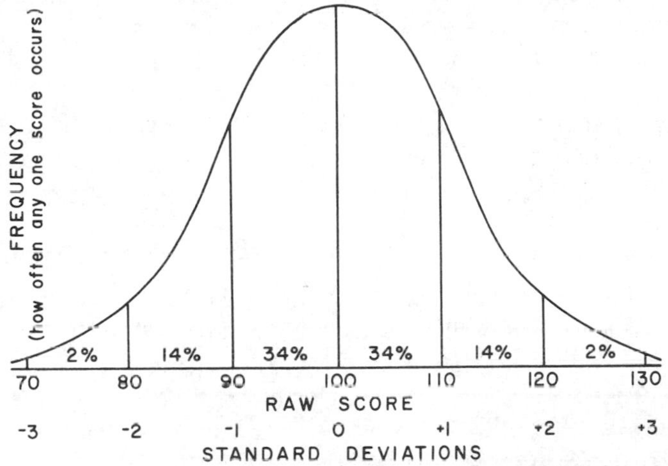

FIGURE 3.4 *Normal curve indicating the approximate percentage of cases falling within each standard deviation interval.*

When a normal curve is divided into SD intervals (note here the SD is 10), 34% of the scores fall between the mean and +1 SD, 14% fall between +1 and +2 SD, and 2% fall between +2 and +3 SD. The same percentages fall into the SD intervals below the mean. It should be pointed out that some small number of cases will fall outside of the ±3 SD range. Whenever a normal distribution is divided into SD intervals, these same proportions will apply. Because of the method used in developing standardized tests and because of the large number of scores used to generate descriptive data on these tests, we can assume that the scores on most standardized tests are approximately normally distributed. Knowing this we can make statements about the relative position of an individual within a group when given that individual's score and the mean and the standard deviation of the test. For example, a student whose score is two SD's above the mean (i.e., his score $= 120$, $\overline{X} = 100$, $SD = 10$) on a standardized test has scored higher than approximately 98 percent of the students who have taken the test.

Derived scores. Although knowledge of raw score means and standard deviations can be useful in the interpretation of test scores, the test manufacturers have developed various types of "derived scores" which can make interpreting test scores even less painful for the counselor or classroom teacher. The percentile score or percentile rank is one such derived score. A student's percentile rank indicates the percentage of students whose scores fall below that of the given individual. Thus, if Sally has a percentile rank of 45, this means 45 percent of the students scored below her on the test. The percentile rank provides an easy way to interpret or report test scores. It is especially helpful because it takes little explaining and seems to provide the information most parents desire.

A second commonly used type of derived score is the standard score. The basic standard score is the *z*-score, which is simply the student's raw score (X) minus the mean score ($\overline{X}$) and divided by the standard deviation (SD); that is, $z = \frac{X - \overline{X}}{SD}$. Notice that if the raw score is identical to the mean, the *z*-score will equal 0. If the raw score is one SD above the mean, the *z*-score will be $+1$. Look back at Fig. 3.4 and notice that the label reading "standard deviations" could be changed to read "*z*-score" and the entries (-3, -2, -1, 0, etc.) would still be appropriate.

Now answer the following questions. If you have trouble with them we suggest that you reread the last few pages.

A. Dan gets a z-score of $+1$. What is his approximate percentile?

B. Carl receives a raw score of 80 on the test illustrated in Fig. 3.4. What is his z-score? What is his percentile rank?

C. What raw score must you achieve to get a z-score of exactly 0? With a z-score of 0 what is your percentile?

The answers appear on p. **103.**

Since plus and minus signs can be hard to work with, standard scores other than the *z*-scores have been developed. These other standard scores are based on the *z*-score and differ from it only in the numerical value given to the established means and standard deviations. These differences in means and standard deviations are given in Fig. 3.5. Included in this figure are the two commonly used types of deviation IQ scores which, as the figure indicates, are also a form of standard score.

Score	Mean	Standard deviation
z	0	1
T	50	10
CEEB (College Entrance Examination Board)	500	100
Stanford Binet IQ	100	16
Wechsler Intelligence Scale IQ	100	15

FIGURE 3.5 *Means and standard deviations of some commonly used standard scores.*

The *T*-score is an easy-to-use standard score that is used by many test producers, whereas the CEEB (College Entrance Examination Board), Binet, and Wechsler scores are seldom used with other than their parent tests. To convert a given z-score to one of these other standard scores is an easy matter. Simply (1) multiply the desired standard deviation by the obtained *z*-score and then (2) add the desired mean to this product. For example, to convert a *z*-score of 1.5 to a *T*-score you use the formula $T = 10(1.5) + 50$. Remember the *T* distribution has a mean of 50 and an SD of 10. If you want to convert from a *z*-score to a CEEB score, multiply the *z*-score by 100 and add 500, $\text{CEEB} = 100(1.5) + 500$. These other types of standard scores, like the *z*-score, are easily translated into percentiles. This is an especially useful feature when reporting test scores to parents since parents may be eager to find out how Johnny ranks in history achievement, but will seldom be prepared to sit through the explanation required if you report test results in standard-score form.

One major advantage of standard scores is that they provide an equality of units between different tests given to the same students. This makes it possible, for example, to compare how Johnny stands in arithmetic with how he stands in spelling. Comparisons of IQ scores must be handled cautiously, however, for although most deviation IQ's have a mean of 100, their standard deviations may vary (as is evidenced in Fig. 3.5).

On the elementary-school level teachers often find test scores reported as grade equivalents or age equivalents. Grade and age equivalents are derived scores designed to allow the teacher to compare the performance of her students with the "average" performance of students at other grade and age levels. Grade equivalents are generally expressed as a whole number and a decimal, the whole number indicating a year and the decimal indicating a month of that year. For example, the typical performance of a student in his fourth month of grade five would be indicated by the number 5.4. Age equivalents are also reported using two digits. In this case the first digit indicates a year and the second indicates a number of months over and above that year. For example, a student whose raw score is the same as the average score of students who are nine years and ten months of age would receive an age-equivalent score of 9-10.

To make it easy for the teacher to compare his students with norm groups, derived scores are usually presented in tables along with the equivalent raw scores. Such a table is presented in Fig. 3.6. Once the teacher has the raw scores of his students in hand, he merely finds these scores in the table and locates the equivalent derived score. The derived score will either tell how the student stands in the norm group, in the

Raw score	T-score	Reading grade	Reading age
10	35	3.3	8–3
11	37	3.5	8–7
12	39	3.7	8–10
13	40	3.9	9–0
14	43	4.0	9–4
15	45	4.3	9–7
16	47	4.8	9–11
17	50	5.0	10–3
18	53	5.3	10–7
19	56	5.8	11–0
20	58	6.5	11–9

FIGURE 3.6 *A sample norm table indicating the T-score, grade and age equivalents of raw scores obtained on a hypothetical test of reading achievement.*

case of standard scores, or at what grade or age level his test performance would be typical.

Despite their apparent simplicity of interpretation, grade and age equivalents should be used with extreme caution. As has been illustrated in Fig. 3.6, the relationship between raw score points, and grade and age equivalents, differs considerably on different parts of the scale. In Fig. 3.6, notice that an increase of one raw score point on the lower end of the scale has only a minor effect on the grade or age equivalent, while a similar increase at the upper end of the scale has considerable effect. Tests using grade and age equivalents often require an unwarranted amount of faith in the ability of one or two test items to cover extremely large segments of the scale. Academic development from year to year and grade to grade is not even. Furthermore, grade and age growth as measured by standardized tests is very dependent upon the specific subject matter covered between testing periods. Since this subject matter can be expected to vary considerably from state to state, school to school, and teacher to teacher, the problems of interpreting grade and age scores are compounded.

Profiles. A test profile is used to compare the various strengths and weaknesses of an individual student. It is a graphic representation of one student's performance on many tests or subtests. Profiles make use of the fact that standard scores put scores from different tests on the same scale and therefore allow direct comparison of a pupil's performance across different tests. In using profiles the teacher should be careful, however, not to attribute to the test more precision of measurement than it possesses. Test manufacturers are aware of this common problem and many have attempted to avoid it by using score

Answers to the questions on p. **101.**

A. Dan's z-score of +1 is equivalent to a percentile rank of about 84.

B. Carl's score of 80 yields a z-score of −2 (remember $z = \frac{X - \overline{X}}{SD}$ or in this case $\frac{80 - 100}{10}$) and a percentile rank of about 2.

C. A raw score of 100 is equal to a z-score of 0 and a percentile rank of 50.

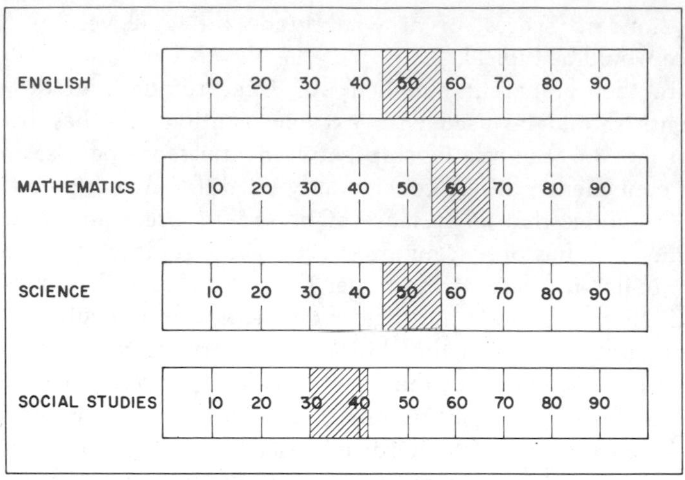

FIGURE 3.7 *Percentile bands used to report test scores on a hypothetical achievement battery.*

bands rather than points on a scale when reporting test scores. This technique is illustrated in Fig. 3.7, where hypothetical achievement scores in English, mathematics, science, and social studies are presented in profile form. Taking into consideration the accuracy or reliability of the test, this profile presents a band of scores extending one standard error above and below the pupil's obtained score.

There are approximately two chances out of three that a pupil's true score will fall within one standard error of his obtained score. Therefore, if the teacher only considers cases in which the standard error bands do not overlap as indicating true differences, he can be reasonably sure that he is not making overly refined distinctions between scores. In interpreting the scores in Fig. 3.7, for example, he should report that there is no important or significant difference between the English, mathematics, and social studies scores of this student since the score bands in these areas overlap. However, he should report that the student is significantly lower in social studies achievement than in any of the other three areas since the score band for social studies does not overlap any of the other bands. Evaluation instruments are limited in reliability, and we should not attempt to get more information from them than they are able to give.

Standardized Tests of Student Achievement

Standardized achievement tests measure just what their name implies, achievement. However, since these tests are produced for nationwide use, it may well be the case that there is little in common between your curriculum and the specific areas covered by the test. These tests are generally not designed to evaluate student progress on small units of work, or to probe specified factual knowledge. The latter is especially the case in such rapidly changing areas as science and social studies. Rather, standardized achievement tests are aimed at (1) assessing the *general* educational development of the student in basic skills and in learning outcomes which are common to many courses of study, (2) diagnosing relative strengths and weaknesses of students in commonly taught content areas, and (3) evaluating pupil progress of a general nature over long periods of time (one or several years). They are generally not appropriate for assessing the progress of a student toward the objectives of one particular course or diagnosing the strengths and weaknesses of students within a particular course.

Achievement tests frequently come in the form of test batteries, sets of short tests each of which measures one basic area of educational achievement. On the elementary level all achievement batteries contain subtests concerned with reading, language, and arithmetic skills; and some also contain subtests on work-study skills, science, and social studies. The content of high school achievement batteries is much more diversified, as is evidenced by the following list of subtests of the Iowa Tests of Educational Development (ITED).

1. Understanding Basic Social Concepts.
2. Background in the Natural Sciences.
3. Correctness and Appropriateness of Expression.
4. Ability to do Quantitative Thinking.
5. Ability to Interpret Reading Materials in Social Studies.
6. Ability to Interpret Reading Materials in the Natural Sciences.
7. Ability to Interpret Literary Materials.
8. General Vocabulary.
9. Uses of Information.

The ITED is an example of a test battery designed to measure educational progress, which does not depend, supposedly, upon any particular series of courses. Other test makers have taken different approaches to the assessment of high school achievement. Some make their tests a continuation of elementary achievement batteries by building them around the basic skills of reading, arithmetic, and language. This approach is especially evident in a test like the *California Achievement Tests*. Other tests, like the *Essential High School Content Battery*, are tests of specific course content in basic areas of study such as mathematics, science, social studies, and English.

Not all standardized achievement tests are test batteries. There are hundreds of tests of specific subject matters. These may be used to check the progress of students against national norms. Other tests, which we might label as "diagnostic tests," are specifically designed so that subscores help the teacher to identify rather specific areas of weakness.

Standardized Tests of Intelligence

Tests of scholastic aptitude are generally used to get an indication of the academic potential of students. These tests are relatively good predictors of future academic success. However, one should not be led to believe that aptitude tests measure only inherent abilities (Honzik, MacFarlane & Allen, 1948). Rather, they are a measure of the current academic ability of a student. Changes in study habits or training, for instance, can have considerable effect on scholastic aptitude as measured by most standardized tests. Scholastic aptitude tests differ from achievement tests only in the degree to which they measure specific academic attainments. Thus, achievement and aptitude tests fall along a continuum. This continuum extends from tests which measure achievement in specific content areas through tests, like the ITED, which measure achievement in more basic academic skills. The continuum extends through the closely related aptitude tests, which measure school-related scholastic aptitude, and on to the more "culture-free" aptitude tests, which attempt to measure general problem-solving ability. This continuum is depicted in Fig. 3.8.

Aptitude tests are of many types, and the information they yield comes in many forms. Group tests of aptitude are widely used. They can be administered by classroom teachers after only minimal training, and generally require only about twenty to forty minutes of administration time.

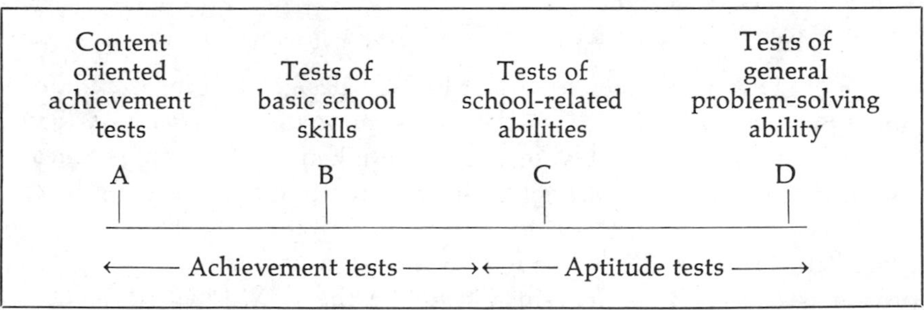

FIGURE 3.8 *The continuum of achievement and aptitude as measured by standardized tests.*

Some of these group tests yield only one score, an index of general scholastic aptitude. Commonly used tests falling into this category are the *Otis Quick-Scoring Mental Ability Test*, the *Henmon-Nelson Tests of Mental Ability*, the *Kuhlmann-Anderson Intelligence Tests, Sixth Edition*, and the *Davis-Eells Games* (subtitled the *Davis-Eells Tests of General Intelligence or Problem Solving Ability*). This last test is an example of a supposedly "culture-fair test." It attempts to overcome the social-class bias which is a problem inherent in all tests which have a middle-class vocabulary base. The language experience of various subgroups of one population (i.e., upper class, urban, rural, culturally deprived, etc.) can vary greatly. Written tests, therefore, give advantages to portions of the population whose language patterns are most like those used in the test. The *Davis-Eells Games* test attempts to measure aptitude apart from that which is determined by language experience by using items in picture form and by requiring that all instructions be read by the test administrator. Both the pictures and instructions used in the test are designed so that all American urban children can easily understand them. No matter how well designed, such measures do not insure that the test will be completely free from social-class bias.

In an attempt to yield more usable information, some standardized tests have been developed so that they yield two or more measures of a student's potential. One of these scores is generally referred to as the verbal score. Verbal scores are intended to indicate abilities in language-related skills. Because verbal skills are so important in school learning these scores generally prove to be excellent predictors of school success.

The second score to be found in the two-score aptitude test may be either a nonverbal score, as is the case in the *Lorge Thorndike Intelligence Tests*, or a quantitative score, as in the case of the *Cooperative School and College Ability Test* (SCAT) and the *Kuhlmann-Anderson Intelligence Tests, Seventh Edition*. Nonverbal scores, as one might imagine, are obtained from items which place little emphasis on the student's ability to use language. Some examples of these items are presented in Fig. 3.9. Nonverbal scores are generally considered to be measures of a student's unrealized potential (i.e., potential which is

The first three drawings are alike in some way. Find the drawing at the right which goes with these three.

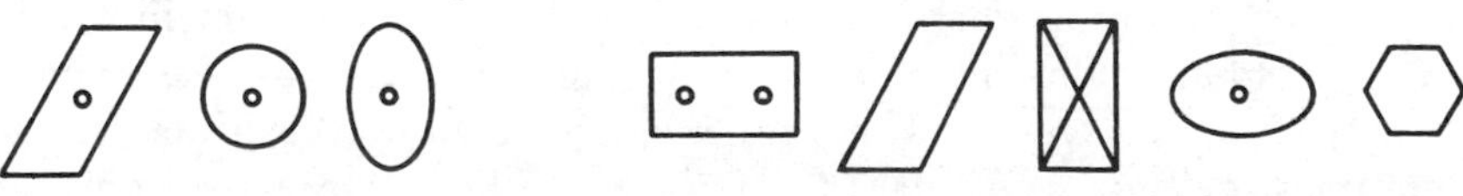

FIGURE 3.9 *An example of a nonverbal test item.*

camouflaged by a poor verbal background). Many feel that proper language training might convert this unrealized potential into a more usable form. Quantitative scores, on the other hand, measure ability in the realm of mathematics and are thus used to predict success in courses stressing mathematics or related concepts (e.g., geometry, physics, chemistry).

Multiscore aptitude tests are available for those who want an even broader look at student potential than is provided by the two-score tests. Included in this category are the *SRA Primary Mental Abilities Test* (PMA) and the *Differential Aptitude Tests* (DAT). These tests are designed to measure several specific yet relatively unrelated aptitudes. The DAT, for example, provides scores on Verbal Reasoning, Numerical Ability, Abstract Reasoning, Space Relations, Mechanical Reasoning, Clerical Speed and Accuracy, Spelling and Grammar. Most of the multiscore tests provide scores in similar areas; however, the number and names of subscores varies, so test manuals must be consulted to determine just what is measured by each of the subscores of any particular test.

For the most part teachers are satisfied with relatively rough measures of student aptitude. However, in cases where students receive extreme scores or scores which conflict with other evaluations, either formal or informal, the teacher may desire a more intensive evaluation of the student's aptitude. This may be accomplished with an individually administered test. Such a test allows the tester to better control or evaluate the influence of factors like motivation, testing environment, and particular student disabilities. Commonly used individual tests include the *Revised Stanford Binet Intelligence Scale, 1960 Revision,* the *Wechsler Preschool,* the *Wechsler Intelligence Scale for Children* (WISC), and the *Wechsler Adult Intelligence Scale* (WAIS). These tests require considerable time for administration, and must be given by persons trained in the administration of the particular test. For this reason they are not recommended as rough screening devices. They should, however, be employed when important or far-reaching educational decisions, such as placement of students in classes for the mentally handicapped, need to be made.

Heredity versus environment. To what extent is intelligence inherited and to what extent is it shaped by the environment? This is an age-old question which has been the subject of a great deal of controversy in recent years. The prominent psychologist Arthur Jensen (1969) has reviewed a number of studies which he interprets as showing that about 80 percent of the variation among people in IQ scores is due to inheritance. By subtraction, this leaves 20 percent accounted for by environment. There are questions about the validity of the assumptions upon which these calculations depend; however, there can be little doubt that intelligence is highly "heritable" (Crow, 1969).

It is important to understand precisely what heritability means. While a thorough discussion is beyond the scope of this text (see Jensen, 1969, pp. 33–46), several points should be made. First of all, heritability is not a universal constant like the speed of light. A heritability estimate holds for a certain population at a certain time under certain environmental conditions. If there is a great range of relevant environmental conditions, then heritability will be relatively low. If a narrow range of environmental conditions affects the population, then heritability will be relatively high. A change in the environment can cause heritability to change.

Second, the fact that intelligence is highly heritable does not mean that intelligence is immutable. Height is another characteristic that is highly heritable, even more heritable than intelligence, yet there have been spectacular increases in the average height of people in Japan and the United States in recent years. These increases are probably due to changes in the environment, such as improved nutrition (Crow, 1969, pp. 158–159).

An improved environment can also raise average intelligence. To illustrate, one dimension of intelligence is called "numerical facility." This is the ability to solve arithmetic problems quickly and accurately. It is quite likely that the average school child of today has more numerical facility than such great thinkers of the past as Plato, Aristotle, Moses, and Ptolemy. The reason for this is simply that arithmetic as we know it today had not been invented when these men lived. Thanks to mathematical developments and universal schooling, there has been a substantial increase in functional mathematical intelligence.

Just as intelligence can be raised so can it be lowered due to environmental or nutritional deprivation. Children in ghetto areas continually lose ground on their contemporaries in more enriched environments as far as *measured* "intelligence" is concerned simply because they do not receive the experience necessary to progress in test-related skills.

One must be very cautious about drawing social and educational policy implications from the fact that intelligence is highly heritable. This fact does not mean, for instance, that compensatory education programs are doomed to failure. However, it does suggest that naive optimism is unwarranted. Simply providing everyone with a "rich," "middle-class" environment may not be sufficient. The best hope is to develop intensive, specialized programs aimed at overcoming specific functional deficiencies

(Bereiter & Engleman, 1966). Whether these deficiencies arise because a person is culturally disadvantaged or genetically disadvantaged is unimportant.

It is commonly said that inheritance limits a person's potential. This is a half-truth. Genes irrevocably limit a person's potential only when he is subjected to a fixed environment which does not take account of his individuality. In years gone by, lack of visual acuity was a very serious handicap. At present, poor vision is a trivial impairment. Most persons fitted with eyeglasses have functionally good vision. We may suppose, too, that there are children who fail to learn to read when taught by conventional methods because of genetic disabilities. If so, a minor genetic deficiency could have disastrous social consequences. However, if specialized methods of instruction were developed and used so that the person learned to read despite his deficiency, then his handicap would be no more serious than poor vision.

Thus, the task of the educator is to find ways to teach all children. There is good reason to believe that if they are taught properly, almost all children can learn the skills and concepts necessary to function in modern society.

Tests of Personality

Tests which are used primarily to collect information about the adjustment, motives, interests, and attitudes of students are included in the broad class of tests which we shall call "personality tests." The information provided by these tests is collected on an informal basis by almost all teachers. In fact, standardized personality tests are merely a formal evaluation technique which can be used to gain information that might otherwise be collected in the course of an informal interview. Because of their efficiency and objectivity, however, standardized tests are generally preferred to interviews. Formal interviews are simply too costly to be used extensively. When they are used, the information obtained is not the same for all students, may be colored by subjective judgments, and is not very easily recorded. Like interviews, personality tests are limited in that they yield only that information which the student is willing to divulge. This is especially true in the case of older and more sophisticated students. Standardized personality tests take many forms. The most commonly used are checklists, personality inventories, interest inventories, and projective tests.

Checklists provide the teacher and counselor with a simple, straightforward, and easy-to-use method for gathering information about students. One common type of checklist is the problem checklist. Problem checklists provide the student with a convenient means of expressing problems which might otherwise go unmentioned or unnoticed, presenting him with a long list of problems on which he merely checks those which trouble him. Fig. 3.10 presents test instructions and a small sample of such problems taken from the *Mooney Problem Checklist.* The *Mooney Problem Checklist* contains problems in eleven fields including morals and religion, finances, living conditions, adjustment to school work, and social relations. Students who check many problems should most likely be referred for counseling. Of all the standardized personality tests, problem checklists are generally best suited to use by the classroom teacher.

FIRST STEP: Read the list slowly, and as you come to a problem which troubles you, underline it.

1. Being underweight
2. Being overweight
3. Not getting enough exercise
4. Getting sick too often
5. Needing to learn how to save money
6. Having to ask parents for money
7. Frequent headaches
8. Weak eyes
9. Too few nice clothes
10. Having to quit school to work

FIGURE 3.10 *Sample items from the* Mooney Problem Checklist *(The Psychological Corporation, 1950).*

Personality or adjustment inventories are much like the problem checklist in the type of information they provide. However, they vary in the format used. Some personality inventories merely ask the student to answer yes, no, or uncertain to questions like:

Do you tire easily?
Do you have trouble making friends?
Are you frequently irritable?
Do you get embarrassed easily?

Others require the student to make a choice as to which of two statements is most characteristic of him. Still others require students to check their problems and the degree to which they are troubled by them. Personality inventories may provide a single adjustment score or separate scores for many adjustment areas such as those presented in the *Mooney Problem Checklist.*

Interest inventories help the student to understand himself, by helping him to identify his areas of academic or vocational interest. The *Kuder Preference Record-Vocational* is typical of this type of test. It presents the student with several sets of three activities. Within each group of three, the student is instructed to indicate which of these activities he likes best and which he likes least. Students receive scores in ten areas: Outdoor, Mechanical, Computational, Scientific, Persuasive, Artistic, Literary, Musical, Social Service, and Clerical. These scores are reported in the form of a profile which indicates areas of strong and weak interest. Another scoring procedure is used in the *Strong Vocational Interest Blank* (SVIB). The SVIB consists of 400 items, the majority of which require the student to indicate whether they like, are indifferent toward, or dislike each of a long list of activities or topics (e.g., fishing, hunting, gardening, painting, being an aviator, producing a play). This test is scored by comparing students' response profiles with those of persons who are successfully engaged in various occupations. The SVIB is therefore scored with a different key for each of the occupations. Norms are provided for 54 male and 31 female occupations. This test yields information on how much student interests are similar to those of persons engaged in the various occupations, but like all interest tests it does not measure ability in these areas. Since both ability and interest are important in the predictions of occupational success, interest test scores are most useful when accompanied by information on student abilities.

No discussion of personality tests would be complete without some mention of projective tests. These are the clinically oriented tests which attempt to probe the more hidden aspects of an individual's personality. These tests are relatively unstructured and rely upon the clinical training of the tester for their reliability. Typically, the individual is shown a series of ambiguous forms or pictures and is asked to describe and interpret what he sees. Responses are then analyzed in an attempt to discover "reflections" of the individual's personality which have been "projected" during the test. Two examples are the *Thematic Apperception Test* (TAT) and the *Rorschach Inkblot Test.* These tests are primarily used as aids in the clinical study of individuals with adjustment problems. A projective test for achievement motivation is described in Chapter 11.

Standardized Tests and Instructional Planning

Now that we have shown how standardized tests are developed, what kinds are available, and how they may be interpreted, we are ready to evaluate their potential as aids in instructional planning. An important point is that since standardized tests are not course specific, they are unable to provide teachers with measures of students' entering behaviors. In addition, although standardized achievement and intelligence tests are relatively good predictors of academic success, they are generally not very helpful in prescribing instruction which is best suited to individual students. The reason for this is that there are few instructional methods which interact with general achievement or ability factors (Cronbach, 1967). That is, we usually find that instructional methods which work well with bright or learned students also work well with their less fortunate contemporaries.

Many of the aptitude batteries are of value in diagnosing deficits in learning skills and abilities (e.g., general verbal ability) which can cause problems in many academic areas, and which cannot be easily overcome by direct, content-oriented remediation. However, specific teacher-made tests of entering behaviors are still more useful in prescribing the instruction for individual students, and when such tests are developed and used properly there is little need to use general achievement or aptitude tests for instructional planning. Furthermore, using general measures of achievement and aptitude can have some undesirable side effects.

There is danger that knowledge of scores on standardized tests may cause teachers to pigeonhole students. Teachers who expect some students to do poorly and others to do well may treat them differently. Rosenthal and Jacobson (1968), for instance, gave teachers a fictitious report about the abilities of their students. They told teachers that a randomly selected group of elementary school students had "unusual potential for intellectual growth." After eight months these students, who at the beginning of the study had no real intellectual advantage over their fellow students, showed significantly greater gains in IQ than their classmates. Here is a documented case of the self-fulfilling prophecy. The teacher's "expectation" of gain was realized, probably because the "bright" students received special attention. Despite recent criticism of the Rosenthal and Jacobson study (Baker, et al., 1969; Gephart and Antonoplos, 1969), it does illustrate a real danger of standardized achievement or aptitude test scores. We would rather see such tests used on the administrative level for selecting students for advanced courses or special counseling, while teachers use specially tailored tests of entering behavior for determining the instruction to be received by individual students.

Homogeneous grouping. The wide range of achievement and aptitude to be found in most classrooms creates problems for the teacher. Must the student who characteristically learns quickly mark time while others catch up? Or should the teacher pitch instruction to the brightest and most eager students, leaving the rest to struggle along as best they can? A seemingly sensible solution to these problems is to use test scores (and sometimes other information) to sort children into classes. Herein lies one possible value of standardized achievement tests, aptitude tests, and personality inventories. Depending upon the size of the school, at each grade there might be a class for the gifted, a class for slow learners, and a class for average children. Secondary schools, for instance, have honors classes and remedial classes and often feature "track systems" comprised of a college, a general, and a business curriculum. Nongraded schools also group children according to achievement and aptitude instead of number of years in school.

A reasonable argument can be made for homogeneous grouping. The idea is that instruction can be geared at just the right level, neither too fast nor too slow for any student in the class. If this reasoning is correct, homogeneously-grouped students should learn more. It has also been argued that homogeneous grouping has favorable social and emotional effects. The high-achiever no longer need feel embarrassed because he is a "brain" and the slow learner is not inevitably at the bottom.

While homogeneous grouping has been studied at length, the evidence regarding its effect on learning and emotional well-being is inconclusive. The reasons are not hard to find. Grouping is often not carried out as announced. Allegedly ideal groupings are abandoned because of parental pressure, the logistics of assigning teachers and rooms, and the difficulty of scheduling elective courses and extracurricular activities.

A second reason why homogeneous grouping has not been dramatically effective is that grouping on one or two factors does not eliminate differences on other factors. For example, grouping on general verbal ability still leaves differences in such areas as academic background, aptitude, motivation, to name only a few. An appealing plan is to use achievement measures in specific subject matter areas as the grouping criterion. That is, English classes would be formed on the basis of some type of English achievement test, history classes on the basis of history tests and so forth. Unfortunately, such a plan magnifies logistic and scheduling difficulties.

No matter how conscientiously a grouping plan is implemented, teachers will still find themselves facing groups of individuals with varying abilities, personalities, interests, and academic backgrounds, who will learn any given concept more or less readily when presented the same lesson. Undifferentiated whole-class instruction is inadequate no matter what form of grouping is used. To be effective, the teacher must still attend to individual students.

Socioeconomic and Racial Factors in Education

Recent years have brought an increased awareness that socioeconomic status and race are significant factors in the progress of a child's education. This awareness comes on a wave of increased social conscience and racial unrest, and crashes down on the educational community with all the force of a tidal wave. It has been met by various responses ranging from quiet embarrassment to impatient outrage. The research community has responded with unusual vigor in its attempt to describe the nature and causes of social class and racial differences. And the educational community, after a normal period of confusion and confrontation, has responded with some encouraging attempts at educational reform. Educational technologists have taken the lead in many of these reform movements, and in the following sections we shall briefly discuss socioeconomic and racial differences, how they relate to entering behavior, and how they can and should influence educational planning.

Socioeconomic status. The socioeconomic status of a student can have considerable influence upon his motivation; attitude; and, consequently, his academic success. The high degree of relationship between socioeconomic status (SES) and school achievement is well documented (Havighurst & Janke, 1944; Havighurst & Breese, 1947; Price-Jones, 1959; Wilson, 1963). One need not look far into the lives of lower-class children to discover several reasons for this relationship. Lower-class parents are less likely than middle- and upper-class parents to encourage academic success, or to be satisfied with delayed rewards for academic accomplishment. They are less inclined and less able to provide incentives for educational achievement. They are generally not as well educated as their middle- and upper-class contemporaries and thus less able to help their children with schoolwork. The lack of support for educational endeavors which low SES students find in their homes has its effect upon their opinion of and interest in such endeavors.

Personality traits which are generally associated with academic success suffer a similar fate in the low SES student. These traits—such as initiative, responsibility, persistence, orderliness, punctuality, restraint of sexual and aggressive urges, and willingness to undergo prolonged vocational preparation—are seldom reinforced in the low SES home. This means that low SES students come to school ill-prepared to meet the demands of the educational system and, especially, the expectations of their predominantly middle-class teachers.

Racial differences in achievement. All of the aforementioned characteristics of low SES students apply to a good proportion of the Negro, Indian, and Latin-American students in our schools. Forty-seven percent of our nonwhite students are raised by parents who earn less than $3000 per year (Witmer, 1964). When the problems generated by racial prejudice are added to those of low SES, the probability of academic success (or any other kind of success) diminishes appreciably.

The so-called culturally deprived home may be lacking in stimulation, at least as defined by middle-class whites. The environment may lack new and interesting objects, and those which are available may not be easily manipulable. The basic orientation of the home is sometimes relatively nonverbal. Often a foreign language is spoken, and when English is the spoken language, it may be restricted to a small vocabulary, with speech characterized by short sequences of words (mostly nouns and verbs), much use of slang or dialect, and poor syntax.

Implications for educational planning. In general, the culturally deprived child reports for his first day of school poorly equipped to meet its demands. He is lacking in language, perceptual skills, and motivation. All too often the school with its expectations geared to the middle-class student is not ready to accept the challenge presented by this child. He does not have the minimal entering behaviors assumed when instruction was developed and thus he is unlikely to get the full benefit from what the school has to offer.

The problem is one of a self-propagating deficit in entering behavior. The child who reports for first grade missing some essential skills will necessarily be unable to learn a certain percentage of the material presented during the year (unless the teacher is able to devote considerable extra time to his individual academic needs). Much of what he *should have learned* will be essential for new learning in the second grade. This means that during second grade the child will fall even further behind his classmates. Third grade will be even less profitable and so on until performance is so poor that the student either is removed from school or drops out.

There have been many proposed solutions to this problem. Preschool education which supplements the deprived home environment and gives students the skills they need for entry into first grade seems to be one good solution. However, there is some doubt as to whether or not the "head start" is enough to overcome the constant exposure to an inadequate environment. The multitude of preschool projects now in operation should be shedding some light on this problem soon.

The motivational problem of the culturally deprived may be more difficult to overcome than those of inadequate skills or knowledges. The disadvantaged child is not easily motivated by promises of future job success or eventual improvement in his economic or social status. He is more interested in seeing the immediate results of his efforts. (The use of tangible rewards and other methods of increasing motivation among the disadvantaged are discussed in Chapter 11.)

Although there are many things we know about the likely problems of the culturally deprived, knowledge about a child's SES or race is certainly not enough upon which to plan instruction. Such knowledge can be useful when objectives are laid down. It is important in considering the general direction or emphasis of an educational program. However, once objectives have been set, more detailed information about the specific skills and knowledges of individual students is needed to develop instruction which meets those objectives.

The disadvantaged child needs an education which is designed to build upon his present skill and knowledge base. He needs to have an educational system in which it is possible for him to succeed. If teachers measure entering behavior and design instruction which is sensitive to individual differences in entering behavior, all students—black, white, rich or poor—will have a better chance to benefit from their years of schooling.

Developmental stages and readiness. As children get older their intellectual abilities increase. They become more adept at handling abstract verbal symbols, relationships, and concepts. In general, they become better able to cope with, understand, and explain their environment. Psychologists have long probed the developmental process trying to identify consistent patterns and attempting to increase our knowledge of the processes and mechanisms underlying developmental changes. Educators have followed closely the progress of developmental research. For it seems only reasonable that if children do indeed go through identifiable stages of development, and if these stages can be characterized by the emergence of rather specific intellectual abilities, then an understanding of developmental stages and periods of readiness is essential to sound educational planning. Let us now take a closer look at the concepts of developmental stages and readiness to determine just what value they do hold for the educational planner.

Piaget's theory of intellectual development. The most elaborate theory of intellectual development comes to us from the Swiss psychologist, Jean Piaget. Piaget and his co-workers at the Rosseau Institute and the Centre International d'Epistimologie Génétique in

Geneva, Switzerland, have attempted to develop and substantiate a comprehensive theory of age-level changes in at least four major areas of intellectual functioning: perception, objectivity, structure of ideas or knowledge, and the nature of thinking or problem-solving. Changes in each of these areas affect learning and retention and thus have potential relevance to education.

Piaget's writings describe several stages of development and attempt to demonstrate that there are qualitative differences in the intellectual ability of children at different stages.

In order to more fully appreciate the kinds of differences in intellectual ability which Piaget and other developmental psychologists are concerned with, we shall discuss three of Piaget's stages in some detail. These three stages are those which are of most interest to educators since they are roughly equivalent to the preschool, elementary school, and adolescent-adult periods. Piaget refers to these periods respectively as the stages of preoperational thought, concrete operations, and formal operations.

It is during the period of preoperational thought (2–7 years) that the child develops his ability to construct symbols, use languages, and engage in imaginative or make-believe play. He goes through a period of preconceptual thought, in which he has relatively little ability to understand the nature of classes or class membership, and goes on to a period of intuitive thought, in which he is capable of learning concepts and principles and using these in simple problem-solving situations. However, these concepts and principles are derived through experience with and manipulation of concrete objects and are very much limited by the child's experience with concrete objects. The five-year-old child learning the concept "square," for example, must come into contact with many exemplars and nonexemplars of this concept before he will acquire the concept. Furthermore, once he has acquired the concept he is limited in his use or manipulation of it in problem-solving, since problem-solving during this stage requires considerable overt manipulation of objects or mental manipulation of once-experienced or remembered objects.

When the child reaches the stage of concrete operations (ages 7–11), he begins to learn and be able to manipulate relationships between objects or sets of objects. He is able to produce a mental image of a series of actions and begins to realize that relational terms like *brighter, smoother, taller,* or *fatter* refer to relationships between two or more objects and not to absolute quantities. He is able to reason about the whole and its parts simultaneously, and is able to learn concepts from rules or descriptions of critical attributes. However, he will still require some experience with concrete exemplars of these critical attributes. For example, the child will grasp the concept "square" only if he has seen a square. He will use the square which he has seen as a reference from which to extract his conceptualization of the critical attributes of squares. Unlike a child at the preoperational level, a child at the stage of concrete operations will need only one or a few exemplars of a concept since he has acquired greater facility in generalizing and handling abstractions. Problem-solving during the period of concrete operations involves less matching to real or remembered samples and more comparison with a conceptualization which is remembered with reference to a single previously experienced object or event.

The child's ability to think in abstract terms is still limited during this period. He is very limited, for example, in his ability to conceptualize or hypothesize about that which exists only in terms of potentiality or possibility. But he has "acquired a rudimentary conception of time, space, number and logic" (Baldwin, 1967) and is able to use these conceptions to organize, order, and manipulate objects or events which confront him.

During the stage of formal operations (approximately age 12 and beyond) the adolescent develops the capacity for abstract thought. He extends his problem-solving ability considerably since he learns to consider the various possible ways a particular problem can be solved. For example, if he is attempting to select the shortest possible route to the seashore, he is able to review all of the possible routes, including some he has never taken before making his decision. The tendency to generate and systematically explore all of the possible solutions to a problem is certainly one of the hallmarks of the stage of formal operations (Mussen, Conger & Kagan, 1963). It is during this stage of development that scientific reasoning begins to emerge. Along with the ability to hypothesize and to see possible solutions comes a wave of idealism. The adolescent theorizes about the world and is prone to criticize its present state while dreaming of and often working for his image of what the world could be.

The stages of development outlined by Piaget should not be likened to developmental plateaus reached by mighty maturational leaps on critical birthdays. Rather, they should be viewed as identifiable phases in the slow and orderly progression of development. These phases are identifiable in that they are qualitatively different from adjacent phases, and are generally characteristic of most members of a roughly defined age range. What stage a particular child has reached is determined by many factors both genetic and environmental. For this reason there is considerable overlapping of stages among age groups. Although a particular stage may generally be characteristic of 7–9 year olds, it may include youngsters who range from 5–11 years of age. Furthermore, individual children may function at one level in one field (i.e., literature) and at a higher or lower level in another (i.e., mathematics).

The concept of readiness is closely related to that of developmental stages. It refers to the student's ability to cope with particular intellectually demanding situations and is a function of general intellectual development. An individual child's state of readiness is reflective of his genetic inheritance, incidental experience, general intellectual stimulation, and educational background (Ausubel, 1968).

Just what is the value of a knowledge of developmental stages or periods of readiness when it comes to educational planning?

Suppose you are a teacher in an elementary school. How can a knowledge of child development or particular periods of readiness help you to plan instruction? How would you evaluate the developmental level or readiness of your students? Write your answer on a separate sheet of paper.

The answer is contained in the following paragraphs.

Developmental stages and instructional technology. Although we wish we could present a list of the ways in which the results of developmental research can be used in instructional planning, unfortunately this is not possible. As Ausubel (1968) notes, "it must be admitted that at the present time this discipline can only offer a limited number of very crude generalizations and highly tentative suggestions bearing on this issue." Developmental research has provided teachers and parents with interesting charts and normative data against which to compare the progress of their students and children. It has also led to some attempts to make instruction relevant to pupils' interests, and possibly has increased the likelihood that elementary-school teachers will provide an adequate number of concrete examples when introducing new concepts. On the negative side, however, overzealous attempts to apply developmental theory in the classroom have had deleterious effects upon instruction—so much so that it has been suggested that the term "readiness" was invented merely to excuse poor instructional planning by shifting the blame to the child.

Many of the problems in applying the research and theory of developmental psychology arise from the fact that our notions of developmental stages and readiness are arrived at by studying children who are products of our current educational, cultural, and social systems. Because of this, lower limits of readiness are in large part determined by what is generally taught and what is generally learned at particular ages within the culture. Recent research indicates that when proper training techniques are used, young children can attain skills which have traditionally been considered impossible for them (Anderson, 1965; Gibson, 1963).

Many of the educational constrictions which are attributed to readiness could more accurately be attributed to the child's training history. By getting a clear picture of what the child already knows or is able to do, we are at the same time defining what he is ready to learn to do. He is ready to learn those tasks for which he has the necessary entering behaviors. For the educational planner it is both easier and more helpful to evaluate entering behavior than it is to attempt to evaluate the more general, more ambiguous, and less applicable abilities which define developmental stages.

SELF-TEST ON ENTERING BEHAVIORS

Generally the questions below can be answered with a word or phrase, although some require a few sentences. Write answers to the questions and then check your answers against the scoring key on p. **123.**

1. Define the term "entering behaviors."
2. Which of the following is the most useful statement of an entering behavior?
   a. The student will have successfully completed the fifth grade.
   b. The student will be able to understand the meaning of the word "asymptote."
   c. The student will be able to state the time correct to within two minutes when shown a clock with any time set on it.
   d. The student will have an IQ of at least 110 and be in the upper quarter of his class in reading achievement.
3. After you have determined the objectives of a lesson, what two steps must you take before you know what it is that you must teach to reach these objectives?
4. What advantage does the teacher-made test of entering behavior have over the standardized achievement test when it comes to planning instruction?

5. Is socioeconomic status an entering behavior? Explain why or why not.

6. What do we call the process through which entering behaviors are identified?

7. How do you determine whether or not students meet your assumptions about entering behaviors?

8. Choose a lesson within your field of specialization and specify in proper form the entering behaviors for that lesson.

Summary

Entering behaviors are skills and knowledge which students possess prior to instruction. They include (1) skill at enabling objectives and terminal objectives, and (2) skill at prerequisites. Prerequisite entering behaviors are skills which are assumed rather than taught.

During the task analysis the educational planner should identify the specific entering behaviors which he will assume his students will be able to perform prior to instruction. The teacher should then determine whether or not students possess the prerequisite entering behavior. When feasible, sample students are given a complete entering behavior test prior to the development of any lesson materials in order to verify the presence of assumed entering behaviors, and also to be sure that they don't already know what the lesson materials are supposed to teach them.

A test of all assumed entering behaviors should accompany every lesson. This test determines whether or not students are ready for the lesson, and should be used to identify students who will need remedial instruction before they can successfully complete the lesson. To be maximally effective a course should begin at the point of each individual student's entering behavior and proceed to the point at which terminal objectives are reached. Such can be the case only when entering behaviors are accurately assessed and individualized instruction is available for the full range of entering behaviors encountered.

Individual differences other than those entailed in entering behavior can affect the progress of student learning. These differences and their effects upon rate, extent, style, and quality of learning have long been studied by both psychologists and educators. We have a wealth of information as to the educational effects of differences in intelligence, personality, socioeconomic status, race, and age. This information can be useful to the educator as he determines the objectives of instruction, prepares instructional materials, or selects methods and media of instruction. However, the educational planner should not use it to replace information about course-specific entering behaviors, because it is simply too general to be used in planning particular lessons.

We do believe that teachers should attempt to understand their students and the individual instructional needs which may result from differences in aptitude, personality, SES, race, etc. However, they should recognize the fact that changes in instruction based upon teachers' impressions about student differences "tend to be beneficial, but there is reason to think that intuitive adaptation of this kind will be inefficient and occasionally will be harmful" (Cronbach, 1967). It is most likely that teachers overdifferentiate instruction on the basis of their subjective assessment of individual differences. Cronbach (1955, pp. 182–183) showed that counselors who were asked to predict student's grade averages accentuated differences between students in their predictions. They tended to "expect too much from those who tested high and too little from those who tested low."

The teacher who is genuinely interested in applying technological strategy in the classroom will shift away from the common emphasis upon general measures of individual differences, and will concentrate upon developing instruction which is individualized on the basis of the skills and knowledge possessed by his students. He will measure entry levels of performance and design instruction which bridge the gap between entering behavior and lesson objectives.

SCORING KEY FOR THE SELF-TEST ON ENTERING BEHAVIORS

A satisfactory score is 9 out of the possible 11 points. Score one point per correct answer unless otherwise indicated. You should review all sections of the chapter which relate to the questions you get wrong.

1. *(2 points)*

(1) Entering behaviors are skills and knowledge which students possess prior to instruction.

(1) Entering behavior includes already-acquired skill at lesson objectives and prerequisite skills.

2. c

3. *(2 points)*

(1) Complete a task analysis.

(1) Determine skills and knowledge that you want to assume and, if possible, test a representative sample of students to see if your assumptions are correct.

4. A test of entering behavior is more specific. It provides information about what a student is able to do and say prior to instruction and thus determines where instruction should start. A standardized achievement test, on the other hand, provides only general information about how a student performed on the test relative to others who took the test. It provides little information about what a student can do or say. It gives you no specific information about where a lesson should begin.

5. No. Socioeconomic status provides only general information about what a student may or may not be able to do. It says nothing specific about whether he possesses the skills and knowledge that are prerequisites for attainment of course objectives.

6. Task analysis.

7. You give a pretest before instruction which includes measures of prerequisites.

8. We are unable to help you evaluate your answer to this test item. But remember, entering behaviors are identified through task analysis, should be as specific as objectives, and should indicate the student's present abilities with respect to the objectives of instruction.

Selected Readings

Carroll, J. B., "Instructional Methods and Individual Differences," in Robert M. Gagné, ed., *Learning and Individual Differences.* New York: Charles E. Merrill, 1967.

Cronbach, L. J., "How Can Instruction Be Adapted to Individual Differences?" in Robert M. Gagné, ed., *Learning and Individual Differences.* New York: Charles E. Merrill, 1967.

Gagné, R. B., "Learning Hierarchies," *Educational Psychologist* (1968), *6,* No. 1, 1–6. A discussion of learning hierarchies and their development. This article presents a method for determining the entering behaviors of a lesson.

CHAPTER

4

Evaluation

Anyone who would attempt to teach must be prepared to make decisions—decisions as to which students to call on for recitation, what to ask, how to respond to a question; decisions as to whom to promote or whom to refer to the school psychologist; decisions about books to use, tests to give, and films to show. To make these decisions requires information and judgment. What an educator does to collect information and to render judgments constitutes evaluation.

Much of a teacher's evaluation is informal. He may sense that the class is losing interest and decide to change the subject. He may observe a class discussion and decide that Carol needs to be encouraged to "join in," or that John needs to have some special instruction. Unfortunately, informal evaluation is variable in quality. Formal evaluation, on the other hand—evaluation which involves checklists, systematic observation, and paper-and-pencil tests—is not without its flaws. If properly employed, however, formal evaluation techniques can supply the teacher with valuable information. It is through broader and more appropriate use of formal evaluation techniques that the decision-making of teachers and administrators is most likely to improve. For this reason, the bulk of this chapter will be concerned with the development and use of formal evaluation techniques.

After reading this chapter you should be able to:

1. describe the relationship between evaluation and the other steps in the teaching process.
2. describe and illustrate three ways in which evaluation can be used to facilitate learning.
3. discuss the relative merits of norm-referenced and criterion-

referenced tests with respect to the various purposes of evaluation.

4. select from among various alternatives a test item which is most appropriate for testing a given behavioral objective, and explain the reason for your selection.
5. construct, use, and analyze the results of a test which covers a unit of instruction in your subject-matter specialty in accordance with the guidelines set down in the chapter.

The Purposes of Evaluation

Ask students why tests are given and the majority of them respond, "so the teacher can give us grades." Unfortunately, many teachers would give the same answer to this question. To be sure, assigning grades is one purpose of educational evaluation, but we shall argue that this is its least important purpose. The most important function of evaluation in education is to provide for a system of quality control. There are two aspects to this system. The first is to monitor student attainment of instructional objectives in order to determine what remedial or supplementary instruction is needed. The second is to locate defects in lesson materials and to determine the reasons for the defects.

Educational evaluation also has several subsidiary functions. These include facilitating student learning, describing and judging student progress, making decisions about the relative merits of instructional methods or materials, and providing individualized guidance and counseling for students. These functions of evaluation will be discussed in the following sections of this chapter.

Evaluation for quality control of student achievement. The students in any one classroom always exhibit a wide range of abilities, interests, and academic backgrounds. Individual differences in rate and level of learning are inevitable. The first purpose of evaluation, providing for a system of quality control, is thus to furnish the information required to maximize the achievement of each individual student.

In this regard evaluation has a role to play before, during, and after instruction. Every lesson assumes certain entering behavior, skills, and concepts that the student must already possess if he is to learn much from the lesson. For instance, a child will have trouble learning long division until he can multiply. On the other hand, every lesson assumes there are some skills and knowledge the student does *not* possess already, namely those the lesson is intended to teach him. A lesson teaching things students already know is boring and it wastes time. Chapter 3 has already discussed entering behavior and its assessment. Now let us consider evaluation during instruction.

Student performance should be continuously monitored in order to detect misconceptions and voids in understanding. Minute by minute, teachers have to decide whether to go on to new material or whether to explain more fully the concept now being taught. Which decision should be made depends upon whether students have mastered the current concept. And to find out whether students have mastered concepts, you pose questions, problems, and tasks. Evaluation should follow every explanation, reading, program, film, exercise, and laboratory activity.

Chapter 8 on corrective feedback describes within-lesson evaluation in more detail. Meanwhile, consider this fact: because one student answers a question correctly does not mean that others can. The larger the sample of student performance upon which a classroom decision is based, the better. The data yield from a single question can be increased in several ways. After asking a question, pause to give time for all students to compose an answer. Don't let students know whom you are going to call on until everyone has had time to compose an answer. Have students write answers whenever possible. When you do call on one student, poll the class. Find how many agree and how many have different answers. Discuss the answers and clear up any misconceptions before going on to another topic. The teacher who is as serious about student learning as he is about "covering" the subject matter will probe to discover the reasons a student has answered poorly, or why he may have sat there mutely without answering at all.

As we shall see later, "test-like events" (Rothkopf, 1966) within a lesson serve several important functions. Among the most important is to provide the teacher with the data for moment-by-moment instructional decisions.

Finally, there is evaluation based on the posttest, an achievement test administered *after* a lesson (or unit of instruction comprised of several lessons). The purpose of evaluation at this time is to determine whether objectives have been reached. Unlike a football game, you cannot make a single win-lose judgment about a lesson. Lessons usually have many objectives. It is possible to reach some goals without reaching others. Classrooms contain many students. You do not reach an objective "on the average"; you either reach it, or you do not, with each individual student. Each student should be judged with respect to every objective. If a unit of instruction that entailed 10 objectives were completed with a class of 25 students, a total of 250 judgments would be required.

If the data show that any students have failed to reach any objectives, the teacher should diagnose the reasons for the failure and then provide remedial instruction.[1] Diagnosis will be easier if the posttest includes questions, problems, and tasks to measure competence in subskills and subconcepts, as well as in the skills and knowledge entailed in terminal objectives. The reason is that failure to master a total skill can almost always be traced to failure to master one or more critical prerequisite components.

The usual practice is to assign students a single test score. Depending upon how high his score is, a student either feels good or bad, but neither he nor his teacher knows which objectives he has failed to reach and what can be done about it. Obviously, instructional quality control requires a fine-grained analysis of student performance, and this sort of analysis requires the teacher to consider tests concept by concept, and even item by item.

An illustration of systematic evaluation. The best example of instruction which follows the evaluation-instruction model we have outlined is Individually Prescribed Instruction (IPI). Under the auspices of the U.S. Office of Education, the University of Pittsburgh's Learning Research and Development Center has undertaken to design procedures, materials, and a totally new classroom environment in an elementary school. The major purpose of this project is to increase knowledge about the process of adapting instruction to individual students who learn at different rates. One of the originators of this project, Robert Glaser (1967), has stated six requirements for adapting instruction to individual students. These criteria, which guided the development of IPI, are as follows:

1. The conventional boundaries of grade levels and arbitrary time units for subject-matter coverage need to be redesigned to permit each student to work at his actual level of accomplishment in a subject-matter area, and to permit him to move ahead as soon as he masters the prerequisites for the next level.

2. Well-defined sequences of progressive, behaviorally-defined objectives in various subject areas need to be established as guidelines for setting up a student's program of study. The student's achievement is defined by his position in the sequence of objectives.

3. A student's progress through a curriculum sequence must

[1] Self-tests, accompanying scoring keys and suggested remedial or "enrichment" readings, can help provide students with needed diagnoses and instructional prescriptions at a lower cost in valuable teacher time.

be monitored. A teaching program adapted to the individual student requires adequate methods to assess the student's level of accomplishment.

4. Students must be taught in such a way that they acquire increasing competence in self-directed learning. To accomplish this, the teacher must provide the student with standards of performance so that he can evaluate his own attainment.

5. Special professional training must be provided to school personnel so that they can evaluate, diagnose, and guide student performance in the manner required for individualized learning, as contrasted to the total class management of learning.

6. The teacher must attend to and utilize detailed information about each student in order to individualize instruction. To assist the teacher in processing this information, it seems likely that schools will have to take advantage of efficient data processing systems.

The IPI staff has developed or adapted instruction in each major curricular area from kindergarten to sixth grade. To illustrate, a sequence of 430 instructional objectives was specified in mathematics. These objectives are grouped into 88 instructional units. As a student works through these units, his performance is continually assessed. Teacher and student alike are kept informed as to where the student stands with respect to the objectives. Testing is oriented toward subject-matter mastery. Each unit of instruction has its own pretest and posttest to determine whether a child meets the prerequisites for the unit or whether he has already mastered its objectives. Children who get 85 percent of the questions correct on any posttest are considered ready for the next unit of instruction. Further instruction is prescribed for children who do not meet this criterion.

The teacher's job is to "prescribe" instruction which is suited to the student, depending upon his level of accomplishment. IPI teachers employ an extensive arsenal of prepared instructional units, as well as their own materials and methods, to adapt instruction to individual children. Lectures, programmed texts, group discussions, and projects—as well as teaching machines, tape recorders, and films—are used as needed.

Far from removing the teacher from the educational scene, the IPI system places the teacher at the hub of the educative process. It is he who decides on the course of study each student will undertake. Much like the medical doctor, the teacher collects information as to the student's educational needs, uses his own judgment in diagnosing the child's problems, and prescribes remedial instruction to fill gaps in skill and knowledge. In such an atmosphere a student's motivation as well as his competence increases.

Two problems with individually prescribed instruction are, first, the mass of achievement data that is produced each day and, second, the need for a great library of instructional materials suitable for use with one child at a time. Automatic data-processing equipment and clerks are solving the first problem. The second problem is being attacked using programmed instruction.

Evaluation to improve instructional materials and techniques. Achievement-test data can be used to evaluate instruction, as well as to monitor student performance. When many students do poorly on the test of a concept, this probably means the instruction that preceded the test was inadequate. Not only should the teacher reteach the students who did poorly; he should also revise the instruction so that it will teach more effectively when next used with other students.

Diagnosing a flaw in lesson materials is much like diagnosing a failure in student understanding. In both cases, you need specific information. The average score on a whole test will not do. The particular concepts and skills students failed to master must be determined, which necessarily involves examining scores on subtests or individual items. If performance with respect to an objective is poor, first review the questions, items, or problems in order to judge once again whether they actually test for mastery of the objective. Are there defects, such as additional answers that could reasonably be counted as right? If so, performance may be satisfactory after all. Next to be determined, assuming the test items are valid, is the reason for poor performance. Do students have two terms or concepts confused? Have they missed an important qualification? Often an analysis of student mistakes on the posttest is informative. If necessary, you can ask additional questions to probe further.

Once the reason for unsatisfactory student performance is tentatively identified, the next step is to locate the place where the student was supposed to learn the concept or skill. If he should have learned from reading several pages in a textbook, reread these pages yourself. If he was supposed to get the point from a discussion-dialogue, review what actually took place. Try to find the difficulty.

Of course, there are any number of reasons why a lesson can fail with respect to some objectives, and an equally long list of remedies. Surprisingly often it turns out that the offending concept has not even been taught or has been given only fleeting attention. Other possible difficulties are that the vocabulary and syntax of the sentences in an explanation were too difficult (see Chapter 12); the student was told about a principle but not provided the opportunity to apply it on his own (Chapter 6); the student was expected to perform under conditions too unlike those in which he learned (Chapter 10); the student confused one term or concept with another (Chapters 9 and 12); or the student failed to work hard, pay attention, and complete assignments (Chapters 7 and 11). Each of these problems can be solved, as the rest of this book will illustrate. But before a problem can be solved, it must be identified. This is one purpose of evaluation.

Other Functions of Evaluation

Using tests to facilitate student learning. There is considerable evidence that giving a test is one of the most dependable ways to increase student learning. At this point, the effects of tests will be described briefly. In subsequent chapters we shall explain the processes at work and explicate the conditions under which tests do and do not facilitate learning. To briefly preview the argument that will be detailed later, people learn what they are led to do (see Chapter 6). A test is an opportunity to apply principles actively, as opposed to sitting passively, listening or reading. Educational research shows that tests increase learning and remembering, provided that (1) the student can satisfactorily answer a reasonable number of questions and (2) the questions are directly related to objectives. Both conditions are important. A test on which a student does very poorly may actually teach him misconceptions (see Chapter 9). Furthermore, the student may become frustrated and anxious when he does poorly (see Chapter 11). A test containing trivial questions unrelated to objectives, on the other hand, can interfere with learning because the student is caused to misdirect his attention. In short, as far as the effect on the student is concerned, a test containing trivial or inappropriately-difficult questions is worse than no test at all.

To reap the benefits and avoid the liabilities of tests, give short tests immediately after the students have learned the skills and knowledge the test covers. The student is most likely to answer questions correctly immediately after instruction. The same test, or a similar test, can be repeated later.

You can capitalize on the high motivation that exists prior to exam periods by seeing to it that this motivation is applied in appropriate study. Many students who want to do well on exams, and who are willing to study in order to do well, are frustrated because they are unable to determine what is important and should therefore be studied; or they do determine what is important but teachers do not test on this material. The solutions to both these problems are simple. First, let students know what is the important material and, second, be sure that tests probe mastery of that important material.

It should be hoped that the instruction itself will serve to indicate to students what is important. However, important topics, main points, and even course objectives are often camouflaged in day-to-day classroom activity. To insure that students make effective use of pre-exam study time, teachers should take special pains to indicate what is most important, and what will be expected of students in the examination. The best way to let students know what is expected of them is to give them a list of the course objectives. Lists of possible test questions,[2] study guides, and outlines of major topics—though not so effective—can serve the same purpose. When given out early enough, these materials help students to budget their study time throughout the term and help to eliminate intensive cram sessions. Teachers often balk at employing such procedures because they do not know what their objectives are or what they will cover in a given period of instruction. Even when objectives are carefully prepared, class discussions often lead to new topics. The teacher who is flexible enough to pursue new topics must be prepared to revise his objectives. When a class takes an unexpected direction, revised lists of objectives should be provided prior to tests.

Students commonly learn what teachers want them to study from the tests they are given. In fact, the directive effect that tests have on study habits is even greater and more specific than most teachers realize. Rothkopf and Bisbicos (1967), for example, have demonstrated that focusing test questions on a certain kind of content increases attention to that content. In this study, high school students were asked to read a 36-page passage from Rachel Carson's book *The Sea Around Us.* For each three-page segment of this passage, students were required to answer two questions. Some students saw only questions requiring either a measured quantity (e.g., a distance or a date) or a proper name for an answer. Some saw only questions requiring either a common

[2] A procedure which has met with considerable success in the authors' classes is to emphasize the major point of instruction at the end of each class or unit of instruction with a question—usually a broad question which involves application of a concept or principle, or a synthesis of earlier instruction. At the outset students are told that a certain number of these post-instruction questions will be found on the final exam. It is stipulated that, although students are encouraged to prepare answers to these questions, notes may not be used during the test. Students happily spend many hours preparing answers to these questions, do well on them, and retain the knowledge well. Students like this approach because it affords a clear view of what is expected of them. We like it because it definitely facilitates learning.

English word or a technical word (e.g., *bathyscaphe, phototropic*). On the retention test given later, students did better on test items in the category they had been tested on earlier, but worse on other items. The explanation for this is that when a student receives questions only on technical words, for example, he begins to pay special attention to technical words in his reading. At the same time, his attention to other categories of words is likely to lag.

In the light of this study what characteristics would you try to build into all of your tests?

The answer is contained in the following paragraph.

The Rothkopf and Bisbicos study contains lessons of practical significance to the teacher. Build your tests to cover the material which is important—that is, to cover the objectives. Be sure that tests emphasize the material you wish to have emphasized. In the section on the construction of achievement tests, we shall list some rules to follow so that tests will fit these requirements.

Evaluating pupil progress. Assigning grades consumes much teacher time and it is one of the most noticeable aspects of teaching as far as the general public is concerned. However, grading should not become the primary goal of any teacher's evaluation program. As his title indicates, the chief function of a teacher is to teach.

There are basically two approaches to describing what a student "knows" (more precisely, what a student can do). The first is to describe him with respect to other students. This can be called the "norm-referenced" approach. The performance of any one student is described relative to the performance of other students. The term "norm" refers to a yardstick of comparison established by testing other students. The second approach can be called "criterion-referenced." Here, the student's performance is described with reference to an "absolute" standard.

An illustration will make clear the difference between the two approaches. If you say, "Jones finished third in the 100 yard dash," this is a norm-referenced description. If you say, "Jones ran the 100 in 10.1 seconds," this is a criterion-referenced description.

Standardized aptitude and achievement tests are norm-referenced. As you learned in Chapter 3, the results of such tests are reported in standardized scores, percentiles, or grade equivalents, each of which expresses a score relative to other scores. If a person scores at the seventy-fifth percentile, this means he did better on a test than 75 percent in a reference group and worse than 25 percent. If a child scores at the 6.0 grade level on a reading test, this means that he did as well on the test as the average sixth grader at the beginning of the year. The simplest norm-referenced statistic a teacher could use is rank in class.

The difficulty with norm-referenced description is that it gives the teacher no idea of the competencies of the person who earns a certain score. Consider the child at the 6.0 reading level. Could he read and understand news stories on the front page of the *New York Times?* Would he find *Tom Sawyer* difficult? Could the suitability of a particular textbook for him be determined by a teacher? No one can give precise answers to these questions on the basis of a norm-referenced description.

The alternative is to describe the material the child can read with comprehension. The test-maker might arrange a series of passages in order of vocabulary difficulty and sentence complexity. For each passage, he prepares test questions; and the child's reading level is defined as the most difficult passage for which he can answer, say, 80 percent of the questions correctly after reading the passage. Now criterion-referenced description is possible, and the teacher can determine the textbooks, novels, and newspaper articles the child will be able to read with comprehension. To find out whether a textbook is suitable for a child, he simply compares the most difficult test passage the child passed with selections from the book.

Norm-referenced description is much more widely used than criterion-referenced description—undoubtedly, for one reason, because the latter is more difficult. We feel, also, that the apparent preference for norm-referenced description may reflect an American obsession with ranking people. To paraphrase an old saying, American educators seem more concerned with whether the child wins or loses than how he plays the game.

Once the teacher has a description of the student's performance, couched in either norm-referenced or criterion-referenced terms, he can approach the issue of assigning grades. Let us emphasize that the description does not translate directly into a grade. What must be determined next is the *worthiness* of given levels of performance. What is passable performance in general science? What is an A's worth of competence in high school physics? Students and parents expect more than a description. They expect an expert's appraisal of value.

Two teachers can look at the same student performance, agree on the same ranking of students, and yet assign very different grades. The decision whether to give the top two, the top five, or the top ten students

A's is subjective. While many teachers apparently feel that the threat of a low grade can goad a student into action, there is reason to believe that there is more motivational mileage to be had from generous use of high grades. This matter is discussed in detail in Chapter 11.

One approach that we cannot recommend is "grading on the curve." According to this system, grades are assigned so as to fit the bell-shaped, normal curve. The teacher who adheres strictly to a policy of grading on the curve gives a predetermined, fixed percentage of students each possible grade. For instance, the top 10 percent might receive A's, the next 20 percent B's, the middle 40 percent C's, the next 20 percent D's, and the bottom 10 percent F's. The problem with grading on the curve is that an entire class may do good work, yet if a teacher follows the system rigidly, a substantial percentage of the students will receive grades below C.

Distributions of test scores often approximate a normal curve. However, there is nothing sacred about a normal distribution. Ideally, every student would master every concept. Most students, therefore, would show perfect or near-perfect performance on tests, and should receive good grades.

Grading on the curve is akin to norm-referenced description. The grade a student receives depends on how well he did relative to other students rather than an absolute standard.

The authors of this book favor a criterion-referenced approach and are therefore committed to a policy of describing and evaluating student performance in terms of the skills and knowledge the student possesses rather than in terms of how he compares with other students. The procedure is to define objectives. Each objective entails a standard of performance. Students who reach the standard receive a good grade. The idea is as simple as that. Implementing the policy is not so easy, however. Despite recent advances in specifying instructional objectives, there still can be considerable variance in the intended level of sophistication at which a concept is developed. Then, too, it can be difficult to accurately describe student performance with respect to a standard. An English teacher grading essays may be in a lenient mood at one moment and in a tough mood a few minutes later. Despite a teacher's best efforts, test questions may contain flaws which mislead students or hints which give away the correct answers.

Considering our fallibility in defining absolute standards and measuring performance with respect to them, we believe teachers should approach grading with a certain humility. Whether students will attain a standard of performance depends upon how well the teacher has done the following three jobs:

1. defining reasonable objectives.
2. teaching satisfactorily.
3. preparing tests and exercises which faithfully reflect the extent to which students have attained objectives.

Making decisions about methods and materials. Among the most important decisions a teacher has to make are what methods and what materials to use. These decisions are likely to be better if they are based on evaluation. The typical classroom teacher has neither the time nor the resources for formal evaluation of methods and materials. Herein lies the role of educational research.

Educational research can be divided into two broad categories. Into the first category fall research studies, which attempt to investigate variables of general educational importance. These studies include analytic studies into the nature of the learning or teaching process, and often have as their long-range goal the development of learning principles or teaching techniques which can be effectively applied over a broad range of content areas. The studies are characterized by close control of learning materials and learning situations, relatively microscopic investigation of particular variables or techniques, and, sometimes, generalizable results. As the Introduction has indicated, though, educational research has not yet led to very many broad principles about teaching and school learning; however, a number of conditional conclusions (which will be explained in later chapters) are warranted.

The second type of educational research involves the comparison of lessons or curricula and the assessment of their relative effectiveness. This research is characteristically less controlled than the first type in that it is completed under more or less realistic classroom conditions. The end product of such research should be statements about the particular instructional units employed in the study, not statements about the relative merits of instructional methods. For example, there have been many studies which have compared "programmed instruction" to "conventional instruction" (whatever that is). Although these studies, if properly conceived, do permit conclusions such as "Programmed Instruction Lesson XII results in better student performance than does the lecture-discussion method employed by Mr. Smith," they do not permit general statements about the relative merits of programmed instruction and other forms of instruction. Because of the lack of generalizability of product comparison research, Cronbach (1963) suggests that researchers and evaluators could better spend their time in "process studies" and curriculum "case studies," which do include extensive measurement and thorough description. Scriven (1967), on the other hand, does not share Cronbach's opinion on product comparison research. He believes that educators want and need to know whether one curriculum is better than another, and he concludes that the best way to answer this question is direct comparison. Scriven argues that comparative research helps the teacher and administrator decide which instructional materials to use.

Though achievement testing has had a long history in this country, there is no coherent, generally accepted rationale for the construction and use of achievement tests in educational research. As a consequence, or perhaps as a corollary, testing procedures described in published research reports are shockingly inadequate. The authors of this book surveyed all of the articles published between 1964 and 1967 in two leading educational journals, the *Journal of Educational Psychology* and the *American Educational Research Journal.* We located fifty articles in which the investigators had prepared their own achievement tests. Table 4.1 contains the percentage of articles which reported various kinds of information about the test in question. Most articles included such inconsequential information as the number of test items, but few detailed the essential characteristics. Only 6 percent mentioned the relationship of the examples and wording of the instruction to the examples and wording of test questions, information which, as we shall explain in Chapter 10, is essential to determine whether the test measured "rote" memory or mastery of concepts and principles. Not a single article listed the objectives of the instruction and explained how the test items were related to the objectives. Only 6 percent described the topics the test covered.

TABLE 4.1 *Types of information provided regarding testing procedures in published reports of instructional research in two leading educational research journals.*

Type of information	*% studies reporting information*
1. Response mode	76%
2. Number of items	74
3. Reliability	22
4. Test development procedure	20
5. Assumed level of psychological process	18
6. Some analysis of the wording and examples of test items in relation to instructional content	6
7. Topical content analysis with number of items per topic	6
8. Behavioral objectives	0

Earlier it was suggested that teachers should analyze tests topic by topic, objective by objective, and item by item. Educational researchers should follow the same advice. Consider a hypothetical experiment in which two instructional units on the general topic of fractions are compared. A group of fifty students are instructed using unit A, while another fifty students use unit B. Immediately after instruction the two groups are given the same 30-item achievement test. Suppose that both groups answer correctly the same average (mean) number of items. With only these data the educator would have no reason to believe that the two units differ. He might merely flip a coin or use some equally unscientific method for choosing between the two units. However, had the researcher evaluated his test data in terms of the topics covered in the two units, he might have been able to give the educator more information upon which to base a decision. The graph in Fig. 4.1 is based on the hypothetical experiment.

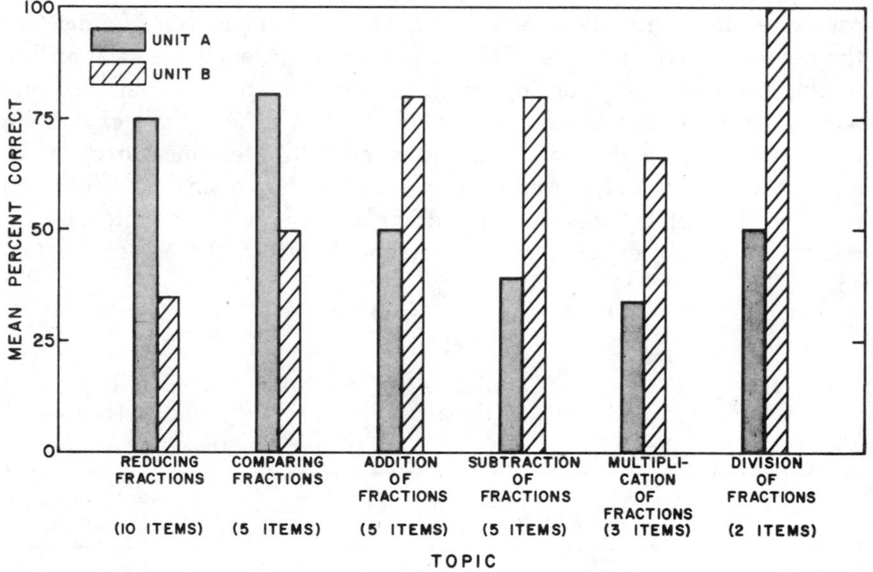

FIGURE 4.1 *A topical breakdown of test data from a hypothetical experiment comparing two instructional units on fractions.*

Fig. 4.1 shows that there is an interaction between the topic being covered and the instructional unit used. Unit A results in superior performance in reducing and comparing fractions, while unit B results in better performance in the areas of addition, subtraction, multiplication,

Please answer the following questions based on Fig. 4.1. A covert response will do.

A. Is there really no difference between the two instructional units?

B. You already have a short and very effective unit on reducing and comparing fractions and a not-so-effective unit on the other four topics. Which of the two units (A or B) would probably be the more valuable addition to your school's curriculum?

The answers appear on p. **141.**

and division of fractions. Knowledge of this interaction changes the interpretation of results. One can no longer conclude that there is no difference in the effect of the two instructional units.

Results such as the one portrayed in Fig. 4.1 are not uncommon. Different instructional units emphasize different topics; no two units devote the same amount of time to each subtopic. Thus, if only the overall average score is examined, the outcome of a comparative research project can hinge on which topics the achievement test happens to emphasize. In the hypothetical experiment, a test which dealt predominantly with the reduction and comparison of fractions would favor unit A, whereas one in which the emphasis was on addition, subtraction, multiplication, and division of fractions would yield results favoring unit B.

The worth or importance of objectives must therefore be considered when choosing between competing sets of instructional materials. Suppose that two reading curricula are evaluated on their effectiveness in promoting vocabulary acquisition, reading speed, oral reading fluency, and reading comprehension. Most reading specialists would give much greater weight to comprehension than to the other objectives. The curriculum which developed comprehension skill most effectively, then, might be the best choice even though it was inferior to the other curriculum with respect to the remaining three objectives.

We believe that publishers and curriculum projects should prepare a manual-technical report to accompany every set of instructional materials. A statement of objectives, a description of prerequisites, evidence demonstrating the effectiveness of the materials in reaching each objective with students of the kind for whom the materials are intended, suggestions for using the materials, and copies of the test of prerequisites and the test of objectives should be included. Unfortunately it is a rare event for the producers of instructional materials to test materials to determine their effects upon students and then to provide users with information upon which to base an evaluation. Instruction would be vastly improved if those who prepare and publish instructional materials followed a policy of trying out and revising their materials until they were effective with students and if schools demanded evidence of effectiveness before purchasing materials.

Evaluation for guidance and counseling. Information about aptitude, achievement, motivation, personality, attitudes, and interests of the individual is needed by those who would help students make vocational and academic decisions, as well as help students with many other of the myriad problems they face.

The counselor in particular often has the task of helping the student estimate his chances of success in certain situations. The kinds of norm-referenced tests discussed in Chapter 3 are available as a means of predicting performance in specified areas with a reasonable degree of reliability. However, such tests used alone are not sufficient for the counselor's purposes. He must temper test results with personal observation and other modes of informal evaluation. In counseling, even more than in other situations, formal and informal evaluation play complementary roles. Both the limitations and potential of each of these types of evaluation must be kept in mind. Good counsel is based on information. The counselor can obtain this information through ingenuity, sensitivity, and the proper selection of formal evaluation instruments.

How to Construct Achievement Tests

As we said in Chapter 3, a good test is *valid* and *reliable.* A test is valid if it is useful for the purpose for which it was designed (Stanley, 1964, pp. 160–196). A test is reliable if scores on the test are stable and consistent. Of these two characteristics, validity is the more important.

Validity. Validity depends upon the purpose of the test. If the purpose of a test is to predict high school grades, then students who score high on the test should go on to earn good grades, and students who score low on the test should go on to earn poor grades. To the extent that a test has this characteristic, it is valid for predicting high school grades. We should not expect it to be equally valid for quite different purposes, however. We assume, furthermore, that the main purposes that teachers have for giving achievement tests will be served if the test can be used to determine whether students have mastered instructional objectives. Therefore, if a test for any one objective were perfectly valid, a student would pass the test *if, and only if,* he had mastered the objective. In other words, on an ideal achievement test, (1) the student succeeds if he has mastered the skill or knowledge entailed in the objective; and (2) the student fails if he has *not* mastered this skill or knowledge.

How do you determine whether a test item, question, problem, or task validly measures competence at a skill specified in an objective? The chief means is to examine the logical relationship of the test to the objective. This may sound complicated, but it is really quite easy, provided objectives are stated in behavioral form.

Consider this objective:

> Given any location in degrees (of latitude and longitude), the student should be able to identify the location on a map.

Which of the following test questions most validly measures the skill named in the objective?

A. Distance east and west around the Earth is measured in degrees ________________.

B. Name the large city closest to 40° North latitude and 80° West longitude. ________________________. To answer this question, you may look at the maps in your geography book.

The answer appears in the following paragraph.

Answers to the questions on *p.* **139.**

A. No. There is a difference in the effect of the two instructional units. Unit A results in better performance on the topics of reducing and comparing fractions while unit B results in superior performance on the topics of addition, subtraction, multiplication, and division of fractions.

B. Unit B. Since you already have an effective unit on reducing and comparing fractions, it would be wise to invest only in unit B.

A behavioral objective is a prescription for a test item. If an objective is clear enough, it usually will be obvious whether a proposed question or problem will measure the skill or knowledge entailed in the objective. Clearly, item B does test the objective above, whereas item A does not.

The results are predictable when a teacher prepares an examination without first clarifying objectives. There is likely to be a quick search of the text for "testable" material. Items are likely to be constructed according to a stream of consciousness in which the test becomes a reflection of what is on the "tip of the pen." Important objectives will be overlooked or badly tested. Instead, memory for names, dates, formulas, and technical terms will bulk large.

The validity of test items can be undermined in two different ways. First, characteristics of the test item may permit the student to answer correctly, even though he has *not* mastered the skill or concept the item is supposed to test. A test item should not contain a hint, or "prompt," which might give away the correct answer. All of the distractors in a multiple-choice question should be plausible and should be grammatically consistent with the stem. Otherwise, the student may be able to arrive at the correct answer by elimination. Luck is an obvious rival to validity in a multiple-choice question, and is even more so in a true-false item. A student has one chance out of two of guessing the correct answer to a true-false question. The prompts in test items can be quite subtle, such as the length of the blank to be filled in a completion item or the relative length of the correct alternative and the distractors (also called "foils" and "decoys") in a multiple-choice item.

A second, and equally important, source of invalidity is characteristics of test items which cause the student to fail, even though he *has* mastered the concepts or skills the items are supposed to test. The stem of a test item should generally be in the form of a question or incomplete positive statement since negative statements are too often misread or misunderstood. When negative statements must be used, underline the words *no* or *not*. Use the clearest, simplest language possible. Do not require the student to go through any steps that are unrelated to the objective being tested.

Examine the following test items, most of which are taken from Gronlund's (1965) book on educational testing. Describe any characteristics of each item that might decrease its validity. Rewrite any items you think should be changed.

1. Which one of the following is not a safe driving practice on icy roads?

   a. accelerating slowly
   b. applying the brakes vigorously
   c. holding the wheel firmly
   d. slowing down gradually

2. An electric transformer can be used

   a. for storing up electricity.
   b. to increase the voltage of alternating current.
   c. it converts electrical energy into mechanical energy.
   d. alternating current is changed to direct current.

3. Who discovered the North Pole?

   a. Christopher Columbus
   b. Ferdinand Magellan
   c. Robert Peary
   d. Marco Polo

4. The shading on the map below is used to indicate

   a. population density.
   b. percentage of total labor force in agriculture.
   c. per capita income.
   d. death rate per thousand of population.

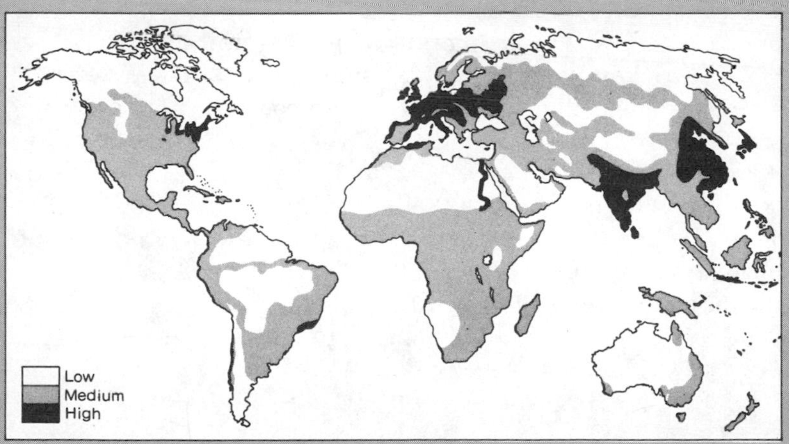

5. Most of South America was settled by colonists from

    (a.) Spain.
    b. England.

The authors' comments on these test items appear in the paragraphs that follow.

Question 1. The first question contains a negative. The best policy is to rewrite negative statements as positive ones, which does not seem feasible in this case. Therefore, *not* should be underlined or italicized. Also, the language of the first question is ponderous. The following is better:

When driving on icy roads, it is *not* safe to

a. accelerate slowly.
b. apply the brakes vigorously.
c. hold the wheel firmly.
d. slow down gradually.

Question 2. Not all of the alternatives in the second question are grammatically consistent with the stem. A test-wise student will have a good chance to guess the correct answer. The item would be better revised as follows:

An electric transformer can be used to

a. store up electricity.
b. increase the voltage of alternating current.
c. convert electrical energy into mechanical energy.
d. change alternating current to direct current.

Question 3. The problem with the third question is that the student may be able to discover the correct answer by elimination. In other words, Columbus, Magellan, and Polo are not plausible distractors. The version below is improved.

Who discovered the North Pole?

a. Roald Amundsen
b. Richard Byrd

c. Robert Peary
d. Robert Scott

Question 4. Gronlund presents the fourth question as an example of a good test item. This item illustrates that it is possible to test understanding of a principle, as well as memory for a fact, using a multiple-choice question.

Question 5. The problem with the fifth question is simple. The student has a 50 percent chance of guessing the correct answer even if he does not know it. The version below is better.

Most of South America was settled by colonists from

a. Spain.
b. England.
c. France.
d. Holland.

The validity of test items can be improved with experience. No matter how hard a test writer may try to develop valid items, many will have flaws. These flaws often can be detected in an *item analysis.* To complete an item analysis the teacher gives the test and then examines student performance on each and every item. Test specialists use various kinds of statistics in item analyses. In our judgment, the most useful information is simply a listing of the answers, right and wrong, that students give to each question, and the percentage giving each answer. If a sizeable percentage of the students give a certain "wrong" answer, the teacher should consider the possibility that this is really a right answer, or the possibility that something about the item confused students. If students do well on one item intended to measure a concept and poorly on another item designed to measure the same concept, it is likely that one of the two items contains a defect.

Fig. 4.2 shows an example of a test item whose defects were made apparent in an item analysis (the item was actually used in a nationwide evalution of a high school biology curriculum.) Only 32 percent of the students checked (B), which was the answer keyed as correct, yet performance on other test items indicated that most students understood quite well that particles diffuse from regions of high to regions of low concentration. Why did they do poorly on this item? First, many students probably overlooked the information at the top which states that

The dots show sugar molecules which cannot pass through the cell membrane.

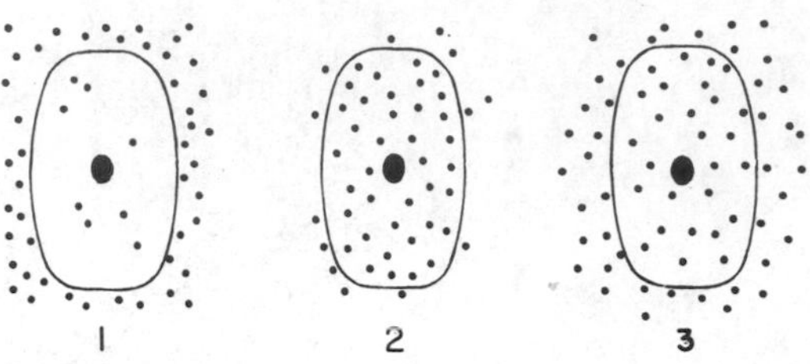

In which of the cells will most water molecules diffuse from outside in?

(A) 1 only
(B) 2 only
(C) 1 and 2 only
(D) 1, 2, and 3

FIGURE 4.2 *A test item with low validity (from Biological Sciences Curriculum Study, 1968, Form B, Item 17).*

the dots represent sugar molecules. If you think that the dots represent water molecules, the best answer is (A); 44 percent chose this answer. The student who did notice that the dots were supposed to portray sugar molecules had to reason that since the concentration of sugar molecules was relatively high in cell 2, the concentration of water molecules must have been relatively low. This inference was not taught nor was it expected from students of the curriculum under evaluation. The item could be repaired easily, however. Remove the sentence above the diagram. Rewrite the question below to read: "The dots show molecules inside and outside three cells. In which of the cells will most molecules diffuse from the outside to the inside?"

Whether or not one is interested in improving the validity of test items, item analysis is an important technique in diagnosing the reasons for student misunderstanding. As indicated earlier, judging whether test items actually measure a certain skill or knowledge is the first step in this process.

A worthwhile teaching practice is to discuss tests thoroughly with students after the papers have been graded. There is evidence that such discussions promote student learning (Sassenrath & Garverick, 1965). The discussions can also provide valuable feedback about the validity of test items. One trick is to give the student credit when he is able to convince you that his answer is reasonable. Under these conditions, students can be counted on to provide searching criticism.

Below is a problem to give you practice at using the data from an item analysis.

Assume the following objective, which is, incidentally, an enabling objective.

> Given a definition of "longitude" or "latitude," the student should be able to supply the correct term.

Here is a test item, a listing of the answers students gave, and the percentage of students giving each answer. What does this information tell you about the validity of the test question? the level of understanding students have of the knowledge being tested? What changes could be made in the test item to improve it?

> Distance east and west around the Earth is measured in
> ______________________________.
>
> 42% degrees of longitude (keyed correct)
> 16% longitude
> 12% degrees
> 10% degrees of latitude
> 9% miles
> 4% latitude
> 7% no answer

The authors' discussion of this test item appears in the following paragraph.

First of all, let us agree on what the information definitely shows. The 10% who answered "degrees of latitude," the 4% who answered "latitude," and the 7% who gave no answer are clearly wrong. Thus, 21% of the students have not learned the concept and should be given further instruction. Now consider the 16% who said "longitude." While this is not the best answer, it is obvious that these students have the concept. It would be unfair to them to count the answer wrong. Moreover, if this answer were counted wrong, the teacher would have to conclude that only 42% of the students possessed the knowledge, hardly a satisfactory level of performance. Considerable reteaching would be indicated with such a poor level of performance. Finally, there is the problem of the 12% who said "degrees" and the 9% who said "miles." Neither of these answers is actually wrong. In fairness to the students, the teacher must count them correct. However, it is not clear whether these students have the concept the teacher is interested in. Maybe they do; very likely they don't. The item would be much improved if these ambiguous answers could be ruled out. The following version of the test item, which appeared earlier in this section, does rule out "degrees" and "miles" as sensible answers, and therefore increases the validity of the item.

Distance east and west around the Earth is measured in degrees of ______________________________.

Reliability. Chapter 3 indicated that a test is reliable if it yields stable and consistent scores. On a reliable test, a person's score will be in about the same position, relative to the scores of other persons, when the test is repeated (provided that during the interval between the tests he does not receive special instruction, training, etc.). Equivalent forms of the same test should give similar results. A test cannot be valid unless it is also reliable. However, not all techniques to increase test reliability are desirable, since some of them may actually undermine validity. For example, a traditional method used to increase reliability is to increase the difficulty of test items. This increases the spread of the distribution of students' scores and generally makes the results of tests more consistent. However, when this results in more of the test being devoted to unimportant material and when the purpose of the test is to assess students' attainment of objectives, this method of increasing reliability may result in a decrease in validity.

Since any extraneous influence can decrease the reliability of a test, one form of test that is often rather unreliable is the essay test. A severe drawback of such a test is that people can't score essays consistently. The standard of performance they employ shifts from one moment to the next. When people rescore essay tests, they usually don't agree very well with themselves, let alone with one another. Essay graders tend to be inconsistent for several reasons. For instance, Stalnaker (cited in Stanley, 1964, p. 258) has observed that, "A C paper may be graded B if it is read after an illiterate theme, but if it follows an A paper, if such can be found, it seems to be of D caliber." Specific suggestions for improving the reliability of essay examinations will be described later in the chapter.

Carefully developed and standardized procedures for administering and scoring tests will improve reliability. (Nothing mysterious is intended by the word "standardized." It simply means following the same procedure on each occasion a test is used.) Variable test directions can reduce reliability and therefore also reduce validity. By the same token, a standardized scoring procedure improves reliability. It is a good technique always to prepare a scoring key rather than depend upon memory, reasoning and judgment—even when grading true-false and completion tests. A key makes mistakes less likely and usually makes grading easier and faster. Each scoring mistake decreases reliability (and validity).

A good way to improve test reliability is to increase the length of the test. By increasing the length we mean increasing the number of items, problems, or questions. Consider a test to measure skill at the multiplication tables. If you presented just one multiplication problem, you might happen to hit one of the few combinations the pupil knows (or one of the few he doesn't know). The pupil might make a lucky guess, or, on the other hand, he might accidentally misread a digit or suffer a momentary lapse of attention. Consequently, a single problem would not give a stable estimate of the student's proficiency. A two-problem test would give a more stable estimate than a one-problem test, and a ten-problem test would be even better. The longer the test the less likely it is that scores will be affected by good or poor luck (random factors). Luck balances out in the long run; talent or lack of talent shows itself.

The main purposes of classroom achievement tests are to determine whether students have mastered instructional objectives, and, if not, to help diagnose the reasons for failure. For these purposes, the reliability of an entire achievement test is unimportant. Each test should contain a subtest for every terminal objective and enabling objective.[3] At the very least, an entire test should contain at least one item for each objective. Subtest reliability will be greatly strengthened if this number is increased to two or three. Also, subtests of greater length will have enhanced diagnostic value.

Test specialists universally recommend two additional methods for increasing test reliability. They argue, first, that test items should be chosen so that about half the students will get each item right after instruction. This procedure makes sense if the purpose of the test is to arrive at the most dependable ranking of students. However, if the purpose is to test for mastery or to assist in diagnosis, rigging the difficulty level of test items may have some disadvantages. The claim is that very difficult items should be avoided, or eliminated on the basis of an

[3] Items covering enabling objectives are included in order to assist diagnosis. A failure to master a skill can usually be traced to failure to master a component skill. If items covering enabling objectives are included in achievement tests, the teacher can identify the missing subskill.

item analysis, because an item that most people get wrong is not efficient for dependably discriminating among people. But, if you want to determine which concepts *are* difficult for students, in order to reteach students or revise instructional materials, you need to leave such items in the test. It is also claimed that very easy items should be avoided. In fact, after any kind of decent instruction, a great many items will be "too easy" according to the rule that only half of the students should get each test item right. A person trying to apply this rule may be forced to split hairs and test on trivialities instead of the main themes of instruction. There may be an irresistible temptation to load test items with irrelevant obstacles to success and to require discriminations finer than those specified in the objectives. Furthermore the rule forces some students to do badly, which has a detrimental effect on learning and motivation (see Chapter 11). Our conclusion is that a procedure of selecting test questions on the grounds that half the students fail them has no place in classroom achievement testing. This rule misses an important point of typical classroom evaluation, which is to discover the percentage of students who will fail. Given this purpose it doesn't make sense to rig the percentage of failures in advance.

A second procedure for increasing reliability that comes highly recommended is to select test items according to their ability to discriminate between good and poor students. To determine the index of discrimination, select the group of students who did best on the whole test (the top 27% is a conventional cutoff point) and the group of students who did worst on the test (e.g., the bottom 27%). Then, compare the performance of the best and worst groups on each item. On a perfectly discriminating item, all of the members of the best group will succeeed and all the members of the worst group will fail. Good discrimination is a critical virtue of items in a test whose purpose is to rank people dependably from best to worst. A whole test will discriminate well between individuals only if the items in the test have this power.

Discrimination between individuals is a less important quality of tests whose purpose is to assess level of mastery, though information about discriminating power can be helpful in locating items with flaws. There is something odd about an item which the students who have best mastered a set of concepts get wrong more frequently than the students who have shown a poor grasp of these concepts. Probably the item contains an ambiguity that is apparent only to the sophisticated student. While a negative or very low discrimination index may signal a defect, high discriminating power is not necessarily a virtue in an item intended to assess whether a student has acquired a specified concept. The fact that an item is highly discriminating may mean that it contains difficult grammar or vocabulary, or requires a logical inference which, let us assume, is irrelevant to the concept being tested. The group of students who do best on an entire achievement test will inevitably have larger vocabularies and more highly developed reasoning skills than the group of students who do worst on the test. Consequently items selected because they discriminate between these two groups are likely to measure general verbal ability, and to that extent are less sensitive to mastery of specific concepts and principles. The conclusion is that item discrimination should not be a major consideration in the construction of classroom achievement tests.

> Below is a figure that presents the scores of ten students on each of two history achievement tests. Assume that you must select the *one* student who will receive an award as the outstanding history student. Which of the two tests makes it easier for you to select reliably an outstanding student?

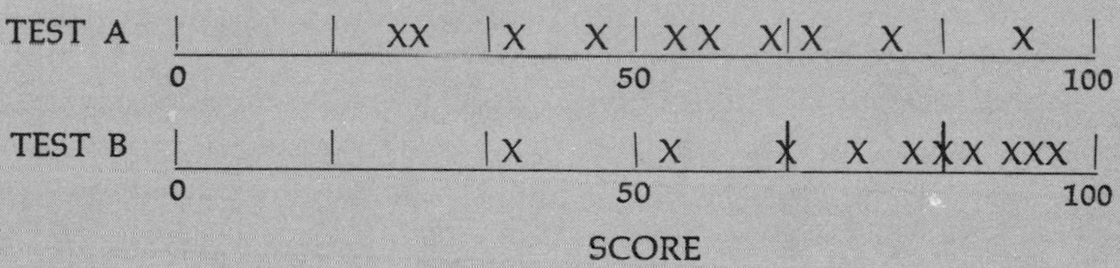

> *The answer to this question is explained in the paragraphs to follow.*

Test A makes it easier to select one outstanding student. Since there is a certain amount of error associated with every test score, in test B it is doubtful whether the difference between the first two or three scores is reliable (i.e., caused by actual differences in achievement). The top three scores are so closely bunched together that the differences may be due to chance fluctuations. For example, it may have been that neither of the first two students knew the answer to one of the questions on the test. However, it is possible that one of these students guessed the correct answer, thus outscoring his nearest competitor by one point. In such a case chance, not academic proficiency, has determined who is "best."

The reliability with which a test differentiates between students depends, as you have just seen, upon how spread out the scores on that test are. For this reason those who take a norm-referenced approach to testing want test scores to be spread out. In order to insure that test scores are sufficiently spread out, these test developers often prefer items which are highly discriminating and of medium difficulty.

The use of item difficulty and discrimination as the basis for selecting items for a test does insure that the test will discriminate between students. It makes ranking students, competitive grading, and awards systems easier and perhaps more equitable. However, such a system cannot be used to evaluate how students are progressing toward instructional objectives. It cannot be relied upon to indicate specific content areas where instruction is weak or where students need remedial work. Nor can it be relied upon to indicate to students what material is important and should be studied. Consequently, a system based on item difficulty and discrimination should not be employed if you wish to use tests for the majority of purposes discussed earlier in this chapter. Criterion-referenced tests are better for these purposes, and are usually adequate for ranking students.

Criterion-referenced tests are designed to compare students' performance with a standard or criterion of good performance. Whether or not an item is selected for a test depends upon the match between the performance required by the test item and the desired terminal performance described in an instructional objective. Using such an approach, item difficulty becomes a measure of the effectiveness of instruction and not a criterion against which to judge test items.

Evaluation of Complex Student Performance

It is perfectly obvious that paper-and-pencil tests are not satisfactory for many objectives. If you want to determine how well a student can make a chair, paint a picture, examine a specimen under a microscope, play a musical instrument, plan and execute an experiment, give an extemporaneous speech, write an essay, lead a discussion, or defend a position on a controversial political issue, you will have to observe the student performing. In some cases, you may be able to study the product he produces (e.g., chair, painting, or essay). However, in none of the cases listed will a paper-and-pencil multiple-choice or completion test adequately assess performance. For instance, a test item that requires the student to label the parts in a diagram of a microscope will not indicate whether the student could use a microscope to locate the choloroplasts in a plant cell. The student who can "list four characteristics of a good speech" may not be able to give a good speech.

To the extent possible, an achievement test should require the student actually to perform the behavior named in an objective under the conditions described in the objective. As already noted, the essay makes an unreliable test. It is also a sad but true fact that having students give speeches, design experiments, or complete graphic art projects are often equally unreliable as tests. Judgments about complex performances are subject to shifting standards. There are, however, steps that can be taken to increase the reliability of these evaluations.

Two kinds of evaluations of complex performance need to be distinguished. In the first kind, performance is judged by its resulting product. For instance, the student makes a bookcase or writes a short story. The teacher need not observe the performance itself, although this might be helpful sometimes. In the second kind, the performance does not result in a tangible product and must, therefore, be observed while it occurs. Gymnastic routines and extemporaneous speeches are examples. Performances that must be evaluated while they occur will be considered first.

Systematic observation of on-going performance. In the evaluation of on-going performance, the characteristics to be observed should be very definite and specific. Each characteristic should be defined in terms of aspects of concrete student behavior. Ratings of overall qualities of performance are unsatisfactory. The evaluation should describe rather than judge goodness or badness. The evaluator should look for specific behaviors that are either present or absent at any given moment in time. Ideally, the aspects of behavior that are to be observed should be defined so clearly that the average junior high school student could readily collect the data once the task was explained to him. If the judgment of an "expert" seems to be required, then the analysis probably hasn't been carried far enough, and the evaluation probably will prove unreliable.

To illustrate adequate and inadequate procedures, we shall examine a difficult case, evaluating whether a speech is "well organized." One way of making such an evaluation is to rate the speech on a rating scale:

A. Extremely well organized
B. Very well organized
C. Fairly well organized
D. Poorly organized
E. Very disorganized

However, a rating such as this violates all of the rules for a satisfactory procedure listed in the preceding paragraph. There are several reasons why such a rating is unsatisfactory. First of all, "organization" is left undefined. This means that different raters will use different definitions.

It also means that a single rater is vulnerable to shifts in his definition from one time to another. Most important of all, the lack of definition means that the rating has poor validity for one of its chief purposes: to diagnose and help surmount poor student performance. The student who is told that his speech is "fairly well organized" will not know what he did right that he should repeat in the future, or what he did wrong that he should try to correct. The modifiers "extremely well," "fairly well," and so on are subjective and arbitrary. A student may be pleased to hear that he has improved from "fairly good organization" to "very good organization." In truth, though, the "improvement" may be attributable to a change in the teacher's mood, or the fact that just before the second speech the teacher heard an even less well-organized speech which he rated "fairly well organized." Another kind of extraneous influence is called the "halo effect." The halo effect is the influence that outstanding performance in some respects has on ratings of unrelated aspects of performance. For example, a very fluent speaker might get undeservedly high ratings of organization.

What is often needed to satisfactorily evaluate speech organization is a checklist instead of a rating scale (see Fig. 4.3). The checklist is used both for observation during the speech and for evaluation of written material after the speech. During the speech the observer takes notes on the points the speaker says he will cover, the ones he actually covers, and the ones he summarizes. *After* the speech, the observer looks at a written outline of the speech and a statement of the main idea, which have been prepared by the speaker. On the basis of his notes and the material prepared by the speaker, the observer then answers the questions in the checklist.

Not all teachers of speech will agree that this particular checklist (Fig. 4.3) captures the essence of good organization. Those who have a different conception will wish to augment or modify it. Nevertheless, the checklist illustrates a sound approach to the evaluation of complex performance.

Using a checklist will help the teacher to diagnose student shortcomings as well as help the student to overcome them. Using it, the teacher should be able both to highlight things the student has done satisfactorily and those in which he has been weak. We can, for example, imagine the following teacher comments based on the checklist:

> You certainly got your main idea across. All but two people in the class got the idea you wanted them to get. I also liked the fact that you stated at the beginning the points you were going to cover. However, I was puzzled by the fact that you talked about the points in an order different from the order in which you introduced them. Unless you say otherwise, the audience naturally

Speaker ____________________

Date ____________________

Title or Topic of Speech ____________________

Observer ____________________

I. List each point the speaker says that he *will* cover.

II. List each point the speaker actually *does* cover.

III. List each point the speaker says he *did* cover.

IV. What do you believe the speaker feels was his single most important point?

V. What does the speaker say was his most important point?

Yes	No	
_____	_____	In the introduction, did he list the points he was going to cover?
_____	_____	Did he actually cover *all* of the points he said he would cover?
_____	_____	Did he cover any *additional* points not mentioned in the introduction?
_____	_____	Did he cover the points in the *order* he indicated he would in the introduction?
_____	_____	In his summary, did the speaker mention *all* of the points he actually covered?
_____	_____	Did he summarize the points in the same *order* he covered them in the body of his speech?
_____	_____	Does your list of the points actually covered in the speech correspond to the speaker's outline?
_____	_____	Is your statement of the main idea of the speech the same as the speaker's statement of the main idea?

FIGURE 4.3 *Sample checklist for evaluating speech organization.*

assumes that you will discuss points in the same order you introduce them. Try to do this in the next speech you give.

An important purpose of classroom evaluation is to determine whether instructional objectives are reached. Suppose that a speech teacher rates only 35% of the first speeches of the year as "very well organized" or better. He rates 85% of the last speeches given in the year as meeting this criterion. Can he be sure the students improved? The answer is "no." His definition of organization may have changed during the year. He may have consciously or subconsciously graded harshly at the beginning of the year in order to get students to work harder. The high marks assigned for organization at the end may reflect the halo caused by improvement in other aspects of public speaking. In short, the teacher has no dependable, objective evidence of improvement.

Now imagine that the speech teacher uses the checklist instead of the rating scale. Suppose that 35% of the students introduced their first speech of the year with a list of points that enumerated in one-to-one fashion the points actually covered in the speech. At the end of the year 85% of the student speeches meet this criterion. While it is not foolproof, the information collected using the checklist is fairly objective and reliable. The teacher can conclude that there was real improvement.

We would not care to debate whether the average junior high school student could *readily* use the checklist contained in Fig. 4.3—as we suggested earlier he should be able to do, given clear definition of the aspects of behavior to be measured—though we are certain he could learn to do so. People must be trained to do systematic observation. Every checklist involves rules and definitions that must be employed faithfully. These rules and definitions should be written down in a manual, or if the scheme is less elaborate, on an instruction sheet. The manual or instruction sheet could answer such questions as what is a "point"? How do you determine whether the speaker has moved from one point to the next or whether, on the other hand, he is just elaborating the previous point? Under what circumstances is the observer's statement of the main idea "the same as" the speaker's statement? The answer to the last question should of course indicate that two statements should be judged the same when they mean substantially the same thing. They do not need to contain identical wording in order to be counted the same. Examples of pairs of statements which are the same or different should be provided. (It is worth noting that when a checklist or observation scheme is used in social science research, the observers—whether students or teachers—receive extensive practice. The research does not begin until the observers can score standard practice tasks the same way an expert does, or until all the observers who will participate score the same way when working independently. This training improves reliability and validity.)

Using a checklist is likely to be an unusually effective way for a student to learn. The student who can accurately score the organization of a classmate's speech is likely to be able to present a well-organized speech himself. For this reason, we urge that students participate extensively in the evaluation of each other's work. While it is true that a student may not be as accurate as a teacher, this difficulty can be overcome by asking many students to evaluate each performance. The modal (most frequent) score these students assign is a good measure of performance, quite probably more reliable and valid than the teacher alone would assign.

The organization checklist presented in Fig. 4.3 deals with only one aspect of public speaking, yet using the checklist would occupy most of an observer's time. Indeed, if he were burdened with further aspects of performance to judge, he would begin to make mistakes. Since the observer can at one time use only one checklist covering one fairly limited aspect of performance, different checklists are required to evaluate different aspects of performance. The teacher who wishes to evaluate many aspects of performance will therefore have to employ student evaluators who are assigned to score different aspects of performance. A teacher might introduce the different checklists one at a time, each being introduced when the aspect of performance it covered was the focus of class activity. On a rotating basis some students could continue to score aspects of performance treated earlier in the year. Furthermore, after experience with a few checklists, students could begin to participate in their development.

A most important attribute of a reliable and valid observation scheme is that the observer should judge behavior which takes place at a *particular moment.* The observer should *not* be asked to summarize performance over a period of time. For instance, it would be wrong to ask an observer, "During the last term, did the student list the points he was going to cover in the introduction to his speeches?" The observer may not remember what the student did, or the speaker's performance may have varied from speech to speech so that neither "yes" or "no" is a proper answer. Ideally, the observer should make a mark on a record form the *instant* the looked-for behavior appears. Take distracting mannerisms of public speakers for illustration. An observer could be directed to make a tally mark each time a speaker says "Ah," or each time he runs his hand through his hair, or each time he handles the change in his pocket. Using this procedure, there is no chance for the observer to forget; he does not have to guess.

Checklists can also be used to assess the behavior of teachers, or even principals. Fig. 4.4 contains the multiple-choice checklist teachers in Tulsa, Oklahoma, irked at the rating system for them, devised to evaluate principals.

To summarize: An achievement test can consist of an attempt to perform a complex skill. Observers equipped with checklists can score the

PROMPTNESS:

_____ Is faster than a speeding bullet.
_____ Is as fast as a speeding bullet.
_____ Would you believe a slow bullet.
_____ Misfires frequently.
_____ Wounds self while handling guns.

INITIATIVE:

_____ Is stronger than a locomotive.
_____ Is as strong as a bull elephant.
_____ Almost as strong as a bull.
_____ Shoots the bull.
_____ Smells like a bull.

QUALIFICATIONS:

_____ Leaps tall buildings at a single bound.
_____ Leaps tall buildings at a running start.
_____ Can leap short building if prodded.
_____ Bumps into buildings.
_____ Cannot recognize buildings.

ADAPTABILITY:

_____ Walks on water.
_____ Keeps head above water under stress.
_____ Washes with water.
_____ Drinks water.
_____ Passes water in emergencies.

COMMUNICATION:

_____ Talks with God.
_____ Talks with the angels.
_____ Talks with himself.
_____ Loses arguments with himself.

FIGURE 4.4 *A checklist for teachers to evaluate principals.*

performance to generate the information needed for the various purposes of evaluation. A checklist that yields reliable and valid information will specify point-at-able, countable acts of the performer. The behaviors observed should be tallied as they occur. The observer should not be asked to summarize performance over a period of time nor to rate qualities of overall performance. Serving as an observer is likely to be an educationally useful experience for the student. The teacher who has students use checklists can gather a wide array of useful information and cause students to learn at the same time. While systematic observation was illustrated with aspects of public speaking, the same approach to evaluation can be used to appraise skill at platform diving, singing, playing musical instruments, dancing, and executing laboratory procedures. The techniques of systematic observation can be applied to evaluate any student behavior.

Systematic analysis of student products. Many student activities result in tangible end-products. The techniques for evaluating these student products are much like the procedures for evaluating ongoing student performance, only easier to use. This is so because in evaluating end-products the judge can take his time: if his mind wanders, he won't miss something important.

The most important step in systematic observation is to define the characteristic to be evaluated in terms of concrete observable *behavior*. In parallel fashion, the aspects of a product to be evaluated must be defined in terms of specific, observable *features*. It should be easy for a judge to determine whether the feature in question is present or not. In analyzing student products, qualitative evaluations should be avoided. The judge should not be asked to give an overall summary; if he is, he will be forced to give subjective weighting to many different features of the product. In the instructions to the judges, and later to the student whose work is being evaluated, precise language should be used. Such terms as "often," "many," "few," and "very" should be avoided since

POOR	BETTER
Your spelling was poor.	You misspelled the seven words noted on your paper.
Your style was "heavy." Try to write in a "lighter" style. Your writing will be more interesting if you do.	Fifty-eight percent of your sentences were written in the passive voice. For instance, you said "Tom was scratched by the bush," when you could have said, "The bush scratched Tom." I counted twenty-one nominalized verbs in your story, which is over six per one hundred words. Here is one example: you said "The reaction of the boy was prompt." This could be written, "The boy reacted promptly." The passive voice and nominalized verbs make for a "heavy," uninteresting style. Use the active voice. Use verbs as verbs. Your style will be "lighter" and more interesting if you do.

they can be interpreted in various ways. For the same reason, metaphorical language should be avoided.

Naturally, no English teacher is going to have the time or the patience to classify and count every important aspect of students' prose. Some teacher-saving procedure is essential. Paraprofessional paper readers are one solution. We believe, however, as we stated in the preceding section, that the best solution is to have students evaluate each other's work. With students collecting and summarizing descriptive information, intensive analyses of student work are possible. Moreover, as we said earlier, a student will learn something of value from assessing another student's work.

Teachers are likely to accept the position that features of student work should be defined in precise, concrete terms. However, many teachers will not be enchanted with the idea that aspects of student work should be counted and then summarized in percentages or proportions. Such teachers must realize that no lesser degree of precision will satisfy the purposes of evaluation.

A system for analyzing student products can be made more reliable than a scheme for observing on-going performance because it is possible to control for additional extraneous influences. For instance, a technique for analyzing products that controls some aspects of the halo effect is to score student work "blind." That is, the name of the student and any other information about him is concealed from the judge. This prevents a judge from grading too high because he has been influenced by the good performance of the student on other occasions. Scoring blind also prevents the reverse halo effect in which there is implicitly a higher standard for good students than poor. A blind scoring system is easily implemented. When students have finished a project, pass around a sheet containing numbered spaces. Ask the students to write their names into the spaces in an irregular order. Each student identifies his work with the number that appears next to his name. Save the sheet with the names and numbers on it to decode the names later.

Thus far all of our examples have involved *stylistic* features of performance. Student performance can also be scored for *content.* This is true of both on-going performance and the end-products of performance. A checklist is essential for reliable and valid scoring of the content of student work. The checklist for an essay test, for example, names the points that will be included in a satisfactory answer to each question. (The scoring guides for the self-tests in many of the chapters of this book illustrate content checklists.) A judge who attempts to give an overall score to an essay without a checklist is vulnerable to many biases. Furthermore, an overall score, fair or unfair, is useless for determining whether specific objectives have been reached as well as for diagnosing weaknesses in student performance.

A comparison of evaluation techniques. Insofar as possible, a test requires the student to actually perform the behavior named in instructional objectives under realistic and lifelike conditions. However, tests which simulate on-the-job performance have a number of limitations, and in several respects compare unfavorably with familiar types of paper-and-pencil tests. It is not always possible to ask the student to attempt the performance ultimately desired from him. For instance, consider the first-aid objective presented in Chapter 1: although the student is expected to be able to stop the blood gushing from a patient's artery, patients bleeding from the arteries are unlikely to be available in the ordinary classroom when needed for testing. The teacher will have to settle for a description from the student of what one should do when faced with arterial bleeding, or maybe the student can demonstrate the procedure on a classmate. In other cases, a realistic performance test is possible, but would be very expensive and time-consuming. Finally, there is the problem that evaluations of complex performance are ordinarily less reliable than paper-and-pencil tests.

The procedures outlined in the preceding sections for systematic observation of on-going student performance and systematic analysis of student products will make evaluations of complex performance more reliable. Research shows that trained judges using a checklist can score essays very reliably (Stanley, 1964, p. 259). Indeed, satisfactory reliability can be expected whenever these procedures are employed. Furthermore, the teacher who is willing to make extensive use of students as observers and judges will not be troubled by the fact that systematic observation and analysis are time-consuming.

A technique that gives a strong a priori appearance of measuring what it purports to measure is said to have "face validity." If the objective is for students to be able to design experiments, systematic assessment of an actual attempt to design an experiment is a procedure with great face validity. Unfortunately, we cannot always take things at face value. In a particular case under consideration there may be several factors to detract from validity, factors which could permit the student to perform well even though he has not mastered the objective. The student could get the idea for his experimental design from a book. His father might solve the problem for him. A classmate might help him. The project can also be regarded as a one-item test: the fact that the student does well in a single case is not dependable evidence that he has a generalizable skill at experimental design.

Many aspects of a complex performance are verbal or symbolic, and often these aspects can be assessed perfectly well using paper-and-pencil tests. Paper-and-pencil tests could be used to determine skill at many aspects of experimental design, as the following item used by the Biological Sciences Curriculum Study (1968, Form B, Item 18) illustrates:

> Does the air contain bacteria? Which one of the following experiments would you use to get an answer to this question? Each test tube contains sterilized food for the growth of bacteria.
>
> A B C D

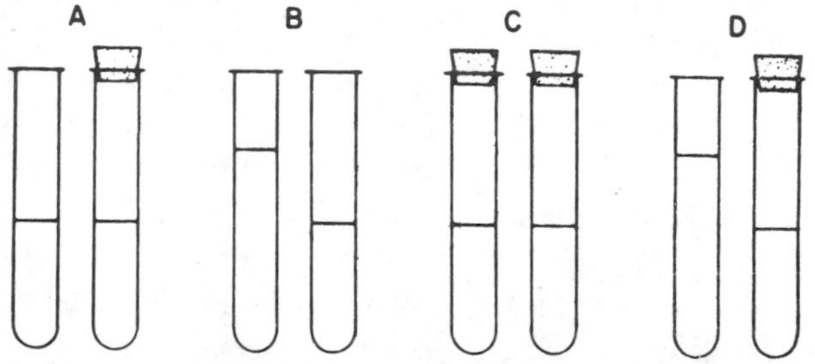

Since evaluations based on more information are generally more reliable and valid, a test consisting of a number of items like the one above could provide a valuable supplement to the project in which the student actually designs an experiment. When the verbal, symbolic, and conceptual features are the major components of a skill, lifelike test conditions are often unnecessary. It hardly seems essential for the testee to be on a schooner in the middle of the Atlantic in order to assess whether, given degrees of latitude and longitude, he can identify a location on a map.

In summary, instructional objectives frequently name skills that cannot be assessed as a whole using paper-and-pencil tests. When this is true, evaluation must consist of systematic observation of on-going performance or systematic analysis of the products of performance. However, supplementary evaluation employing paper-and-pencil tests seems prudent. A single attempt to perform a skill is like a one-item test. It is subject to various influences that undermine reliability and validity. Paper-and-pencil tests, on the other hand, can provide a broader base of information.

Many of the objectives of education are of a verbal, symbolic, or conceptual nature. This is especially true of enabling objectives, which often require the student to describe, define, identify, or differentiate between. Attainment of these objectives can be adequately tested using paper-and-pencil tests. We should not, however, be fooled into believing that the verbal skills probed by these tests are the only ones which are taught or the only ones which should be tested. The validity of a test, it should be remembered, is determined by how accurately the test probes attainment of desired performance. Often we want students to manipulate objects or perform actions. Whatever the teacher's field, he should be sure that he does not fail to test critical objectives merely because they cannot be probed with a paper-and-pencil test.

Teaching to the test. This chapter has emphasized that a satisfactory test completely embodies the skill or knowledge named in an objective. It has also been argued that instruction should continue until every student masters the objective. This may seem to imply that it is proper to "teach to the test," meaning to give instruction and arrange student practice directly related to specific test questions.

Teaching to the test is entirely appropriate whenever the student is to learn a sequence of behavior that is always performed in a fixed order. An example is learning to recite the Pledge of Allegiance from memory. If this objective is to be reached, teaching to the test is not only permissible, it is necessary.

When the test *samples* the total set of skills and concepts the student is to learn, however, a limit must be placed on teaching to the test. Consider the 100 basic addition "facts." As long as the test consists of all 100 facts, there is no problem with teaching to the test. Suppose it is decided that a test of ten facts will satisfactorily measure competence at the entire set. Now teaching to the test is no longer proper. If the students get extra practice on these ten, the test will no longer accurately represent performance on the complete set of 100 facts. A test which samples from a total array of skills and knowledge is invalidated if the questions sampled are singled out for special attention during the lesson.

Examine the following objective and a test item that probes mastery of it.

OBJECTIVE: The student should be able to compute the difficulty index of a test item given the number of students taking the test and the number of students getting that particular item right.

TEST ITEM: Sixty students took a test. Twenty of the students correctly answered the first item of the test. What is the difficulty index of that item?

Here the *procedure,* not the answer to a particular problem, should be taught. It is improper to test for mastery of a concept, principle, or generalized skill using any of the examples or practice tasks that were employed to teach. When a student has mastered a concept, he should be able to deal successfully with an instance he has not encountered before. The student who "really knows" a principle will be able to apply it in a novel situation. As will be explained in detail in Chapter 10, a test for mastery of a concept or principle must include examples and situations different from those used during the lesson.

SELF-TEST ON EVALUATION

1. Describe the role of evaluation in a system of instructional quality control.
2. Describe some steps which you could take to insure that your testing facilitates student learning.
3. Criterion-referenced tests are best described as tests which
   - **a.** can be used to compare student's performance with those of his age or classmates.
   - **b.** can be used to compare student's performance with some desired level of performance.
   - **c.** can be used to compare student's performance with his own past performance.
   - **d.** generally have fixed instructions, administration, and scoring procedures and are accompanied by a manual for use and interpretation.
4. The validity of a classroom achievement test should depend upon how well the test
   - **a.** produces about the same scores each time it is given.
   - **b.** can be used to predict success in other, related courses.
   - **c.** measures attainment of course or lesson objectives.
   - **d.** spreads students out on the grading scale.
5. Explain why criterion-referenced testing is to be preferred over norm-referenced testing when your goal is to improve instructional materials and techniques.
6. Which of the following tests would you use to measure attainment of this objective? Why?

   OBJECTIVE: The student will be able to identify oak trees, elm trees, and maple trees.

   TEST: a. Ask students to describe the distinguishing characteristics of oak, elm, and maple trees.
   b. Give the student six leaves of different sizes (two oak

leaves, two elm leaves, two maple leaves) and ask him to name the tree from which each came.

c. Take the student into the field and have him point out and name the oak, elm, and maple trees which he encounters.

7. What guidance would you give to a colleague who must evaluate his students' performance in a panel discussion?

8. Consider a small segment of a lesson in your subject-matter area. Write out the objectives of that lesson segment and develop a pretest and posttest for the lesson.

Summary

Classroom evaluation serves several purposes, the most important of which is to provide for a system of instructional quality control. Student performance on exercises, projects, and tests should be continuously evaluated to determine whether performance matches standards. When a student's performance is deficient in any respect, the reasons for the deficiency should be diagnosed, and more instruction should be provided. A student should be directed on to new objectives only when he has mastered preceding ones. The most prominent example of such a system in public education is the Individually Prescribed Instruction (IPI) plan.

Evaluations of student performance can be used to identify weak aspects of instructional materials and teaching procedures. In addition to reteaching individual students, when performance is poor the teacher should revise the lesson so that students will learn better when the lesson is used again.

Other purposes of evaluation include assignment of students to homogeneous groups, facilitation of student learning, and grading. Grading is the traditional purpose of educational evaluation, a fact which has had an unfortunate impact on evaluation technique.

Two approaches to educational evaluation may be distinguished. In the norm-referenced approach, any one student's performance is compared to the norms established by testing other students. In the criterion-referenced approach, the individual's performance is judged against an absolute criterion. The norm-referenced approach predominates in educational measurement.

A good test is both valid and reliable. For most of the purposes of educational evaluation, an achievement test is valid when students pass the test if, and only if, they have mastered the objectives the test covers. The principal method to determine the validity of a test exercise is to examine the relationship of the exercise to the objective the exercise is supposed to embody. This is not difficult when objectives are formulated in behavioral terms, since a behavioral objective is a prescription for one or more test exercises. An item analysis is also useful to check test validity.

A reliable test yields stable and consistent scores. A test is valid only to the extent that it is reliable. Increasing the length of a test and standardizing the procedures for administering and scoring a test will improve reliability. Two other methods for increasing reliability cannot be recommended because they impair the validity of tests for the chief purposes of educational evaluation. These methods are (1) selecting test items which only about half the students will get right, and (2) selecting test items which discriminate well between students whose overall performance is high and students whose overall performance is low.

Many important instructional objectives entail skills that cannot be assessed satisfactorily with paper-and-pencil tests. These skills can be evaluated while the student is performing them. The key to systematic observation is a checklist that specifies point-at-able behaviors of the performer. A scheme that requires an observer to summarize or rate overall qualities of performance will prove unreliable, and the information will have little utility for determining whether objectives have been reached or for diagnosing and surmounting student difficulties. Similar conclusions hold for the evaluation of student products.

An important principle of classroom evaluation is to assess the student while he is actually performing the skill or using the concepts entailed in an objective, under lifelike conditions if possible. Still, there is a role for paper-and-pencil tests. They compare favorably in several respects with direct assessments of complex performance. They are more convenient to use. When constructed carefully, they are very reliable, ordinarily more reliable than evaluations of complex performance. And, of course, much of what we want students to learn is verbal or symbolic.

SCORING KEY FOR THE SELF-TEST ON EVALUATION

Score one point for each correct answer unless otherwise indicated. The lowest acceptable score is ten out of a possible thirteen points. Reread sections of the text which relate to questions you miss.

1. (*3 points*) Your answer should indicate that it is through evaluation that we determine the adequacy of the other steps in the teaching process. Specifically

(1) Evaluation based on the pretest can indicate whether students possess prerequisite skills and concepts and whether, on the other hand, they have already mastered objectives.

(1) Evaluation based on the posttest can indicate which students have failed which objectives. It shows who needs remedial instruction.

(1) Evaluation based on the posttest can identify weaknesses in the instruction. It indicates aspects of the instructional materials and procedures which should be revised.

2. (*3 points*) Score one point for each of the following.

(1) Let students know what the instructional objectives are and therefore what they should study.

(1) Test on objectives so that test emphasis and instructional emphasis are parallel.

(1) Test as soon after instruction as possible so that students will be likely to respond correctly.

3. **b**

4. **c**

5. (*2 points*) Norm-referenced tests do not indicate how well students have achieved lesson objectives. Therefore they cannot be used to indicate where a course needs improvement and where it does not. Criterion-referenced tests compare students' performance with a standard (attainment of objectives) and can be used to indicate which objectives have been achieved and which have not.

6. One point for choosing *c* and indicating that this test employs realistic, lifelike conditions, or one point for choosing *b* and indicating that while this test is not as lifelike as *c*, it is sufficiently realistic and much more practical.

7. (*2 points*)

(1) Develop a checklist covering specific, well-defined aspects of student performance.

(1) One point for naming one or more of the following: (a) tally the behavior as it occurs; (b) prepare a manual explaining how to use the checklist; (c) train the observers; (d) use student observers.

8. *No credit.* If you have performed well on the preceding questions, this means you should be able to judge for yourself whether your objectives, pretest, and posttest are satisfactory.

Selected Readings

Gagné, R. M., "Instructional Variables and Learning Outcomes," in M. C. Wittrock and David Wiley, eds., *The Evaluation of Instruction: Issues and Problems*. New York: Holt, Rinehart and Winston, 1970.

Glaser, R., and Klaus, D. J., "Proficiency Measurement: Assessing Human Performance," in Robert M. Gagné, ed., *Psychological Principles in System Development*. New York: Holt, Rinehart and Winston, 1962.

CHAPTER

5

When Instruction Fails: Diagnosis and Prescription

The strategy of instructional planning which has been detailed in the preceding chapters is a process for developing effective lessons, but the classroom teacher invests only part of his time in lesson development. His chief commitment is to the students now in his classroom. He is less concerned with perfecting lessons to use with future classes than he is with providing the best possible instruction for the class (or classes) he now teaches.

The major components in instructional planning from the perspective of the classroom teacher are diagrammed in Fig. 5.1. The heart of the teacher's task is represented by the loop consisting of "Teach," "Evaluate," "Diagnose causes of poor student performance" (when necessary), and "Prescribe remedial instruction" (if required). The teacher shares the responsibility for selecting and clarifying objectives with scholars, other educators, and social philosophers. Subject-matter experts and other specialists analyze tasks; and these analyses are (hopefully) embodied in the lesson materials prepared by curriculum projects, textbooks, manuals, films, and so on which teachers use. But with the exception of assistance rendered in unusual cases by such persons as school psychologists and speech therapists, the classroom teacher is solely responsible for the other functions represented in Fig. 5.1.

The second half of this book is devoted to techniques of teaching in relation to the principles of learning. But before considering these matters in detail, we must consider what is to be done when instruction fails.

How good is good enough? The teacher has the main responsibility for maintaining a standard of excellence. What should this standard be?

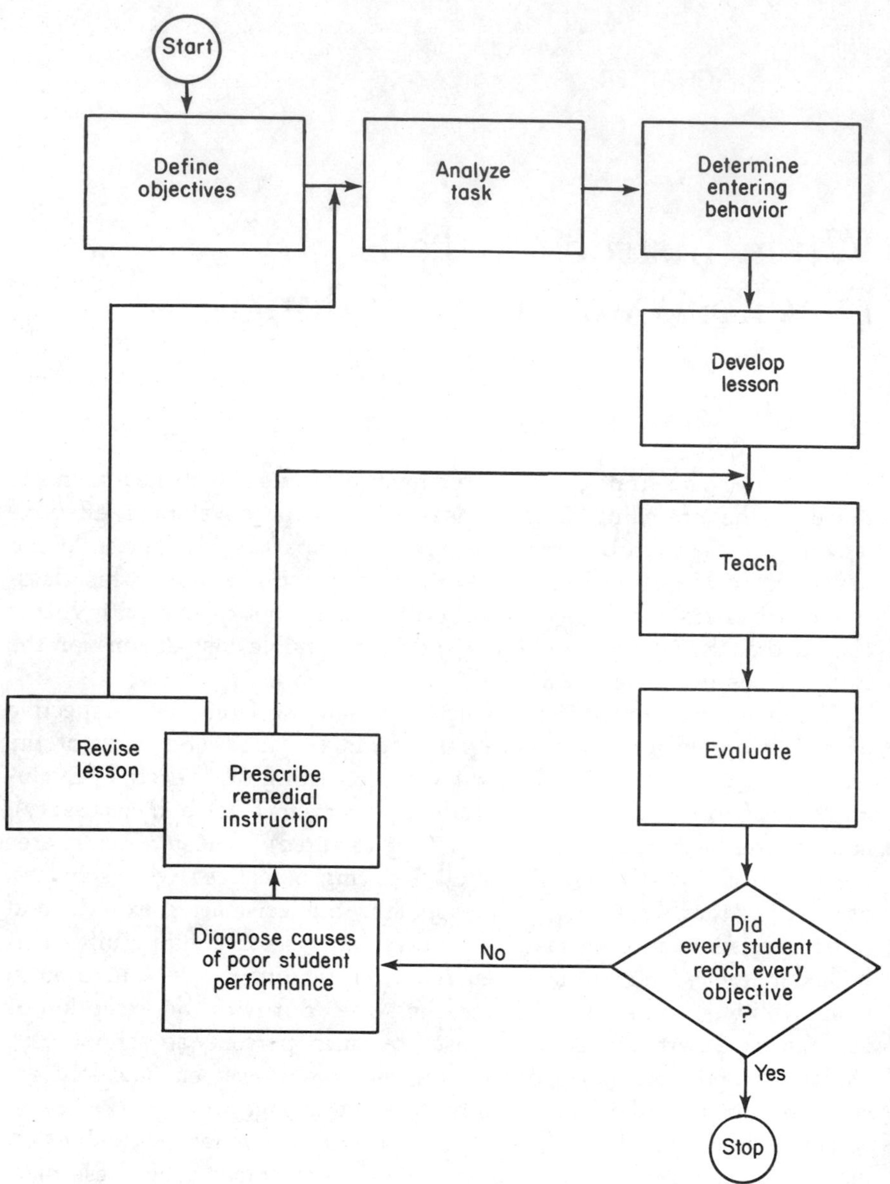

FIGURE 5.1 *A task analysis of the major components of instructional planning.*

Twenty-four of twenty-five students in a class reach all objectives. One student reaches every objective except for one. According to Fig. 5.1, what is the next step?

The answer appears on p. **173.**

We believe that instruction should continue until every student masters all of the basic objectives of a lesson or unit. The number of pages in a textbook completed in a school year and the number of topics covered in a course of study are irrelevant criteria. The criterion must express what the student masters, not what he "covers." To be sure, there will be instances in which an objective turns out to be unrealistic for some students. Either the objective is impossible to reach, or accomplishing it will take so much time that little will remain to attain other important objectives, or attempting to reach it will place undue stress on the child (and maybe the teacher, as well). However, assuming objectives that are both realistic and important, we believe that teaching is not good enough until all students master every objective. Persons who develop self-instructional programs have a motto which could well be adopted by educators generally: "When the student fails, the programmer flunks."

Diagnosing the causes of poor student performance. One of the teacher's most important tasks is to discover the reasons for unsatisfactory student performance. Consider first some "diagnoses" which are not very helpful:

1. The student has low intelligence.
2. The student's motivation is poor.
3. The student suffers from an inadequate home life.
4. The student is culturally disadvantaged.

Make no mistake, such factors are frequently contributing causes of poor student performance.[1] The teacher's main job, though, is to deal with more immediate and concrete problems. An analogy with the physician will make this point clear. A doctor cannot be satisfied with the explanation, "The patient has a disease which could be due to his unsanitary living conditions," true though it may be. The doctor must

[1] The teacher should be alert to signs of impaired hearing, impaired vision, malnutrition, and emotional disturbance, among other conditions. When symptoms of such conditions are detected, the child should be referred to appropriate auxiliary school personnel or community agencies.

discover the patient's specific disease in order to prescribe therapy. Likewise, the classroom teacher must discover the student's specific difficulty in order to prescribe remedial instruction.

A good task analysis is essential to the diagnosis of learning difficulties. The reason is that the task analysis specifies the subskills and subconcepts which comprise a total skill. And, usually, poor overall performance can be traced to failure to master one or more critical subskills or subconcepts.

Identifying the weak link (or links) requires a close look at student performance. The operative phrase here is "a close look." Merely noting that a student gets a low total score on a test covering some objectives is not enough. The low total score indicates only that the student has a problem; it seldom clarifies the reasons for the problem. A good way to locate the student's specific problem is to analyze his mistakes. Often a detailed examination of the student's performance on the test covering the objectives will reveal his specific difficulty. In other cases, it will be necessary to observe the student in different test situations, to pose new problems, or to ask further questions.

A fifth grader gets 15 items wrong on a 30-item long-division test. Typical of his mistakes was the following: given $13.1\overline{)187.33}$ he answered 143. What subskill has he failed to master? Refer, if you wish, to the task analysis of long division diagrammed in Fig. 2.3.

The answer appears on p. **175.**

For self-evident reasons, teachers (including textbook authors, who, usually *are* teachers) illustrate concepts and principles using examples with which their students will be familiar. Most of the illustrations in this book are chosen from the elementary school curriculum because almost everyone will understand them. To use a wide variety of examples is another principle of good teaching. Following this principle, even at the risk that many persons will not understand the subject matter, the next example involves concepts in genetics which might be taught in high school or college biology courses. The purpose of this example is to illustrate that essentially the same techniques can be used to diagnose the causes of poor student performance when the subject matter entails a complex set of interrelated concepts as are used with a so-called skill subject.

Assume this objective:

Given a description of variation or change in a trait possessed by a population, the student will be able to select the most probable explanation from among the following four:

a. the gene for the trait is dominant (or recessive).
b. the trait appears because of mutation.
c. the trait is expressed under some environmental conditions but not under others.
d. the frequency with which the trait appears has changed because of natural selection.

An adequate test for mastery of this objective will include several problems of each of at least four types, three of which are illustrated below. The correct answers are starred.

1. All of a species of rabbits populating an island off the coast of Alaska have white ears when they are young, but as they mature their ears always turn black. Several young rabbits from this population are raised in Mexico. Their ears remain white. Which of the following is the best explanation of these facts?

   a. the gene for white ears is recessive.
   *b. black ears develop only under certain environmental conditions.
   c. white ears develop because of mutation.
   d. black ears no longer develop because of natural selection.

2. Most of the flowers in a certain species are pink; some are white. Two pink flowers are crossed. All of the F_1 generation are pink. Several white flowers appear in the F_2 generation. The best explanation of these facts is that

   *a. the gene for white flowers is recessive.
   b. white flowers appear only under certain environmental conditions.

Answer to the question on p. **171.**

Diagnose reasons for poor student performance.

c. white flowers appear because of mutation.
d. white flowers appear because of natural selection.

3. A population of bees gets its food only from the bottom of the narrow tube-shaped flowers of two species of clover. The bees' tongues range from 3mm to 6mm in length. The tube-shaped flowers average 6mm in length in one species of clover and 3mm in the other species. A blight kills all of the clover with short-tubed flowers. Two years later it is found that most bees' tongues range from 5mm to 6mm in length. Which of the following is the best explanation of these facts?

   a. the gene for short tongues is recessive.
   b. short tongues appear only under certain environmental conditions.
   c. long tongues appear because of mutation.
   *d. short tongues no longer appear because of natural selection.

Assume that three students correctly answer items 2 and 3 and that they also correctly answer several items (not illustrated) in which the inference of mutation is reasonable. However, each of the three answers item 1 (and other items like it) incorrectly, choosing natural selection as the best explanation. A competent biology teacher should be able to conclude from this information that these students have a poorly differentiated conception of the effects of environment on trait appearance, variation, and change. Obviously, they do not understand that a trait may appear under some environmental conditions but not others. Furthermore—and this is the important point—they have not mastered the concept of natural selection. They seem to regard natural selection as the name for any environmental influence.

Natural selection occurs when individuals with a certain trait are poorly suited to live in a given environment. The trait may, for instance, make these individuals more vulnerable to predators or less able to obtain food. Therefore, individuals with this trait contribute fewer offspring to the next generation, and as a consequence the trait appears less frequently in subsequent generations. The concept of natural selection, furthermore, has several subconcepts:

1. Natural selection operates over generations. It cannot explain changes in the characteristics of living individuals.

2. Natural selection operates on trait variation which already exists within a population (or is introduced by mutation). Natural selection alone cannot account for the appearance of a new trait.

3. Natural selection works gradually over many generations unless the trait selected against is closely related to survival. It cannot explain sudden shifts in traits which have little effect on chances for survival.

Further questioning will reveal which aspects of natural selection the three students do not understand.

Sometimes it will happen that a student has apparently mastered all of the component skills and concepts identified in the task analysis, but he still cannot perform the total skill. This probably means that there is a gap in the task analysis, an important missing subskill which was not identified in the analysis nor taught in the lesson. Some students may "leap the gap," but others cannot. For instance, an inference may be required which is obvious to some students (and the teacher) but not obvious to others. It may be necessary to teach this kind of inference explicitly, if making such inferences is critical to performance of the complete skill. Or it may be possible to revise the task analysis (and the lesson or remedial lesson) so that the inference is no longer required.

Prescribing remedial instruction. The word "remedial" may suggest instruction in exceptional cases at a special time, in a special place, conducted by a special teacher. We intend it to mean simply the reteaching of a thing not learned the first time through a lesson. In this broader sense, remedial instruction should be going on every hour in every classroom. Remedial instruction may consist of a brief oral explanation from the teacher, reading or rereading a passage from a text-

Answer to the question on p. **172.**

He has not learned how to "set the decimal point" correctly. In fact, an even more precise diagnosis—which could be checked by reviewing the child's solutions to other problems—seems possible. He appears to be eliminating the decimal points in both the divisor and the dividend and simply setting the decimal point for the quotient above and to the right of the right-hand digit in the dividend.

book, new problems presented in such a way that the student is likely to see and circumvent his difficulty, or a sequence of activities especially tailored to help a certain student overcome a specific weakness. (Many concrete suggestions for teaching or reteaching various kinds of concepts and skills appear throughout the remainder of this book.)

Neither diagnosis nor remediation is a mysterious process. Most teachers will be able to develop considerable skill at these functions, provided they understand that they are essential to successful teaching. It should be noted that remedial instruction aimed at specific student difficulties is likely to be more successful than a "brute force" approach. Further drill on problems (concepts, writing exercises, or whatever) with which a student is having trouble is unlikely to be effective unless the sources of trouble are identified and remedied beforehand. Likewise, repeating an explanation using the same words and examples is likely to be ineffective (unless the student was absent or not paying attention the first time). After all, if a student could not learn from an explanation the first time, why should he learn any better from it a second time? Undifferentiated practice is often ineffective, and it is usually dull and punishing. A few minutes of instruction which gets precisely at the student's difficulty can be worth more than hours of general review.

Planning for individual differences. Not all students will have the same difficulties with a lesson. This means that the teacher must make individual diagnoses for individual students and groups of students. And of course it also means that it will be necessary to provide as many as several different kinds of remedial instruction. Accommodating individual differences in rate of learning introduces a serious problem in instructional management. What will students who have already mastered an objective do while other students receive further instruction?

The simplest plan for dealing with individual differences among students is to have all students continue to receive instruction until every student has mastered the objective. A reasonable amount of review and continued practice beyond the point of mastery is desirable because (as is detailed in the chapter on memory) such "overlearning" improves memory over the long haul. However, constant review of things already learned can be a deadening experience. Furthermore, it wastes the student's time. He could be learning other things instead of marking time.

A second plan for dealing with individual differences in rate of learning involves a variable standard of performance. The objective is the same for all students and all students are expected to meet a minimum standard of performance. Students who quickly meet the minimum standard spend the rest of their time working toward a higher level of proficiency. For example, a reading comprehension objective should specify the minimum difficulty of materials which the pupils are supposed to be able to read with comprehension.[2] Under this plan, pupils who easily master materials of minimum difficulty will spend their remaining time developing proficiency with harder reading selections. Under the first plan, fast learners would continue to practice with easy materials.

A third plan involves different objectives for different students. Everyone is expected to reach basic objectives. Those who do so quickly spend their remaining time working toward optional "enrichment" objectives. This plan works especially well when the rapid learners are able to complete additional work more or less on their own. The teacher is then able to focus his attention on the problems of the slow learners.

Each of the three plans already described is based on the assumption that students will spend a fixed amount of time completing their formal schooling. A fourth plan allows students who master objectives quickly to graduate early. The old procedure of permitting some students to skip grades and requiring others to repeat grades is an application of this plan. Some nongraded primary schools allow children to enter upper elementary school as soon as they have mastered all primary school objectives, whether this takes two years, three years, four years, or even longer.

The teacher's role in revising and improving lessons. When the teacher himself is preparing instructional materials, it is to be hoped that he will carefully delineate objectives and painstakingly analyze the task. To develop lessons to a high level of effectiveness often requires several cycles of tryout, evaluation, diagnosis, and revision. The lone classroom teacher, however, seldom has fresh groups of students with whom to try successive revisions of lessons. Often a whole year will pass before a given lesson is taught again. Hypotheses about what went wrong with the lesson taught today and ideas for its improvement will grow cold with time. For this reason "Revise lesson" is included as a step accompanying "Prescribing remedial instruction" in Fig. 5.1. While teachers are always under pressure to get something ready for tomorrow, there is much to be said for at least making a few notes on today's lesson before preparing tomorrow's. Otherwise the teacher is likely to repeat the same mistakes year after year. Note too, that while a given lesson may be taught no more than once a year, curricula entail many similar skills and similar sets of concepts. Teachers should be encouraged to undertake really thorough postmortems several times a

[2] There are procedures for grading the difficulty of reading selections. See Chapter 12 on memory.

year, if not more often. Undoubtedly particular lessons will benefit from such analysis and revision. Perhaps even more important, teachers will thereby learn ways to do a better job of teaching other lessons which involve similar skills and concepts.

Much of the time teachers use prepackaged instructional materials (textbooks, laboratory manuals, workbooks, programs, films, etc.) prepared by others. *To be most effective, a teacher must have a clear picture of objectives and a complete analysis of component skills and concepts, even when using prepackaged materials.* A teacher *may* be able to present a prepackaged lesson without knowing the components of the skills and concepts it is supposed to teach, but he surely will not be able to make very penetrating diagnoses of student problems without such knowledge.

As a general rule teachers should assume that prepackaged lessons can be improved. *Very few published lessons have been through a process of tryout and revision until they are demonstrably effective in reaching objectives.* Therefore the classroom teacher should not be overly impressed by the fact that the reading primer contains illustrations in three colors, or the fact that the laboratory exercise was prepared by a famous curriculum project, or the fact that the textbook was written by a professor at a prestigious university. The teacher should have no reluctance to modify and supplement prepackaged instructional materials and procedures. If an explanation in the textbook proves confusing, he should substitute a simpler, clearer one of his own. If the lesson guide puts the student in the position of always hearing about concepts and principles but seldom using them, the teacher should prepare supplementary exercises which lead the student to use what he has learned in new situations.

SELF-TEST ON INSTRUCTIONAL PLANNING

This test is designed to teach—as well as to test for mastery of—the skills, concepts, and principles which have been described. After each question compare your answer with the authors' answer before attempting the next question. Our answers are scattered across several pages so that you will not see the answer to one question while looking for the answer to another. To get the most benefit from this exercise, you should prepare a complete, careful answer to each question before you look at the authors' answer.

1. Imagine you are a kindergarten teacher. The curriculum includes teaching the children to tie their shoes. State this objective in behavioral terms. Our statement of the objective can be found on p. 188.

2. Complete a task analysis of the skill of tying shoelaces. Draw a flow chart to illustrate your task analysis. This will take a few minutes of your time, but it should be worth the trouble. If necessary review Chapter 2 on task analysis. (IMPORTANT NOTE: In this case, it is not possible to judge whether the analysis contains enough detail by asking the question, "Can the student perform the subskill upon being asked to do so?") The authors' task analysis appears in Fig. 5.2 on p. 182.

3. In your judgment, which of the following teaching procedures would be most useful in teaching kindergartners to tie their shoes? See p. 190 for the authors' answer.

    a. A brief explanation using simple words, perhaps illustrated with drawings of the important components of the skill.
    b. A puppet show in which the hero can tie his shoes and the scapegoat cannot.
    c. A demonstration of each of the components followed by practice.

4. How many children do you think you could teach at once? What seating arrangement would you use? The authors' opinions are on p. 194.

5. Many of the children learn to tie their shoes but a few have trouble. What should you do? See p. 192 for our answer.

6. Despite your best efforts, a few children have not learned how to tie their shoes, and they seem to be getting frustrated. What should you do now? The authors' answer is on p. 191.

7. Suppose you have decided that you can work with only two children at a time. Assume that you do not have a student teacher or a regular assistant. How are you going to handle the rest of the class while you teach one pair of children? See p. 197 for the authors' solution.

Part I: Overview and Summary

The best strategy for preparing effective lessons, in our view, consists of specifying objectives in behavioral language, determining the component skills and knowledge entailed in the objectives, and preparing techniques and materials to teach the components that are not included in the student's entering repertoire. The next step is to experiment with the lessons to determine whether objectives are reached, and, if not, to discover the reasons for shortcomings. On the basis of the evaluation of student performance, the lessons are revised, and then tried again. This process of tryout and revision continues until the lessons are demonstrably effective, or until the decision is made that it is impossible to reach the objectives within the limits of available time and resources.

Development of instruction begins with an instructional need or requirement. This need or requirement is generally stated in broad, nonspecific terms and often comes to the *instructional designer* (person who is preparing the lesson) in the form of a memo, a suggestion, or a lesson or course title. The first job of the instructional designer is to translate this broad statement of needs or goals into specific statements about desired student outcomes: that is, the designer must prepare statements of *behavioral objectives* (see Chapter 1). Once objectives have been prepared, and to insure that tests measure attainment of objectives and not merely "material covered" during instruction, it is a good idea to develop the criterion test (see Chapter 4).

With his objectives stated in terms of observable behaviors and the criterion test prepared, the designer is ready to break down terminal objectives into sub- or *enabling objectives.* To determine the specific tasks, skills, and knowledge which the student must possess, the designer goes through a process called *task analysis* (see Chapter 2), which breaks each objective down into its behavioral components. A task is broken down until the designer reaches the level at which component subskills are part of the student's assumed *entering behavior.* Entering behaviors (see Chapter 3) are skills and knowledge which are components of *terminal behavior* and are also part of the student's behavioral repertoire prior to instruction. As the task analysis proceeds, a test of enabling objectives and finally a test of assumed entry skills should be developed.

If at all possible, assumptions about required entry skills should be checked prior to the development of instruction. This can be done by selecting a sample of students who represent the intended student population and giving them the test of prerequisite entry skills. If this testing reveals that students do not have the required entry skills, the designer must either adjust his assumptions about entering behavior to a more realistic level, which may require further task analysis, or prepare special instructional materials which can be used by students who do not meet requisite entry standards. In many cases, appropriate students are not available for testing prior to the development of instruction and the instructional designer must simply estimate entering behaviors and build the course accordingly.

In any case, the designer should be prepared to handle individual students who do not have some prerequisite skills (see Chapter 6). The preparation of course materials and determination of course content should follow directly from the statements of objectives, task analysis, and estimation of student entering behavior. The teacher's task is to take the student from the level of entering behavior and guide him to attainment of course objectives. To do this efficiently and effectively will take imagination, creativity, and considerable expertise in the organization and structuring of instructional content and the technique of instruction. These subjects are covered in the second part of this text.

With instructional materials prepared, the teacher is ready to administer the *pretest* to students beginning his course. This pretest should include a test of prerequisite entry skills, so that the teacher can identify students who are not yet ready for the lesson, as well as tests of enabling objectives and terminal objectives, so that he can identify areas in which students are already proficient and therefore do not need instruction. Students who do not meet prerequisites can be shifted to some lower level course (one for which they do have the prerequisites), if such a course is available, or they may be given some precourse instruction to bring them up to the required level of performance. Students who have attained some course objectives should not be required to sit through instruction on these objectives and can either be sent on ahead or given additional, enrichment material (e.g., projects, self-instructional programs, group discussions, etc.) while other members of the class work to attain these objectives.

Once students have received instructions on previously unattained objectives, they are ready to be given the *posttest* or achievement test. This test should be criterion-referenced and should include items covering both enabling and terminal objectives. Such a test can be used to diagnose areas where more instruction is needed and identify aspects of the instruction that should be upgraded. Teachers who do not present additional work to those who need it are not meeting their responsibility to reach instructional objectives, while teachers who provide this instruction but do not change main-line instruction are not improving the likelihood of future success with the course. Of course, the decision to revise main-line instruction should be made only when substantial numbers of students have failed to reach an objective; when only a few students fail to reach an objective, the provision for remedial instruction should be sufficient.

We believe that instruction should be judged satisfactory only when every student reaches every important and realistic objective. When one tries to live by this standard, instruction is necessarily individualized.

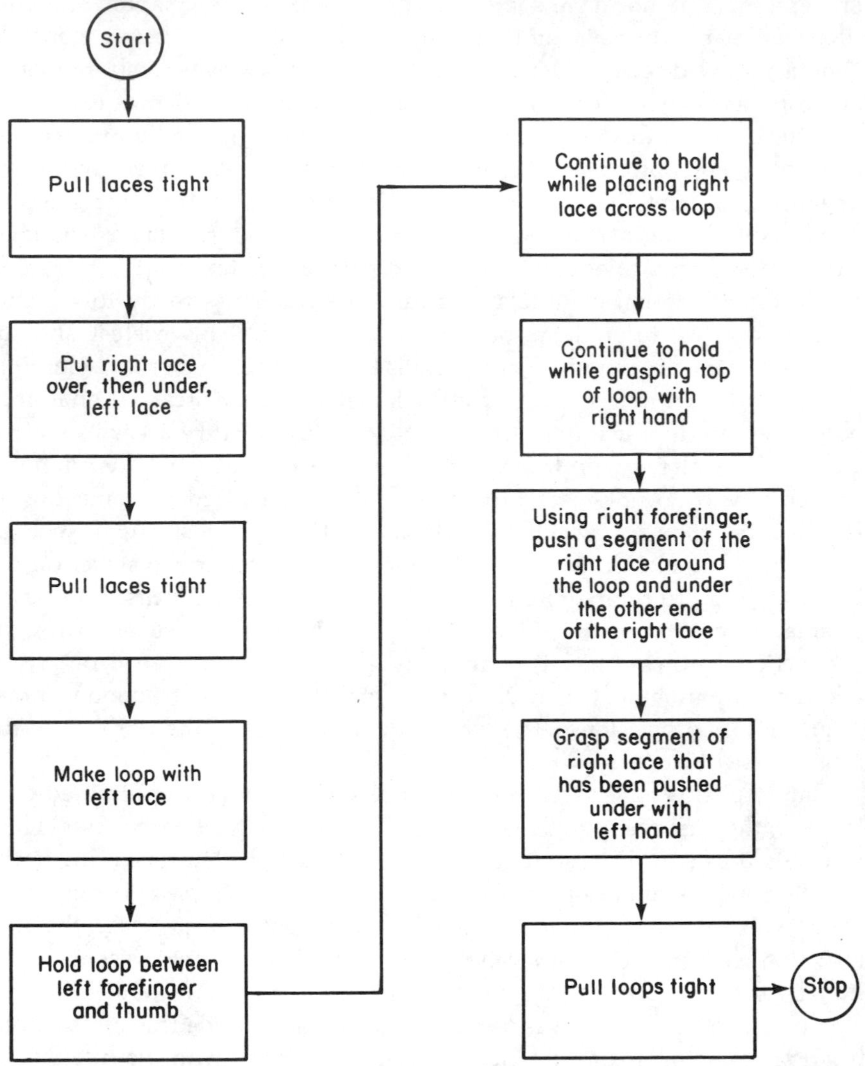

FIGURE 5.2 *Flow chart showing one of several possible analyses of the skill of tying a shoe. More details could be included.*

Given the same instruction, students learn at different rates. Students who do poorly will do so for different reasons. Remedial instruction that gets to the heart of the student's difficulty is likely to be more effective than undifferentiated drill and review.

To be successful, the classroom teacher must have a clear conception of the goals of instruction and a complete task analysis even when using prepackaged instructional materials. Otherwise, the teacher will not have adequate criteria for evaluating student performance nor adequate guidelines for diagnosing the causes of student failure. There is a close parallel between the strategy for developing instructional materials and the tactics for day-to-day instructional decision-making in the classroom. The developer is trying to improve lessons. While the classroom teacher is also interested in improving lessons for future use, his main job is to teach the students now in his class. Consequently, when a failure in student understanding is identified and diagnosed, the classroom teacher gives most of his attention to prescribing remedial instruction, whereas the developer concentrates on revising instruction.

PART

TEACHING AND THE SCIENCE OF LEARNING

Introduction: A Model of Teaching

Part I of this book has described a general, practical strategy for developing and conducting instruction. Included in this strategy are two steps which we have labeled "develop lesson" and "teach" (see Fig. 5.1). The remainder of this book is devoted primarily to a treatment of these two steps. To be considered are the arrangements of instructional materials and the techniques of teaching that are likely to be effective for different purposes under a variety of conditions.

Instruction can be viewed from the perspective of the teacher or the perspective of the learner. We shall use both perspectives. Let us begin with the teacher.

A complete teaching episode consists of the three components diagrammed below:

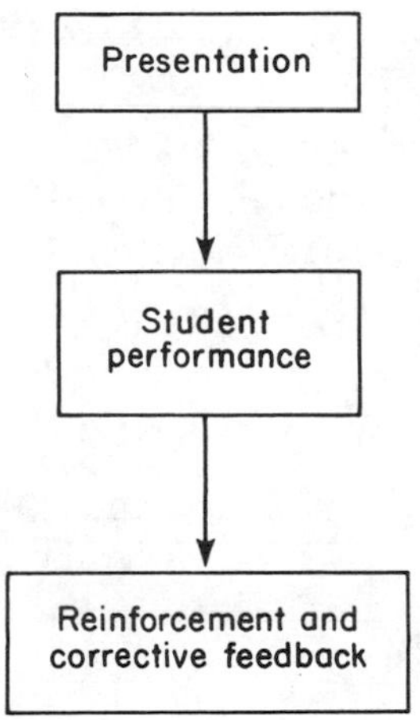

Presentation includes giving reading assignments, demonstrating, displaying pictures and diagrams, lecturing, writing on the chalkboard. Note that presentation can involve not only the activities of live teachers but also the material in books, films, and programs. *Student performance* includes taking tests, solving problems, answering questions orally, writing term papers, practicing a skill, completing exercises, running experiments. For reasons which will become clear in the next chapter, we exclude watching, listening, and reading (except when reading itself is being taught) from the definition of student performance. *Reinforcement and corrective feedback* include telling a student he is right or wrong, offering praise, tokens, giving and withholding privileges, criticism, and remedial instruction. Corrective feedback may also include asking further questions or posing new problems.

Although a complete teaching episode includes presenting, arranging for student performance, and giving feedback, different teaching strategies emphasize different components. Some strategies may omit one of the components. It may take days or even weeks to complete a cycle of all three components; or, a cycle can be completed in as little as thirty seconds. Some of these variations are illustrated in the table on p. 189. Note that presentation takes the bulk of the instructional time in this (hypothetical) college lecture course, whereas most of the time in the (hypothetical) laboratory unit is devoted to student performance. Each frame in a program, on the other hand, involves a cycle of all three components in a brief period of time; and the entire program contains many cycles. Discussions also typically involve many cycles. The laboratory unit illustrated in the table has the overall form of a complete

Answer to question 1 on p. **179.**

Our statement of the objective is given below. There are at least several acceptable ways to express this objective, so if yours does not match ours it does not necessarily mean that yours is inadequate.

Given a shoe on his own foot with free lengths of laces at least six inches long when the laces are pulled tight, the child will be able to tie the shoe in a minute or less without assistance so that:

a. the bow contains two loops of about the same size.
b. the knot is snug to the shoe and pulled tight.
c. the child can easily untie the shoe.

	College lecture course	*Single frame from a self-instructional program*	*Laboratory unit in a high school science course*
Presentation	Three 40–50 minute lectures, and a 60-page reading assignment.	One sentence.	A problem is posed in a 15-minute lecture.
Student performance	Students take 20-minute quiz on material presented.	Students fill blank in a second sentence.	Over a 5-day period, teams of students design experiments, develop procedures, record observations, graph results, draw conclusions.
Feedback	Teacher returns graded quizzes. Major points about which many students were confused are discussed for 15 minutes.	The word or phrase which goes in the blank appears on the next page.	Teacher gives suggestions, asks questions to get students to reconsider what they are doing. At the end of the unit, differences in design, procedure, results, and conclusions are discussed.

Three Illustrations of the Components in a Teaching Episode present–perform–feedback cycle. Furthermore, embedded within the laboratory unit, there would typically be a number of shorter cycles.

Now let us consider instruction in the light of what students must learn. Speaking very broadly, two categories of learning may be distinguished. The first is *response learning.* This includes the acquisition of motor behavior, verbal-symbolic behavior, and emotional behavior. A person may acquire single, discrete responses, but more frequently in school he learns sequences or chains of behavior. The second category is *learning when and under what circumstances one should behave in a certain way.*

The environment contains cues which should signal skills into action. Unless a person has learned to pay attention to these cues, his repertoire of behavior will be valueless. Other cues guide behavior once a performance is under way. If a person has not learned to notice these latter cues and react to them precisely, his performance will be erratic, uncoordinated, and ineffective.

Answer to question 3 on p. **179.**

We favor answer c, demonstration of each component, followed by practice of that component. Some authorities recommend "backward chaining" for skills of this sort (Gilbert, 1962), meaning that the child would start with a nearly-tied shoe and learn the last subskill first, then the next to the last, and so on. In this case, we prefer "forward chaining" in which the child learns the first component, then the second, then the third, and so on. As he learns new components the child should review the previous ones.

While there might be some value to drawings, you should have learned from completing the task analysis that it would be almost impossible to teach an adult, let alone a child, to tie his shoes using a "brief explanation." The steps are difficult to describe in words and would be more difficult still to comprehend. Most kindergartners will not know right from left. *Over, under, across,* and *loop* will be difficult, ambiguous terms for many of the children. A wordy teaching procedure will not work.

A puppet show might have some value if there were a motivational problem. However, we feel most children will *want* to be able to tie their shoes. Their problem will be learning *how,* a problem which a puppet show could not solve.

The organization of Part II can be explained in terms of the three components of teaching—presentation, student performance, and reinforcement and corrective feedback—and of the two categories of learning—learning responses, and learning the conditions under which these responses are appropriate.

The first component of teaching, presentation, is not considered in a single chapter. Rather, it is considered from different perspectives in Chapters 9, 10, 11, and 12.

Chapter 6, "Teaching New Responses," emphasizes the second component of the teaching model and the first category of learning. This chapter appears first in Part II because it considers the student's first task, response learning. The main point of this chapter on practice is that students learn what they are led to *do*.

Chapter 7, "Reinforcement," considers part of the third component of the teaching model. Procedures are described for influencing student behavior, using praise, attention, money, tokens, toys, grades, privileges, and punishment. The chief conclusion is that rewards should be made contingent upon the student's reaching a clearly-defined standard of performance. This chapter also contains suggestions for dealing with discipline problems.

Chapter 8, "Corrective Feedback," considers the other part of the third component of the teaching model, describing strategies and tactics for altering unsatisfactory student performance. These range from simply telling a student he is wrong to presenting counter-examples and posing further questions to cause the student to reconsider his position.

The following chapters consider the first component of teaching, presentation, from different perspectives.

Chapter 9, "Stimulus Control," is concerned with teaching students *when* to behave in a given manner, the second category of learning. In order to act appropriately in various situations, students must be able to distinguish the critical features of things, events, patterns of symbols,

An answer to question 6 on p. **179.**

Choose a lower minimum standard of performance. Spend a little time trying to think of a simpler way to tie shoes which has these qualities: the child can do it himself; it will stay tied; the child can untie it easily himself (an ordinary knot will not do because it is hard to untie). After you have invented a simpler knot (bow), see p. 199 for a description of the authors' solution.

and other people's behavior. When the differences between things are subtle, a fine discrimination is required. Specific procedures are detailed for teaching students to make difficult discriminations.

Chapter 10, "Concepts and Principles," considers one of the teacher's most important tasks, the analysis and teaching of concepts and principles. It also deals with the question of when and under what circumstances a given behavior is appropriate. However, whereas Chapter 9 deals with *narrowing* the range of occasions which will evoke a certain response, in order to exclude those occasions on which the response is inappropriate, Chapter 10 discusses *broadening* the range to include all circumstances in which a certain behavior is appropriate. Concepts and principles encompass *classes* of things, events, or situations. Thus, when a person really knows a concept or principle, he should be able to use it in any situation to which it applies.

Chapter 11, "Motivation," compares the psychologist's and the educator's conceptions of motivation, and suggests techniques for engaging motivational processes in the learning situation and also for dealing with excessive motivation (often aroused during examinations, contests, public performances, and the like).

Every teacher hopes that students will use the skills and concepts they learn outside the classroom and later in life. The conditions which promote wide application and continuing use of things learned in school are quite complex and are discussed in several different places in the remainder of this book. Whether skills and concepts will be used depends partly on motivation, partly on whether the student has learned to recognize signals that the skill or concept is relevant (Chapters 9, 10), but also on whether the student can remember the skill or concept. Chapter 12, "Memory," therefore considers explanations of why forgetting occurs and suggests methods to reduce forgetting and to promote remembering over the long haul.

Answer to question 5 on p. **179.**

Try to figure out what they are doing wrong. Try to help them overcome their difficulties. If a child makes too small a loop, get him to make a larger loop. If he lets go of the loop held with his left hand too soon, get him to hold it longer. In addition to demonstrating you may be able to guide the child's fingers with yours.

CHAPTER

6

Teaching New Responses

The three components of teaching are presenting a task or materials, providing for student response, and giving reinforcement and feedback. We shall begin our detailed consideration of the teaching process with the middle component, providing for student response. This is a sensible starting point because the first task of the student is to learn the responses which will be required of him. The person who completes this chapter should be able to:

1. describe the optimum length of a presentation preceding student response.
2. identify the relationships which should exist between a presentation and the student response that follows.
3. identify the conditions under which student response is most important.

We have already referred to the distinction between (1) learning new responses and (2) learning when to make these responses. This is an important distinction. Consider a case which does *not* involve new response learning. Assume that the word "wolf" is part of a first grader's speaking vocabulary; however, when he comes to the word in a sentence he is reading he does not say "wolf." He does not need to learn the response, since he can already say the word. What he must learn is another circumstance in which to say the word, either to himself or out loud. He must learn to say "wolf" when the sequence of letters *w-o-l-f* appears.

Now consider a case which *does* involve new response learning. Assume a fifth grader who has never encountered the word "analogy."

He will have to learn to say the word and perhaps to spell it. Of course he will also have to learn to recognize the word when it appears in printed or oral form and learn the word's meaning, but these learnings have to do with when to use the word, not with how to make the response itself. A person can learn the response before or at the same time he learns when to give the response. But, obviously, he cannot learn *when* to behave in a certain way before he is capable of that behavior.

The singular expression "*a* response" is a little arbitrary because it suggests a unit of behavior which is not divisible into smaller components. Often it would be more accurate to say "sequence of responses" instead of "*a* response." What is the functional unit of behavior which could rightly be called "*a* response"? A rough answer is that a single response is all of the behavior which, once started, will almost always run off in an automatic, invariant fashion. By this definition, the conventional greeting, "How are you?" is usually a single response, even though it contains several words. On the other hand, for a beginning reader sounding out an unfamiliar word, the functional unit of behavior is smaller than a single word. Tying a shoe certainly involves many responses for a kindergartner, but could perhaps be regarded as a single response for an adult. Note the parallel between the definition of a "single response" and the definition of an "intact entering skill" (Chapter 3).

Responses are seldom wholly new. Frequently "new" responses entail a synthesis of other responses of which the student is already capable. Or the student must learn to make a response similar to one already in his repertoire. In such cases, teaching the response involves only modifying behavior of which the student is already capable. Response learning is involved when responses in the student's repertoire are strengthened or made more probable. For instance, everyone has words in his vocabulary which he seldom if ever uses. Response learning is entailed in getting a person to use such words more frequently. In short, in addition to the acquisition of entirely new responses, response learning covers the synthesis, modification, and strengthening of previously acquired responses.

Answer to question 4 on p. **179.**

We feel that it would be best to teach no more than two children at once. Seat one child on each side of you. It is important that the children see your hands move from the perspective from which they see their own hands (Roshal, 1961).

Which of the following entail new response learning?

A. a novice violinist learning to hear the difference between an A and an A♯.
B. an offensive lineman learning to keep low when he blocks.
C. a basketball player learning the situations in which he should pass instead of shoot.
D. an actor learning his lines.
E. a rookie policeman learning to squeeze the trigger of his revolver.
F. an infant learning that "dada" applies only to his father.

The answer appears on p. **197.**

Teaching responses using verbal instruction. The simplest way to get a person to make a new response is to describe the response he should make. This procedure will work whenever the response is easily describable in words and the student understands these words. For instance, seventh graders could be taught how to find the area of rectangles by saying, "To find the area of a rectangle, multiply the width by the height." A complete teaching episode would include arranging for student response (e.g., asking "What is the area of a rectangle 10 inches high and 5 inches wide?") and providing reinforcement and feedback (e.g., "10 inches times 5 inches is 50 inches. The area of the rectangle is 50 square inches.")

When response learning entails strengthening responses already in the student's repertoire, describing the general form of the response is often a satisfactory first step. Suppose a high school English teacher receives from a student a short story which begins with the following sentences:

A young man was standing in a forest clearing. He was rather handsome. As he stood there, he noticed an unusual bird. The bird was brightly colored. The bright colors excited his imagination.

The teacher believes the student uses too many short, choppy sentences and too few complex, deeply embedded ones. To change the student's behavior the teacher might say, "Your writing would be more interesting if you used more long, complex sentences. Why don't you try to rewrite the beginning of your story in a single sentence containing no independent clauses? In other words, don't just string the sentences together with 'ands'." The following revision meets these criteria.

The bright colors of an unusual bird he noticed excited the imagination of a rather handsome young man standing in a forest clearing.

It should be emphasized that this illustration, like the others in this section, is incomplete in the sense that to produce an enduring change in behavior usually requires much more practice and a systematic schedule of reinforcement and feedback.

Verbal instruction can be a very effective means of teaching verbal-symbolic responses. Verbal instruction is usually less effective for teaching motor responses. You probably learned from the exercise in Chapter 5 that it would be difficult to teach a kindergartner to tie his shoes solely by describing the component movements in words. Adults cannot easily learn complex movements from verbal explanations either. While a professional dancer might be able to approximate a dance step from a verbal description, such a description would be futile for the average person. This is not to say that words have no role in teaching motor responses, but only that words cannot bear the main burden of instruction. (Teaching by telling is discussed at greater length in Chapter 10.)

Teaching responses using demonstrations. A generally useful technique is to demonstrate the response for the student. The teacher can serve as the model and so can other students. Demonstrations can be filmed. Still pictures and diagrams can also be used to depict responses, although somewhat less effectively than moving representations.

Demonstrations have their place in teaching verbal-symbolic responses. Consider teaching a student to pronounce words in a language containing phonemes (sound units) not found in his native tongue. The best way to teach a person to pronounce, for instance, the German umlaut, as in *schöne,* is for the teacher to articulate the phoneme himself and ask the student to mimic him. Naturally, demonstrations are of special value when the response does not lend itself to verbal description. As already indicated, this is usually true of motor responses. (A lengthy illustration of motor skill teaching using demonstration appears later in this chapter.)

Frequently, if not always, "Actions speak louder than words." Whether intended or not, students are going to learn from watching what a teacher does as well as listening to what a teacher says should be done. From an early age children learn by imitating. Everyone to some extent mimics his peers in matters of speech, dress, hair style, and in sundry other ways. Research indicates that attractive people with status are likely to be selected as models. This is so even for children. Enrolled in a kindergarten class taught by the wife of one of the authors was the only son of a college choral music director and a professor of speech. The boy had been nearly mute until the age of four, but when he did begin to speak his diction was flawless. After a few weeks of kindergarten, to his parents' understandable dismay, the boy began to lisp. Investigation revealed that the biggest, toughest boy in the class lisped. For this child, and for a number of other children as well, lisping was the first evident new response acquired in school.

People can even acquire emotional behavior by imitation. Albert Bandura and his associates (Bandura & Walters, 1963) have completed a large number of studies in which children learned patterns of behavior by observing adult models. Certain children in one of these experiments (Bandura, Ross & Ross, 1963) observed either an adult or a cartoon character punch, slap, squash, kick, throw, and shout at a large, inflated plastic doll. Other children saw an adult play with the doll in a gentle, nonaggressive manner. When given the opportunity to play with the doll themselves, the children who had observed the aggressive model made twice as many aggressive responses as the children who had seen the nonaggressive model. (Fig. 6.1 contains photographs of children reproducing the behavior of an aggressive model.) Incidentally, research indicates that the notion that antisocial behavior can be curbed by encouraging an aggressive person to release his pent-up feelings is probably false. People encouraged to act aggressively are likely to display more rather than less aggressive behavior in the future (Kahn, 1960).

Answer to the question on p. **195.**

B, D, and **E** involve response learning.

Answer to question 7 on p. **179.**

It *may* be possible to arrange something that the rest of the children can do on their own. Bear in mind, though, that kindergartners usually cannot sustain an activity for more than a few minutes without supervision. The children you are teaching to tie their shoes will need your undivided attention. To teach every child in the class will require a number of hours. You probably will need help. Maybe you can borrow a junior or senior high school student, or, if they are not available, a fifth or sixth grader, for a couple of hours a week. Or, perhaps you could ask some mothers to help you.

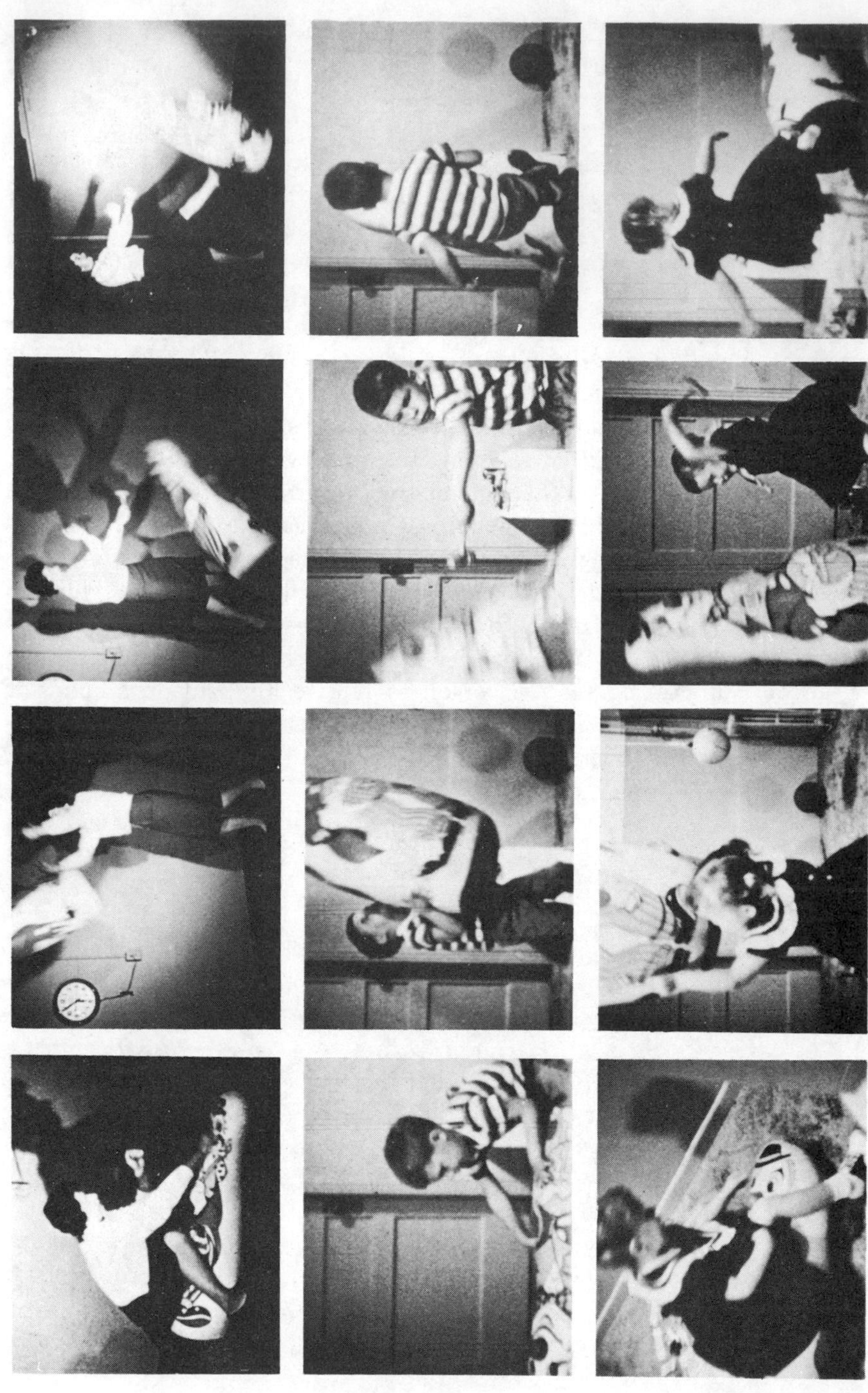

FIGURE 6.1

Like all other people, teachers do as they have observed others doing. A person spends sixteen or more years as a student before he becomes a teacher. One reason teaching practices are resistant to change is that it is difficult to escape the patterns of a lifetime. Even those most careful about instructional technique tend to teach as they were taught. Not uncommon is the professor of education who does nothing but lecture about the value of discussion and the importance of active student participation.

When he learns from a demonstration, the student's first response will entail copying, echoing, or imitating. Such responses constitute only a first approximation to the desired behavior. By the end of the teaching sequence the student should be able to respond on his own without a model to copy from. He should be weaned from his model as soon as possible. (The reasons for this rule are made clear later in this chapter, with special reference to the copying drill for teaching spelling, and are considered again in a different perspective in Chapter 9.)

Other methods of teaching responses. Verbal instruction and demonstration can be combined to teach responses. In addition, it is sometimes possible for students to *discover* the response without directive verbal instruction or demonstration. A discovery method will work when the new response, usually a principle or rule, involves a synthesis of responses already in the student's repertoire. (Discovery teaching is discussed in detail in Chapter 10.)

When teaching new responses, reinforcement and feedback are of the greatest importance. Verbal direction and demonstration, when properly planned, will evoke an approximation to the desired response. The re-

One answer to the question posed in the answer to question 6 on p. **191.**

Tying a one-loop bow might be acceptable minimum performance. The most difficult part of tying the usual bow is the maneuver that produces two loops. A one-loop bow is simply a square knot or granny knot in which one of the two ends tied together is a loop instead of a single strand. With a little experience, a teacher should be able to recognize early in instruction the child with poor small muscle coordination and teach him to tie one-loop bows. Children with good coordination should be encouraged to tie more elegant bows.

sponse is then "shaped" into its final form using reinforcement and feedback. In fact it is possible, through employing reinforcement, to shape responses without an introductory presentation. (The technique of shaping is described in Chapter 7.)

The Role of Student Response

One of the most important principles in this entire book is that *students learn by doing.* For purposes of discussion three levels of active response may be distinguished. At the first level the student is required to read, listen, or watch. At the second level he is required to make a particular *covert* response. And, finally, at the third level, he is required to make a particular *overt* response.

When a student reads silently, he is making active responses. To be sure, unless he moves his lips, no one else can see these responses. Nonetheless, silent reading does entail active responding. When active responding stops, for any practical purpose, reading ceases. Most people have had the experience of beginning to read a book and of finding that they have turned several pages without the slightest idea of what has passed before their eyes. This phenomenon occurs when active engagement with the text stops. Similarly, listening and watching entail active responding. If the student is not actively engaged with what a speaker is saying, then he is not really listening.

At the next level, the student is requested to make particular covert responses. Of course the responses involved in reading, watching, and listening are also largely covert. But, unlike reading or listening, the response requirement at this level is quite definite and structured. For instance, the student may be asked to answer a question or solve a problem. The covert response is not publicly observable. Hence, the student is directed to "think" the answer rather than to write it or to check an alternative. Or he is asked to work a problem in his head without writing down the result or any of the intermediate steps. There is considerable evidence, however, that requiring particular covert responses within a lesson increases learning.

There were many investigations of the effects of requiring particular overt responses—or as such responses were then called, "recitation"—between 1900 and 1920. Much of the early research was summarized by the famous educator, Arthur I. Gates (1917). This research generally shows that requiring active recitation increases learning. Gates also completed the classic experiment on the relative effects of reading and recitation. In his experiment several hundred elementary school children memorized either lists of three-letter nonsense syllables (trigrams), or they memorized short biographies such as the following:

JAMES CHURCH, born in Michigan, February 15, 1869. Studied in Munich, and later studied Forestry and Agriculture. Director of Mt. Rose Weather Observatory in 1906. Studied evaporation of snow, water content, and frost.

JOHN CLARK, born in Indiana, June 4, 1867. Studied Surgery and became a doctor in Philadelphia. Taught at Johns Hopkins. Has visited Italy and Russia. Has a brother in Vancouver.

MORTON CLOVER, born in Ohio, April 25, 1875. Studied Chemistry at Michigan. Worked in Manila for eight years. Wrote articles on the content of dogwood, of sugar, and acids. Now lives in Detroit.

In particular, Gates investigated the effects of spending an increasing proportion of total study time in active recitation. Although all groups spent the same total amount of time studying, one group spent the entire period of time reading the material; another group read for the first 80% of the time and then engaged in active recitation for the remaining 20%; another group read for the first 60% of the time and recited for the remaining 40%; and so on. The children were told that while reading: "you should never look away from the paper; never close your eyes to see if you can say the words; in fact never say a single word unless you are actually looking at it; actually reading it" (p. 30). When the experimenter gave the signal to recite, the children were supposed to begin trying to repeat the material to themselves without looking at the text. They were instructed not to look at the words unless absolutely necessary. Immediately following the period of study a test was given in which the child wrote as much as he could remember. The test was repeated four hours later. Figures 6.2 and 6.3, which are based on Gates data, picture the results of the experiment for the trigrams and biographies, respectively.

When the response is publicly observable or leaves a publicly-observable record, it is said to be an overt response. Just as there is evidence to suggest that active recitation, as compared to reading, increases recall, there is evidence that the requirement to make overt responses increases learning to a somewhat greater extent than the requirement to make covert responses. For instance, Michael and Maccoby (1961) showed 49 classes of high school juniors and seniors a 14-minute film entitled, *Patterns of Survival,* which describes civilian defense against atomic bombing. The experiment was completed in 1950 and 1951, not long after the Soviet Union had successfully tested its first atomic device, so

Study Figs. 6.2 and 6.3 and write down the principal conclusions that can be drawn from the Gates experiment.

The authors' interpretation can be found on p. **204.**

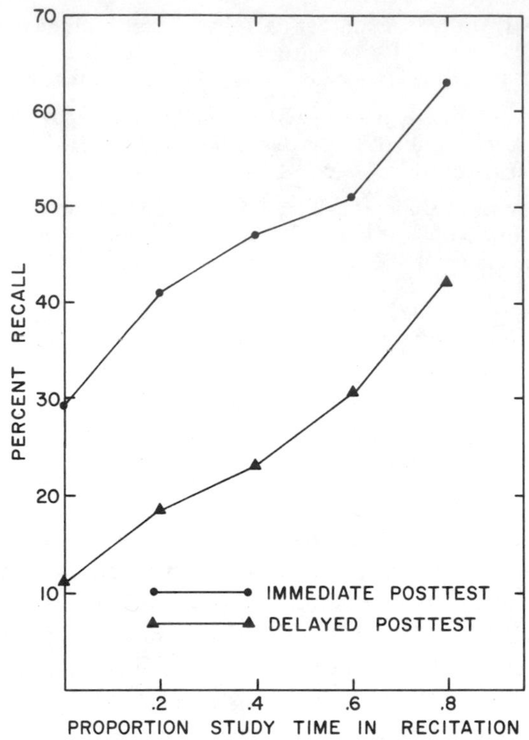

FIGURE 6.2 *Percent recall of trigrams immediately following learning and four hours later as a function of proportion of study time spent in recitation. Each point represents 120 fourth, sixth, and eighth graders.* (*Based on Gates, 1917.*)

the subject matter was of immediate and pressing interest. Some classes only saw the film. For other classes there were four "participation sessions." These occurred during three breaks in the film and at the end of the film. During participation sessions the teacher read questions covering some of the points presented in the preceding section of the film. In the overt-response groups, students wrote their answers to the questions on answer sheets. In the covert-response groups, students were instructed to "think" the answers. After the film, a 30-item test was administered. The questions, which were all of the short-answer variety, involved information directly covered in the film. On questions from the posttest which had been asked and answered during participation sessions, students who only saw the film got 52.5% correct; those who made covert responses during participation sessions got 66.1% correct; while those who made overt, written responses got 70.4% correct. Note that there was a fairly big advantage from requiring covert responses as opposed to simple viewing of the film, and a smaller addi-

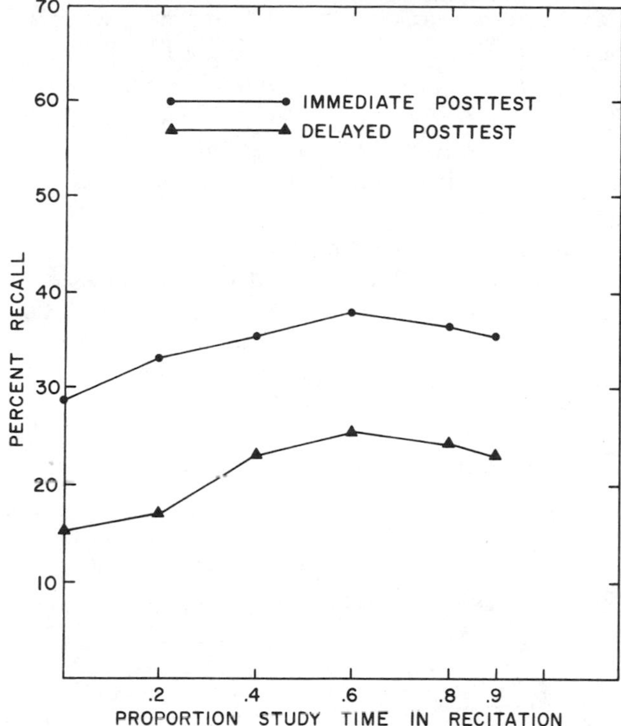

FIGURE 6.3 *Percent recall of biographies immediately following learning and four hours later as a function of proportion of study time spent in recitation. Each point represents 200 third, fourth, fifth, sixth, and eighth graders. (Based on Gates, 1917.)*

tional advantage from requiring these responses to be written. There was no difference among groups on questions about the film which were not asked during participation sessions. This fact indicates that, in this case at least, all of the positive effects of asking questions during the film must be attributed to the practice the student got from answering them, rather than from any stimulating of students to pay closer attention: if the students who were asked questions were, as a result, paying closer attention, they would have done better on all of the posttest questions, not just the ones they had practiced during the lesson.

Conditions under which overt responding facilitates learning. The requirement to make overt responses is one of the main features of programmed instruction. It was a distinct surprise, therefore, and a great disappointment to some investigators when study after study involving programmed instruction found that students who were required to make overt responses didn't learn any more than students who made covert responses or read programs with the blanks filled in (Alter & Silverman, 1962; Crist, 1966; Della-Piana, 1962; Hartmann, Morrison & Carlson, 1963; Lambert, Miller & Wiley, 1962; Stolurow & Walker, 1962; Tobias & Weiner, 1963). Fortunately, the failure to find what almost everyone expected to find had the desirable effect of leading to research that has clarified the conditions under which overt responding does facilitate learning.

Relevant overt responses occurring for the right reasons increase learning. The requirement to make irrelevant overt responses, on the other hand, may actually interfere with learning. Suppose that the purpose of a frame in a self-instructional program is to teach about reflexes. Which of the following frames is the better version?

The doctor taps your knee with a ____________ in order to test your reflexes.

The doctor taps your knee with a hammer in order to test your ____________.

The latter frame, of course, is better because it leads the student to write "reflexes," whereas the first frame leads him to write "hammer."

Answer to the question on p. **201.**

A. For both the trigrams and biographies the greater the proportion of time spent in recitation, the greater the recall, except that the effects were less pronounced for the biographies than the trigrams. In fact, the recall of the biographies reached a maximum when .6 of the time was spent in recitation. These are the chief conclusions. Those that follow are less important.

B. Overall, the children seemed to recall a greater percent of the trigrams than the biographies. (This is not a typical result. Other things being equal, people learn and recall a higher percent of meaningful than unmeaningful material.)

C. The amount forgotten in the four-hour interval between the immediate and delayed posttests is roughly constant across all proportions of time spent in recitation. This fact indicates that varying the recitation time influences the amount learned (represented by the immediate posttest) and not (except indirectly by affecting the amount learned) the amount remembered.

D. Over the four-hour period between the two tests, the students forgot more of the trigrams than of the biographies.

James G. Holland (1965b), one of the pioneers in programmed instruction, to demonstrate that the requirement to make overt responses does indeed increase learning, altered 377 frames from the *Analysis of Behavior* (Holland & Skinner, 1961—the psychology program upon which the two frames presented above are based) in such a way that the content was identical to the normal program, except that in each frame a different word was chosen to be left blank. One experimental version required responses that were judged to be irrelevant to the critical material in the program. A second version was modified so that, while dependent upon critical content, correct responses were difficult to make—so difficult that students made errors on 74 percent of the frames. In a third version the blanks were filled in; consequently, the student was required only to read. The final version was the standard program, constructed, the authors hoped, so that the student was required to make relevant overt responses. The results of the experiment appear in Fig. 6.4. As you can see, students who received the standard program made

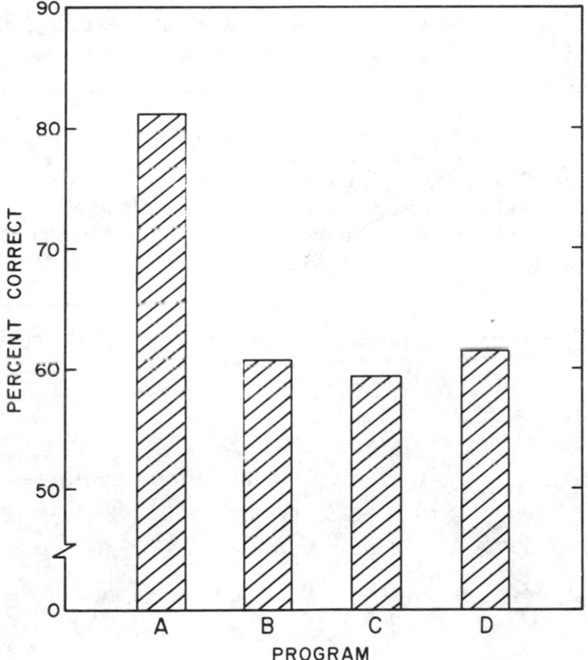

FIGURE 6.4 *Percent correct on the posttest for four versions of a psychology program. (Adapted from Holland, 1965.) Program A is the normal program, with response determined and dependent on critical content; Program B has responses determined, but answers relatively unrelated to critical content; Program C has responses relatively undetermined, but dependent on critical content; and Program D has only complete statements with no responses.*

only about half as many errors on the achievement test given after the program as students who received any of the other versions. The experiment shows that if responses are relevant to critical content and the student is capable of making these responses correctly, there is an advantage to the requirement for an overt response.

Krumboltz (1964) has completed a similar experiment with similar results. College students who got the version of a program on tests and measurements calling for trivial responses did significantly worse on the posttest than those who simply read completed statements or those who took the standard program; but the latter two groups did not differ. This study shows that requiring a trivial response can actually disrupt reading habits that are normally adaptive.

Only relevant overt responses, then, increase learning. Furthermore, these responses must occur for the right reasons if learning is to benefit. A student should be able to respond correctly if, and only if, he goes through the steps which the teacher intends. (See the frames in Fig. 6.5, for example, which come from a program on money and banking. "Bill of Exchange" is the correct response in several preceding frames.)

22. A *B - - - of Exchange (Draft)* is convenient for the payment of debts.
23. The seller of merchandise by sending a *Bill of E - - - - - - -* drawn on the buyer and attaching the shipping documents to a bank for collection can be assured that the merchandise will not be delivered to the buyer until the buyer pays for it.

FIGURE 6.5. *Two frames from a monetary program. (Adapted from Holland & Kemp, 1965.)*

Examine Fig. 6.5 and consider the following question before proceeding. Will it be necessary for the student to read all of the text in order to complete the blanks correctly?

The answer appears in the following paragraph.

Holland and Kemp (1965, 1966) have invented a simple but nonetheless ingenious procedure called the "blackout technique" to measure the extent to which the responses required in a self-instructional program are dependent upon the content of the program. People trained in this technique are prepared to cross out with a black crayon every word in a program which can be obliterated without making it more difficult to respond correctly. In Fig. 6.5, for example, people can make the correct responses to the frames even though everything except the phrases "Bill of Ex   " and "B   of Exchange" are blacked out. This fact indicates that the responses are not contingent upon the critical material in the frames.

According to Holland & Kemp (1966), the "blackout ratio" is the percentage of words in a program that can be covered without influencing error rate. In the money and banking program as a whole, 69% of the words could be covered without making it more difficult to complete the blanks correctly. Holland and Kemp (1966) computed blackout ratios, which ranged from 11% to 75%, for programs used in twelve experiments which had previously compared overt responding with covert responding and reading. The lowest four blackout ratios were obtained for programs with which a significant advantage for overt responding had been found previously. The remaining eight ratios were obtained for programs which had been employed in studies that showed no difference between overt responding and covert responding or reading. The research with the blackout technique demonstrates that the requirement to make overt responses facilitates learning, provided the responses are contingent upon the critical content of the lesson. It is important to note that while this research was done with programmed instruction, the same principle should hold for any form of instruction.

Just what the relationship between the response and the critical content of the lesson should be depends upon the purpose of the teacher. The student may have to read a passage critically, examine a map or a graph, or solve a problem. Whatever the precise connection may be, as a general rule in a well designed lesson, the student can respond correctly when, and only when, his responses are contingent upon the critical content of the lesson.

Another way to say the rule is to say that the student must be led to make relevant responses for the right reasons. A notorious example of a violation of this rule occurs in the spelling exercise in which the student repeatedly copies the to-be-learned word. The response *is* relevant, since the student is doing exactly what he later will be doing when he spells the word. The problem lies in the reasons which govern the writing. When a student repeatedly copies a word, he is not spelling, he is copying. By definition spelling is writing or saying the letters of a word without a model to copy from. In the copying drill, however, the student is able to make correct responses without really spelling. If the spelling of any word is learning from repeatedly copying it, it must be regarded as an accident, since the copying drill is, if anything, an exercise in penmanship rather than spelling. Copying from a model might be used to introduce the spelling of a new word, but a complete spelling exercise must involve more than copying.

The prospective teacher may wonder how to get a student to spell new words for the first time, especially ones with irregular spellings. Here is an improvement upon the copying drill: (1) say the word and then write it on the board; (2) erase the word; (3) say the word and have each student write it on a sheet of paper; (4) rewrite each word on the board so that the students may check their spellings. Teach about eight to ten words at a single time. Do not repeat a word until all of the others have been presented. Present the words in different orders on each run through the list. Use the procedure described several times, then present the words several times more, omitting the first two steps for each word. For best results, review the words a day or two later, once again omitting the first two steps.

Why does overt responding increase learning? The fact that requiring the student to make particular covert responses improves upon simple reading, watching, or listening, as well as the fact that overt responses are, in turn, superior to covert responses may suggest that the causative factor is "degree of activity." The more active the response that the student makes, the more he apparently learns. This is a plausible interpretation. There is, to the authors' knowledge, no data to prove that it is false. Nonetheless, the effective difference among the kinds of response is probably *not* degree of activity.

Before reading further consider the difference between the two following activities. Do they require the same response from the student?

A. Read the following: The square of the hypotenuse of a right triangle is eaual to the sum of the squares of the sides.
B. Answer the following question: What is the relationship between the hypotenuse and the sides of a right triangle?

The answer appears on p. **211.**

The difference between these activities illustrates an important point. Though both activities "cover the same topic," and though both entail active responses, the responses are qualitatively different. Therefore, *since the student learns what he does,* he cannot be depended upon to learn the same things from successfully completing the two activities. The student *may* stop and "think" about what he is reading (meaning that he tests himself to see if he can explain the relationship). If he does correctly explain the relationship to himself while he reads, then he will probably learn the same thing as the student who is required to complete the second activity. Otherwise he probably will not. One cannot be sure what a student is doing when he is looking at the pages of a book. He may be reading every line or he may be skimming. He may test himself on the implication of what he reads; but, then again, he may not. He may be giving selective emphasis to certain sections, as, for example, students seem to do when they underline portions of a text. The student's emphasis, it should be mentioned, is not necessarily the emphasis that the teacher desires. The student may give special attention to sections that he has trouble understanding or, on the other hand, he may skip difficult sections. If the student gets bored or tired, he may begin to daydream or even go to sleep.

Listening and watching have most of the potential difficulties of reading plus some additional ones. If a reader is stimulated by what he reads to think some thoughts of his own, he can at least return to the same spot in the book when he wishes. The person who is stimulated by a lecture, however, may "tune in" again only to have missed an important remark.

How does the requirement to make particular responses, either overt or covert, help to overcome the problems inherent in reading, listening, or watching? The answer is that such a requirement makes it highly likely that the student will make the responses necessary to learn: a student is more likely to learn something if he has correctly answered a question than if he has been present during a lecture which covered the point in question or been exposed to a page which dealt with the topic. It should be pointed out that while one can urge a student to make a covert response, one cannot effectively require him to, because there is no way to monitor covert responses short of requiring overt ones. A student can, however, be held accountable for his overt responses. Whether he receives rewards or faces sanctions necessarily depends upon overt responses. Covert responses, then, are fine as long as the student makes them. The problem is that students, particularly less conscientious ones, often stop making covert responses when they get bored or tired, or the material gets difficult.

It must be emphasized that throwing out a question every now and then is not enough to satisfy the principle of active responding. If one takes seriously the principle that the student learns what he does, then an active response will be required for each significant aspect of the subject matter. Not just any response will do either. The student must be led to make each of the responses designated in the behavioral objectives for a lesson. A typical concept taught in school will ordinarily entail at least the following five general types of objectives.

1. Given the rule or generalization, the student should be able to name the concept.
2. Given the concept, the student should be able to state the rule or generalization.
3. The student should be able to discriminate between examples and nonexamples of the concept.
4. The student should be able to list examples of the concept.
5. The student should be able to describe the differences between the concept and similar concepts.

In the blanks below, match the appropriate type of objective (using the numbers from the list above) with each of the questions on prime numbers.

______ **A.** Define a prime number.
______ **B.** Name four prime numbers greater than 20.
______ **C.** Distinguish between a prime number and an odd number.
______ **D.** What is a number called if it is divisible only by itself and one?
______ **E.** Which of the following are prime numbers: 2, 7, 12, 15, 19, 37, 39?

The answers appear on p. **212.**

Finally, it is not enough to require *a* single response, even when it is relevant. The student must be led to make *each* of the responses it is hoped he will learn, under the conditions in which he is expected ultimately to make them. This means, for instance, that the student should be led to answer all of the kinds of questions about prime numbers rather than just one or two of these.

When to require explicit responses. The timing of active practice is important. In programmed instruction the student is often required to make a response for every one or two sentences that are presented. On the other hand, many classroom teachers require the student to respond only on occasional quizzes covering what has been presented during a preceding week. The question is how long a time interval should occur between watching a demonstration, listening to an explanation, or reading a passage and active practice by the student.

Spitzer (1939) performed a large experiment which gives a rather clear answer to this question. Nine groups of sixth graders, totaling 3,600 students, read a 577-word passage describing a United States Department of Agriculture Experimental Station. At various times thereafter the groups received a 25-item multiple-choice test covering the passage. At no time were the students told the answers to any of the questions. The solid line in Fig. 6.6 traces the performance of groups the first time

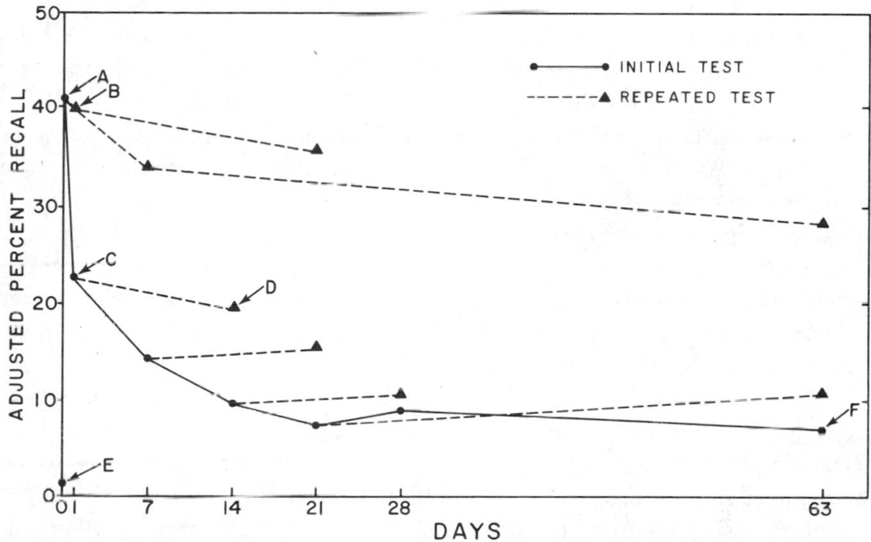

FIGURE 6.6 *Recall as a function of time of testing. (Based on Spitzer, 1939.) The solid line represents recall the first time the test is presented. The broken lines represent recall at the second or third testing. Each point represents about 400 sixth graders.*

Answer to the question on p. **208.**

No, the responses are different. Of course the student might be able to do **A** and not be able to do **B.**

they received the test. The dashed lines represent performance on the test for a second or third time. For instance, one group took the test for the first time one day after reading the passage (*C*) and then took the test again 14 days after the reading (*D*). A control group (*E*) took the test without reading the passage. As one can see, the control group registered only slightly above zero; therefore, it is safe to assume that the scores of the other groups represent what they actually learned and remembered rather than what they already knew before reading the passage or what they could figure out with a little common sense. By comparing the group that took the test immediately after reading the passage (*A*) with the group that received the test for the first time one day later (*C*), one can see that there was a drop of about 15%.

Looking at the difference between the group that took the test for the first time after one day (*C*) and the group that took the test for the first time after 63 days (*F*), one finds a drop of about 13%. These comparisons show that half of all the forgetting that occurred over seven weeks took place during the first 24 hours. One group which took the test immediately after reading the passage (*A*) repeated the test one day later (*B*). This group forgot only 0.6% during the first 24 hours or about 1/25 as much forgetting as the group that took the test for the first time one day after reading. In general, the effect of taking the test was to help preserve what the student could remember at that point. However, the test was not effective in helping the student to recover what he had already forgotten. The clear implication of the Spitzer experiment is that the student should be required to practice actively as soon as possible after instruction.

In a printed text, a student may be required to answer questions after completing a whole chapter, after completing major subtopics, or even after completing individual paragraphs. However, if learning is to be maximized, how much material should be presented before the student is required to engage in active practice? Webb and Schwartz (1959) completed an experiment that suggests an answer to this question. In their study, 345 naval air cadets read three stories, averaging 741 words in length, from Bullfinch's *Mythology*. All of the cadets completed 45 true-false questions covering the material presented in the stories, but different groups of cadets answered the questions at different times. One

Answers to the questions on p. **210.**

2A, 4B, 5C, ID, 3E

group answered a question or two after every paragraph. Another group answered a batch of 15 questions after each story. A third group read the three stories and then answered all 45 questions. A final group read the three stories that everyone else read, plus three additional stories, before answering the questions. The achievement test scores from the Webb and Schwartz experiment, corrected for guessing, are graphed in Fig. 6.7.[1] As one can see, the results of the experiment seem to support

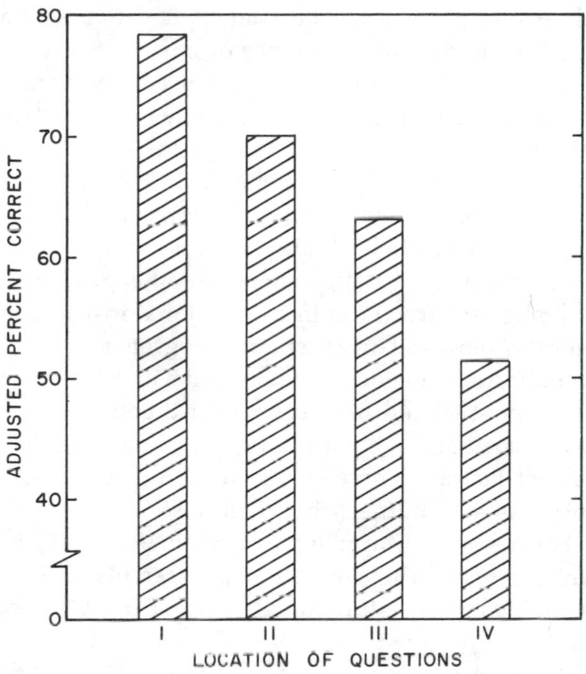

FIGURE 6.7 *The effects of spacing active practice. (Based on Webb & Schwartz, 1959.) Questions were asked after each paragraph (I), each story (II), three stories (III), or six stories (IV).*

the programmed instruction practice of "small steps," that is, the practice of presenting only a very small amount of material before requiring an active response from the student. Because they were actually conducting this experiment for a different purpose (to determine the best

[1] The formula to correct a true-false examination for guessing is $R - W$ (Rights minus Wrongs). The rationale for this formula is simple. Even if he is just guessing, a person will get a true-false question right about half the time. So for every question he got wrong, the chances are he got another one right just by guessing. Therefore, $R - W$ should give the number of questions he knew without guessing.

procedures for reading comprehension tests), Webb and Schwartz did not present the test again later. This is unfortunate since it is possible that the differences between groups would have decreased sharply on a later test.

Sheffield (1961) and Margolius and Sheffield (1961) have developed the concept of "demonstration-assimilation span" to deal with the issue of how much material to present before the student engages in active practice. They argue that the teacher (or film, or book) should present only as much at one moment as the student is capable of assimilating. Then it is time for the student to practice or answer questions. Just how long a segment the student can assimilate must be determined from experience. These authors suggest that a segment of instruction is the proper length when the responses of the typical student are 75 percent correct immediately following the segment. If the instructional unit is any larger, the student will make too many errors, whereas, they argue, shorter segments are inefficient. It should be noted that the instructional segments which Sheffield, et al., believe are the proper length, while certainly much shorter than those in conventional instruction, are longer than the frames in most self-instructional programs.

In actual application Sheffield, et al., believe that the length of an instructional segment should be a compromise between the demonstration-assimilation span and the natural units of a task or the logical divisions of a subject matter. These so-called natural units can be thought of as the subskills which the process of task analysis identifies (see Chapter 2). For instance, Margolius and Sheffield (1961) judged that a black-and-white film on the step-by-step assembly of an automobile distributor contained three natural units. Two of these were also roughly the same length as a demonstration-assimilation span. However, experimentation showed that the remaining natural unit was too long and complex to be assimilated in one showing; therefore, it was subdivided into two demonstration-assimilation span units.

It should be emphasized that the demonstration-assimilation span is not calibrated against the length of the material (as, number of printed words or number of minutes running time of a lecture or filmed demonstration). Rather, it is the other way around. The length of the presentation is determined by how much the student can assimilate in one stretch. The span will vary according to the student. Thus, children usually can assimilate less than adults. The amount that can be assimilated in one stretch also depends upon the complexity of the material, and complexity may vary within a single lesson. Consequently, instructional segments will be of varying length if these segments are determined according to how much the student can assimilate. For example, the

18-minute film on assembling a distributor was divided into four sections —each corresponding to a demonstration-assimilation span—yet one section of the film had a running time of six minutes, whereas another section, a more difficult one, ran only 2.5 minutes.

Margolius and Sheffield (1961) completed an experiment, using the film that has just been described, which shows the value of the concept of demonstration-assimilation span. Four groups of college undergraduates learned to assemble an automobile distributor using the film. The first group saw the film in the four sections, each calibrated to be one demonstration-assimilation unit in length. The film was stopped after each section and the students in this group attempted to assemble the part of the distributor which had just been described. The second group saw the film in large segments, consisting of two of the sections of the film, then attempted to assemble all that had been described in the preceding large segment. A third group saw the whole film, then tried to assemble the entire distributor. Every student in the groups described so far completed three cycles of film viewing and practice with the same sized segments of film each time. Students in a fourth group received what was called the "transition condition." On the first cycle they alternated between small film segments and practice. The second time they saw the large film segments before practicing. On the third and final trial those in the transition group saw the whole film and then tried to assemble the entire distributor. All students received a final test which consisted of trying to assemble the distributor. For both the practice sessions and the final test, all of the pieces of a standard distributor of the same model used in the film, plus five "confusion pieces," were arrayed in a standard pattern in front of the student. A screwdriver and tweezers were provided. The measure of performance was the number of pieces correctly assembled per minute. The results of the experiment appear in Fig. 6.8 on page 216.

Before proceeding examine Fig. 6.8 and determine (a) which instructional technique was *least* effective and (b) which two techniques were *most* effective. A covert answer will do.

The answers are contained in the following paragraph.

This experiment demonstrates once again that short presentations followed by short periods of practice are more effective than longer presentations followed by longer periods of practice. Whether still

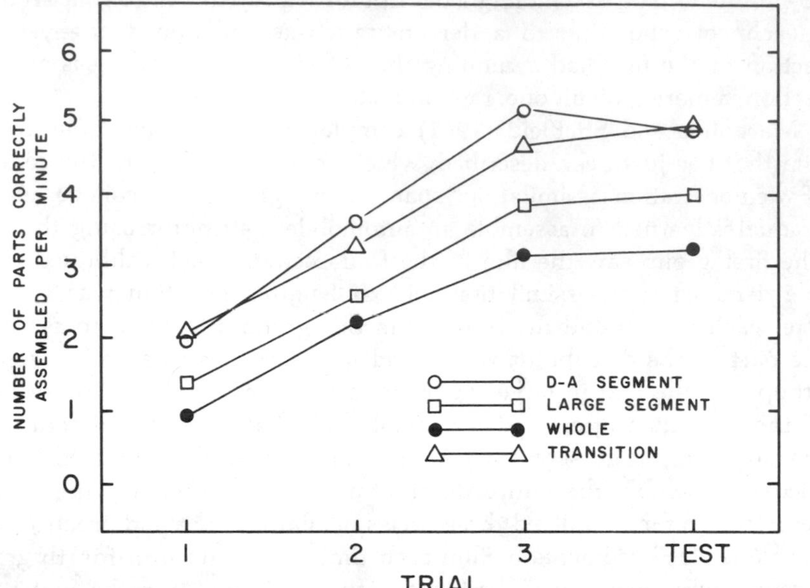

FIGURE 6.8 *Average rate of assembly of an automobile ignition distributor for three practice trials and a test trial. (Adapted from Margolius & Sheffield, 1961.)*

smaller units of material than those employed by Webb and Schwartz (1959) or Margolius and Sheffield (1961) would be even more effective is a moot question. It may well be that even smaller steps, such as those found in programmed instruction, are most effective, but this has not yet been proved experimentally, to the authors' knowledge.

In summary, experimental evidence seems to indicate that students learn more when required to make active responses immediately after small segments of a lesson.

Response difficulty. It is especially important to require an overt response from the student when the response itself is difficult. When a difficult response must be learned, as we have suggested, then the requirement for overt responses is usually superior to the requirement for covert responses. Response learning, it should be noted, is ordinarily involved in the acquisition of physical skills, or, as they are called, *motor skills*. While there is some benefit from imaginary "practice" (thinking through the sequence of movements) of a motor skill, research shows that overt practice results in much greater improvement

(Perry, 1939). Indeed, it seems unlikely that great skill at, say, swimming could ever be acquired without overt practice.

Response difficulty is also a factor in verbal and symbolic learning. Psychologists have accumulated a good deal of systematic knowledge, for instance, about the relative difficulty of the three-letter verbal combinations called *trigrams*. Which of the following do you suppose would be the easiest and which the most difficult to learn?

DOG
DGL
DIL

Undoubtedly, DOG would be the easiest to learn. In fact you have already learned a response for DOG. You know what this verbal unit means and you can pronounce it. In the ordinary sense of meaning, neither of the other two trigrams means anything. They are both nonsense syllables. Yet DIL "suggests more" than DGL. DIL can be pronounced easily and may make a person think of a dill pickle or "diligent," or some other word containing the same sequence of letters. Tables of norms have been developed which give the "association-value" (indicating the relative difficulty which people have in thinking up an association for a trigram) of all possible consonant-vowel-consonant (CVC) nonsense syllables (Glaze, 1928; Archer, 1960). The association value (Archer, 1960) for DIL is 94 percent, meaning that DIL ranks rather high among the 2,480 CVC nonsense syllables which can be formed in English. Many psychologists refer to association-value and related characteristics such as pronounceability as measures of "meaningfulness," even though it may seem odd to speak of the meaningfulness of a nonsense syllable. In any event, association value and pronounceability are known to have a very powerful effect on the ease with which trigrams are learned (Underwood & Schultz, 1960).

With respect to words in a living language, frequency of usage is a good predictor of response difficulty. Research workers have undertaken the tedious task of actually counting the number of times that words appear in various kinds of printed reading material, including textbooks, novels, and popular magazines. A summary of four word counts totaling 18,000,000 words appears in the best known and most widely used source of this sort, *The Teacher's Word Book of 30,000 Words*, by Thorndike and Lorge (1944). The following words beginning with *A* were selected from the Thorndike and Lorge list to give an idea of the differences among words which appear with different frequencies in ordinary usage.

Less than one occurrence per million words:

abaft
agnostic
ambulatory
aseptic

Between one and 50 occurrences per million words:

absorb
alien
appointment
available

Between 50 and 100 occurrences per million words:

active
addition
ancient
apply

Among the 500 most frequent words:

about
after
anything
ask

Eigen and Margulies (1963), experimenting with verbal learning, have demonstrated that the more difficult the response, the greater the advantage of the overt as compared to the covert response. Groups of students received short self-instructional programs within which the responses were either three-letter words (easy), consonant-vowel-consonant (CVC) trigrams such as DIL (moderately difficult), or consonant-consonant-consonant (CCC) trigrams such as DGL (very difficult). Within each group half of the students were required to write their responses, whereas the remainder were asked to "think" the answers. The performance of the various groups on the achievement test given immediately after the program is graphed in Fig. 6.9. The results indicate that there is only a tiny advantage for overt responding when the responses are easy, but that there is a larger advantage as the responses become more difficult. Relatively speaking, those who made overt responses recalled about half again as many CVCs and twice as many CCCs as those who made covert responses.

Overt responses have proved to be important in actual school lessons, as well as in laboratory experiments, when the responses are difficult.

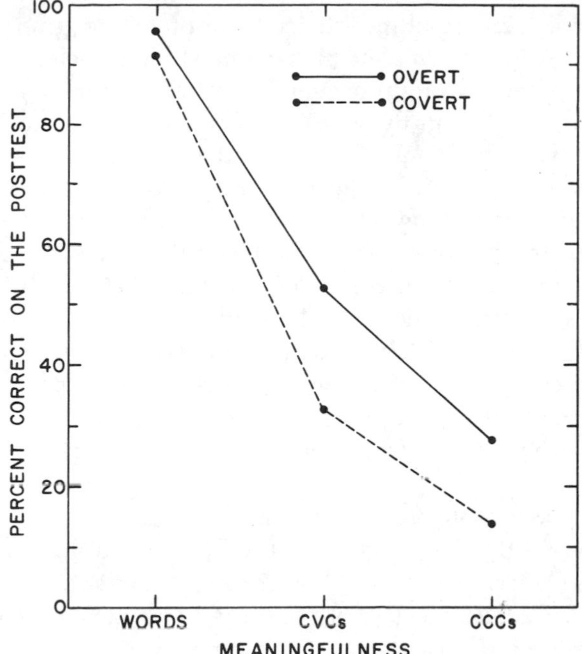

FIGURE 6.9 *Posttest performance for three sets of materials at different levels of meaningfulness. (Based on Eigen & Margulies, 1963.)*

At this point a further distinction must be made. Overt responses may involve choosing among alternatives, as in multiple-choice questions, or producing the response, as in short-answer questions. For example, consider the following two questions:

An event that increases the likelihood of responses it follows is a

____________________________.

An event that increases the likelihood of responses it follows is a (circle one)

A. conditioned stimulus
B. reinforcer
C. oversure stimulus
D. refractory phase

The student must produce or "construct" the answer (which is, incidentally, "reinforcer") to the first question, whereas all he must do is recognize it in the second. This distinction turns out to be important. Williams (1963) prepared four versions of a self-instructional program to teach introductory psychology to college undergraduates. One group of students received a multiple-choice form of the program. Instead of writing out answers to complete blanks, the students selected one of two alternatives. A second group made constructed responses—that is, they were required to write out the words to fill blanks. The third group read the program with the blanks filled in and with the words which filled the blanks underlined. A final group read the program with the blanks filled in but no underlining. The overall achievement test performance of the constructed-response group and the multiple-choice group did not differ. However, both of these groups scored significantly higher than either reading group,[2] which, in turn, did not differ. When just those test items which required the student to produce a novel, technical term were considered, it was found that the constructed-response group was superior to each of the other groups, including the multiple-choice group, whereas the other groups were not significantly different from one another.

Williams (1965) confirmed these results using a zoology program with sixth graders. In this later experiment, there was no difference between the multiple-choice group and the constructed-response group on a multiple-choice achievement test, but the constructed-response group proved superior on the short-answer achievement test. As predicted, the constructed-response group was significantly better on test items which required a novel, technical term as an answer, whereas the groups did not differ on items that could be answered with familiar vocabulary. Clearly, according to these experimental findings, an overt, *constructed* response should be required from a student if he is expected to be able to produce an unfamiliar technical term. However, if he merely has to recognize the term or if he is already capable of emitting the response, as is the case with high-frequency words in the language, then selecting a multiple-choice alternative or just thinking the answer may do as well. Most of the systematic knowledge we have about response difficulty in verbal and symbolic learning concerns nonsense syllables and single words. Obviously, more complicated and lengthy responses such as those involved in solving problems in arithmetic and algebra, writing poetry, or preparing research papers in history also entail response difficulty. Presumably, then, the requirement to make overt responses

[2] "Significance" is a term with a technical meaning in the biological and behavioral sciences. Statistical procedures are applied to the data gathered in experiments to determine the likelihood or probability that a result could have occurred by chance. As a matter of tradition and convention, a result is "significant" if it could have occurred by chance less than 5 times in 100, or 1 time in 100, or even 1 time in 1,000—the exact value or "level of significance" depending upon the scientific speciality. A scientist will not claim that he has confirmed an hypothesis unless his results are statistically significant.

will facilitate learning any of these more complex skills. In fact, it seems reasonable to suppose that overt responses are even more important in learning to solve, say, algebra problems, than they are in learning technical terms. Presumably this is the case, but there is no direct experimental evidence to demonstrate that it is so.

Explicit responses and attention. A person learns what he does, therefore, as the previous pages have detailed, learning is facilitated if the student is led to make relevant responses correctly. This may be called the "direct instructive effect" of the requirement to make explicit responses. Could it also be that the requirement to answer questions or perform now and then keeps the student on his toes so that he learns more from material upon which responses are not contingent? The answer seems to be yes, to some extent, under some conditions.

The Michael and Maccoby (1961) experiment, described earlier in this chapter (involving lessons based on the film on defense against atomic attack), was designed in part to determine whether requiring students to answer pertinent questions in the course of a lesson causes them to pay closer attention. The reasoning behind the experiment was that if asking questions increased attention, then students should perform somewhat better on all the questions on the achievement test, not merely those that were asked and answered during the lesson. However, in this experiment, and in a further experiment (Maccoby, Michael, & Levine, 1961—also employing the film on defense against atomic attack), students who were asked questions during the lesson performed better on those same questions which appeared later on the achievement test, but were no better on additional achievement test questions which were not asked during the lesson. Hence, in these experiments, requiring students to make responses during the lesson had a direct instructive effect but did not seem to have an indirect effect on attention.

Maccoby, et al., then argued that asking questions during a lesson may not have influenced attention in the previous experiments because the lesson was intrinsically interesting and students were already paying attention. So they completed an experiment in which nearly a thousand air force trainees were shown a dull, "educational" film that traced the history of world map concepts from ancient times to the Air Age. Half of the students engaged in "active review" sessions, two following brief sections of the film and one at the end. During these sessions, a total of ten factual questions were asked, students wrote answers, and then the correct answers were announced. The remainder of the students just saw the film. An achievement test was announced before the film for half of the active-review groups and half of the groups that got no review. The test consisted of ten factual questions which were "practiced" during the film, twenty additional factual questions which were not practiced during the film, and five "principle" questions which were not practiced.

The results of the experiment (which appear in Fig. 6.10) show, first,

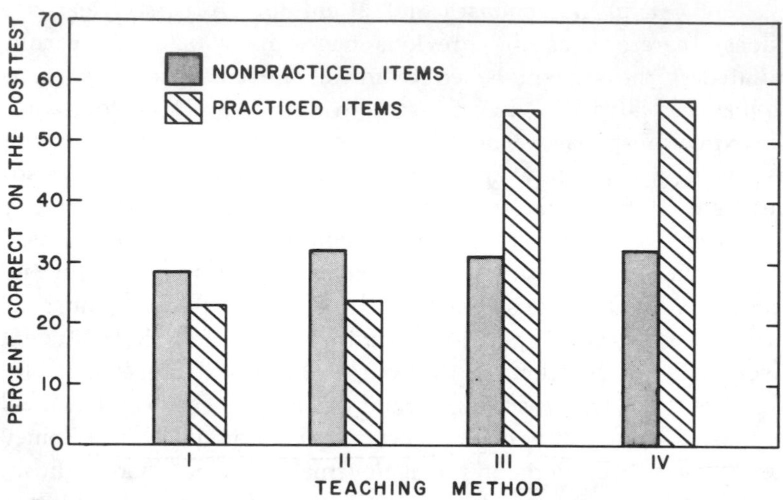

FIGURE 6.10 *Performance on a posttest according to teaching method. Group I did not participate in practice sessions during the film nor get an advance announcement of the test; Group II did not receive participation sessions but did receive an announcement of the test; Group III participated in practice sessions but received no test announcement; Group IV got both participation sessions and a test announcement. There were about 250 air force trainees in each group. (Based on Maccoby, Michael, & Levine, 1961.)*

that engaging in active review resulted in about a 33 percent advantage over no review on practiced items. The indirect effects of active review were much smaller. Either having the test announced beforehand or active reviewing during the lesson resulted in less than a 4 percent increment in the nonpracticed items; however, if the test was announced there was no additional advantage from active review. The results with the "principle" items showed the same trends as the nonpracticed factual items; however, the differences among conditions were not statistically significant (i.e., they could have occurred by chance). While this experiment did show a statistically significant effect attributable to increased attention, the important point is that the direct instructive effect of active practice during the lesson was ten times as great as the indirect effect.

The clearest demonstration that asking questions during a lesson may influence attention is to be found in the research of Ernst Rothkopf, a research scientist at Bell Telephone Laboratories. In one experiment, Rothkopf (1966) divided a 5,000-word chapter from Rachel Carson's book *The Sea Around Us* (1961) into seven sections, each three multilithed pages in length. Two questions of the short-answer variety were developed for each section. A total of 159 college undergraduates read (or, in the case of one group, did *not* read) the chapter under one of several conditions which differed, first, according to whether the student was required to answer the questions, and if so, differed according to when the questions were asked and whether the student was provided the correct answers after he responded. The conditions are detailed below:

1. *Shortly before, with answers* (SBA). Just before starting any section, the student read the two questions for the section and was instructed to try to guess the correct answer for each. After writing his guess, the student obtained the correct answer.
2. *Shortly before, no answers* (SB). This condition was the same as SBA, except that the correct answers were not provided.
3. *Long before, with answers* (LBA). Just before starting the chapter the student was given all fourteen questions in one block. He was instructed to guess an answer to each question and write it into the appropriate space. The correct answer was then provided.
4. *Shortly after, with answers* (SAA). Immediately after reading each section, the student was asked to respond to each of the two questions based on the section that he had just read. The correct answers were provided.
5. *Shortly after, no answers* (SA). The condition was the same as SAA except that answers to the questions were not provided.
6. *Control A.* No questions were given under this condition; the students simply read the chapter. The directions stressed, as they did for each of the other conditions, that the student should try to remember as much of the chapter as he could, since he would be tested later.
7. *Control C.* This was the same as *Control A* except that the direction included statements that the chapter contained a good deal of detailed information and that the student should read the chapter slowly and carefully.

8. *Control T.* Those students who were tested under this condition did not read the chapter at all. Instead they studied the experimental questions and the correct answers to them until they could answer each question perfectly regardless of the order in which the questions were presented.

Immediately after reading the chapter, students were given a criterion test that consisted of twenty-five questions that had not been practiced during the chapter, then a test that consisted of fourteen experimental questions that had been practiced. Students in Control T were unable to improve their scores on the criterion test as a result of learning the answers to the experimental questions, indicating that the concepts covered by the two sets of questions were independent. The results for the other conditions in the Rothkopf experiment appear in Fig. 6.11. Comparing the other conditions with Control A, you can see that about 40 percent more of the practiced items were learned when the questions

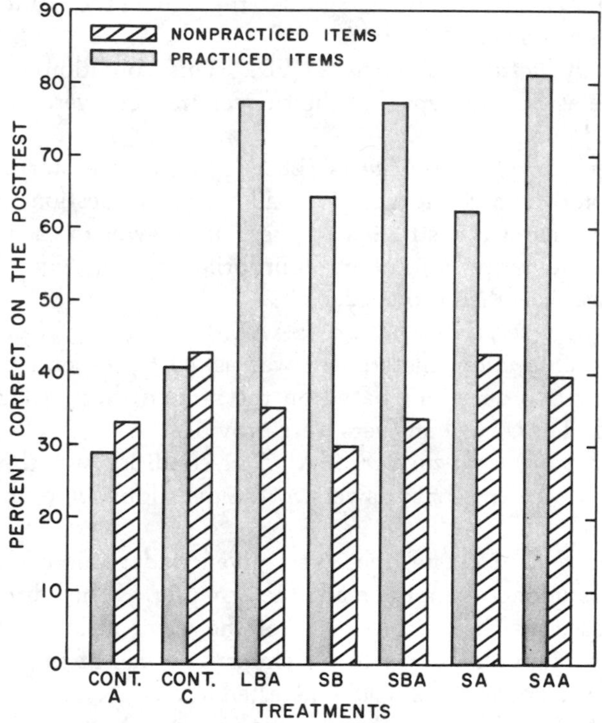

FIGURE 6.11 *Performance on a posttest according to treatment (treatments given to each group are described in the text). There were 21 college students in each group. (Adapted from Rothkopf, 1966.)*

were asked during the chapter, demonstrating that asking the questions then had a large direct instructive effect. Turning now to the nonpracticed items and once again comparing Control A with the other conditions, there is a small (about 7 percent) but statistically significant effect from asking questions *after* a student has read a passage—an effect which Rothkopf attributes to increased student attention. Asking questions *before* the student reads the section, on the other hand, does not have a beneficial influence on attention. However, Control C, a group in which students were asked to read with care and pay attention to detail, performed significantly better than Control A, in which students were merely given general directions.

Rothkopf and Bisbicos (1967) reasoned that if the increase in learning of answers to nonpracticed items that results from inserting questions within a lesson is caused by getting the student to pay closer attention, then by focusing the questions on a certain kind of content it should be possible to strengthen attention to this kind of content. In this experiment high school students read a passage from *The Sea Around Us* thirty-six multilithed pages in length. For each three-page section of this passage, they were asked two questions. Some students only saw questions requiring either a measured quantity (a distance, date) or a proper name for an answer. Some saw only questions requiring either a common English word or a technical word (*Bathyscophe, phototrophic*). On the achievement test, which was shown experimentally to be independent of the questions asked within the passage, it was confirmed that asking questions *after* the student has read the relevant three-page section improves achievement, whereas asking questions *before* the section upon which they are based does not. As was predicted, presenting a restricted category of questions within the passage facilitated performance on achievement test items in that category.

The research which has been completed to this point may underestimate the effects on student attention of asking questions and giving tests. The experiments, notably the ones employing educational films, have employed rather short lessons. Rothkopf (1966), who used a somewhat longer lesson than that of the film studies, got somewhat stronger results. Rothkopf and Bisbicos, however, specifically designed their experiment to see whether the effect on attention was greater for the second half of the lesson than the first half. The results demonstrated that it was. Studies of eye movements during prolonged reading suggest that the effect on attention of asking questions might become quite important in really long lessons or under the daily routine of school. Hoffman (1946) had thirty college undergraduates read a history textbook for four consecutive hours in a chamber that resembled a library carrel. A sensitive apparatus made a continuous record, called an "electroculogram," of the eye movements of each reader. Analysis of the electroculograms revealed that the pattern of eye movements associated with reading steadily deteriorated over the four-hour period. For instance, half hour by half hour there was a regular increase in the frequency of eye blinks and the variability of eye movements, and a regular decrease in the number of lines read per minute. Carmichael and Dearborn (1947) completed another study of eye movements during prolonged reading in which twenty high school students and twenty college students read for continuous six-hour periods. They found that when brief tests were given after every twenty-five pages of reading material, there was no deterioration of eye-movements. Evidently the tests maintained attention and careful reading.

In summary, research shows that questions asked during a lesson can improve achievement by causing students to pay closer attention. However, the same research also shows that the direct effect (on achievement) of asking questions—specifically, learning the answers to the questions that are asked—is much stronger than the effect on attention. Thus, while it does seem possible that the research completed so far has not revealed the full effects of asking questions, the prudent advice at the present time is to concentrate on asking every type of question students should learn to answer. Teachers should not lean too heavily on questioning and testing simply as a means to maintain attention.

SELF-TEST ON STUDENT RESPONSE

Please answer the following questions and then check your answers against the scoring key on p. **228.**

1. A student in a cabinet-making course must learn to use the drill press (a machine which is generally unfamiliar to the students before this course). What method of instruction would you choose to teach the operation of this machine? Explain why you made this choice of method.

2. Jennifer Sweet, a sixth-grade teacher, likes to ask many questions of her students. She says that this seems to keep the students more attentive and that she read in an educational psychology text that it is good to require overt responses (in this case, answers to her questions) from students. We agree with Jennifer, but there are some conditions when requiring an

overt response is especially likely to facilitate learning. Describe at least three of these conditions.

3. When would you require students to make a simple copying or mimicking response during instruction?
4. What danger is there in requiring only covert responses during instruction?
5. To increase learning and retention, how soon after a lecture should you require students to respond to that instruction?
6. You are writing a text in your subject-matter specialty. What besides writing in a clear and interesting style can you do to improve the chances that students will attend to the wise words you will undoubtedly fit into that book?

Summary

A student can be taught a first approximation to a new response either from hearing or reading a verbal description, or watching a demonstration. Verbal instruction is effective when the response can be described easily in words which are in the learner's vocabulary. Motor and emotional behavior, as well as verbal-symbolic skills, can be demonstrated or modeled. While copying, echoing, and imitating are important for initiating new forms of behavior, the student should be weaned from his model as soon as possible.

Students learn what they are led to do. Consequently, lessons should be planned so that during the course of the lesson the student actually practices the skills and applies the concepts which the lesson is designed to teach him. According to the principle of active responding, to learn foreign language vocabulary the student must pronounce the words, use them, and distinguish their meanings; to learn to prove theorems the student must in the process begin to prove theorems; and to learn to write essays the student must, necessarily, write essays. Being "active" and "busy" are not enough. In fact, active responses which are irrelevant to the purpose of the lesson can interfere with learning.

Research indicates that the student should be required to make a response as soon as he is capable of making it. This means that immediately after reading a passage, listening to a lecture, or watching a demonstration, the student should be asked to attempt a performance, answer questions—do whatever the presentation was intended to teach him to do. The student's ability to respond correctly will deteriorate rapidly with even short delays. By much the same reasoning, student achievement is improved if lessons are divided into short segments in which brief presentations are followed by student practice.

While reading, listening, and watching do involve active responses, there is a great deal of evidence that the explicit requirement specifically to answer questions or solve problems produces a sizeable increment in achievement. When the student thinks the answer to a question to himself, works a problem in his head, or engages in imaginary practice, he is said to be responding "covertly." An "overt" response, on the other hand, is one which is publicly observable or leaves a publicly observable record. The covert response usually takes less of the student's time than the overt response and seems to be satisfactory as long as the student actually makes the response. The problem is that students, especially less conscientious ones, may stop making covert responses. The teacher, of course, has greater control over overt responses. Consequently, when the lesson is long or dull, when the responses to be taught are difficult, or when the students are slow or disinterested, overt responses are preferable to covert ones. Multiple-choice questions require a form of overt response which saves the student's time and, as compared to covert responses, keeps him from backsliding. However, the "constructed," or written-out, response is superior to the response to a multiple-choice question when the student must learn to produce a difficult response, such as an obscure technical term.

SCORING KEY FOR THE SELF-TEST ON STUDENT RESPONSE

There are 9 possible points on this test. A score of 7 is satisfactory. Review the sections of the text which deal with questions which give you trouble.

1. (*2 points*)

(1) The best method is likely to be either a demonstration or a combination of telling the students how to use the machine *and* demonstrating its use.

(1) Demonstrations are particularly effective in teaching new responses or series of responses when the response(s) do not lend themselves to verbal description. Many of the manipulations one has to make of a drill press fall into this category.

2. *(possible 3 points)*

Jennifer should remember that overt responses are most effective when:

(1) the response is relevant to the instruction.
(1) the response is one the student can make correctly.
(1) the response is one the student can make correctly if and only if he has done what the teacher intends (i.e., studied, listened in class, etc.)
(1) the student must learn to make a difficult response (such as pronouncing a foreign word, manipulating objects or machines, using technical terms, etc.).

3. *(1 point)*

When they are engaged in learning to make that particular response (i.e., pronouncing words, etc.).

4. *(1 point)*

The instructor cannot be sure that covert responses are made. They may "drop out" or not be made as precisely as overt responses. Also note the instructor cannot give individualized feedback to covert responses.

5. *(1 point)*

As soon as possible. The sooner you require a response the more likely students will remember what they were told. For this same reason periodic questioning *during* lectures will increase learning and retention of the lecture material. Remember, you want to require responses while students can still make them correctly.

6. *(1 point)*

Make some provision for student responses (i.e., inserted questions, projects, tests, etc.) in the book itself.

Selected Readings

Anderson, R. C., Faust, G. W., Roderick, M. C., Cunningham, D. J., & Andre, T., eds., "Section IV. The Student Response," *Current Research on Instruction.* Englewood Cliffs, N.J.: Prentice-Hall, 1969. Included are six chapters describing research on the role of the student response in instruction.

Bandura, A., "Behavioral Modification Through Modeling Procedures," in L. Krasner & L. P. Ullman, eds., *Research in Behavior Modification*. New York: Holt, Rinehart & Winston, 1965. An excellent case is made for the importance of modeling and imitation in human learning.

Lumsdaine, A. A., ed., *The Student Response in Programmed Instruction*. Washington, D.C.: National Academy of Science—National Research Council, 1961. This book contains over thirty heretofore unpublished reports of research on student practice. Despite the title, none of the studies directly involves programmed instruction.

CHAPTER

7

Reinforcement

This chapter deals with reinforcement, one of the aspects of the third component in teaching. Reinforcement techniques are the chief means the teacher has for arranging and maintaining attention, encouraging persistence and effective study habits, and minimizing discipline problems. When you have finished this chapter you should be able to:

1. describe the relationship between reinforcement and motivation.
2. define the terms and recognize instances of
   a. reinforcement (both positive and negative, intrinsic and extrinsic).
   b. extinction.
   c. operant conditioning.
   d. superstitious behavior.
3. describe and recognize the behavioral effects of the various types of schedules of reinforcement.
4. describe the procedures and potential value of differential reinforcement and shaping.
5. recognize conditions under which various forms of reinforcement or punishment can be used to facilitate student attention, persistence, and effective study habits, as well as to minimize discipline problems.

When a person or animal is rewarded (i.e., *reinforced*) for what it does, the same behavior will tend to be repeated with increasing frequency. This fact is so generally true of both animals and humans that it can be regarded as a fundamental law of psychology. Indeed, it was so designated by Edward L. Thorndike, one of the greatest of American psychologists (who was, incidentally, primarily an educational psychologist).

Thorndike (1913, p. 4) expressed the law as follows: "When a modifiable connection between a situation and a response is made and is accompanied by a satisfying state of affairs, that connection's strength is increased. When made and accompanied by an annoying state of affairs, its strength is decreased." Thorndike called this principle the *Law of Effect* because behavior is strengthened according to the *effects* of behavior. The Law of Effect describes a process that might be characterized as "psychological Darwinism." Just as mutations that have adaptive consequences are selected by the environment and perpetuated, likewise behavior is selected by its consequences. Behavior which has "favorable" effects is perpetuated, whereas behavior which fails to have these effects is not.

The working of the Law of Effect can be illustrated with reference to a representative experimental procedure. Fig. 7.1 pictures a pigeon in a Skinner box. A food tray can be raised into place at the opening in the side of the box, allowing the pigeon to feed. The apparatus is rigged so that every time the pigeon pecks the key, the food tray is raised to the

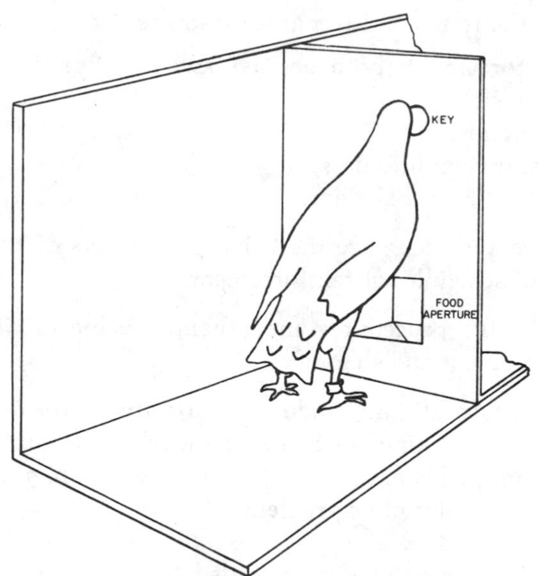

FIGURE 7.1 *A pigeon in a Skinner box.*

feeding position. Typically, the birds used in the Skinner box are placed on a restricted diet so that their body weights are 75%–80% of that which the birds would maintain if unlimited access to food were permitted. When a pigeon is placed in the Skinner box for the first time, it behaves erratically and exhibits "emotional behavior." Consequently, before being expected to peck the key, the bird is allowed a period of time in the box for "adaptation" of emotional responses and "magazine training," so that it will go to the food tray and eat at the sound of the mechanism which raises the tray into place. At this point, if food is made contingent upon pecking the key, sometimes a considerable period of time will pass during which the bird engages in various kinds of behavior but not the behavior of pecking the key.[1] If and when the pigeon does peck the key a single time, the process becomes remarkably orderly and predictable. It is almost certain that the bird will soon peck the key again and that in a relatively short period of time the pecks on the key will occur at a moderate, stable rate. The process is depicted graphically in Fig. 7.2. The graph in this figure contains a cumulative record of the

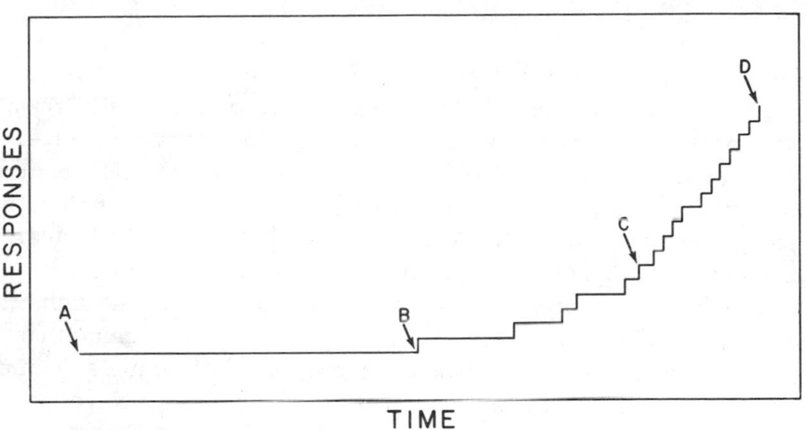

FIGURE 7.2 *Cumulative key-pecking responses of a naive pigeon.*

pigeon's responses. A pen is held against a moving sheet of paper. As long as there are no pecks on the key the pen traces a straight horizontal line. When a peck on the key occurs the pen moves up a notch. When the pigeon pecks at a fast, steady rate the line on the paper has a steep slope.

[1] Since the occurrence of the first responses is uncertain, in practice they are usually "shaped" (see pp. 237–242).

The following questions are based on Fig. 7.2

1. In a cumulative response record, horizontal distance measures (a) ———, whereas vertical distance measures (b) ———————.

2. Looking at the lettered segments in Fig. 7.2, between which two points did the pigeon make no pecking responses?

   a. A–B
   b. B–C
   c. C–D

3. Between which points did the pigeon show the highest rate of response?

   a. A–B
   b. B–C
   c. C–D

The answers appear on p. **236.**

The distinguished psychologist B. F. Skinner has restated the Law of Effect to include the word "reinforcer" instead of the word "reward" or the phrase "satisfying state of affairs"; the term "reinforcer" is broader than the term "reward" and is also noncommittal about the reason the law functions as it does. Reinforcers include all of the things which can be classified as rewards, such as food given to a food-deprived pigeon, but also include things and events which are not at all like rewards. Skinner expressly refuses to speculate about the subjective experience of the organism so of course he does not claim that the organism is being "satisfied" when it is reinforced. Skinner's definition of "reinforcement," then, can be stated as follows: a reinforcer is anything or any event that increases the likelihood of responses that immediately proceed it. This definition leaves open the question of what things and events are reinforcers. An indefinitely large number of things and events can serve as reinforcers. Whether any particular thing is a reinforcer is a simple question of fact to be answered by research.

Educators sometimes use the term "reinforcement" as a synonym for drill or repetition, as when, for instance, the explanation of a concept is repeated several times. While repetition is often a desirable educational practice, it is entirely different from reinforcement in the technical sense used here. In technical discourse there is a clear distinction between repetition and reinforcement.

The process whereby behavior is strengthened through reinforcement is called *operant conditioning,* so called because the organism learns behavior which *operates* on his environment.[2] While reinforcement may be "artificial" in the sense that it is contrived by an experimenter, trainer, or teacher, it may also follow as the inexorable "natural" or physical consequence of the behavior. For instance, if a pigeon in a park turns a leaf and finds a peanut, leaf-turning behavior is reinforced. This is an instance in which the natural consequences of an act that operates on the environment are reinforcing. There are, of course, countless other instances. When a basketball goes through the hoop, the behavior that launched the ball is reinforced. The baby's approximations to "Daddy" are reinforced by the father's expressions of delight. Looking at *Playboy Magazine* is reinforced by the stimulating events portrayed within it.

When a response is no longer reinforced, the process of *extinction* occurs (i.e., the nonreinforced response occurs less and less frequently). If it is never reinforced, a response will eventually extinguish completely. Typically when reinforcement is withheld, the first effect is a brief *increase* in the magnitude or rate of response, followed by the characteristic decline. Eventually a point will be reached at which no more responses are emitted or at which responses are emitted no more frequently than they were before conditioning. After a period of time, additional responses may occur despite the fact that extinction was apparently complete at the earlier date. This phenomenon is known as *spontaneous recovery.* Extinction is one way to weaken unwanted behavior, if not eliminate it entirely. As a practical matter, extinction is usually used in combination with other techniques to combat undesired behavior.

The process of extinction should be distinguished from forgetting. In extinction, the response occurs repeatedly but is not reinforced. Forgetting, on the other hand, refers to the decrease in the strength or likelihood of a response over a period of time during which the response in question is not made.

Conditioned Reinforcers and Generalized Reinforcers

A reinforcer which serves an obvious biological function is called a *primary reinforcer.* A stimulus which accompanies or slightly precedes such a primary reinforcer may therefore take on the power to reinforce. Such stimuli are called *conditioned reinforcers*[3] ("conditioned" means

[2] Operant conditioning is also called "instrumental conditioning." Another basic process through which behavior is modified, called "classical or respondent conditioning," will be described in Chapter 9.

[3] Conditioned reinforcers are also called "secondary reinforcers."

"learned" or "acquired"). An example of a conditioned reinforcer is the sound of the food dispenser in a Skinner box raising into the feeding position. In commonsense terms the noise of the food dispenser becomes a reinforcer because it is a signal that food will follow. The pigeon can be made to work and learn new responses when reinforced with the noise of the food magazine alone even when food doesn't follow. Of course, if food never follows the noise of the mechanism, this sound will lose its power to reinforce. Money is an example of a conditioned reinforcer for humans. Note that money, like other conditioned reinforcers, has no intrinsic value. One cannot eat money nor wear it on one's back when one is cold. Conditioned reinforcers gain their power to reinforce by virtue of their relationship to other previously-established reinforcers.

A pigeon in a Skinner box will not peck a key to get food unless it has been deprived of food. Furthermore, even when it has been deprived of food, it will continue to peck the key only until it gets as much food as it will eat. Technically speaking, the bird stops pecking the key when it is *satiated* with food. Of course, after it has once again been deprived of food, the bird will peck the key in order to get food. In other words, for food to function as a reinforcer, food *deprivation* is necessary. Conditioned reinforcers, too, depend for their effectiveness on the organism's state of deprivation. The noise of the food mechanism will be a less effective reinforcer when the pigeon has not been deprived of food.

An important class of conditioned reinforcers is the generalized conditioned reinforcer, or, more simply, the *generalized reinforcer*. A conditioned reinforcer becomes a generalized reinforcer when it is associated with several primary reinforcers relevant to several kinds of deprivation or arousal. Generalized reinforcers have two important characteristics. First, they do not depend for their effectiveness on a *specific* state of deprivation (e.g., lack of water). Second, they are less subject to satiation than other reinforcers. Money is a good example of a generalized conditioned reinforcer. People will work for money even when they are not hungry, thirsty, cold, and so on. The reason money is such a pervasive reinforcer is that it is related to many kinds of gratification.

Answers to the questions on p. **234.**

1. (a) time
(b) responses, cumulative responses, or pecks on the key

2. a

3. c

Negative Reinforcement and Punishment

If an organism works in order to receive something, this something is called a *positive reinforcer*. Thus far, only positive reinforcement has been illustrated. If an organism works to avoid or escape a stimulus, the stimulus is functioning as a *negative reinforcer*. Electric shock is an example of an aversive (painful, unpleasant, annoying) stimulus which may function as a negative reinforcer—one, incidentally, that has been studied extensively in the laboratory. Positive and negative reinforcement have the same effect on behavior. Both increase the likelihood or strength of a response. For instance, if an organism escapes a severe electric shock by making a certain response, this response is likely to be repeated in the future.

Negative reinforcement is different from punishment. In punishment when the response occurs, an aversive stimulus *begins*. In negative reinforcement when a response occurs, an aversive stimulus *ends*. The two processes have different behavioral consequences. Behavior is strengthened by negative reinforcement. Punishment does a variety of things, but certainly does *not* strengthen the behavior preceding it.

Differential Reinforcement and Shaping

Whatever a person or animal is doing at the precise moment that it is reinforced will be strengthened. For example, if a mother gives her baby a bottle of warm milk while it is crying, the baby will probably cry more frequently in the future. Similarly, if a dog is let in from the cold while it is scratching on the door, the likelihood that the dog will scratch on the door in the future will increase.

It is the end of the school day. The class is noisy and somewhat rowdy. The teacher is tired and he would like to dismiss the class immediately. Or he could wait until it is quiet. What will probably happen in the future if the teacher dismisses the class while it is noisy? Why? A covert answer will do.

The answers appear on p. **239.**

Each of the preceding examples has stressed the importance of the *contingency* between the reinforcement and the behavior which precedes it. Prospective teachers are often encouraged to maintain a warm, supportive classroom "climate" and to give lots of individual attention, but seldom are they advised on just when to show warmth and give attention. This is unfortunate since the contingency of reinforcement is all-important. There is no reason to believe that indiscriminate praise, warmth, and attention will have educationally useful effects.

Indiscriminate reinforcement has been studied in the laboratory and it produces what Skinner calls "superstitious behavior." Pigeons were reduced to 75 percent of normal body weight by placing them on a restricted diet. A clock was rigged so that it delivered food in a Skinner box at regular intervals *"with no reference whatsoever to the bird's behavior"* (Skinner, 1959, p. 405; italics in the original). In six out of eight cases, the bird developed clearly-defined responses that two observers could agree on perfectly. According to Skinner, one bird learned to turn in circles about the cage, making two or three turns between reinforcements. Another thrust its head repeatedly into one of the upper corners of the cage. A third developed a "tossing" response. Two birds acquired "a pendulum motion of the head and body, in which the head was extended forward and swung from right to left." Another pigeon learned to make "incomplete pecking or brushing movements directed toward but not touching the floor." The movements that have been described came to be repeated rapidly—typically five or six times in the 15-second interval between reinforcements. The behavior was also quite stable and persisted over long periods of time. One bird that developed a hopping motion from one foot to the other made over 10,000 such responses after the clock was turned off and food was no longer presented.

The pigeons might be said to have learned a form of superstition since each of them behaved as though there were a logical connection between its behavior and the food, where in fact there was no relationship. The process can be understood as follows. Whatever the pigeon is doing when the food is presented for the first time is accidentally reinforced. As a result, this behavior is strengthened and the chances increase that the same behavior will occur just when food is presented again. In the initial stages, the form of the response may "drift" but eventually it will stabilize when a certain response is reinforced several times.

There are countless examples of superstition in humans that have been acquired and are maintained as the result of accidental contingencies of reinforcement. Indeed, probably far more of the behavior in which we engage is superstitious behavior than we realize or would care to admit. Athletes and coaches provide many interesting examples. On most campuses one can see a coach who on the day of the game wears a certain tie, a peculiar pair of socks, or a battered hat in order to bring himself luck. The team had happened to win when the coach was wearing his "lucky" clothes, thereby making it more likely that he would again wear the same items on the day of a subsequent game. An accidental contingency and a superstition was born. The popularity of patent medicines and home remedies of no medical value can also be understood as forms of superstition. Many ailments will get better without any therapy. However, if a person feels better soon after taking a remedy, he is likely to try it again. Thus, several accidental contingencies may lead to a persistent superstition. Similarly, indiscriminate praise and attention to maintain a "warm classroom climate" may result in accidental reinforcement of educationally undesirable behavior and may lead to forms of superstitious behavior.

The teacher who deliberately controls contingencies of reinforcement has a powerful tool for modifying student behavior. To reinforce one form of behavior and to withhold reinforcement for another form is called *differential reinforcement.* An illuminating case showing the effects of differential reinforcement was reported in the *Journal of Educational Psychology.* Harris, Johnston, Kelley, and Wolf (1964) treated a three-year-old girl who had regressed to crawling instead of walking about 75 percent of the time when at nursery school. The child, whose name was Dee, had been walking normally before she started nursery school. Her parents were "a pleasant and likeable young couple." Both held college degrees. The mother "seemed a warm and responsive person whose primary interest was her family."

> On the first day of school Dee showed strong withdrawal behavior. That is, she crouched on the floor most of the time, turning her head away or hiding her face in her arms whenever an adult or a child approached. She did not attempt to remain close to her mother, who sat in one corner of the room or of the play yard. Dee spoke to no one and crawled from indoors to outdoors and from place to place as school activities shifted . . .
>
> Typically, Dee removed and put on her wraps while sitting on the floor in the locker area, and then either left them on the floor or crawled to her locker and stuffed them in. Sometimes she pulled herself to her feet with her hands on the locker edges and hung her wraps on the appropriate hooks. Then, dropping to hands and knees, she crawled to an out-of-the-way spot and sat or crouched. . . . She usually accepted and ate a snack, but remained impassive, somber, and silent. The rest of the group talked, laughed, and in general responded freely to

Answers to the questions on p. **237.**

The likelihood of noise and rowdiness in the future will probably increase because being dismissed from class is undoubtedly reinforcing for many of the students.

both teachers and to other children. The usual teacher approaches to Dee (friendly, warm, and solicitous) resulted in strong withdrawal behavior. . . .
By the end of the second week of school Dee was avoiding all contacts with children or adults and avoiding the use of most material and equipment. A half-hour record written at this time showed Dee in a standing position for only 6.5% of the time, once at her locker and once at a bathroom sink. For 93.3% of the observation period she sat or crouched on hands or knees. . . .

At this point the nursery school teachers began differentially to reinforce standing and walking on Dee's part. Attention was withheld from Dee whenever she was off her feet. The teachers avoided conveying the impression that they were angry, disappointed, or disgusted; they simply occupied themselves with other children or tasks whenever Dee was sitting, crouching, or crawling. On the other hand, "on-feet" behavior was reinforced immediately with attention. According to the report,

Such attention [consisted] of going immediately to her and making appropriate interested comments about what she was doing. Sample comments might be, "You hung that up all by yourself, you know just where it goes," and "It's fun to let water slide over your fingers. It feels nice and warm, doesn't it?" A teacher's attention behavior was to convey to Dee that she was liked, appreciated, and considered capable.

Differential reinforcement had a dramatic effect on Dee. After two weeks the girl's behavior was indistinguishable from that of the rest of the children. She walked and ran as much as any of them. "She talked readily, often with smiling animation, to the teacher administering the planned schedule of social reinforcement."

In order to prove that differential reinforcement had been the significant causative factor in Dee's change in behavior, the procedure was reversed. The teacher now gave attention when she was not on her feet. During the second morning under the reversed procedure, she spent 82 percent of the time off her feet. Finally, on-feet behavior was again differentially reinforced. Within a single morning, Dee began to spend most of her time on her feet, a pattern of behavior which persisted from that day on.

Note that differential reinforcement entails *extinguishing* one form of behavior, a form sometimes quite similar to the one being reinforced. The technique enables a person such as a teacher to strengthen desired behavior and simultaneously to weaken unwanted behavior.

Differential reinforcement is obviously a technique with great potential, but consider the following kind of problem. Suppose that you are an animal trainer. You have a food-deprived pigeon in a Skinner box. Assume that you have a switch on the end of a long cord (something like a remote control for tuning a TV set) that operates the food magazine. By depressing the switch you can instantly raise the food tray into place. Your task is to get the bird to turn repeatedly in clockwise circles. How would you go about it? If you simply sat watching the bird, ready to reinforce the behavior of turning in circles when it occurred, you might have to wait a long time. In fact the bird probably never would repeatedly turn clockwise circles if left to its own pursuits.

Instead of waiting for a complete turn in a clockwise circle, first reinforce any approximation to this behavior. Initially reinforce any slight turn of the head to the right. Next reinforce only somewhat greater turns, then only turns which go at least a quarter of the way around, and, next, only turns that go halfway around. After reinforcing a couple of turns to the halfway point, wait for the bird to make a full turn. If it does not do so within a few seconds, it may be necessary to back up and reestablish turns to the halfway point. Eventually the bird will make a full turn. If a full turn is the only behavior reinforced at this point, the bird will turn repeatedly in circles until it is satiated. After this training the pigeon will begin immediately to turn in circles when it is again placed in the Skinner box following a period of deprivation. With some skill on your part in judging how much can be demanded from the pigeon before a reinforcement, and a little luck, turning behavior can be established within a few minutes.

The procedure which has just been described for getting a pigeon to turn in circles is called *shaping*. Shaping consists of *differential reinforcement of successive approximations to the desired behavior*. The trick lies in determining an acceptable approximation at any point. If the standard is set too high, the behavior that has been acquired up to that point may extinguish. If the standard is kept too low, the procedure is inefficient and there may be difficulty in moving on to the next step. The extraordinary power of the shaping procedure to modify behavior must be seen to be appreciated.

The technique of shaping was discovered more or less accidentally by Skinner and a few of his associates. Skinner tells the story as follows (1959, p. 132):

> In 1943 Keller Breland, Norman Guttman, and I were working on a war-time project sponsored by General Mills, Inc. Our laboratory was the top floor of a flour mill in Minneapolis, where we spent a good deal of time waiting for decisions to be made in Washington. All day long, around the mill, wheeled great flocks of pigeons. They were easily snared on the window sills and proved to be an irresistible supply of experimental subjects. We built a magnetic food-magazine, which dispensed grain on the principle of an automatic peanut vendor, and conditioned pigeons to turn at the sound it made and eat the grain it discharged into a cup. We used the device to condition several kinds of be-

havior. For example, we built a gauge to measure the force with which a pigeon pecked a horizontal block, and by differentially reinforcing harder pecks we built up such forceful blows that the base of the pigeon's beak quickly became inflamed. This was serious research, but we had our lighter moments. One day we decided to teach a pigeon to bowl. The pigeon was to send a wooden ball down a miniature alley toward a set of toy pins by swiping the ball with a sharp sideward movement of the beak. To condition the response, we put the ball on the floor of an experimental box and prepared to operate the food-magazine as soon as the first swipe occurred. But nothing happened. Though we had all the time in the world, we grew tired of waiting. We decided to reinforce any response which had the slightest resemblance to a swipe—perhaps, at first, merely the behavior of looking at the ball—and then to select responses which more closely approximated the final form. The result amazed us. In a few minutes, the ball was caroming off the walls of the box as if the pigeon had been a champion squash player. The spectacle so impressed Keller Breland that he gave up a promising career in psychology and went into the commercial production of behavior.

Intermittent Schedules of Reinforcement

This section will detail the effects of intermittent schedules of reinforcement on the rate at which a pigeon will peck a key. Since the educator wants to be able to understand the behavior of children in classrooms, this may seem to be a strange topic for an educational psychology text. The authors believe, however, that one good way to approach this ultimate goal is to begin with an intensive study of simple behavior occurring in well-defined circumstances. The alternative view, that a psychology based on research with rats and pigeons is irrelevant to an understanding of complex human behavior, is often voiced in educational circles.

Consider the development of the science of genetics during the last century. Much of the really critical research was completed with sweet peas, fruit flies, and bread mold. These organisms were employed—instead of, say, oak trees, elephants, or people—mainly because they are convenient to study. It was an article of faith that the hereditary mechanisms underlying, for instance, the presence of straight wings or curly wings in the fruit fly would shed light on the genetics of living things in general, including people. Such has proved to be the case. Similarly, it is reasonable to hope that a science of learning and motivation based in part on research with pigeons and other birds and animals will contribute to an understanding of human behavior. The research on the rate at which pigeons will peck a key is important, then, because it may reveal the basic processes involved when an organism works with vigor and persistence.

Returning, therefore, to our experiments with pigeons, let us suppose that a pigeon in a Skinner box has pecked a key for several hours on continuous reinforcement with food—that is, every peck is followed by the opportunity to eat. (In *continuous reinforcement* every response which meets the criterion is reinforced. Some important effects can also be obtained from *intermittent reinforcement,* in which some but not all acceptable responses are reinforced.) Now arrangements are changed so that food is available only after every 10 pecks on the key. Initially there will be some disruption in behavior under the new arrangements, but eventually the pigeon will peck the key at a high rate. In fact, the rate will be much higher than it was under continuous reinforcement. The arrangement in which the pigeon gets food after a fixed number of responses is called a *fixed ratio schedule* because a fixed or constant number of responses, in this case 10, is emitted per reinforcement.

A pause or rest period during which the organism makes no responses after each reinforcement is characteristic of a fixed ratio schedule. The pauses are quite lengthy when the number of responses required per reinforcement is large, say 50, 100, or even 200. An organism on a fixed ratio schedule typically performs at a zero rate or at a high rate. Responding seldom occurs at intermediate rates. The change from the zero rate to the characteristic high rate usually occurs abruptly.

Fig. 7.3 contains a segment of the cumulative response record of a

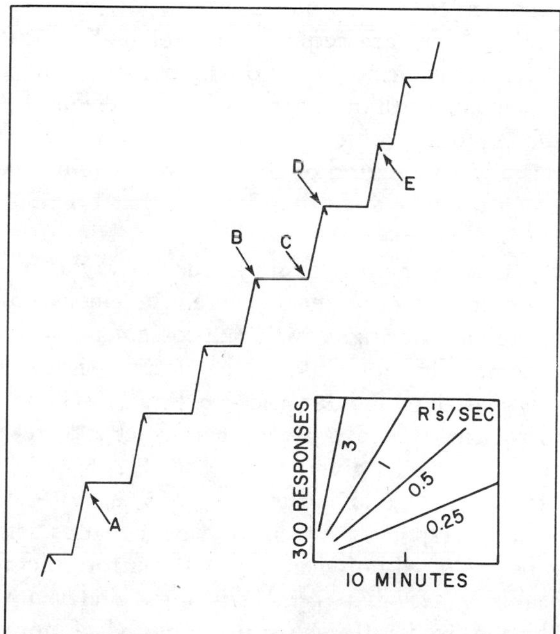

FIGURE 7.3 *Cumulative record of performance on a fixed ratio schedule in which every 120th response is reinforced.*

pigeon being reinforced on a fixed ratio schedule for every 120th response. The *slope* of a cumulative record represents the rate of response. The radiating lines in the small graph in the lower right corner of the figure indicate the rates of response for representative slopes. The "pip" (see *A* in Fig. 7.3) marks the occurrence of reinforcement.

The following questions are based on Fig. 7.3.

A. About how many responses did the pigeon make between *B* and *C*?
B. Approximately what was the rate of response between *C* and *D*?
C. What does the small slanting line extending below the record at *E* signify?

The answers appear on p. **247.**

The stair-step pattern pictured in Fig. 7.3 always occurs under fixed ratio schedules. When only a few responses are required per reinforcement (i.e., at low ratios), the pauses after reinforcement are brief and the rate of responses following pauses is very high. When more responses per reinforcement are required (i.e., at high ratios), the pauses are longer and the rate of response following pauses is lower.

How could the pause following each reinforcement be eliminated? The key to solving this problem is the fact that under a fixed ratio schedule there is always a period of time following reinforcement before reinforcement will occur again. It is known that organisms learn this fact.

The trick is to modify the procedure in such a way as to eliminate the relationship between the occurrence of reinforcement and the period immediately thereafter during which reinforcement will never occur. This can be accomplished by making the occurrence of reinforcement unpredictable or variable. Under the fixed ratio schedule considered thus far reinforcement is always given after exactly 10 responses. Now imagine that reinforcement is given after either 1, 3, 5, 7, 9, 11, 13, 15, 17, or 19 responses in an irregular pattern (e.g., 15, 3, 7, 19, 11, 1, 7, etc.). The *average* ratio of responses to reinforcement in this series is 10, but the actual number required between any two reinforcements is variable; thus, this is called a *variable ratio schedule.* Under a variable ratio schedule, unlike the fixed ratio schedule, a period of nonreinforcement does not systematically follow each occurrence of reinforcement. For this reason, the organism typically does not pause after reinforcement. Research shows that high, stable rates of response, such as that pictured in Fig. 7.4, are characteristic of variable ratio schedules.

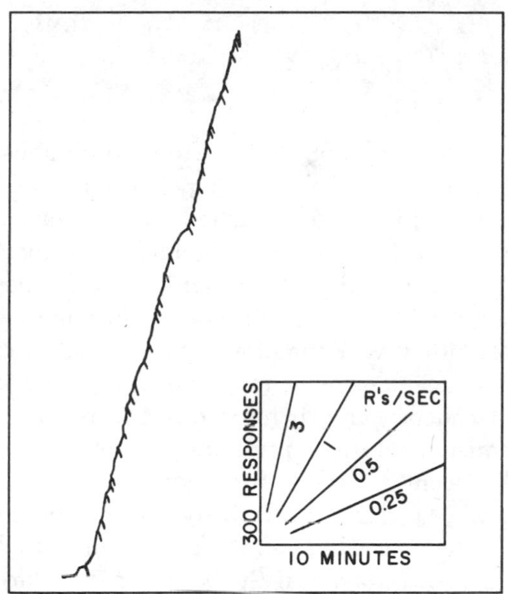

FIGURE 7.4 *Cumulative record of responses under a variable ratio schedule.*

Ratio schedules that deal with the key-pecking behavior of the pigeon typically entail differential reinforcement of high rates of response. The reason is that the pigeon is unlikely to complete a ratio with an isolated peck. The ratio is much more likely to be completed, and therefore reinforcement is more likely to occur, during a "burst" of responses. Consequently, a high rate of response is usually reinforced and a low rate extinguished. This is typically the case, but not always. Sometimes a pigeon will complete a ratio with an isolated response emitted after an interval of no responding. Should this happen, a low rate will have been reinforced and the high stable rate of response may not develop. To guarantee that the pigeon will peck at a high rate, a high rate is reinforced directly—that is, the pigeon is reinforced only when it completes the required responses within a limited period of time.

It is, of course, impossible to start a bird on a high ratio. If the schedule is to take hold, the number of responses required per reinforcement must be gradually increased, beginning with continuous reinforcement and slowly approaching the desired ratio.

Why will the high stable rate of response typical of the variable ratio schedule *not* appear if a pigeon is changed abruptly from continuous reinforcement to a variable ratio schedule in which one out of every 200 responses is reinforced?

The answer is in the paragraph that follows.

The difficulty with an abrupt change from continuous reinforcement to a high ratio is that pecking behavior may extinguish before the bird is reinforced. Similarly, it is well-established that organisms, both animals and people, acquire new behavior most rapidly when they are reinforced 100 percent of the time or close to it (Jenkins & Stanley, 1950). It is equally well established that behavior extinguishes more slowly when it is reinforced intermittently. Extinction, you will recall, entails nonreinforcement of behavior. If a response is not reinforced it will diminish in strength and frequency until it no longer occurs (or at least until its strength and frequency return to pretraining levels).

The rule is this: continuous reinforcement results in relatively rapid acquisition of new behavior but relatively quick extinction. Reinforcement on an intermittent schedule, on the other hand, results in relatively slow acquisition of new behavior, if the behavior is acquired at all. However, once behavior is acquired, it will be relatively slow to extinguish.

The practical thing to do in training an organism to respond is to combine the best features of both continuous and intermittent reinforcement. To produce rapid acquisition of new behavior, use continuous reinforcement. Then, to maintain this behavior and to increase resistance to extinction, shift to an intermittent schedule. The higher the average number of responses required per reinforcement, the greater—up to a point—will be the resistance to extinction. Pigeons on schedules requiring many responses per reinforcement have pecked a key thousands of times over many hours without ever receiving reinforcement before the behavior extinguished. However, after only continuous reinforcement the total responses emitted before the behavior extinguishes numbers in the hundreds, and the process of extinction is completed in a few hours.

Two other schedules of reinforcement that have been extensively studied are the *fixed interval schedule* and the *variable interval schedule*. Under an interval schedule the first response that is emitted after a specified period of time is reinforced. For instance, under a fixed interval schedule in which a one-minute delay is imposed between reinforcements, the pigeon will not be reinforced more frequently than once a minute no matter what it does. Notice that the interval between reinforcements might be longer than a minute because reinforcement is contingent upon both a one-minute delay and, then, following the delay, the emission of the appropriate response. (If reinforcement occurred at one-minute intervals without reference to what the pigeon was doing, superstitious behavior would result.) Under a variable interval schedule, the *average* length of the interval between one reinforcement and the point at which reinforcement next becomes available is specified. The delays actually imposed are variable, sometimes longer and sometimes shorter than the average value.

Generally speaking, the fixed and variable interval schedules have consequences resembling those of fixed and variable ratio schedules, respectively. One difference is that the rate of response is not as high under interval schedules as under comparable ratio schedules. Like the fixed ratio schedule, there is a pause following reinforcement under the fixed interval schedule. However, the cumulative record of performance under the latter schedule typically inscribes a "scalloped" pattern instead of the stair-step pattern characteristic of the fixed ratio. The scalloped pattern (see Fig. 7.5) appears because the pigeon first pauses following reinforcement and then steadily increases its rate of pecking, reaching the highest rate shortly before the next reinforcement.

The variable interval schedule produces a very stable rate of response, even more stable than that produced by the variable ratio schedule. An interesting difference between these schedules appears during extinction. A pigeon that has been on a variable interval schedule will gradually reduce its rate of response over a long period of time, with few if any abrupt shifts in rate (although eventually the rate will approach zero in rate). Performance following variable interval schedules, in other words, is very resistant to extinction; birds have pecked a key as many as 18,000 times without reinforcement before the response extinguished (Ferster & Skinner, 1957, p. 413). In contrast, the bird that has been on a variable ratio schedule will begin to alternate between periods of no responding and periods in which there is a high rate of response. As the process of extinction continues, the periods of no responding grow longer and the bursts of response at a high rate become shorter.

The schedules of reinforcement that have been considered thus far can

Answers to the questions on p. **244.**

A. none
B. approximately three per second
C. the occurrence of reinforcement

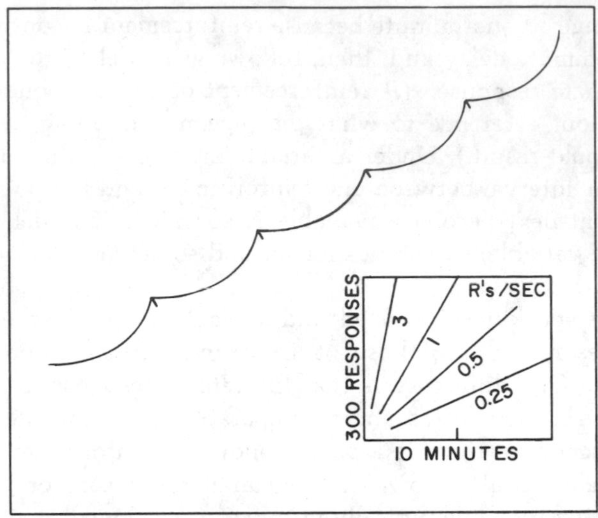

FIGURE 7.5 *Cumulative record of performance under a fixed interval schedule.*

be combined in various ways to form more complex schedules. One fact that has been revealed by research with complex schedules is that an organism will learn to adjust its rate of response to the prevailing schedule. For instance, a pigeon reinforced at a low ratio when the key is green and at a high ratio when the key is red will peck at a higher rate when the key is green than when it is red.

In summary, if an intermittent schedule of reinforcement is gradually introduced a pigeon can be made to peck a key at a higher rate than it will maintain under continuous reinforcement. Perhaps more important because of its practical implications, intermittent schedules sustain performance indefinitely with little reinforcement. If a schedule has predictable features, then performance will be periodic, its exact features determined by the particular contingencies of reinforcement that are in effect. If, on the other hand, the pigeon is reinforced on a variable and therefore unpredictable schedule, remarkably stable rates of performance can be sustained. The general conclusion to be drawn from the research on schedules of reinforcement is that the rate and consistency of an organism's performance are precisely controlled by the frequency and contingencies of reinforcement.

What Functions as Reinforcers for Humans?

Social reinforcers. There is a great deal of evidence that praise, attention, friendly remarks, and encouragement can serve to reinforce human behavior. Greenspoon (1955), one of the pioneers in the study of social reinforcement, showed that the frequency with which people used plural nouns could be increased by saying "Mmm-hmm" to them after they had used a plural noun. Since then, there have been literally dozens of studies of the effects of social reinforcement on behavior. Many of these studies have concerned verbal behavior, for instance, the frequency with which plural nouns or the pronouns "I" and "we" are used. In one of the most interesting of these studies, Verplanck (1955) investigated the effects of expressions of agreement with and paraphrases of a speaker's opinions. Conversations were carried on with 24 people, mostly college students, on a wide variety of topics and in a wide variety of places (e.g., a telephone booth, a bar, a street corner). None of these people realized they were subjects in an experiment, yet it is reported that all 24, when reinforced by agreement and paraphrase, increased the rate at which they gave opinions. When reinforcement was terminated, the rate of presenting opinions decreased for 21 speakers. The overall rates of speaking were not affected by reinforcement.

The standard practice in research on the effects of social reinforcement on verbal behavior has been to interview subjects after the experiment to determine whether they were aware of the contingency of reinforcement. That is, if the experiment concerned the frequency with which personal pronouns were used, the experimenter wanted to find out if the subjects could tell him "You said 'Good' whenever I started a sentence with 'I' or 'we'." Early research seemed to indicate that people were generally not aware of the contingency of reinforcement (Krasner, 1958), a fact which was seized upon as evidence that reinforcement is an automatic, inexorable process which does not depend upon "thinking" in order to be effective. The research upon which this conclusion was based was challenged, however, on the grounds that the questioning after the experiment was too brief and too vague to elicit adequate information about subjects' awareness of the contingency of reinforcement. Subsequent research employing lengthy interviews and detailed questionnaires showed that when reinforcement was effective in increasing the frequency of some response, subjects did report the contingency of reinforcement. More important, reinforcement did not work for subjects who could not describe the contingency of reinforcement. Those who believe that reinforcement is an automatic process challenged this research on the grounds that the method of questioning put words into the mouths of the subjects. While some of the research may be criticized on this basis, not all of it can. The evidence now available suggests that when reinforcement is effective, the subject usually will be aware of the contingency of reinforcement—that is, he will be able to report a "correct hypothesis" about the behavior on his part which leads to reinforcement (Spielberger & DeNike, 1966). The practical significance of this fact is that reinforcement will be more successful when the recipient understands what behavior will be reinforced. There is no practical reason in the classroom, therefore, for concealing the contingencies of reinforcement. The teacher should strive to set clear standards of performance.

Differential social reinforcement can be a powerful tool for classroom management. Convincing evidence of this has been obtained by Becker, Madsen, Arnold, and Thomas (1967), who studied five elementary school classrooms. Two especially disruptive children in each class were chosen as target students. For five weeks trained observers scored the frequency of deviant behavior on the part of the target children, while the teacher taught the class in her usual style and handled discipline in her usual manner. During this five-week "baseline" observation period, the ten target children were engaging in deviant behavior 62 percent of the time. Two of the children were described as follows:

> Albert (age 7 years, 8 months) tested average on the Stanford-Binet [an intelligence test], but was still on first grade materials during his second year in school. He was selected because he showed many behaviors which made learning difficult. He talked, made other noises, did not attend to teacher, and got in and out of his seat a lot. He loved to be "cute" and make his peers laugh. (Becker, et. al., 1967, p. 11.)

> In the words of his teacher, Albert "was a very noisy, disruptive child. He fought with others, blurted out, could not stay in his seat, and did very little required work. I had to check constantly to see that the minimum work was finished. He sulked and responded negatively to everything suggested to him. In addition, he was certain that he could not read. (Ibid., p. 11.)

The second child, who was enrolled in a different class, was called Edward.

> Edward (age 6 years, 8 months) tested 95 on the Stanford-Binet. [His teacher] considered him to be "distractible," to have poor work habits, show poor attention, and not to comprehend what he read. He never finished assignments. He could sight read and spell first grade words. The baseline observations showed high frequencies of wandering about the room, turning around in his seat, talking at the wrong time, and making odd noises. He also showed little [tendency to play with his classmates]. A psychological examination . . . stressed Edward's poor social history (his parents had not talked to each other for three years), his lack of enthusiasm and emotional unresponsiveness . . . (Ibid., p. 24.)

Following the five-week baseline observation period, the participating teachers followed a planned reinforcement policy for a nine-week experimental period. The three general rules the teachers agreed to apply are given below:

1. Make rules for each period explicit as to what is expected of children. (Remind of rules when needed.)

2. *Ignore* (do not attend to) behaviors which interfere with learning and teaching, unless a child is being hurt by another. Use punishment which seems appropriate, preferably withdrawal of some positive reinforcement.

3. Give *praise* and *attention* to behaviors which facilitate learning. Tell child what he is being praised for. Try to reinforce behaviors incompatible with those you wish to decrease. (Ibid., pp. 7–8.)

Systematic observation of the ten target children showed that deviant behavior decreased from 62 percent during the baseline period to 29 percent during the nine-week experimental period. This is a striking change of considerable practical significance. While some of the children were affected more than others, all of the target children changed in the desired direction. The objective record of Albert's behavior showed that he was one of those who had made a large change for the better. Albert's teacher stated:

> Albert has improved delightfully. He still blurts out, but makes an effort to stop this. He is often seen holding his hand in the air, biting his lips. He completes his work on time, and it is done well. Often when he has to re-do a paper, he takes it cheerfully and says, "I can do this myself." No sulking. He still finds it difficult to sit for a long period of time, but time on task has increased. He works very hard on his reading and has stated that he can read. (Ibid., p. 12.)

Similar results were achieved with Edward, who greatly reduced the time he spent in aimless wandering, twisting in his seat, and talking. It is reported that he began to complete assignments, showed better give and take with his peers, and, while still "distractible," worked independently for longer periods of time. The policy of differential reinforcement had the greatest effect in Edward's class, probably because previously his teacher had leaned heavily on negative control. A report during the five-week baseline period stated that "the noise level for the entire classroom was extremely high and went higher just before recess. Some behaviors noted included whistling, running around the room (5 occasions), yelling at another child (many times), loud incessant talk, hitting other children (7 times), pushing, shoving, and getting in front of each other in the recess line." (Ibid., pp. 22–23). The teacher would attempt to establish control by threatening, scolding, and shouting, which would work for a while but then the noise level would rise again. There was a marked change in this classroom when the teacher began to make her rules clear, ignore objectionable behavior, and praise and pay attention to children when their behavior facilitated learning. By the teacher's own estimate better than half of the members of the class "definitely profited" from her change in behavior.

Tangible reinforcers. It is well known that money, toys, trinkets, candy, cigarettes, food, and the like can be effective reinforcers. Educators have been reluctant to use tangible reinforcers, but there is evidence that such reinforcers could have considerable value in specialized educational programs, and perhaps in classroom instruction more generally.

Tangible reinforcers appear to be more effective than social reinforcers with preschool children. Arthur W. Staats and his associates have completed a program of research on beginning reading skills (Staats, 1965). Under their typical procedure the child receives a marble for each correct reading response. The marbles may be exchanged for pieces of candy or trinkets, or the child may accumulate a large number of marbles to exchange for a small toy. Under these procedures four-year-olds received sight vocabulary training for eight 40-minute sessions in which they paid close attention, worked steadily, and learned a number of new words. Then, three four-year-olds were introduced to the training but were given only social reinforcement. Two of the children wanted to stop after only 15 minutes of the first session and one wanted to discontinue the activity 15 minutes into the second session. At the point at which the child wished to stop, tangible reinforcement was started. In each case the child then worked steadily throughout the remainder of training. Three other children completed two sessions with tangible reinforcement. Then reinforcement was terminated. These children continued to work for three or four sessions before requesting to discontinue the lesson. When reinforcement was reinstated, two of the children again began to work steadily. It was concluded that the system of tangible reinforcement solved the major problem in teaching young children; namely, to keep them at the task over long periods of time.

Tangible reinforcement may have important advantages for special populations—for instance, for students diagnosed as mentally retarded, emotionally disturbed, or brain damaged. Birnbrauer, Wolf, Kidder, and Tague (1965) completed a study with seventeen mentally retarded children in a classroom in which both social reinforcement and tangible reinforcement were used as standard practice. The tangible reinforcement system in the study consisted of the following. Each pupil carried a special booklet into which the teacher placed a check mark whenever the pupil's behavior merited. When a child accumulated enough check marks in his booklet, he exchanged them for candy, a small toy, or other items of his choice immediately after he finished his work for the day.

Birnbrauer and his colleagues studied the children for several weeks during which the tangible reinforcement system was in effect, then for several weeks in which marks were not given nor tangible reinforcers provided, and finally for several weeks in which the tangible reinforcement was again used. It should be emphasized that the teachers continued to use social reinforcement during the period when tangible reinforcement was not used. The results indicated that the system of marks or "tokens" backed up by toys, candy, and other items was not necessary to maintain cooperation and satisfactory levels of accuracy for five of the children. However, five additional children showed a decline in the care with which they completed their work when tangible reinforcement was terminated. The decline was substantial enough to have serious consequences for their educational progress. Moreover, three children were not only more accurate but clearly more cooperative with tangible reinforcement than without it. "In fact their disruptive behavior [during the period when no tangible reinforcers were used] was such that dropping them from school would have been in order under ordinary circumstances." (Ibid., p. 234.)

Staats and Butterfield (1965) have completed a case study which further illustrates the value of tangible reinforcers in dealing with problem children. They worked with a fourteen-year-old Mexican-American delinquent boy who had a long history of school failure and misbehavior, as well as only a 2.0 grade reading achievement level. He had been referred to juvenile authorities nine times for such offenses as running away, burglary, incorrigibility, and truancy. The boy was described by a school official as having "been incorrigible since he came here in the second grade. He has no respect for teachers, steals and lies habitually and uses extremely foul language." (Ibid., p. 928.)

In the study, the boy was given forty hours of reading instruction, which extended over a four and one-half month period. Science Research Associates reading materials were adapted for use with the tangible reinforcement system. The boy received tokens—in this case poker chips —for making correct responses and for paying close attention to the reading materials. The tokens were later exchanged for a variety of items including a pair of "beatle shoes," hair cream, a phonograph record, an ice cream sundae, a ticket for a school function, and money for his brother, who was going to reform school. The total value of the items the boy received was $20.31, for which he made an estimated 64,307 single-word reading responses. During the training, the boy's attention and participation were maintained in good strength by the reinforcers: he learned and retained 430 new words; his reading achievement increased to the 4.3 grade level; he passed all of his high school courses for the first time (earning a C and three *D*'s); and his misbehaviors in school decreased steadily from the beginning of the sessions to zero at the end.

O'Leary and Becker (1967) introduced token reinforcement into a third-grade "adjustment" class consisting of children described as "emotionally disturbed." Two observers scored the frequency of deviant behavior—which included "pushing, answering without raising one's hand, chewing gum, eating, name calling, making disruptive noises, and talking" (Ibid., p. 638)—three times a week during a baseline period of several weeks, and then during a two-month period while a token reinforcement system was in operation. On the first day of the token period the experimenter placed the following words on the blackboard to remind the children of the rules of conduct: *In Seat, Face Front, Raise Hand, Working, Pay Attention,* and *Desk Clear.* The children received tokens consisting of ratings entered in booklets on their desks, ratings which reflected the extent to which they followed instructions. The tokens or ratings could be exchanged for "back-up" reinforcers such as candy, pennants, comics, perfume, and kites. The total cost of the reinforcers used during the two months was $80.76. Fig. 7.6 shows that there was a sharp drop in the percentage of deviant behaviors as a result of token reinforcement. All of the children displayed less deviant behavior and the average dropped from better than 70 percent during the baseline period to less than 20 percent during the period in which token reinforcement was in effect.

Grades. According to McKeachie (1963), in his review of research on teaching at the college and university level, grades are the most important motivational device that the college teacher has.

> Whatever a student's motivation for being in college, grades are important to him. If he is genuinely interested in learning, grades represent an expert's appraisal of his success; if he is interested in getting into professional school, good grades will unlock the graduate school doors; if he wants to play football, grades are necessary to maintain eligibility. Most students are motivated to get passing grades, and thus grades are a powerful motivational tool for teachers. (Ibid., p. 1119.)

What McKeachie has said is quite probably correct; however, there is surprisingly little research on grades and grading practices. Indeed, while procedures for constructing tests in order to grade students were discussed, not one of four widely-used educational psychology texts that were consulted (Klausmeier & Goodwin, 1966; Smith & Hudgins, 1965; Stephens, 1965; Travers, 1967) even mentioned the effects of grades on

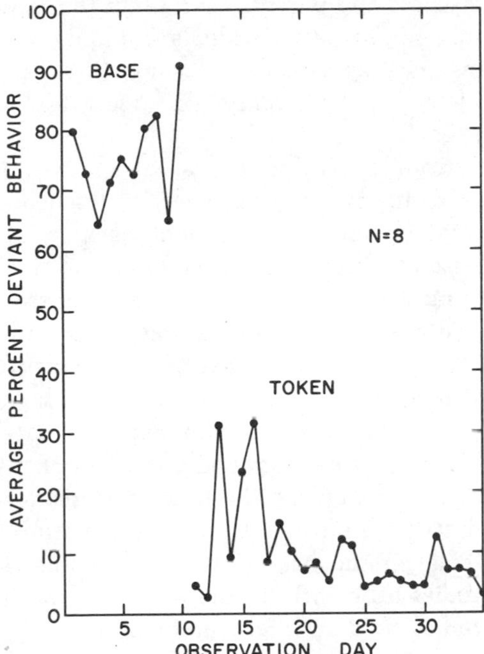

FIGURE 7.6 *Average percentages of deviant behavior during the base and token periods. (Redrawn from O'Leary & Becker, 1967, p. 640.)*

the student. Fortunately, it is possible to make a theoretical analysis of grading practices with reasonable confidence that the analysis is correct.

A grade is a kind of token. It has no intrinsic value. A grade is worth something because of its relationship to actual gratifications. In other words, a grade is a conditioned generalized reinforcer. A high grade probably acquires its power to reinforce because it is associated with praise, attention, affection, and encouragement from primary school teachers. In this respect, parents—at least middle-class parents—back up the teacher. They too bestow praise and affection for high grades. Special privileges are made contingent upon satisfactory grades. Some children are paid a sum of money for each high grade. Low grades, on the other hand, are met with restriction of privileges, signs of disappointment, or worse. Later, the reinforcing power of grades is maintained and accentuated by factors such as those described by McKeachie.

Conditioning—that is, learning—must occur, however, if grades are to function as reinforcers. Not all parents and teachers will reinforce (with approval, attention, etc.) children who earn good grades. Furthermore, not all children will receive grades high enough to elicit reinforcement from their teachers and parents. It follows that good grades will be strongly reinforcing for some individuals but only weakly reinforcing for others. For instance, as a matter of conjecture, one would suppose that grades would tend to be weakly reinforcing for "culturally disadvantaged" youngsters.

If grades are strongly reinforcing, student work rates should be controlled by the frequency, contingencies, and schedule of grades. A problem here is that in junior high schools, senior high schools, and, especially, colleges and universities, a student may be graded on only few occasions during a term. During a college course, he might get a grade on only a midterm examination, a final examination, and a paper. This arrangement roughly parallels that of a pigeon pecking a key on a fixed interval schedule of food reinforcement. As you will recall, there is a period of little or no responding immediately after reinforcement under a fixed interval schedule. Gradually the rate of response increases until it reaches a peak just before the next reinforcement. Our impression is that this description also characterizes the study habits of many high school and college students. If we are not mistaken, the all-too-typical student studies little early in the term. As the time for the final grows near he studies harder. The culmination is a frenzy of activity and all-night cram sessions a day or two before the final. This work pattern has several obvious shortcomings.

The remedy for the goof-off-then-cram cycle of studying is to change the conditions of reinforcement. Instead of, or in addition to, a final examination, several shorter midterms could be given. Regular quizzes and graded assignments could be introduced. Several short papers could be considered as an alternative to one long paper. When a long paper or project is inescapable, consideration could be given to requiring its completion in stages, each of which is graded.

The procedures just described will increase the frequency of reinforcement and reduce the interval between reinforcements; however, the student will still know the occasions upon which he will be graded and, therefore, he will still study and work in cycles. The way to produce a high, sustained work rate with a pigeon is to reinforce on a variable schedule such that it is impossible for the bird to predict just which responses will be reinforced. By analogy it may seem that the surprise quiz is the ideal technique to get students to work hard and consistently. However, we hesitate to recommend surprise quizzes, because of the possibility that the payoff would be made too uncertain, and that instead of working hard, many students would reduce the amount of time spent studying. Under analogous circumstances—as when a bird is abruptly shifted to a high ratio or interval schedule—the key-pecking behavior of a pigeon often extinguishes; the schedule does not "take hold." Another problem with the surprise quiz is that it is frustrating and anxiety provoking. To be sure, a certain amount of unpredictability is tolerable—indeed, necessary—to maintain student work output. This is the lesson of the intermittent reinforcement research. The questions are how much and what kind of unpredictability must be considered, in the light of the most important issue in any program of reinforcement—namely, the contingencies of reinforcement.

The usual test samples from among the things the student is expected to know. The quantity of material for which the student is held responsible may be very large. When this is true, there is a high ratio of material covered to material tested, and, as a corollary, there will have to be a high ratio of "studying responses" to "test responses" if the student is to earn a high grade. If this ratio gets too high, studying behavior will extinguish. In other words there is some point at which it becomes so improbable that studying will pay off that the student will stop studying.

Write a paragraph answering the following question.

A teacher says:

> Here is a list of important concepts. The final examination will contain questions on two of these concepts chosen at random.

What is the probable effect on the total amount of time the student will spend studying when the list contains two concepts? four concepts? twenty concepts? one hundred concepts? one thousand concepts? Give an explanation to support your answer.

The answer appears in the next paragraph.

It is impossible to be *sure* what would happen to the total amount of time a student would spend studying depending upon the number of concepts the student is held responsible for. As far as the authors know, no one has ever done research on this matter. However, a theoretical prediction can be made based on the established facts regarding intermittent reinforcement (and a couple of assumptions). Up to a point the total amount of time the student will spend studying should *increase* as the number of concepts for which he is responsible increases. After this point, as the number of concepts for which he is responsible increases still further, total studying time should decrease. For most students there will come a point when the responsibility is so great that he will study little or not at all. What might be called the procrastination or where-do-I-begin syndrome is then in evidence. There is no way to know at the present time that optimum theoretical point at which total studying time will be at a maximum. This point will undoubtedly depend upon the subject matter, the student, and the recent experience of the student. While we have no hard facts to back up our opinion, it is our belief that the typical high school or college teacher holds students responsible for too much at any one time, and that most students could be induced to study harder and longer if they were held responsible for less.

The contingency of reinforcement is a most important issue in any practical program of reinforcement. Grades in high school and college depend heavily upon examination performance. If examinations contain trivial questions, students will be led to study trivia. In the Rothkopf and Bisbicos study (1967) referred to earlier, questions were asked after students read brief passages from a book. Three questions were categorized by the form the answer could take. Some questions could be answered with numbers (i.e., dates, measurements, quantities) while others could be answered with names of persons, places or things. If questions which could be answered using numbers were asked after earlier passages students did better on this same category of questions after later passages, but did less well on other categories of questions. This experiment showed that the nature of test questions will influence that which the student emphasizes when he studies. Preparing examinations which require the student to deal with centrally-relevant concepts is important because the student is likely to study concepts which are tested.

But preparing good examinations is not enough. The student may misjudge the nature of the exams. For instance, though a history professor may regard certain broad concepts and principles of historiography as the meat of his course and his examinations may reflect this intent, the student may generalize inappropriately from previous experience and spend his time memorizing names and dates. Eventually, after he has had experience with several tests prepared by a given teacher, a student *may* learn what is required of him in order to do well. This, however, is an inefficient and uncertain way to teach him.

There is a remarkably simple way to get students to try to master the important concepts which will be represented in a well-prepared examination: tell students exactly what the examination will include. Merely suggesting in a general way what the test will cover is not likely to help. The evidence indicates that best results will be obtained when what the student must master to obtain a good grade is made unmistakably clear, stated in language he cannot fail to understand. Tiemann (1968) provided some sections of an introductory college course in economics with a detailed list of behavioral objectives at the beginning of each class session. The objectives specified in complete and concrete terms that which the student was expected to learn from the lesson. Other groups did not get the lists of objectives. Since the course was televised, all groups received identical instruction. On the final examination those who were provided with objectives did significantly better than those who were not. Moreover, students who received lists of objectives expressed a significantly more favorable attitude toward the course.

Making explicit to the student what he must master in order to earn a good grade on examinations will make the exams easier. Thus, more students will earn good grades. For this very reason, many teachers will be reluctant to follow such a policy. Grades are a two-edged sword. If good grades are reinforcing, then poor grades are punishing. The latter possibility, unfortunately, bulks large in the thinking of a great many teachers. Their strategy is to make school difficult enough so that the student is constantly afraid that he will not make the grade. Large amounts of work are assigned. Objectives and standards of performance are kept ambiguous. Examination questions are tricky and surprise quizzes are given often. The underlying assumption is that students will not work except for the threat of something unpleasant—fear of embarrassment, say, or fear of failure. Hence, it is necessary continually to "challenge" them.

It cannot be denied that a fear of doing poorly is one goad which, under some conditions, will drive a student to work hard and pay attention (Sax & Reade, 1964). However, there are other responses to poor grades and the threat of poor grades. The student may try to "psych out" the instructor. He may cheat. He may drop out of school.

Indeed, if a student often receives poor grades it is inevitable that he will lose interest in school, stop paying close attention, and stop completing assignments. If he does not literally drop out of school, he will begin to daydream or become a discipline problem—that is, he will become a "mental dropout." A perennial complaint of the teacher faced with a student making poor progress is, "If he would only complete his assignments, stop daydreaming, and pay attention, I know he could succeed." The implicit diagnosis is that "quitters" tend to be "losers." While this statement has the ring of truth, the direction of causation is obscure. In our view the more pregnant maxim for the teacher is that "losers" tend to be "quitters."

We do not object to typical grading practices for humanitarian reasons, though a case could be made on these grounds. Nor are we arguing, though it would be possible to do so, that students should not work for grades alone but for some other, deeper reason, such as love of learning for its own sake. Our objection to typical grading procedures is pragmatic. If the preceding analysis is correct, grading practices could be modified in such a way that students could be induced to pay closer attention, to spend more time studying, and to learn more.

Significantly here, little is accomplished by simply awarding higher grades, or by grading on effort rather than performance. Improvement will not come from lowering standards but rather from clarifying them. If high grades are reinforcing and if the student knows exactly what skills and concepts he must master in order to earn high grades, then it can be predicted with considerable confidence that he will try to master those skills and concepts.

The Premack Principle. In addition to praise and tangible items of value, the opportunity to engage in a preferred activity is reinforcing. This fact is called the Premack Principle, after David R. Premack (1965), who has stated that "for any pair of responses, the more probable one will reinforce the less probable one." (p. 132). By a "more probable response," Premack means the response the person (or animal) would give if he had a free choice in the matter—in other words, his preferred activity. To paraphrase, then, if the more probable response is reinforcing, the rate or strength of the less probable response should increase if the organism must make it in order to have the opportunity to engage in the more probable response (the preferred activity). Premack has completed a series of experiments that show the soundness of this principle. His research and analysis recasts and sharpens the concept of reinforcement and broadens the range of things that can be predicted to function as reinforcers.

Homme and his co-workers (Addison & Homme, 1966; Homme, et al., 1963) have made an application of reinforcement, termed the "Contingency Management System," which incorporates many of Premack's ideas. Under this system, the student is provided with a "reinforcing event menu"—the RE menu for short. The RE menu lists or, in the case of children, pictures, the things the student can get provided he completes a required amount of work. The amount of work to be completed for a certain entree is negotiated with the "contingency manager," also called the "RE administrator." The menu lists not only items such as toys, candy, and cigarettes (for high school dropouts), but also, after Premack, lists activities in which the student may engage. For instance, pushing the RE administrator around the office in his swivel chair has proved a very popular entree with preschool Indian children. In another instance, students were induced to spend more time working on arithmetic problems (initially a low probability response) when this led to the opportunity to talk about baseball (a high probability response). It is reported that the Contingency Management System has been used successfully with a wide variety of students—ranging from high school dropouts to grade school children with academic achievement problems—and has been used in a variety of settings—ranging from the psychiatric ward to the ordinary classroom—with promising results.

Negative reinforcement and punishment. Punishment cannot be recommended as a general method of classroom control. Make no mistake; severe punishment will suppress unwanted behavior. Solomon (1964) has shown that dogs given severe electric shocks several times will continue to make avoidance responses indefinitely even though they are never again punished. The military is able to maintain rather good control of the behavior of troops because orders are backed up with severe punishment. But, for very good reasons, society does not permit teachers to use really severe punishment. Mild punishment can occasionally be used to good advantage; however, it must be warned that mild punishment loses its effectiveness when used repeatedly (Azrin & Holz, 1966). Punishment, furthermore, has undesirable side effects. While you may temporarily get a child to do what you want by using punishment and threats of punishment, in the long run he may learn that learning is an unpleasant business and that school is a hateful place. Still another problem is that what the teacher intends as punishment may actually be reinforcing. The attention from the teacher and from peers which accompanies punishment may actually increase the likelihood of disruptive behavior on the part of some pupils. There is a certain notoriety in being a "bad boy."

To be sure, there are occasions upon which punishment can be used successfully and indeed should be used. Punishment is always in order in cases of flagrantly objectionable behavior. To be avoided is a gradual escalation in which pleading is followed by scolding, which is in turn followed by threats and finally punishment. The rule of conduct which has been violated should be restated once, at most. If the objectionable behavior continues, its next occurrence should be met with the strongest punishment that is appropriate considering the nature of the offense.

"Time out" from positive reinforcement can be effective punishment. Under this procedure the organism is isolated or otherwise prevented from getting reinforcement for a period of time after each instance of unwanted behavior. A case study performed by Hawkins, Peterson, Schweid, and Bijou (1966) illustrates the value of the time out procedure. A mother had come to a university mental health clinic because she felt she was helpless in dealing with the frequent disobedience and tantrums of her four-year-old son. During a baseline observation period, psychologists observed the boy in his home with his mother and confirmed that he engaged in a large amount of objectionable behavior including "(1) biting his shirt or arm, (2) sticking out his tongue, (3) kicking or hitting himself, others, or objects, (4) calling someone or something a derogatory name, (5) removing or threatening to remove his clothing, (6) saying 'No!' loudly and vigorously, (7) threatening to damage objects or persons, (8) throwing objects, and (9) pushing his sister." The observers noted that many of the boy's undesirable behaviors appeared to be maintained by attention from his mother. "When [the boy] behaved objectionably, she would often try to explain why he should not act thus; or she would try to interest him in some new activity by offering toys or food." (Ibid., p. 100.)

After the baseline observation period, the mother implemented a planned treatment with the help of a psychologist-observer who sat in the home. The psychologist gave hand signals to the mother which indicated how she was to deal with her son. When the boy misbehaved, the mother warned him once. If he persisted, he got a five-minute time out, during which he was locked in a bare room. The boy was released at the end of five minutes provided he had been quiet for at least the last thirty seconds. When the boy engaged in desirable behavior, the psychologist signaled the mother to give attention, praise, and affectionate physical contact. This treatment brought about a sharp decrease in the frequency and strength of objectionable behavior, changes which were still in evidence during a follow-up nearly a month after the psychologist had left the home.

Extrinsic versus intrinsic reinforcement. There is a vein of opinion among educators that in the long run, for really important objectives, students cannot be "bribed" with grades, money, privileges, attention, affection, and the like. Over the long haul, it is believed, the student must read because he enjoys reading, solve problems because doing so satisfies his curiosity, and learn history because it increases his understanding of the world in which he lives. The implication in this opinion is that intrinsic reinforcement is somehow more potent or more effective than extrinsic reinforcement. There is not, as far as we know, any body of evidence to support such a conviction.

For the purposes of the discussion here, extrinsic reinforcement is defined as reinforcement contrived by a teacher which would not occur except for the intervention of the teacher. Intrinsic reinforcement arises as the "natural" physical or social consequence of a response, and need not be planned by a teacher. When a person reads novels because he enjoys them, "enjoyment" is simply a nontechnical term for intrinsic reinforcement. All cases in which a person does something "for its own sake" entail intrinsic reinforcement.

Behavior cannot be maintained indefinitely by a teacher's reinforcement. Reinforcement must continue when the student leaves the classroom; otherwise the behavior will extinguish. Intrinsic reinforcement can continue when the student is no longer in the classroom. It should not be imagined, though, that the only source, or most important source, of reinforcement beyond the classroom is intrinsic reinforcement in the narrow sense of doing a thing for its own sake. For instance, a musician may practice for long hours because he enjoys his own music and/or because of pride in reaching a standard of excellence, but also because of applause from audiences (social reinforcement), favorable comment and esteem on the part of his fellow musicians (social reinforcement), money (token reinforcement), and the things which money will buy (a variety of kinds of reinforcement).

An obvious disadvantage of intrinsic reinforcement is that it will not always occur at educationally desirable times. Maybe a boy should play the violin because of the thrill of hearing the music he produces. But what if he finds his own music less than exciting? Maybe if his teachers and parents keep him going with extrinsic reinforcement, he will eventually come to enjoy his own music. The point is that intrinsic reinforcement will not occur unless performance meets a certain standard. The beginner may not be able to meet the standard.

Our best guess is that a persistent tendency to engage in an activity, and to do so with evident pleasure, begins with a first effort which is reinforced. If the first effort seems to be spontaneous and the reinforcement seems to be intrinsic, that is fine; but there is no substantial reason to believe that this is a necessary condition, or even a very frequent one. Supplementary extrinsic reinforcement arranged by classroom teachers and informal teachers such as parents is probably essential, even when it seems as though the behavior is intrinsically reinforced. The development of the persistent tendency to try to meet standards of excellence, called "achievement motivation," is an example. The development of achievement motivation seems to depend upon the child's receiving attention, praise, and physical affection from his parents, particularly his mother (Winterbottom, 1958).

The tendency to read widely with enjoyment very likely also depends upon extrinsic reinforcement. There may be some intrinsic gratification for a child in reading a new word or completing a primer story on his own. However, it will take several years of hard work before most children will have developed enough competence at reading to make possible a high frequency of intrinsic reinforcement from reading stories, books, magazines, and newspapers. Extrinsic reinforcement in the form, for instance, of attention or praise, is probably vital to the development of reading skill in most beginners.

SELF-TEST ON REINFORCEMENT

Write your answers to each question, then grade your paper using the scoring key on p. **268.**

1. A boy frequently disrupts class by making surreptitious wisecracks, throwing things, and playing the clown. Which of the following is the best explanation of his behavior?

a. He has a strong need for attention.
b. His peers and the teacher react to him when he disrupts class.
c. He may be brain damaged or emotionally disturbed.
d. His parents and teachers have not disciplined him properly.

2. An experienced life insurance salesman continues to contact people in the attempt to sell during a long period in which he makes no sales. Why does he continue to try to sell insurance instead of taking another job?

a. He enjoys meeting new people.
b. In the past he has sold policies to most of the people he contacted.
c. In the past he has sold policies to only a small proportion of the people he contacted.
d. He can draw on his savings during periods when sales are poor.

3. A primary school teacher usually pays attention to children who raise their hands. She ignores children who call out her name. This is an instance of

a. differential reinforcement.
b. negative reinforcement.
c. intermittent reinforcement.
d. shaping.

4. When an unreliable cigarette lighter lights after five tries on the average, the behavior of trying to light it is reinforced on a ____________________ schedule.

a. fixed interval
b. fixed ratio
c. continuous
d. variable interval
e. variable ratio

5. The difference between negative reinforcement and punishment is that

a. negative reinforcement increases the rate or frequency of the reinforced response; punishment suppresses the response.
b. negative reinforcement will increase the *rate* of responding at a progressively increasing rate; punishment increases the rate of responding until it reaches a constant level.
c. negative reinforcement is punishment presented immediately after the response.
d. negative reinforcement is more effective for suppressing undesired responses than punishment.

6. Head scratching, pencil chewing, and table tapping are generally forms of ____________________ behavior.

a. shaped
b. operant
c. superstitious
d. accidental
e. unconditioned

7. A correct statement of the relationship between the response and reinforcement is that

a. the reinforcement is conditioned to elicit the response in the future.
b. the more quickly the response follows the reinforcement, the less reinforcement is needed on the next trial.
c. the more similar the reinforcement is to the response, the

greater is the number of responses for which it can act as reinforcer.

d. response magnitude increases as reinforcement latency decreases.

e. the reinforcement increases the frequency with which the response will again occur.

8. Mr. Jones, a high school history teacher, gives a reading assignment every day. Exactly once a week he gives a surprise quiz covering the preceding day's assignment. Which of the following best describes the care with which his students will read the assignments?

a. They will read all assignments carefully.

b. They will read none of the assignments carefully.

c. They will not read carefully the assignments following the quiz.

d. They will not read carefully the assignments before the quiz.

9. What important practical effect does intermittent reinforcement have on behavior?

10. Briefly describe the procedure of shaping.

11. Briefly describe the conditions which will produce superstitious behavior.

12. A young high school teacher finds that supervising a 50-minute study period in the school library is his most irksome assignment. Many students fail to come to the study hall with books, paper, and pencil. There is much talking and little studying. He finds that frequent warnings and threats and occasional punishment keep the noise level down somewhat; but there still isn't much studying and he does not enjoy being a policeman. Describe in detail reinforcement procedures this teacher could use to improve the situation in the study hall.

Summary

Reinforcement techniques are among the most useful methods a teacher has for arranging and maintaining the behaviors that give birth to learning, such as attentive behavior and persistent behavior. A reinforcer is anything that strengthens behavior it follows. Differential reinforcement involves reinforcing one kind of behavior and simultaneously extinguishing another. Using this technique a teacher can strengthen a desirable response and at the same time weaken undesirable ones. Shaping entails differential reinforcement of successive approximations to the desired behavior.

Continuous reinforcement, in which every acceptable response is reinforced, produces the most rapid learning of new responses. However, to develop persistence over the long haul, intermittent reinforcement is best. Intermittent reinforcement entails reinforcement of some but not all acceptable responses. The most effective practical procedure is to establish responses using continuous reinforcement and then to sustain responses already acquired by using intermittent reinforcement.

If reinforcement is delivered on a regular, predictable schedule, there will tend to be a pause in which few responses are emitted. Steady work rates can be maintained by delivering reinforcement on an irregular, or variable, schedule.

It is most important to make reinforcement contingent upon satisfactory student responses. Maintaining a warm supportive classroom climate is not enough. Indeed, reinforcement given without regard to student performance can lead to superstitious behavior.

Many objects and events function as reinforcers for humans. The list includes social reinforcers such as praise, encouragement, attention, and physical affection. Money, food, candy, toys, cigarettes and the like are usually effective tangible reinforcers. In fact, tangible reinforcers are often more effective than social reinforcers. The opportunity to perform certain preferred activities—for instance, playing a game—can also be reinforcing. Grades are a form of token reinforcement much used in schools. Finally, many activities are more or less self-sustaining because they give rise to intrinsic reinforcement.

The key to maintaining attention, persistence, good study habits, and good conduct is to reinforce satisfactory behavior and ignore unsatisfactory behavior. Teachers easily fall into the trap of paying attention to a student only when there is trouble. The problem with troubleshooting is that it is likely to lead to more trouble in the future. The best way to shape up a student whose performance is unsatisfactory is to be alert about reinforcing him during those moments when he does behave appropriately.

SCORING KEY FOR THE SELF-TEST ON REINFORCEMENT

A total of 15 points may be earned on the test. A score of 11 or better is satisfactory. Review sections of the text dealing with questions that gave you trouble.

1. *(1 point)*

The best answer is *b*. The reactions of the teacher and the other students probably reinforce the boy's disruptive behavior.

2. *(1 point)*

The best answer is c. Making a sale is reinforcing. If he has made sales to a small proportion of the prospects he contacted, he has, in other words, been reinforced intermittently. Therefore, the behavior will be slow to extinguish.

3. *(1 point)* a

4. *(1 point)* e

5. *(1 point)* a

6. *(1 point)* c

7. *(1 point)* e

8. *(1 point)* c

A quiz will lead to a grade, and a grade is reinforcing (or punishing). The schedule of quizzes, and therefore reinforcement, has a predictable feature. Students are likely to study less carefully following the quiz since they know another quiz will not be given. Note that it will not help consistently to give the quiz late in the week because then students will not study early assignments carefully. You should be able to devise a procedure to get the students to read all of the assignments carefully.

9. *(1 point)*

Intermittent reinforcement causes persistence; in technical language, it causes resistance to extinction.

10. *(2 points)*

Shaping is differential reinforcement of successive approximations to the desired behavior. You need not use technical language to be counted correct.

(1) for mentioning differential reinforcement.
(1) for mentioning successful approximations.

11. *(1 point)*

Superstitious behavior is caused by accidental reinforcement.

12. *(3 points)*

(1) for defining the rules students are expected to observe.
(1) for indicating a plan for reinforcing behavior which satisfies the rules.
(1) for indicating that behavior which does not fit the rules will be ignored (unless it is very disruptive).

For an illustration, we believe the following specific plan would work successfully. Indicate to students that each person who brings books, pencils, paper, and other needed materials to study hall and works industriously for the first 35 minutes will earn 15 minutes of free time. Provide a "conversation corner," board games or cards, and light reading material to be used during free time by those who earn it. Ignore students who do not study unless they seriously interfere with the work of others.

Selected Readings

Anderson, R. C., Faust, G. W., Roderick, M. C., Cunningham, D. J., & Andre, T., eds., "Section V. Reinforcement and Feedback," *Current Research on Instruction*. Englewood Cliffs, N.J.: Prentice-Hall, 1969. Several papers on reinforcement and corrective feedback are presented.

Kuhlen, R. G., ed., "Section 9. Methods of Providing Reinforcement in the Schools," *Studies in Educational Psychology*. Waltham, Mass.: Blaisdell, 1968. Reprinted are five papers discussing reinforcement in the schools.

Skinner, B. F. *The Technology of Teaching*. New York: Appleton-Century-Crofts, 1968. Skinner analyzes many issues of education in terms of the frequency and contingencies of reinforcement.

CHAPTER

8

Corrective Feedback

This chapter, like the preceding one, deals with the third component of the teaching model. While the preceding chapter showed that inappropriate behavior can be weakened by withholding reinforcement, it was mainly concerned with strengthening desired behavior. This chapter, on the other hand, considers a variety of additional techniques—some simple and direct, others elaborate and indirect—to cope with errors and unsatisfactory student behavior. To put it simply, the reinforcement chapter concerned mainly the feedback to provide when the student is doing well (or, at least, better), while this chapter focuses on the feedback to give when the student is doing poorly. When you have finished this chapter you should be able to:

1. describe the types of knowledge of results which can be provided and the likely behavioral effects of each.
2. describe problems which can arise when immediate knowledge of results is provided.
3. describe procedures you would use for providing knowledge of results, given various instructional situations.
4. distinguish between knowledge of results and correction procedures; discuss the relative merits of each and the conditions under which each is most appropriate.

We must begin on a cautious note. The case can be made that in an ideal lesson corrective feedback would be unnecessary because at every step in an ideal lesson student performance will be satisfactory. Evidence to support this proposition will be reviewed in Chapter 9. In the meantime, consider the fact that corrective feedback is usually nonreinforcing and may even be punishing. Therefore, the student who receives large doses of corrective feedback may become frustrated and may stop trying to learn. For example, the school child whose grammar is continually corrected by parents and teachers may become frustrated by this barrage of corrective feedback and may even elect to remain silent when with adults rather than receive any more of it. Consider also that the prediction that errors will hinder learning can be deduced from the principle that people learn what they do. A corollary is that if they make errors, students will be learning error tendencies. Errors therefore are not only a sign that the student is doing poorly now, but are also a source of future confusion.

This chapter is divided into three sections. The first deals with several different kinds of information the teacher can provide about the adequacy of student responses. The second describes "correction procedures," so called because the student is required to keep repeating a question, task, or problem until his performance is correct. The final section discusses adaptive teaching procedures, in which the whole sequence of instruction depends upon student performance.

Knowledge of Results

The term "knowledge of results" refers to *providing the student with information (knowledge) about the adequacy (results) of his responses.* Sometimes knowledge of results is provided by another person, for instance, a teacher who says "right" or "wrong," or repeats the correct answer. More generally, the response directly produces feedback as when, for example, a shot at a target causes a hole a greater or lesser distance from the bull's-eye.

There is a wealth of evidence indicating that knowledge of results facilitates learning. Michael and Maccoby (1961), for instance, provided knowledge of results for half of the 49 classes of high school juniors and seniors that took part in a study on the effects of "participation sessions" on learning from an instruction film (see Chapter 6). Those who received knowledge of results in this study averaged 16 percent higher on the achievement test than those who did not.

Knowledge of results facilitates learning for two reasons. It provides reinforcement when the student's response is adequate and it furnishes corrective feedback when the student makes an error. Research seems to indicate that it is more important to tell the student he is wrong when his response is incorrect than it is to tell him he is right when his response is correct (Buss, Braden, Orgel, & Buss, 1956; Travers, Van Wagenen, Haygood, & McCormick, 1964). This fact, among others (Anderson,

1967, pp. 148–150), suggests that knowledge of results functions more as corrective feedback than as reinforcement.

Types of knowledge of results. Listed below are several possible reactions of a teacher to unsatisfactory student responses. We are emphasizing the corrective feedback aspect of knowledge of results, since this is its most important function. Presumably the teacher will also reinforce good performance. When a student makes a mistake, the teacher can

1. ignore the mistake; withhold reinforcement.
2. tell the student he is wrong.
3. tell the student he is wrong and furnish the correct answer.
4. tell the student he is wrong, furnish the correct answer, and explain why the correct answer is correct.
5. tell the student he is wrong and explain why he is wrong.

Consider the first two forms of feedback listed above. Research indicates that it is better to tell a student he is wrong than to ignore errors. Buss and his associates (e.g., 1956) completed a series of studies involving the three feedback alternatives "right," "wrong," and no comment. Their general finding was that either "right" and "wrong," or no comment and "wrong," produced more rapid learning than saying "right" when the student was correct and giving no comment when he was wrong.

The conclusion that students should be told when they are wrong may seem to contradict the advice given in the previous chapter. There it was maintained that the best way to deal with inappropriate behavior is to ignore it. Which procedure is best, in fact, depends upon whether the student is capable of making the desired response. When he is capable of the response, the best technique is to ignore unsatisfactory responses and reinforce satisfactory ones. But when he is not capable of the desired behavior, the student should be given feedback so that he can learn to behave correctly. Consider these two cases: (1) a boy talks out in class without raising his hand; (2) the same boy misspells a word. The boy is perfectly capable of raising his hand and undoubtedly knows he should; therefore, following the procedure suggested above, he should be ignored (unless he is so disruptive that this is impossible). In the second case, the boy can't spell the word correctly or he would have; therefore, he should be told he is wrong. To put the matter in everyday language, ignore unsatisfactory behavior when the problem is one of motivation. When the problem is one of information, furnish the information.

Providing the correct response is more effective than simply telling the student he is wrong. Travers and his colleagues (1964), in a study supporting this view, taught small groups of fourth, fifth, and sixth graders the English synonyms for sixty German words. A card containing a German word and two English words, one of which was correct, was presented. A child was called on and asked to guess the correct English word. In some groups, the child was told "No, that's wrong," when he made an error. In other groups, the corrective feedback consisted of "No, that's wrong; [*German word*] means [*English word*]." Giving the correct answer resulted in significantly higher achievement on the part of the children. This study, moreover, probably underestimates the benefits which would be obtained in most school situations from providing the correct answer, because in the study there were only two alternatives: if one was wrong, the other had to be right. When the student is selecting from a larger set of alternatives or constructing his response, knowing that one answer is wrong will not be very helpful in determining which answer is right. We conclude, therefore, that in most situations, furnishing the right answer is far better than merely telling a student he is wrong.

There has been little research on more complicated forms of knowledge of results. Studies which attempted to determine whether there is an advantage to explaining the correct answer in addition to providing it have yielded equivocal results (Bivens, 1964; Moore & Smith, 1964; Rosenstock, Moore, & Smith, 1965). For reasons which will become clear in a moment, we believe the results of these studies should be discounted because they all involved programmed instruction. In our opinion, it is reasonable to suppose that more elaborate forms of feedback will facilitate learning in many circumstances; though this has not yet been demonstrated experimentally.

One of the fundamental premises of programmed instruction is that knowledge of results is facilitative. It is for this reason that the correct answer is always provided in programmed lessons immediately after the student makes his response. Ironically, though, some research done with programmed lessons has seemed to show that lessons are most successful *without* immediate knowledge of results (Lublin, 1965; see also Krumboltz & Weisman, 1962). This finding can be understood in part by assuming that knowledge of results is a weak reinforcer and one for which students quickly become satiated. More important, it seems likely that the presence of knowledge of results in programmed instruction sometimes allows the student to "short-circuit" the instructional process. Since he will be shown the correct answer, he doesn't bother to study the lesson material carefully. Lublin (p. 299) concluded that when knowledge of results was withheld, "each frame demanded more attention from the subjects and required the subjects to study each frame more carefully." Sullivan, Baker, and Schutz (1967) have also obtained evidence that students given immediate knowledge of results worked more rapidly and made more errors than students who did not receive knowledge of results, though there was no difference between the two groups of students on the final achievement test. They too concluded that immediate knowledge of results permitted the student to short-circuit the instructional process; he could obtain the right answers without carefully studying the text.

Providing the correct answer has undeniable value as corrective feedback when the student is wrong. And it probably serves as a reinforcer, at least a weak one, when the student is right. Yet, as we have seen, the systematic attempt to use immediate knowledge of results in programmed lessons sometimes interferes with learning, probably because students are thereby able to get correct answers without studying carefully. How can the advantages of immediate knowledge of results be realized and at the same time the short-circuiting of instruction be avoided? Herein lies a challenging problem in educational engineering. We believe the problem can be solved in the following ways.

First, insure that the student actually makes the response, answers the question, or tries to solve the problem *before* he receives knowledge of results. Knowledge of results may not have shown up well in the programmed instruction studies because the students often responded *after* they had viewed the correct answer. Lublin's program was printed on long sheets of paper with the correct answer in the margin just below the frame. Such a format makes it easy for students to peek at the answer; indeed, it is difficult for even the conscientious student to avoid seeing the correct answer occasionally. The problem is that the student may just copy the answer into the blank—particularly if he is tired, bored, or disinterested. Even the conscientious student may learn less when he sees the answer beforehand. The problem was expressed well by a graduate student in education who participated in a programmed instruction experiment of our own (Anderson, Faust, & Roderick, 1968), in which, to our dismay, we discovered that it was often possible to read the correct answers through the pages of the program: "I was annoyed at times by the fact that the correct responses on the next page were often visible because of the thinness of the paper. In cases where I had already looked at these responses it's difficult to tell if I really thought out & wrote down the correct response, or just copied the response that was visible through the page." It is known that students learn little from a program when they simply copy correct answers (Brown, 1966; Faust & Anderson, 1967; Anderson & Faust, 1967). Consequently, learning is likely to be undermined unless steps are taken to insure that the student responds before the correct answer is provided.

A second way to gain the benefits and avoid the liabilities of immediate knowledge of results is to increase the incentive for correct performance on the first try. Students may become careless about responding when the correct answer is always provided immediately. The incentive for being right the first time can be increased by supplementing knowledge of results with other positive reinforcers (praise, attention, good grades, privileges). The incentive can also be increased by mild punishment for errors. It has been shown that a brief delay or "time out" following an error will improve accuracy (Zimmerman & Ferster, 1963). One way in which this procedure can be implemented in the classroom is by requiring the student to complete an additional problem or two for each error. Rather than treat these additional problems (questions, examples, etc.) as punishment, they should be represented as part of the regular work which can be bypassed by completing preliminary work satisfactorily. The lesson should be planned so that it will teach well without the extra problems. Such a procedure will improve accuracy and facilitate learning, even though students seldom if ever actually have to complete the extra problems (Geis & Knapp, 1963).

Short-circuiting can also occur in oral give-and-take between teacher and students when immediate knowledge of results is provided. The problem is a little different from the one found in paper-and-pencil programmed lessons, however. The student who is actually called on in class to answer a question is almost sure to profit from knowledge of results. Unlike the situation which sometimes exists in a programmed lesson, the student who answers out loud in class has plenty of incentive for responding correctly on the first try. The problem is that in a discussion or oral exercise, only one student can answer at a time. The silent students are likely to learn less than those who have the opportunity to answer. This conclusion follows from the preceding discussion and from the principle that students learn what they are led to do. As a matter of fact, Travers and his associates (1964) did find that students who actually answered the questions learned substantially more than those who merely listened and watched. We therefore suggest the following techniques to gain the benefits and avoid the liabilities of knowledge of results in oral classroom instruction.

First, ask the question or pose the problem *before* you call on a student. If you call on the student first, others in the class may "tune out." They will have been relieved of the responsibility to compose an answer.

Second, pause before calling on a student. Give enough time for most students to make covert responses.

Third, occasionally after a student has answered, whether rightly or wrongly, ask the rest of the class to commit themselves to agreeing or disagreeing with him. Then furnish the correct answer.

An eighth grader incorrectly explains the difference between an analogy and a metaphor. According to research, which of the following procedures would be most effective for the teacher to use?

A. Praise him for something else he has done in order to avoid embarrassing him.
B. Warn him that he had better study harder.
C. Quickly ask another student a different question.
D. Tell him the correct explanation.

The answer appears on p. **279.**

Correction Procedures

Psychologists use the term "correction procedure" to mean that the student (or subject) is required to keep trying to answer a question or solve a problem until he gets it right. The diagram on the following page shows the simplest form of correction procedure. Correction procedures almost always involve some form of knowledge of results. However, when only knowledge of results is employed, the student remains passive. Correction procedures, on the other hand, require the student to correct his mistake actively.

In research involving simple laboratory tasks, correction procedures usually speed learning for children (e.g., Suppes & Ginsberg, 1962) and sometimes, but not usually, facilitate adult learning. There has been less research involving school-related tasks. What research there is suggests that a correction procedure will help students of all ages when complex subject matter is being learned. For example, Holland and Porter (1961) had graduate students in education complete a self-instruction program in psychology. After each set of about thirty frames, the students in one group were required to repeat items they had missed earlier until each item had been answered correctly. The students in the second answered each question only once, correct or not. On both an immediate achieve-

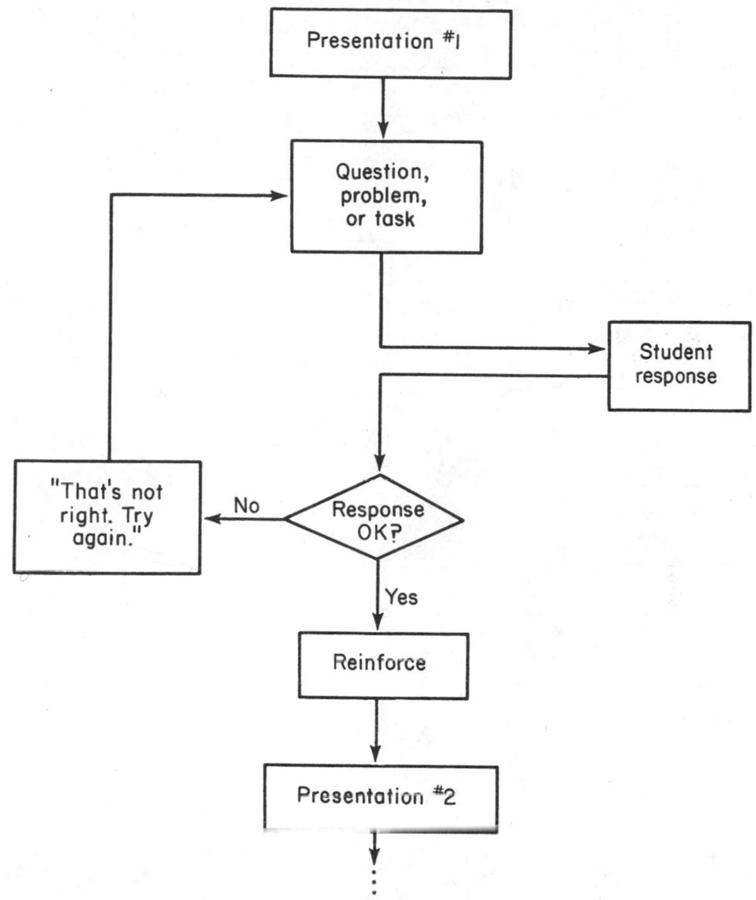

SIMPLE CORRECTION PROCEDURE

ment test and a retest six months later, the group which had had to repeat missed items did significantly better.

Teachers usually use more elaborate correction procedures than the one diagrammed above. Consider the diagram on page 278. The dashed line at (1) indicates that it would be possible, perhaps desirable, to bypass the remark, "That's not right." The remedial sequence can be expanded, if necessary, to include one, two, or even a dozen complete cycles before the student is again asked to try the performance upon which he failed the first time.

Most classroom teachers probably make considerable use of correction procedures resembling the one in the last diagram. "Branching" programs also use correction procedures that sometimes involve lengthy,

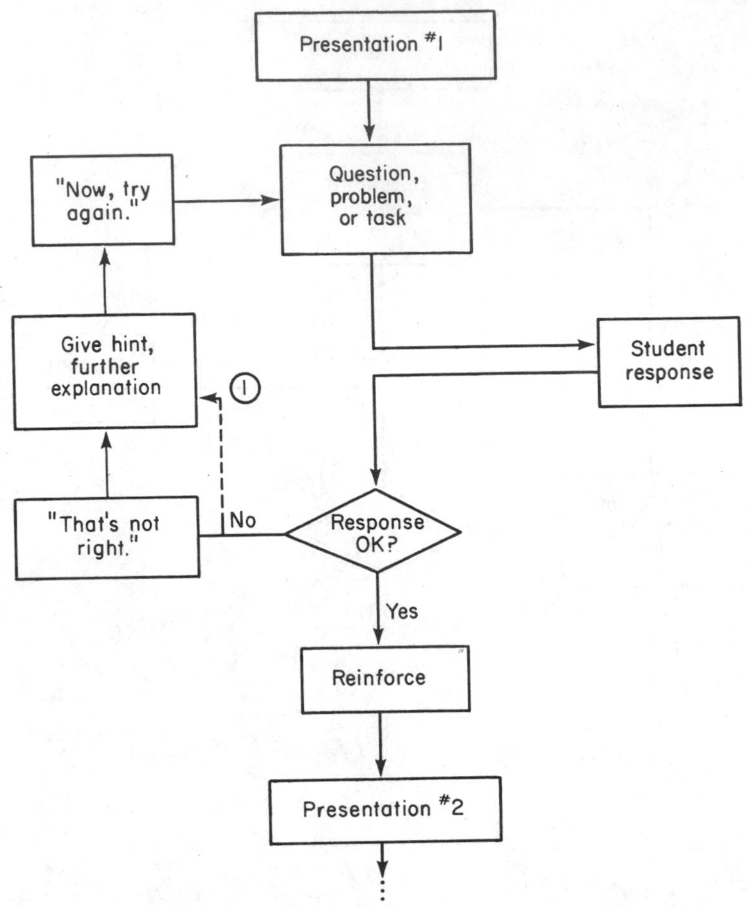

MORE ELABORATE CORRECTION PROCEDURE

remedial sequences. A branching program contains a series of terse presentations. After each presentation, there is a test question. If a student answers the question correctly he goes on to the next presentation. The student who fails to correctly answer the question is "branched" to a remedial sequence.

Surprisingly enough, research with branching programs seems to indicate that correction procedures are not very effective (Anderson, 1967, pp. 151–154). Campbell (1963) prepared three forms of a program to teach set theory. The short, linear version consisted of fifteen frames, one for each of the fifteen "basic required steps" of set theory. The bypass program consisted of the same fifteen basic frames, plus remedial frames which were skipped when the student was correct. If his answer was wrong, the student completed the remedial sequence before attempting the next basic frame. The student could avoid 85 percent of the frames by responding correctly on basic frames. In the long, linear version, the student worked through the entire sequence of both basic and remedial frames with no opportunity to skip any of the frames. Seven hundred and eighty children from the fourth, sixth, eighth, tenth, and twelfth grades received the programs. For every grade the long, linear program gave better results on the achievement test than the bypass program, which in turn gave better results than the short linear program. Learning time followed the same order. Amount learned and time spent corresponded closely to number of frames studied.

Despite these results, we believe that the research with branching programs underestimates the value of correction procedures. Understand that branching programs typically are designed as much to allow the student who already knows a portion of the material, or who masters the portion with minimal instruction, to skip ahead as they are to provide remedial instruction for students who have difficulty. In terms of the bypass function, some branching programs have performed well, saving a good deal of the student's time while maintaining the same level of achievement as the version that requires the student to complete everything (Bisbicos, 1965). The problem arises when teachers and programmers, in their eagerness to avoid boring bright students with unnecessary repetition, prepare a basic instructional sequence which is too fast moving and too difficult. As we shall emphasize in the next chapter, it is far better to teach the student right the first time than it is to permit misunderstandings to arise, which then have to be corrected. The problem is compounded when students are allowed to skip material on the basis of answers to one or two questions. The student may make a "lucky" guess or may only partially understand. One reason branching programs have failed to show up well is probably that the answer to a single question is a fallible basis for a decision, often yielding false positives, so that students miss instruction they need. Coulson and his associates (1962), in a more successful use of this procedure, based the decision on whether to present remedial instruction or go on to new material on the total number of errors a student made on a topic; answers to diagnostic test questions; and student evaluations of their degree

Answer to the question on p. **276.**

D. Tell him the correct explanation.

of mastery of the topics. One group of students received a lesson in symbolic logic to which these procedures were applied. Another group received a 233-frame linear version of the same lesson. The branching group saw an average of 213.5 frames; took less time to complete the lesson than the linear group; and, what is most important, scored significantly higher on the achievement test than the linear group. Using reliable information helped Coulson and his colleagues avoid bad decisions. They could be fairly certain that a student had mastered each skill and concept before he was directed on to new material.

We fear that teachers engaging in whole-class instruction may be even more vulnerable to bad decisions than the authors of branching programs. When two or three or four students have satisfactorily answered questions, solved problems, or performed, it is tempting to conclude that every student has mastered whatever is being taught. This is a weak assumption. People learn what they are led to do. To be sure, students will learn vicariously, by imitation, from observing their classmates perform; however, it cannot be concluded that a student has mastered a principle, concept, or skill until he himself has had a chance to perform, and has done so satisfactorily. A brief written exercise or quiz can make a good sequel to oral give-and-take because *every* student gets the chance to respond. Rather than interrupt the flow of instruction by collecting papers and grading them later, the teacher should have students grade their own papers, on the basis of feedback. If a show of hands indicates that many have done poorly, whole-class instruction should be continued. If only a few have done badly, the rest of the class should be assigned a self-instructional activity such as reading, working on a project, or completing a program. Students whose performance was unsatisfactory should be worked with individually or in a small group.

Despite the conflicting data from research with branching programs, we are confident that classroom teachers can get good results using

A fourth grader spells "rough," *r-u-f-f*. Which of the following teacher tactics are correction procedures?

A. " 'Rough' ends like 'tough' and 'enough.' Now let's see if you can spell 'rough.' "
B. " 'Rough' is spelled like this." Teacher writes *r-o-u-g-h*.
C. "No, that's wrong, but 'rough' is a difficult word. Can you spell 'clown'?"

The answer appears on p. **283.**

correction procedures. Two conditions are important. First, the main instructional sequence should be designed to teach thoroughly. The correction procedure is a backup to be used when needed. Correction procedures should not be relied upon to patch holes in inadequate lessons. Second, enough within-lesson evaluation should be included so that sound decisions can be made as to whether students have mastered the things now being taught and can proceed to new material or, whether, on the other hand, remedial instruction is needed.

Adaptive Teaching Procedures

We shall define an "adaptive teaching procedure" as one in which the instructional sequence depends upon the responses students make. A clear example of a *non*adaptive teaching procedure is a linear self-instructional program, such as the one on behavioral objectives in Chapter 1. As is shown in the flow chart below, each frame in the linear self-instruction program consists of a presentation and a question. The

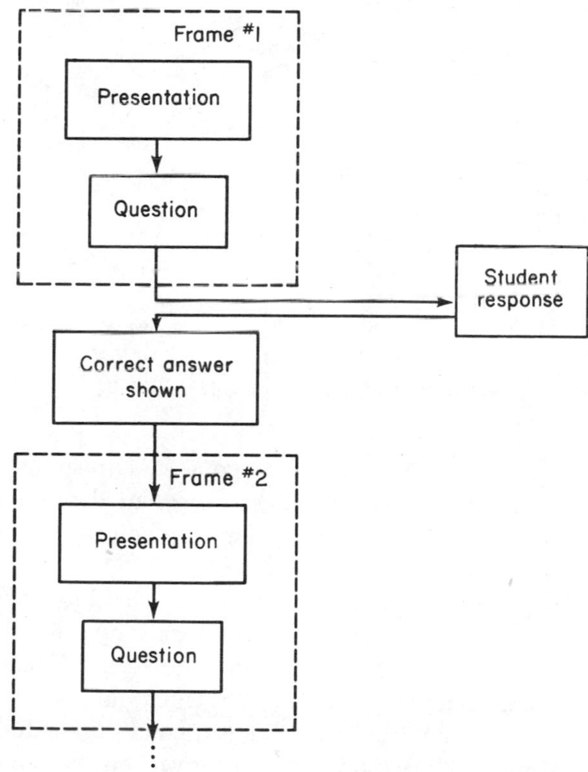

NONADAPTIVE TEACHING PROCEDURE

student gets the same feedback and the same sequence of frames no matter whether his responses are right or wrong. In fact, a program of this sort is called "linear" because the sequence is fixed.

Other examples of instruction which is usually nonadaptive are textbooks and lectures. In some senses, a linear program is certainly more adaptive than a lecture because, for instance, the student paces himself instead of having the pace determined by the teacher. However, in the specific sense used here a linear program is nonadaptive because the instructional sequence is fixed.

Many forms of knowledge of results and all correction procedures are adaptive. The simplest example of adaptive teaching is differential reinforcement.

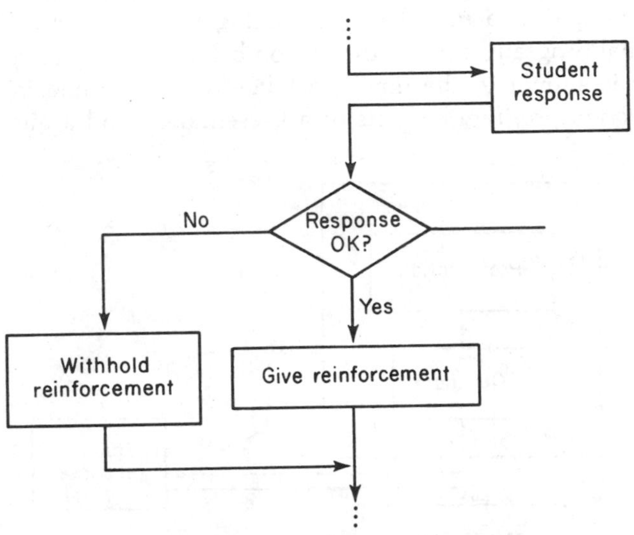

ADAPTIVE TEACHING PROCEDURE

Here at least part of the instructional sequence is response contingent. (As in the previous flow chart, the boxes represent the actions of either teacher or student; the diamond represents a choice point, decision, or discrimination.)

In each of the procedures described so far, the main line of the instructional sequence is fixed. A correction procedure adapts to student differences by making detours from the main sequence. When a student's performance is unsatisfactory, he may be asked simply to try the performance again, with or without further explanation; or he may be led through a lengthy auxiliary sequence. In any event, when such a procedure is used, the teacher or teaching materials direct the student back into the main sequence of the lesson as soon as his performance is satisfactory.

Fully adaptive teaching procedures. There is no overall, preplanned sequence in a fully adaptive lesson. The sequence that emerges depends upon what the student does and says. However, the teacher has a starting point and, hopefully, one or more clear objectives. He has planned various presentations, problems, questions, and tasks to use if certain contingencies arise, planning for the contingencies that analysis and previous experience indicate are likely. Planned activities are not used unless the contingency arises.

The shaping procedure described in the previous chapter is the simplest form of fully adaptive teaching. In shaping, there is no preplanned sequence. The teacher is guided at every step by learner performance. Below is a flow chart of a segment of instruction that employs shaping. (The material enclosed in circles represents the kind of diagnosis or decision the teacher is making.)

In shaping there are just two possible diagnoses at any moment. Either the behavior occurring is the best approximation that can be

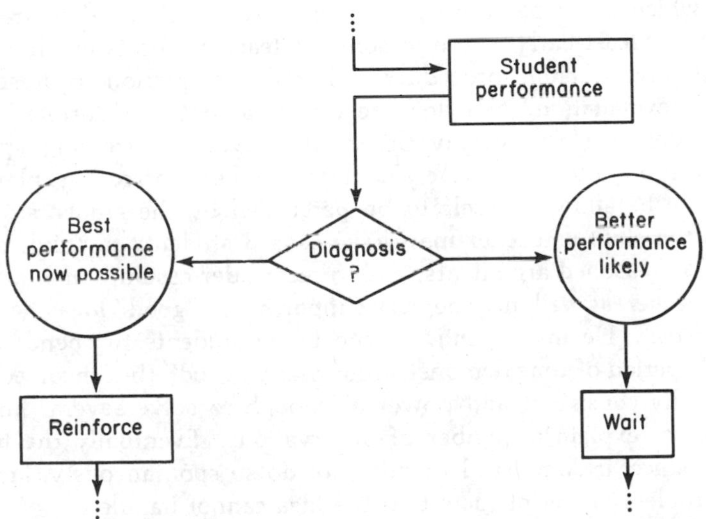

FULLY ADAPTIVE TEACHING PROCEDURE

The answer to the question on p. **280** *is* A.

expected at that time or a closer approximation is likely. And there are just two teacher tactics: reinforce for the first diagnosis; withhold reinforcement for the second.

Following a single student response, skilled teachers frequently consider several possible diagnoses, and for each diagnosis as many as several possible tactics. Fig. 8.1 diagrams some of the "moves" a teacher could consider following a single student response. Each subsequent student response will open up new possibilities. A diagram showing all of the contingencies that could arise and all of the courses of action a teacher could consider during a thirty-minute lesson would be enormously complicated.

Advocates of fully adaptive teaching procedures contend that these procedures have a special value for shaping up student skill at reasoning, inventing solutions to problems, inventing explanations of sets of facts, determining the internal consistency of arguments, and testing the generality of solutions and explanations. When a lesson has one or more of these purposes, the teacher is usually more interested in "good" ideas than in "correct" ideas. This is an important distinction. A "correct" idea is one which matches the theories of physicists, mathematicians, historians, economists, or whoever. A "good" idea, on the other hand, is one which could be true considering only the things known to the student. At least early in the lesson, the teacher who is employing the fully adaptive teaching procedure avoids the temptation to present the "correct" explanation. Nor does he readily accept the "correct" theory from students. He may play the devil's advocate, stressing apparent difficulties or counterintuitive features of the "correct" explanation. Eventually he allows himself to be persuaded by the students. In the process the skillful teacher may have caused students to think deeply, to develop reasoned arguments, and to reconsider assumptions.

The teacher, as well, may be very supportive of "good" ideas he knows are incorrect. He may spend, or encourage students to spend, a considerable period of time demonstrating that a "good" (but incorrect) idea is internally consistent and powerful enough to solve several kinds of problems or explain a number of observations. Eventually the teacher will introduce, if some student does not do so spontaneously, an argument, problem, or set of facts that the idea cannot handle.

Since fully adaptive teaching does not lend itself very well to abstract, general discussions, we turn now to two concrete illustrations.

An adaptive lesson in elementary school mathematics. By observing and then imitating Robert B. Davis, a gifted contemporary

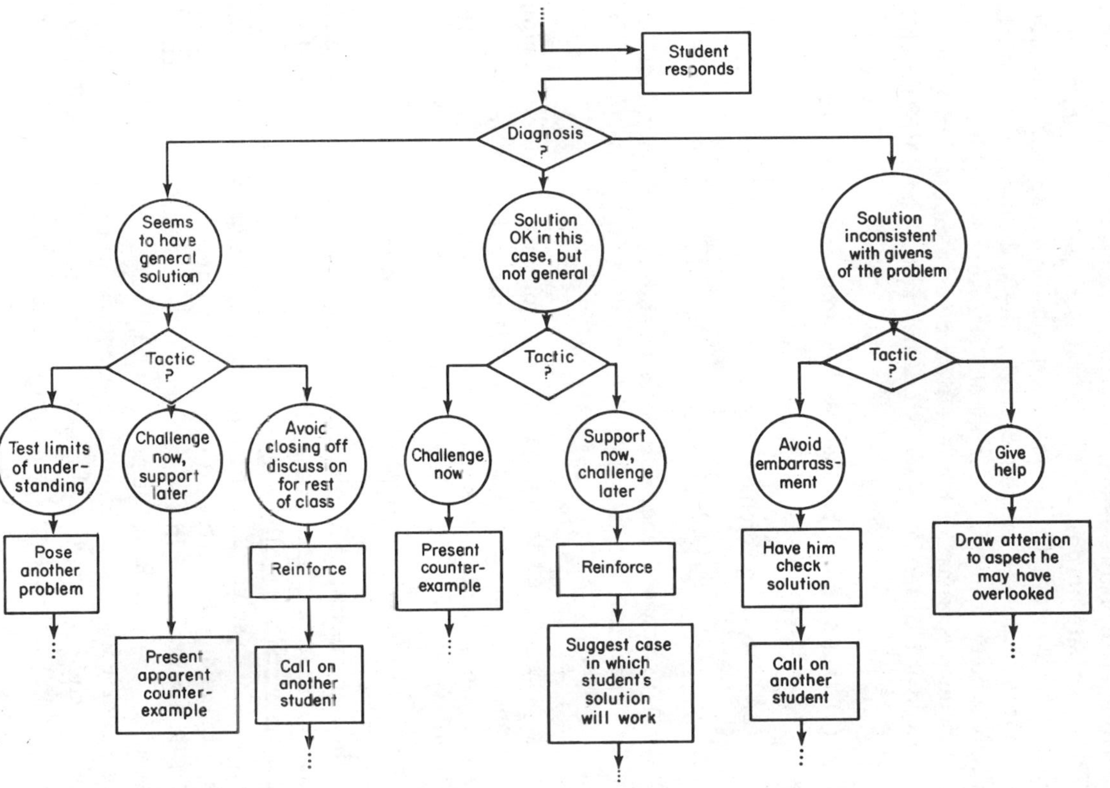

FIGURE 8.1 *Some courses of action after a single student response.*

mathematics educator, one of the authors of this text learned to teach a fascinating mathematics lesson.[1]

The immediate purpose of the lesson is to get fourth, fifth, or sixth graders to discover a rule for solving quadratic equations. It is assumed the children possess as entering behavior the ability to add, subtract, and multiply whole numbers. No previous exposure to algebra is assumed. The introductory phase of the lesson involves a more or less fixed main sequence, with correction when students have difficulty. The children learn

(1) that a □ can be filled with a number to make an expression true or false;

(2) to solve equations of the form

$$2 + \square = 5, (3 \times \square) + 1 = 7, (\square \times \square) = 36$$

(3) to add sequences of positive and negative numbers, such as

$$16 - 26 + 10 = \square.$$

The first phase of the lesson usually takes from twenty to thirty minutes. The second phase of the lesson is fully adaptive. The teacher begins the second phase by writing a quadratic equation, such as the following, on the board.

$$(\square \times \square) - (5 \times \square) + 6 = 0$$

The children are told that "the truth set for this sentence contains two numbers"; that is, in traditional language, there are two values for the unknown which satisfy the equation. (For those whose algebra is rusty, a simple way to solve quadratic equations is to find two numbers whose sum is the middle term [the 5 in the problem above] and whose product is the final term [the 6 in the problem above]. Applying this rule, the answers to the problem above are 2 and 3.)

To begin with, the children are encouraged to guess freely. Each number a child proposes is checked. Later the arithmetic will be completed for only an occasional problem—the teacher usually simply telling the child whether he is right or wrong. When the children finally hit on a correct pair of numbers, the board is erased and another problem is presented. The first several problems all entail small whole numbers, in order to facilitate guessing and checking.

[1] For Davis' own views on the teaching process, see "Discovery in the Teaching of Mathematics," in L. S. Shulman and E. R. Keislar, eds., *Learning by Discovery* (Chicago: Rand-McNally, 1966), pp. 115–128.

After a few problems, the following sequence of events is almost certain to occur:

TEACHER: Writes new problem on the board.
SHIRLEY: Immediately stands at seat, waves hand, and frantically says "I know!" "Please!"..."Please!"
TEACHER: Calls on Shirley.
SHIRLEY: Correctly gives *both* numbers.

Shirley may or may not have discovered the entire rule, but instead of probing Shirley's understanding, the teacher attempts to get the rest of the class to search for a rule. He says, "I think Shirley knows the secret. Don't tell anyone, will you, Shirley?"

After perhaps four or five children know the rule, or think they do, the teacher begins to present problems containing large numbers to those who solve when the numbers are small. For instance:

TEACHER: Writes

$$(\square \times \square) - (9 \times \square) + 14 = 0$$

TOMMY: Volunteers eagerly.
TEACHER: Calls on Tommy.
TOMMY: "2 and 7."
TEACHER: "Right!"
TEACHER: "Here's another one for you, Tommy." Writes

$$(\square \times \square) - (70 \times \square) + 1000 = 0$$

TOMMY: "20 and 50."

Those who are still using trial-and-error will be very impressed by the fact that it is possible to solve a problem involving such large numbers so quickly. The teacher should not assume that all or even most of those who think they have discovered the rule really know the entire rule. When maybe half of the class seems to have discovered something, the teacher should search for a child who will make a mistake like the following:

TEACHER: Writes

$$(\square \times \square) - (11 \times \square) + 24 = 0$$

MARTHA: "6 and 4."
TEACHER: "How many think that's right?"
CHILDREN: Some raise hands.
TEACHER: Substitutes 6 and completes arithmetic, shows that 6 is not correct.

Martha and the other children who raised their hands probably have discovered that the product of the two numbers must equal the last term. They do not appear to have discovered that the sum of the numbers must equal the middle term. Acting on this diagnosis, the teacher presents one at a time a series of problems like the following, replacing the middle term in each case but taking care never to erase the final term.

$$(\square \times \square) - (7 \times \square) + 12 = 0$$

$$(\square \times \square) - (8 \times \square) + 12 = 0$$

$$(\square \times \square) - (13 \times \square) + 12 = 0$$

The purpose of this sequence is to direct attention to the middle term in the equation. If there are still children who have not discovered the rule after a couple of series of this sort, try some problems like this:

$$(\square \times \square) - (1002 \times \square) + 2000 = 0$$

$$(\square \times \square) - (103 \times \square) + 300 = 0$$

An adaptive lesson in high school social studies. One of the most interesting feedback devices in adaptive teaching is the counterexample. A counterexample is a case to which a rule proposed by a student does not apply. Or it may entail a problem which cannot be solved with the technique the teacher infers the student is using. Counterexamples can also involve a situation like the one a student is considering, except that he feels differently about it. Illustrations of counterexamples are easy to find in mathematics and the sciences. For variety's sake, we have selected an illustration from the social studies.

A high school history teacher wants students to consider approaches to social change—revolution versus evolution, the politics of confrontation versus the politics of gradualism. He is as much concerned that his students develop feelings about these approaches as he is that they learn facts and theories. The teacher begins his teaching by reading a newspaper report of an incident in which five draft resisters have broken into a Selective Service office and burned the records. He asks the class how it feels about this incident. As it happens, most of the members of the class believe strongly that the draft resisters behaved reprehensibly. What follows is a condensed version of the dialogue which might take place.

TEACHER: Would you say that it is immoral to break the law?

FIRST STUDENT: Yes.

TEACHER: The draft resisters say the draft is immoral and that it's wrong to obey an immoral law.

FIRST STUDENT: You just can't burn draft cards and stuff like that.

TEACHER: You are saying that you have to obey laws even if you think they are immoral, is that right?

FIRST STUDENT: [No response.]
ANOTHER STUDENT: A protest is all right, but you can't break the law.

At this point, the teacher introduces his first counter-example.

TEACHER: Let's say you lived in this country in the 1770's. The government imposes new taxes. You don't want to pay, but you do because you always obey the law. Right?
STUDENTS: [No response.]
TEACHER: Which side would you have been on during the American Revolution, anyway? How many would have been on the English side? Let's see hands. [No hands.] How many would have been on the American side? [About two-thirds of the class.] Okay, John, [teacher picks an articulate student] *why* would you have been on the American side?
JOHN: Well, the taxes were unfair. The people couldn't vote on the taxes.
TEACHER: That's right. Taxation without representation. [Pause] If it was all right for the colonists to refuse to pay their taxes, why isn't it all right for the draft resisters to disobey the draft laws?
STUDENTS: [Many hands now.]
BILL: Things are different now. We have a democratic form of government. They had a dictatorship then.
TEACHER: You mean a feudal form of government?
BILL: Yes, a feudal system.
TEACHER: I don't see that things are any different. A good share of the people affected by the draft couldn't vote until recently because they were under 21. Isn't that right?
BILL: Well, 18-year-olds can vote now.
TEACHER: But the fact is, they couldn't vote at the time of this incident. Let's get this straight. You say the colonists had a moral right to disobey because they didn't have a voice in the government. Therefore, people under 21 had the right to disobey draft laws, because they didn't have a voice in the government. Isn't that logical?
BILL: [No response.]
TEACHER: Well, is it logical or isn't it?
BILL: It's logical, but I don't think it's right.
SYLVIA: In a democracy the majority rules.
TEACHER: Yes. The majority, or their elected representatives, have passed the draft laws. Thus, you would say everyone has the obligation to obey them. Is that what you are saying?
SYLVIA: Yes, that's right.

The teacher at this point prepares to introduce his second counter-example. Students are asked to read copies of a magazine article describing the Birmingham bus boycott and a speech by Martin Luther King. As they read, students are asked to formulate a personal answer to this question: "In a democracy, no matter what his personal beliefs, a citizen is morally obligated to obey the laws passed by the duly elected representatives of the people." The ensuing discussion may show that many students, because of their reading, have developed a sympathy for civil disobedience. Indeed, a few may have become enthusiastic activists.

The teacher, at this point, begins to suggest problems taking the position that each person should follow the dictates of his conscience instead of the dictates of the law. He asks questions such as, "If Martin Luther King and his followers could place themselves beyond the law, why can't the Ku Klux Klan?" The class is asked to study violent confrontations with the established order, such as riots in the inner city, confrontations between college students and faculty, the French revolution, and the American Civil War. Through these means, and others, the students are led to consider that a frontal assault on social institutions can reap a harvest of human misery, and often fail to achieve the goals of its instigators. In other words, through the use of counterexamples, the failures as well as the successes of revolutionaries, the progress as well as the inertia of moderates, can be illustrated.

The analogy between colonial revolutionaries and contemporary draft resisters can be milked for further discussion. The students seem to be especially outraged by the fact that draft resisters have burned draft cards and destroyed property. Can you think of a counterexample from the Revolutionary War era?

The answer appears on p. **292.**

Donald W. Oliver and James P. Shaver, in their provocative book *Teaching Public Issues in the High Sch*ool (1966), refer to this style of teaching as the "socratic" method. They state (p. 177):

> Socratic teaching, as we conceive it, is clearly adversarial. When the center of discussion is a controversial political topic—as in our work—socratic teaching requires that the student do more than describe the controversy in the terms in which the teacher (or assigned materials) has presented it. Rather, the teacher requires the student to take a position on the issue, state that position, and defend it. Here the emphasis is not only on knowledge provided by the teacher as background for the discussion but on the process by which the student arrives at a decision about the topic under consideration, on the careful consideration of alternative decisions, and on the utilization of analytic concepts and strategies, regardless of the position which is finally reached.

Oliver and Shaver describe a variety of instructional materials which can be used with the socratic method, and they compare and contrast this style with alternative teaching techniques.

Reflections on fully adaptive teaching. Prospective teachers are likely to be intrigued with the fully adaptive teaching procedures illustrated in the preceding sections. It is with regret that we must report that the research to date has failed to demonstrate any significant advantages for these procedures. With respect to the socratic method, Oliver and Shaver (1966, p. 301) have reported that the most striking result of a lengthy comparison of this method with a "recitation method" was "that groups taught by the two styles behaved similarly on every measure of learning administered."

It would be premature to conclude that fully adaptive teaching styles are without merit. Despite eighty years of research in which literally thousands of experiments have been completed, there is still controversy over the processes entailed in something as apparently simple as learning to associate pairs of nonsense syllables. Systematic research on teaching techniques is in its infancy. One can hope that future analysis and research will reveal the ways to make adaptive teaching consistently successful, perhaps even more stimulating and effective than most techniques in use today. In the meantime, we shall offer our opinions, even though they are unsupported by hard data, on how to make fully adaptive teaching work.

We believe that at its best fully adaptive teaching is not a hit-and-miss procedure wandering aimlessly from topic to topic. In our opinion it takes planning to make a fully adaptive lesson successful. We fear that spokesmen for adaptive styles of teaching have placed exaggerated emphasis on such qualities as spontaneity and free student participation. While adaptive teaching does have these qualities, we believe the heart of this teaching process involves (1) diagnosis of the state of the student's knowledge from the responses he is making, and (2) given the diagnosis, the selection of the appropriate teaching tactic. Planning is obviously important in that the teacher will be better able to make diagnoses and select tactics if he has analyzed the contingencies that are likely to arise in the course of the lesson and has planned ways of dealing with them.

SELF-TEST ON CORRECTIVE FEEDBACK

Complete this test on a separate sheet of paper, then check answers against the scoring key on p. 293.

The first three questions are based on the following information.

A teacher has presented an oral explanation to a fifth-grade class of the differences between the three homophones (words with different spellings and meanings which sound alike) *there, they're,* and *their.* He then writes a series of sentences one at a time on the chalk board with blanks to be filled by the students. He writes "__________ over at my house" and a student supplies *their.*

1. Describe three *specific* kinds of knowledge of results which the teacher could give to the student who supplied *their.*
2. Describe the *simplest* correction procedure which the teacher could use with this student.
3. Describe in concrete terms a more elaborate correction procedure that could be employed with the student who misused *their.*
4. What are the chief characteristics of a fully adaptive lesson?
5. Name at least one problem which can arise when students are provided with immediate knowledge of results. Suggest ways to solve each problem.
6. Which of the following is likely to be *least* effective when a student makes a mistake?

   a. Ignoring the student; withholding reinforcement.
   b. Telling the student he is wrong.
   c. Telling the student he is wrong and explaining why he is wrong.
   d. Telling the student he is wrong and providing the correct answer.
   e. Telling the student he is wrong, providing the correct answer, and explaining why it is correct.

Answer to the question on p. **290.**

A counterexample is the Boston Tea Party, which students are likely to regard as a noble, courageous, and patriotic act. When the close parallel between the burning of draft records and the destruction of tea is brought to their attention, students will undoubtedly reconsider their feelings toward violent social change.

Summary

At each step in a well-conceived lesson, the student will have been so thoroughly prepared by preceding steps that he is almost sure to behave satisfactorily. However, should the student err, the teacher must take corrective action. The simplest thing the teacher (or teaching materials) can do is provide knowledge of results. Knowledge of results reinforces satisfactory performance and furnishes corrective feedback when performance is unsatisfactory. Research indicates that knowledge of results is more effective when it contains information about what the correct response should be, rather than merely letting the student know he is wrong. Sometimes when immediate knowledge of results is provided, students get careless and pay less attention. This danger can be avoided by taking steps to insure that the student actually responds before he is exposed to knowledge of results and by increasing the incentive for correct responding.

Knowledge of results alone allows the student to be passive. Correction procedures have the virtue of requiring the student actively to make the correct response before he proceeds. Research indicates that correction procedures are often more effective than only knowledge of results.

The sequence of instruction in a fully adaptive lesson depends at every step upon student performance. The teacher decides after each student response what the next step should be. Unfortunately, research has not yet shown special advantages for fully adaptive procedures nor clarified the techniques for making fully adaptive procedures successful.

SCORING KEY FOR THE SELF-TEST ON CORRECTIVE FEEDBACK

This test will be scored on a point basis. There are 13 possible points. A score of 10 is satisfactory. Review the sections of the text that deal with questions that gave you trouble.

1. (*3 points*) Some possibilities are

(1) No, that's wrong.
(1) The correct answer is *they're.*
(1) *They're* is the right answer. *They're* means "they are." "They are over at my house" makes sense, doesn't it?
(1) That's not right. *Their* means something belongs to them. It wouldn't make any sense to say "over at my house belongs to them."

Give yourself one point for each concrete reply (up to 3) you listed. Your list need not match the one presented here.

2. (*1 point*)

The simplest correction procedure would be to indicate to the student that his response is not correct and then ask him to try again.

3. (*2 points*)

There are many possible kinds of hints, simplified problems, and further explanations that can be given to the student before he is asked to try again. Here is one such sequence for the student who supplies *their* in the expression "__________ over at my house."

TEACHER: *Their* [writes *their*] means "something belongs to them." If you write "their car" you mean the car belongs to them.
Which word goes in this blank?

The boy took one of __________ marbles.

STUDENT: [Writes *their.*]
TEACHER: Very good! Yes, that's right.
TEACHER: *They're* [writes *they're*] is a contraction for "they are." Which word would you put in this blank?

__________ *in the kitchen.*

STUDENT: [Writes *they're.*]
TEACHER: Good! You understand it now. Try this one again.

__________ *over at my house.*

STUDENT: [Writes *they're.*]
TEACHER: Yes, that's right.

While the student has now properly completed this sentence, it cannot be assumed he has mastered the distinctions between the three homophones until he has responded correctly in other sentences in which the grammar is varied. Credit yourself with two points if you

(1) described any specific hint or explanation, not necessarily as involved as the one described here;

(1) then indicated the student would be asked to try again the problem he originally missed.

4. (*2 points*)

Credit one point if you said that the sequence of instruction in an adaptive lesson depends at every step upon student performance. Give yourself one more point if you mentioned that for each student response the teacher makes a diagnosis and selects a teaching tactic.

5. (*4 points*)

One problem is that when the student is wrong, knowledge of results is nonreinforcing and sometimes punishing. The remedy is to design the instruction so that the student is usually right. Give yourself two points for naming this problem and suggesting this solution.

Another problem is that students may become careless and inattentive when immediate knowledge of results is always provided. The remedy is to make sure that the students have responded (overtly or covertly) before knowledge of results is provided and/or to increase the incentive for responding correctly the first time. This problem and solution are worth two points. If you named both problems and described a solution to each, credit yourself with four points.

6. (*1 point*) **a**

Ignoring the mistake is likely to be least effective.

Selected Readings

Anderson, R. C., "Educational Psychology," *Annual Review of Psychology* (1967), *18*, 129–164. See pp. 145–154. This review pays special attention to the question of whether knowledge of results functions as reinforcement or corrective feedback.

Anderson, R. C., Faust, G. W., Roderick, M. C., Cunningham, D. J., & Andre, T., eds., "Section V. Feedback and Reinforcement," *Current Research on Instruction*. Englewood Cliffs, N.J.: Prentice-Hall, 1969. Included are reports of research on knowledge of results and correction procedures, as well as descriptions of research on reinforcement.

Gagné, R. M., & Rohwer, W. D., "Instructional Psychology," *Annual Review of Psychology* (1969), *20*, 381–418. See pp. 398–401. Research since Anderson's review, listed above, is described.

CHAPTER

9

Stimulus Control

The preceding three chapters have considered techniques for teaching students new responses, the conditions under which responses should be requested from students, as well as methods for modifying behavior using reinforcement and feedback. This chapter deals with teaching students *when* to give the responses and use the skills which they have acquired.

People get signals from their environment which tell them when and under what circumstances to use the skills they have acquired. Without such cues skills would be of little value. For instance, a person may report that he didn't "think of" dividing to solve an arithmetic problem. Very likely the person failed to divide because he had not learned to pay attention to the cues which are supposed to signal the division skill into action. The person who completes this chapter should be able to:

> describe specific procedures for teaching students to notice the cues which should signal a response or skill into action.

The generic term for a cue which tends to evoke, guide, or regulate behavior is *discriminative stimulus* (symbolized S^D and pronounced "ess dee"). When behavior is evoked by an S^D, the S^D is said to *control* the behavior. The term "control" is a strong word which may seem to be synonymous with "cause"; however, it should be understood here in a weaker sense. The sound of the doorbell tends to evoke door-opening behavior; a red light at an intersection tends to evoke a stopping response from motorists; and a pretty girl tends to evoke a looking response from most males. We have carefully used the phrase "tends to evoke" in these examples, rather than a strong word such as "cause," for in the examples the stimulus is neither a necessary nor a sufficient condition for a response. For instance, we are not compelled to open the door when the doorbell rings. The doorbell merely "sets the occasion" for the door-opening response; the doorbell makes it highly probable that one will open the door if no other stimuli, such as a cake burning in the oven, are in control of one's behavior at the moment. Thus, a stimulus controls a response if it sets the occasion for this response.[1]

As people grow older, more and more of their behavior comes under stimulus control. In fact, one major difference between a young child and an adult is that the adult "knows" what behavior is appropriate in a wider variety of situations. That is, there are a greater variety of stimuli which control an adult's behavior. In the complex world of the classroom and in the real world in general, however, it is seldom the case that a single stimulus could be said to control a single response. Therefore, it is important to be aware that the concept of stimulus control applies also to more complex cases, in which sets of stimuli control sets of responses. For example, the botany student's response, "This tree is a spruce pine (pinus glabra)," is under the control of various stimuli, which should include short, needlelike leaves that are borne in clusters of two—as well as reddish-brown, shiny cones with minute prickles. Complex sets of stimuli which control one response or a class of responses are often referred to as "concepts." In the next chapter we shall extend the present discussion of stimulus control to include concepts and principles. This chapter will focus on a description of the basic procedures for establishing stimulus control.

In order for a stimulus to control a response, a response must occur in some strength, and the range of stimuli which evoke this response must be narrowed. Consider the case of the parents who are attempting to teach their child to say "dada" in response to daddy's smiling face. The parents' task is twofold. They must first get their child to say "dada" in the presence of his father and then they must limit the range of stimuli which evoke this response.

As the parents narrow the range of stimuli to which the child responds "dada," they are improving stimulus control. Stimuli which are physically very dissimilar from the child's father will be easily discriminated from him; therefore it will be very easy to teach the child to respond to father and these other stimuli differently. For example, the child's father may be easily distinguished from inanimate objects, less easily from females, and still less easily from other males. Although there is some degree of stimulus control in evidence when the child responds "dada" only to males, the child's parents—and especially the child's father—

[1] Stimulus control has nothing to do with political or social control, in which one person or group forces its will on another.

will probably not consider this amount of stimulus control adequate. They will undoubtedly desire a greater degree of stimulus control, in this case control by one and only one stimulus (the child's father). As the child gets older and more adept at using language, the control of the "dada" response may again spread to a variety of stimulus situations—such as when the child is referring to his father (e.g., "Daddy went to work"), or when the child desires attention. Note that these may include situations in which the father is not actually present. However, before this more complex behavior can be acquired, the parents must get the child to attach the verbal response "dada" to his father. In common language, they must teach the child the meaning of the word "dada."

When stimulus control is complete the response will almost always occur in the presence of the S^D and seldom occur in the presence of other stimuli. A hypothetical example of the probability of the child's "dada" response in the presence of various people is plotted in Fig. 9.1. Assume that the people are arranged on the "persons" continuum in terms of how much they look like daddy. Note both aspects of stimulus control at work: as training proceeds (1) the probability of response to the appropriate stimulus increases, while (2) the probability of response to inappropriate stimuli decreases. In other words the child becomes more likely to say "dada" when he sees his father and less likely to say "dada" when he sees his aunts and uncles.

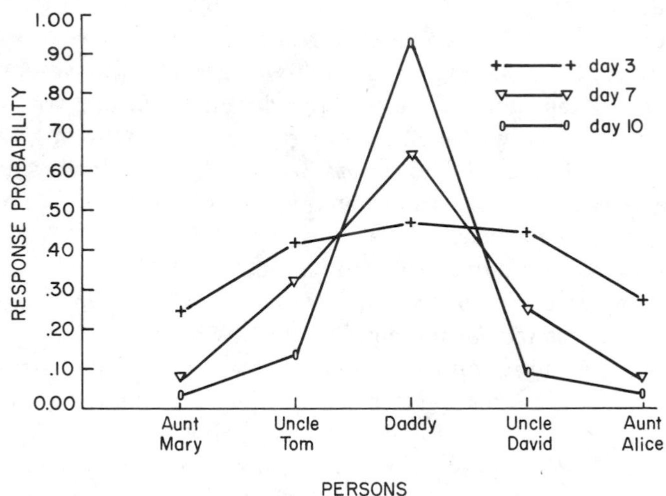

FIGURE 9.1 *Probability of a hypothetical child responding "dada" to several persons 3, 7, and 10 days after the start of training.*

Please make covert responses to the following questions.

A. When a car pulls into his driveway, a certain small boy usually runs to the door shouting "daddy is home." This running and shouting behavior could be said to be under the ____________ of the car-coming-into-driveway stimulus.

B. If the boy makes this response only when his father's car comes into the driveway we could say that ____________ ____________ is perfect (or appropriate).

The answers appear on p. **300.**

Discrimination

In order for a stimulus to control a response, the organism must be able to *discriminate* this stimulus from other stimuli. To discriminate two stimuli means to notice or pay attention to a difference between them.[2]

To some extent attention is observable. One can, for instance, sometimes determine where the eyes are looking. Usually, though, the aspect of a stimulus which a person is paying attention to, or discriminating, must be identified by inference rather than direct observation. This was illustrated in an experiment by Underwood, Ham, and Ekstrand (1962). The task was a paired associate list in which the stimuli were CVC trigrams printed in black on distinctive colored backgrounds. Upon learning the first list, the subjects were tested on a second list identical to the first except that the stimuli were either the CVC's alone or the colors alone. Those who received color stimuli performed almost perfectly on the second list, whereas those who got the CVC's showed no evidence of learning. One can *infer* from this experiment that the subjects discriminated colors instead of one or more of the letters in the trigrams, although one could not observe that behavior directly.

Everything in this world possesses a variety of more or less distinguishable features (attributes, properties, qualities). Any two objects or events acting as stimuli may have many features in common; in other respects they will differ. Obviously, therefore, stimuli cannot be dis-

[2] Many psychologists use the term "discrimination" to refer to making a response to one stimulus and not making it in the presence of other stimuli. By this definition, "discrimination" is synonymous with "stimulus control." We are using "discrimination" to refer to a perceptual or sensory process which is part of, but not the same as, stimulus control.

criminated on the basis of common features. They must be discriminated in terms of differences.

Any difference can provide the basis for a discrimination. This is an important fact. An infant could identify his father by the feel or appearance of a tweedy sport jacket his father often wears. If this were the case, the child would not be able to recognize his father if he were dressed in a T-shirt. It cannot be assumed, then, that a person automatically will pay attention to the predicted or expected distinctive features of an object or event.

The *nominal stimulus* comprises all of the features an object or event physically possesses. The *functional stimulus,* on the other hand, consists of the features an organism looks at, listens to, or otherwise senses. The functional stimulus is seldom the same as the nominal stimulus. Organisms seldom pay attention to all of the features of a stimulus. For example persons watching an auto race pay attention to only selected parts of the entire scene before them and ignore others. Similarly, children learning to sight-read begin by paying attention to only selected parts of the words they are presented. They may learn that they say "red" whenever they see a short word with a tall line at the end. This can be very disconcerting for the teacher, especially when he wants to teach another word such as "rut" or "mad," but it indicates the importance of the distinction between the nominal stimulus (in this case the entire three-letter word being presented to the student) and the functional stimulus (that aspect of the word which the student is focusing on to make his response).

Feature relevance. Different features of stimuli have different degrees of relevance. Completely relevant or critical features allow perfect discrimination, while a person paying attention to partially-relevant features will make some discrimination errors. The father's tweedy sport jacket is an example of a partially-relevant feature. The father undoubtedly possesses characteristics of appearance, speech, or personality which are highly distinctive, if not unique. Such distinctive characteristics are relevant features. The father can always or almost always be discriminated on the basis of them. But it is important to remember that people can respond correctly some of the time by noticing partially-relevant or even irrelevant features.

Answers to the questions on p. **299.**

A. control
B. stimulus control

A first grader correctly reads aloud the sentence, *The sun comes up in the morning.* Can it be assumed that the child actually read the word "morning"?

The answer is in the paragraph below.

A person can read a word if (1) he can always say the word when confronted with the sequence of letters which represents the word; and (2) he never says the word when presented with the letters which form other words. Technically speaking, when these two conditions are met, the printed form of the word controls the reader's response. It may be that the reader can say the word easily, almost spontaneously, when he sees the printed form—in which case the word would be said to be in his sight vocabulary. Or, he may sound out the letters and then blend the sounds until he can say the word. In any event, a person is not reading a word unless he is paying attention to the distinctive features of the letters in the word and discriminating these letters from other possible combinations of letters.

Suppose that a first grader cannot read "morning." He might, nonetheless, be able to say "morning" if it were included in the sentence, *The sun comes up in the morning.* The word "morning" can be guessed from this context. Consider that many children would probably say "morning" if asked to complete *The sun comes up in the* __________. Or, the child might sound out the first letter of "morning" and guess the rest of the word from the context. If this were the case, he would "read" any one of the following three sentences the same way.

The sun comes up in the morning.
The sun comes up in the mortuary.
The sun comes up in the meadow.

If a child can actually read the word "morning," he will be able to do so either when the word is presented alone or in a sentence in which the context is not helpful; for instance, *Spot came home in the morning.* The point is that context provides cues which are only partially relevant. While a reader can and should use context cues to some extent, he is not reading if all he is doing is guessing at words from the context.

Physical capacity to discriminate. What factors determine the features of a stimulus which an organism will notice? The first factor is the physical capacity of the organism to discriminate. The smallest unit of difference that an organism can detect is called a *just* *noticeable difference* (*jnd*). Human *jnd's* have been determined for such stimulus features as brightness, hue (color), loudness, and pitch. The procedure is to ask experienced judges (working under optimal conditions) to try to detect differences between pairs of stimuli. The smallest difference which the judges can reliably detect is a *jnd*. For an example, a pitch *jnd* for adults in the octave above middle C is about three cycles per second, or, in other words, about one-eighth of a musical half step.

The role of sensory experience. Experience is a second factor which influences whether a person or an animal will discriminate a stimulus feature. Organisms discriminate features of stimuli which they have learned to pay attention to in the past. Caucasians are sometimes heard to say that all Chinese or all Negroes look alike. In reality Orientals and Negroes are just as discriminable as Caucasians.

Previous experience with a stimulus feature greatly facilitates discrimination and the development of stimulus control. Ganz and Riesen (1962) have performed an interesting experiment with Macaque monkeys which illustrates this fact. They separated two groups of monkeys from their mothers immediately after birth. For the next ten weeks one group was raised in darkness, while the second was raised under normal visual conditions. Both groups received identical treatment in all other respects. Then both groups were placed in the dark and trained in daily sessions to press a key to get water. Reinforcement was given when a light of a certain hue was on but not given when no light was present. Dark-reared monkeys took an average of one month longer than light-reared monkeys to learn to respond only when the light was on. After training, the monkeys were given tests for stimulus control. The test stimuli consisted of lights with various degrees of similarity in hue to the light which was present during training. The light-reared monkeys showed evidence of stimulus control. That is, they seldom responded to lights of a different color than the training light. Their dark-reared counterparts responded almost equally to all of the test stimuli, indicating that they were not paying attention to color differences, only to the presence or absence of light. After several exposures to the test stimuli, the dark-reared monkeys began to show some evidence of stimulus control but never to the degree that the light-reared monkeys did.

The Ganz and Riesen experiment, among others (e.g., Peterson, 1962), indicates that organisms will much more readily learn to pay attention to a stimulus feature if they have had previous experience with it. The same principle applies to humans. Before they enter school, children have experience with a great variety of forms, color, sounds, and so on. Formal schooling builds on this experience. It is believed that one reason culturally-disadvantaged children tend to do relatively poorly in school is a deficit of the kind of experience—particularly in the area of language—that most middle-class children have had. Fortunately, there is some evidence that the deficits of the culturally-disadvantaged can be overcome with intensive, carefully-conceived training (Bereiter & Engelmann, 1966).

As people grow older, they typically become better able to discriminate the countless numbers of features which the stimuli in the environment exhibit. For instance, Duell and Anderson (1967) investigated pitch discrimination among first, second, and third graders. Their results appear in Table 9.1. Notice that third graders detected smaller differences than second graders, who in turn detected smaller differences than first graders. The first grader is as physically able to discriminate pitches as the third grader, so the improvement from first to third grade must have been due to experience, probably music instruction in school and incidental experience with sounds and music.

TABLE 9.1 *Cumulative percentage of children who consistently discriminated pitch differences of given sizes (from Duell & Anderson, 1967).*

Interval	*Grade*			
	First	*Second*	*Third*	*All grades*
Sixth	94	94	100	96
Fourth	91	91	100	94
Sharpened second	78	86	95	86
Half step	59	66	80	68
Two-thirds half step	36	40	60	45
One-third half step	6	12	20	13

Generalization

Generalization and discrimination are complementary processes. To discriminate is to notice a difference between stimuli and act accordingly. To generalize is to fail to notice or to ignore a difference. Another way to describe generalization is to say that it involves paying attention to *similarities* among stimuli. An organism is generalizing when it makes the same response to two or more distinguishable stimuli. For instance, the infant who calls his aunts and uncles "dada" is generalizing. In simple language, generalization means treating different stimuli as though they were equivalent.

An organism will always generalize when it is not physically capable of detecting differences among stimuli. An organism will make the same response to stimuli less than one *jnd* apart. Previous experience also affects generalization. The dark-reared monkeys in the Ganz and Riesen (1962) experiment were physically capable of discriminating colors; however, the dark environment in which they were reared had not prepared them to notice color differences. Consequently, unlike the light-reared monkeys, the dark-reared monkeys pressed the key no matter what the color of the light. The light-reared monkeys discriminated. The dark-reared monkeys generalized.

Sometimes generalization is appropriate and sometimes it is not. Parents want their child to discriminate his father from other men. But if the same parents take their child to the zoo and teach him to call a grizzly bear a bear, they hope that he will generalize to brown bears, polar bears, and koala bears. Whether the child will generalize depends upon his previous experience. The child is perfectly capable of telling polar bears and grizzly bears apart. Nonetheless, he may spontaneously generalize among bears if he has, for instance, learned to call various creatures dogs despite differences in size, color, fur length, and texture.

Education requires both generalization and discrimination. The child must learn to discriminate between letters but generalize among different representations of the same letter (upper case and lower case, cursive and printed, etc.). The general point is that school learning always entails noticing similarities and ignoring differences, as well as noticing differences and ignoring similarities.

Due to the enormous influence of such psychologists as Clark L. Hull (1943), generalization has long been regarded as an automatic process. Once an organism learned a response to a certain stimulus, it was presumed to be inevitable that it would generalize to other, similar stimuli. As will be detailed later in this chapter, recent evidence indicates that neither generalization nor discrimination is automatic. Which will occur and to what extent depends upon the general experience of the organism and on specific training. This fact is of practical importance to education. Students cannot be counted on to discriminate when discrimination is appropriate nor to generalize when generalization would be desirable. Teachers must not rely on automatic processes to take the place of instruction.

It may seem that generalization is antithetical to the development of stimulus control, and, indeed, it can be. In the real world, though, a single stimulus seldom controls a response. Usually it is hoped that several stimuli will control the response. The learner must generalize from these stimuli. A single object can appear in different guises. It can be viewed from different perspectives, from a short distance or a long distance, in the light or in the dark, in one context or another. The learner must generalize across these variations. Generalization is especially important in the learning of concepts. A person "knows" a concept when a certain class of stimuli control a response. All bears comprise a class of stimuli. When a child calls any bear a "bear" (and calls no other creature by this name), he knows the concept. The child must generalize among bears to learn the concept. Procedures for teaching people to generalize will be detailed in the next chapter. This chapter will emphasize discrimination learning.

Stimulus Control and Respondent Conditioning

We turn now to a consideration of procedures for establishing stimulus control. The first procedure is to pair a stimulus with another stimulus which already controls the response. Under the proper circumstances, the first stimulus will acquire the power to evoke the response. This process is called *respondent conditioning.*[3]

It has long been realized that events which occur together tend to become associated. The laws governing the associative process have been a major topic of discussion for philosophers and psychologists since the time of Aristotle. It was not, however, until the advent of systematic and objective research that much light was shed on the specific mechanisms of the associative process. Surprisingly, some of the first great insights into the associative process came neither from a psychologist nor by design.

While studying the digestive activity of dogs, Ivan Petrovich Pavlov, a Russian physiologist, devised an apparatus which allowed him to collect and measure the flow of saliva secreted by his dog subjects in response to the stimulus of food placed in the mouth. As his experiment progressed, Pavlov noticed that the dogs often began to salivate before the food actually reached the mouth. Just the sight of the food dish or the approach of the attendant who customarily brought the food caused the dogs to salivate. Pavlov realized that the sight of the food dish and the approach of the attendant, which were not natural stimuli for salivation, had, through experience, come to be a signal to the dog that food was coming. Moreover, he felt that research on this "conditioned reflex" would lead to new insights in the area of brain physiology. Excited by his discovery, Pavlov designed many experiments to demonstrate the conditioning process, to test its limitations, and to test his own hypotheses as to the nature of brain functioning during conditioning.

The essential features of Pavlov's conditioning procedure can best be

[3] Respondent conditioning is also called "classical conditioning."

introduced by describing a typical Pavlovian experiment (Anrep, 1920). After a minor operation in which a duct of the parotid gland was diverted so that saliva flowed through an opening in the cheek, a small glass funnel was firmly attached to the opening to collect the saliva. The dog was then placed in a harness (see Fig. 9.2) and left quiet for a while.

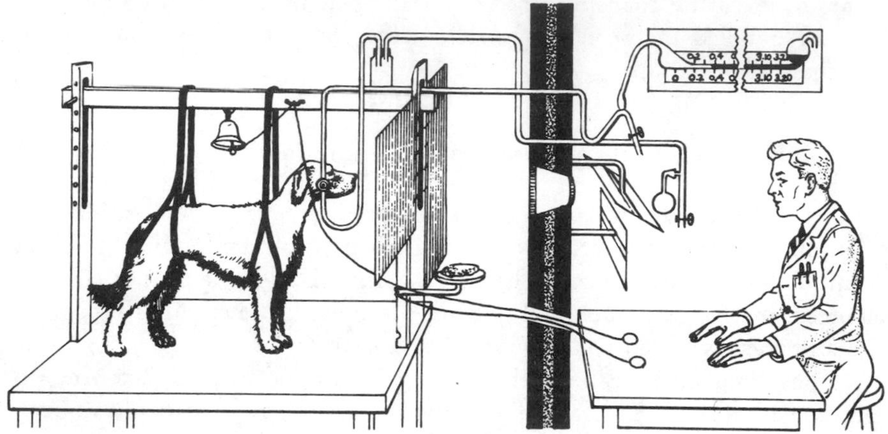

FIGURE 9.2 *Pavlov's arrangement for the study of salivary conditioning (from Morgan & King, 1966.)*

The experimenter occupied an adjoining room, and could observe the dog through a small window. From this vantage point he presented stimuli by means of automatic devices. Once the dog had become adapted to the harness, a tuning fork was sounded. Seven seconds later a plate holding a small measured amount of food powder was placed in front of the dog and he was allowed to eat it. The tone and food were presented together three times during each daily session. The three trials were spaced from 5 to 35 minutes apart at random intervals over an 18-day period. The strength of the conditioned response (salivation to the tone) was determined by presenting the tone alone for 30 seconds on trials 1, 10, 20, 30, 40, and 50 and then measuring the amount of salivation and the elapsed time between the presentation of the tone and the onset of salivation. Table 9.2 shows data typical of this type of experiment.

Notice that on the first trial the tone did not elicit salivation. On this trial the tone can be said to be a *neutral stimulus* (*NS*) with respect to the salivation response. The *NS* is a stimulus which has no effect on the to-be-conditioned response prior to conditioning. The food powder, on the other hand, does elicit salivation in this situation without any conditioning and is therefore referred to as an *unconditioned stimulus* (*UCS*).

TABLE 9.2 *Magnitude of response (number of drops of saliva) and response latency (time between onset of tone and salivation) by trials in a respondent conditioning experiment in which a tone is presented in conjunction with food powder.*

I	*II*	*III*
Trial number (tone presented alone)	*Drops of saliva*	*Time between onset of tone and salivation (in seconds)*
1	0	—
10	6	18
20	20	9
30	60	2
40	62	1
50	59	2

In Pavlov's experiment (Fig. 9.2) only nine pairings of the neutral stimulus (tone) and the unconditioned stimulus (food powder) were necessary to show evidence of conditioning (salivation to the tone alone). Once conditioning has begun, the formerly neutral stimulus is customarily referred to as a conditioned stimulus (*CS*), because through conditioning it has come to elicit the conditioned response (*CR*). In the language used throughout the rest of this book, both the *UCS* and the *CS* are considered as discriminative stimuli. The *UCS* is an S^D before conditioning and the *CS* becomes an S^D because of conditioning. In the remainder of this section, we shall use the language and notation customarily used in discussions of respondent conditioning.

Look again at Table 9.2. What happens to the conditioned response as conditioning proceeds? A covert response will do, but be sure to study the entire figure before answering.

The answer is presented in the following paragraph.

As conditioning proceeds the *magnitude* of the *CR* increases (i.e., the number of drops of saliva elicited by the *CS* increases from test trial to test trial). At the same time the *latency* (i.e., time before beginning) of the *CR* decreases. These two measures, magnitude and response latency, are indices of the strength of the conditioned response; and in this experiment these measures give evidence that the *CR* increases in strength as conditioning proceeds. As can be seen in Table 9.2, the magnitude of the *CR* does not increase indefinitely, but rather stabilizes at around sixty drops. Likewise, the latency of the *CR* stabilizes at about two seconds. When response magnitude has reached its maximum and response latency has reached its minimum, conditioning is complete. This does not mean, however, that conditioning is permanent. If the *CS* and *UCS* do not occur together for many trials, the magnitude of the response will begin to decrease, and the latency of the response will increase. This process—like that in operant conditioning when reinforcement no longer follows a previously reinforced response—is called *extinction*.

Respondent conditioning can involve various stimuli since either the *CS* or the *UCS* can take several forms. However, there is a general pattern or model for respondent conditioning which includes the essential ingredients of the process. In science such general models are often referred to as *paradigms*. The respondent conditioning paradigm is presented in Fig. 9.3. The *NS*, which prior to conditioning does not elicit the response, is presented *before* the *UCS*, a stimulus which does elicit the response prior to conditioning. Sometime after the presentation of the *NS* the *UCS* is introduced and it elicits (draws out) the response. Through conditioning the *NS* acquires some of the eliciting function of the *UCS*, and will therefore elicit the response when presented alone. At this point the *NS* has become a conditioned stimulus (*CS*).

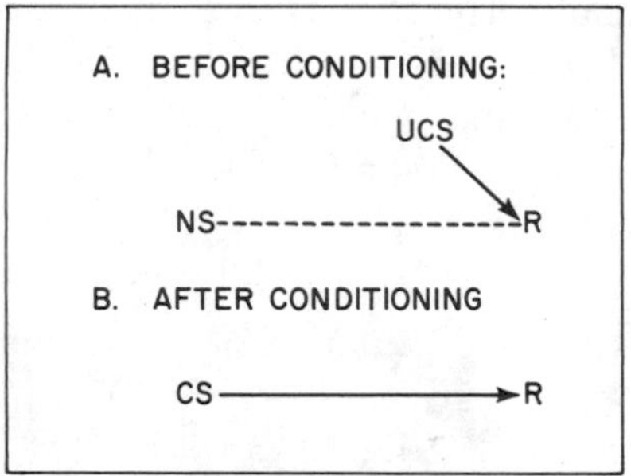

FIGURE 9.3 *The respondent conditioning paradigm. The dashed line is used to show the passage of time, whereas the arrow indicates the eliciting function of the stimulus.*

It should be mentioned that the response to the *CS* is not exactly the same as to the *UCS*. For instance, the dog does not make chewing or swallowing responses to the tone, whereas he does to the food powder. The responses to the *UCS* may not always be qualitatively different from those to the *CS*, but there are always differences in at least the quantitative characteristics of the reaction (i.e., amount of salivation, latency of response, etc.). Because of this, psychologists have postulated that the response to the *CS* can be considered either a fractional component of the response to the *UCS* or a preparation for the unconditioned stimulus.

The sequence of events in respondent conditioning is critical. It has been amply demonstrated that the *NS* must precede the *UCS* if conditioning is to take place. Many attempts have been made to produce conditioning by presenting the *UCS* before the onset of the *NS*, a procedure often referred to as *backward conditioning.* These attempts have generally had little or no success (Bernstein, 1934; Cason, 1935; Porter, 1938). Conditioning has been achieved, however, through many variations of the forward conditioning paradigm. In some experiments the *NS* appeared prior to the *UCS* and continued up to the time of the *UCS* presentation. In still other cases the *NS* was terminated either before or after the presentation of the *UCS*.

The time interval between the onset of the *NS* and the onset of the *UCS*, called the *interstimulus interval,* has been shown to markedly affect the conditioning process. The *NS* must be presented almost immediately before the *UCS* if conditioning is to proceed efficiently. Pavlov experimented with various interstimulus intervals and found that intervals of 0–5 seconds produced the fastest conditioning. He referred to experiments using these short intervals as instances of "simultaneous presentation" of *NS* and *UCS*, and apparently could find little differences in ease of conditioning between intervals within this range. More recent research in the United States, however, indicates that the optimal interval is much shorter than 5 seconds, and is more likely .5 seconds (Kimble, 1947; Kimble, Mann & Dufort, 1955; Moeller, 1954; White & Schlosberg, 1952).

Respondent conditioning has been demonstrated to have considerable generality with respect to the organisms, stimuli, and responses. Laboratory experiments have employed flatworms, crabs, octopi, pigeons, rats, sheep, monkeys, and men as subjects. The elicited responses have varied from involuntary (probably) gastrointestinal responses, such as stomach contractions, to responses generally considered to be voluntary, such as swallowing and finger withdrawal. The unconditioned stimuli have naturally varied with the reactions being considered.[4]

The range of conditioned stimuli is limited only by the experimenter's ability to manipulate the stimulus (make it occur at the right time) and

[4] It should be remembered that the *UCS* must elicit the response prior to conditioning. Therefore an electrical shock is an appropriate *UCS* if one wishes to condition a finger withdrawal, whereas food may be a good *UCS* to use in conditioning a swallowing response.

by the organism's ability to perceive it. Experiments in Pavlov's laboratory even demonstrated that once conditioning has been produced, the *CS* can be used as the "unconditioned stimulus" in conditioning the same response to yet another stimulus. When conditioning involves a *CS* in place of a *UCS,* the process is called *higher-order conditioning.* The dog used in Pavlov's experiment could, for instance, be taught to salivate in response to a black square flashed on a screen by pairing the black square with the previously conditioned tone.

A great deal of human learning and behavior can be explained in terms of respondent conditioning. When a child has flu his parents will say things like *Poor Johnny is sick. . . . Are you going to be sick to your stomach? . . . . If you're going to be sick, run into the bathroom.* Because it is repeatedly paired with unpleasant sensations in the stomach, the word "sick" will become a conditioned stimulus. It will acquire the power to elicit *some* of the responses involved in being sick. The conditioned stimulus, however, elicits only a fractional part of the responses which would be elicited by the unconditioned stimulus. Hearing the word "sick" will not induce sickness, or even make a person feel sick; but it will evoke to some extent some of the responses associated with actually being sick. Arthur W. Staats (1968, pp. 10–50), one of the leading contemporary investigators of respondent conditioning in humans, has stated that a conditioned stimulus, such as a word, can elicit two overlapping kinds of responses, emotional responses and sensory responses. Examples of emotional responses to the word sick are a nauseous feeling and the sensation of an acrid taste and a slimy coating in the mouth and throat. The image or mental picture of a person vomiting is an example of a sensory response. Indeed, even this description may elicit these feelings and sensations to some extent in many readers.

Now suppose that "sick" has become a conditioned stimulus (we could also say discriminative stimulus) which controls some of the responses associated with sickness. Suppose further that a certain child has never heard the word "disgusting." He hears it for the first time in the following utterance: *That's disgusting. It makes me sick to my stomach.* If "disgusting" is paired several times with "sick," it will acquire the power to evoke the responses already controlled by "sick."

Respondent conditioning is one of the processes by which people learn from words. Staats (1968, pp. 48–49) has written:

> Through words the individual can have experiences that provide learning similar to that which the actual events would have provided. The individual can thus acquire new sensory experience without ever having had contact with the objects themselves. For example, many people have never had contact with a jellyfish. If they were told, however, that a jellyfish is "mottled purple,

pink and white," is "gelatinous in its flexibility," comes in "various sizes around eighteen inches across," and gives a "stinging sensation on contact," these words would elicit grossly appropriate sensory responses. Even in this simple example, the individual so conditioned by these verbal means will acquire a constellation of sensory responses that approximates to some extent the sensations he would receive if he had direct contact with the organism. Furthermore, other behaviors that he might learn under the control of the organism itself as a stimulus could also be learned to the conditioned sensory responses. That is, if told to avoid touching the organism, although he had never seen such an animal, he would avoid one on the very first direct contact.

While respondent conditioning is very important to an understanding of learning and behavior, several qualifications are necessary. Conditioning a dog to salivate to a tone is only distantly related to teaching a person a new word by pairing it with its definition or a synonym. The sentence is an extraordinarily effective conditioning paradigm for an experienced user of the language. It speeds up the conditioning process and changes the process in many ways. To illustrate, it might take many simple pairings of "azure" and "blue" before "azure" controlled the responses already controlled by "blue." However, the sentences *Azure means blue* or *Azure is the color of the sky on a clear day* could produce the effect in a single presentation.

Stimulus Control and Operant Conditioning

Stimulus control can also be established using *operant conditioning.* The procedure in this kind of conditioning is to reinforce only those responses that occur in the presence of a certain stimulus. Eventually this stimulus will become a discriminative stimulus which controls the response. For instance, if a pigeon is reinforced with food for pecking a key when a light is red, it will begin to respond more frequently when the light is red and less frequently when the light is different colors. Notice that this procedure entails differential reinforcement. Responses when the light is not red are extinguished.

For many years errors were regarded as inevitable during discrimination learning because of the presumably automatic process of generalization. So, if a pigeon were reinforced for pecking when a light was red, it was assumed it would generalize to lights of other hues. To teach the bird to peck only when the light was red, it was thought necessary to extinguish the tendencies that were believed to arise because of generalization. We now know that errors are not inevitable in discrimination learning and that generalization is not an automatic process. Herbert S. Terrace (1963a) showed that pigeons could learn a red-green discrimination without making errors. In his experiments, the key that the pigeon pecked was a translucent disc which could be made to change colors by shining a red or green light through it from the rear. The pigeons learned to peck the key when it was red to receive food reinforcement. As soon as a bird consistently pecked the key when it was red, the green light was introduced. At the beginning, the key was green for only a few seconds and green was introduced when the pigeon had moved back from the key. Also, on the first appearance of green, the key was very dimly illuminated, almost dark. Gradually the intervals during which the key was green were increased until the key was red or green equally often. At the same time the illumination behind the green key was gradually increased until the key was equally well illuminated whether red or green. Using this procedure, the birds made virtually no errors; that is, they seldom if ever pecked the key when it was green. On the other hand, birds that began with green and red lights equally well illuminated and of equal duration made from 2000 to 4000 errors while learning the discrimination.

(For an example of operant conditioning in humans, see *A practical application of prompting and fading,* p. 322.)

Learning from one's mistakes. Educators are likely to be unimpressed by the fact that organisms can learn without making errors. Firmly entrenched in educational folklore is the notion that people learn from their mistakes. To be sure, it is possible to learn from one's mistakes. But psychological research indicates that errorless learning is better. In Chapter 6, it was argued that organisms learn what they are led to do. A corollary of this principle is that organisms permitted to make errors will learn error tendencies. Terrace (1963a, p. 24) found that pigeons that made errors while learning developed "permanently faulty discrimination performance." Even after the discrimination was acquired, birds that had learned with errors made from 100 to 500 errors. These errors tended to occur in consecutive series, or "bursts," following periods of correct responding. Furthermore the pigeons that made errors while learning showed signs of agitation when the green light was on; they would "usually flap their wings, stamp on the floor of the chamber, and orient themselves away from the key" (Terrace, 1963a, p. 13).

Research with school-related tasks also shows that errors have negative consequences. Kaess and Zeaman (1960) asked college undergraduates to complete a multiple-choice examination in psychology covering difficult, unfamiliar material. Each student used a punchboard device which informed him as to whether he had selected the right answer. The student kept punching on each question until he chose the correct answer. Students completed the examination five times. On the first time through, one group of students received an abbreviated form of the test in which only a single answer was listed, the correct one; therefore, errors were impossible. Other groups received forms of the test listing either two, three, four, or five possible answers, including just one correct answer. Naturally, the more alternative answers listed, the greater was the percentage of errors. After the first presentation of the test *all* groups received the form of the test in which five alternatives were listed. The results of the experiment are diagrammed in Fig. 9.4. As you can see, the effects of making errors on the first attempt at the test persisted over five exposures.

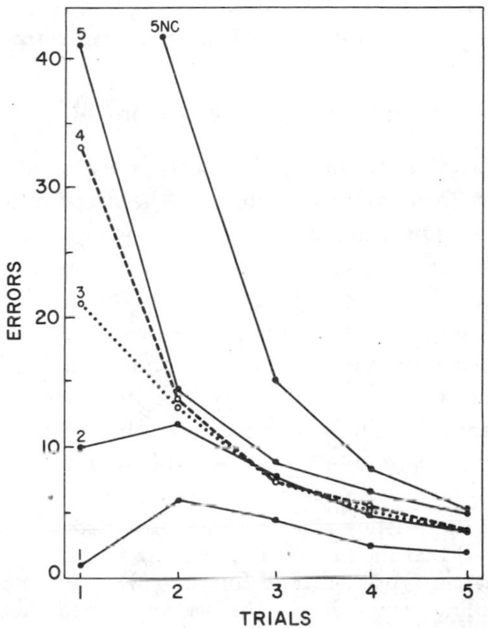

FIGURE 9.4 *Mean errors made on punchboard by groups having one to five alternatives available on Trial 1. The label for each curve indicates the number of choices on Trial 1. Condition "5NC" had five choices without confirmation on Trial 1. Items for Trials 2–5 had five choices with confirmation for all groups. (Based on Kaess & Zeaman, 1966.)*

Melaragno (1960) has also demonstrated the undesirable effects of errors. He taught college undergraduates symbolic logic concepts using a 50-frame, self-instructional program. Five ambiguous frames were inserted in the middle of the program. One group was called wrong on these five frames no matter what answers they gave, while individuals in another group were always called right. The group that made "errors" earned significantly lower scores on the achievement test. Since the ambiguous frames were unrelated to the content of the program and the test, making errors on these frames must have had an undesirable emotional or motivational effect. A third group was also called wrong on each of the ambiguous frames; however, in this case the ambiguous frames appeared at widely spaced intervals throughout the program. This group did well on the test, indicating that an occasional error is not disruptive.

It may be argued that important goals which involve, for instance, teaching the student to discover relationships for himself or to solve problems, necessarily involve student errors. We do not believe this to be the case. The issue will be treated in detail in Chapter 10.

Procedures for Establishing Stimulus Control

As the chief illustration in this section we shall use the learning of letter-sound correspondences, which is the first important task of the beginning reader. During the thirty or forty years prior to 1960, the sounding out of words was deemphasized in beginning reading instruction. Children were expected to learn whole words through a "look-say" approach. Reexamination of the research evidence and further analysis of the task of learning to read indicate that systematic instruction in letter-sound relationships is probably the best way to begin reading instruction. Jeanne S. Chall in her comprehensive book, *Learning to Read: The Great Debate* (1967, pp. 83–84) concluded

> My analysis of the existing experimental comparisons . . . tends to support [the linguist's view] that the first step in learning to read one's native language is essentially learning a printed code for the speech we possess. It does not support the prevailing view that sees the beginning reader as a miniature adult who should, from the start, engage in mature reading. Early stress on code learning, these studies indicate, not only produces better word recognition and spelling, but also makes it easier for the child to read with understanding. . . . The correlational studies . . . show a significant relationship between ability to recognize letters and give the sounds they represent and reading achievement. Although knowledge of letters and their sounds does not assure success in reading, it does appear to be a necessary condition for success. In fact, it seems to be more essential for success in the early stages of reading than high intelligence and good oral language ability.

Teaching the response and establishing gross stimulus control. In teaching a child to name the letter *b*, the teacher might begin by writing *b* on the chalkboard and saying "This is a *b*." Pause. Then the teacher points to the *b* and asks "What is this?" After reinforcing or correcting as needed, he erases the board and writes *b* again. He asks, "Is this a *b*?" Erasing the board and writing *b* once more, he asks "What is this?" If the child has answered these questions correctly, he has learned the response. He has also discriminated the stimulus, though probably not adequately; he may only have noticed the difference between a chalk mark and an empty space on the board.

Sharpening stimulus control. The teacher will not be satisfied until the child can always say "b" when presented with *b* and never calls any other letter "b." In other words stimulus control must be sharpened, which is mainly a matter of teaching a fine discrimination. The child must learn to pay attention to the features of *b* which distinguish it from other letters.

At this point a new technical term must be introduced, *S-delta* (symbolized S^{Δ}).[5] Responses to an S^{Δ} are inappropriate and they are not reinforced. Responses to the discriminative stimulus, or S^{D}, on the other hand, are appropriate. The letter *b* is an S^{D} for the response, "That's a *b*." The letter *m* is an S^{Δ} for this response.

The first rule for teaching a fine discrimination is to begin introducing S^{Δ}'s as soon as the student consistently makes the correct response to the S^{D}. With respect to a child learning to name the letter *b*, this means other letters should be introduced as soon as a brief teaching sequence, like the one described above, is successfully completed. If the student practices responding to the S^{D} for a considerable period of time before S^{Δ}'s are introduced, he may have trouble learning a fine discrimination. The pigeons that in Terrace's (1963a) experiment spent three sessions responding to the red light (S^{D}) alone before the green light (S^{Δ}) was presented for the first time, made many errors while learning the discrimination, and even after acquiring the discrimination occasionally made bursts of errors.

Methods of presenting stimuli. There has been fairly extensive research on four methods of presenting stimuli to teach a discrimination. In *successive presentation* one stimulus appears at a time, either the S^{D} or an S^{Δ}. The S^{D} and the S^{Δ} alternate in an irregular order. Using a chalkboard, a teacher could present *b*'s and *d*'s successively. The child would be asked to answer the question, "Is this a *b*?" for each letter, or he might be asked to name each letter as it appears. In the latter case he should first be taught to say "d" and associate this response with the letter.

In *simultaneous presentation* the S^{D} and one or more S^{Δ}'s are presented

[5] An S-delta is sometimes called a *negative stimulus* (S—).

at the same time. A teacher using a simultaneous presentation method might write the following pairs of stimuli on the chalkboard, one pair at a time.

b d
d b
d b
b d
d b
b d
b d
b d
d b
b d

The child could then be asked to point to the *b* in each pair. In this kind of presentation, the spatial position of the S^D should vary in an irregular fashion, otherwise the organism might learn to respond on the basis of position without paying attention to the critical features of the S^D. Simultaneous presentation is not limited to pairs of stimuli. The S^D could be presented together with two or more S^{Δ}'s.

Research involving discrimination between colors or shades of gray usually shows that simultaneous presentation leads to slightly faster learning than successive presentation, especially when the discrimination is difficult (Loess & Duncan, 1952). However, Ackerman and Williams (1969) reported that successive presentation was better for a difficult letter discrimination (*b* versus *d*), while simultaneous presentation was better for an easy discrimination (*b* versus *s*).

Probably neither successive nor simultaneous presentation is as effective as a third method called *matching-to-sample.* In this method, the sample is the S^D, while the possible matches include the $S^D$and one or more S^{Δ}'s. In matching-to-sample, the sample and the matches are visible together. The position of the S^D among the matches, however, should vary irregularly from presentation to presentation. A teacher could teach a *b* discrimination using matching-to-sample by printing the letter *b* on the chalkboard and then below, or alongside, the letter *b* again and one or more other letters. For instance:

b
b d

Erase and write:

b
d b

Erase and write:

b

d b

Continue presenting problems of this sort until the child is consistently correct. When the matches are printed, the child should be asked "Which is the *b*?" or "Point to the *b*." Some children display the annoying tendency of not looking at the sample. A refinement which often eliminates this tendency is to ask the child to point to the *b* on the top and then point to the *b* on the bottom. Another refinement to get the pupil to pay attention to the sample is to present the sample, pause briefly (one or two seconds), then present the matches while the sample is still visible.

A variant on the matching-to-sample method is to remove the sample before presenting the matches. This procedure is called *delayed matching-to-sample.* The available evidence suggests that people will learn more rapidly using matching-to-sample than delayed matching-to-sample. Samuels (1969) taught kindergartners to discriminate *b, d, p,* and *q* using either matching-to-sample or delayed matching-to-sample. Each of these four letters was the sample in some presentations. The matches always consisted of the four letters in different orders. The children who received delayed matching-to-sample required almost twice as many presentations to discriminate the four letters perfectly.

People will probably learn discriminations most easily using matching-to-sample and least easily using simultaneous or successive presentation methods. Delayed matching-to-sample would probably fall somewhere in between. It may seem that matching-to-sample is obviously the best procedure to use; however, there is a very important qualification. People who can perform perfectly on a matching-to-sample task will not necessarily be able to discriminate stimuli which appear in isolation. Samuels (1969) found that while kindergartners learned most quickly using matching-to-sample, they did much better on another task that required discriminating the letters in isolation when they had been taught using delayed matching-to-sample.

For practical purposes we recommend a combination method for sharpening stimulus control when hard discriminations are required. *First,* teach the pupil to give the response to the S^D (see the section on establishing gross stimulus control and the first section of Chapter 6). *Second,* require the pupil to discriminate the S^D in several matching-to-sample problems. *Third,* when the pupil can perform perfectly on matching-to-sample problems, present delayed matching-to-sample problems. *Fourth,* present single S^D's, using the successive method, after the pupil can discriminate perfectly under delayed matching-to-sample.

The combination method which has just been described makes discrimination easy at the beginning. Errors are unlikely. At the same time, by the end of the sequence, most students will be able to respond correctly when the S^D is presented in isolation. Often there are many similar S^D's, each of which must control a different response. This is true, for instance, of naming the letters of the alphabet. Several letter-name correspondences could be taught at once using the method described above. Complete the first two steps with two letters, then present matching-to-sample problems in which the first letter is the S^D in some problems and the second letter is the S^D in others. As each new letter is introduced, include problems in which this letter is the S^D and review problems in which the other letters serve as S^D's. When all of the letters have been introduced and performance is perfect on matching-to-sample problems, move on to the third and fourth steps, intermixing problems involving all of the letters being taught.

While we have illustrated discrimination learning with tasks involved in beginning reading, bear in mind that discrimination learning is critical in all subject matters and for people of every age. The cook must be able to discriminate when the hollandaise sauce should be removed from the stove. The mechanic must be able to discriminate symptoms of carburetor malfunction from ignition system failure. The student of political science must be able to discriminate feudal and rational-legal systems of government. And the art critic must be able to discriminate a Rembrandt from a forgery.

Identifying difficult discriminations. Discrimination involves learning to pay attention to the critical features of stimuli. It is, therefore, useful for the teacher to identify critical features. This may be regarded as an aspect of task analysis (see Chapter 2).

A student may discriminate two stimuli on the basis of any difference between them. For example, he may discriminate an *A* from an *O* because an *A* "looks like a teepee" or is made up of straight lines or is open at the bottom, or he may learn the critical features of *O* and ignore those of *A*. However, when the task changes to one of multiple discrimination, such as among *all* of the letters of the alphabet, the child cannot pay attention to just any difference if he is to discriminate accurately. He must notice the critical features. Critical features are those which cannot be changed if the stimulus is still to be classified the same. For example, the uppercase letter *A* must remain an open figure if it is to remain an *A*. Closed transformations of *A* such as 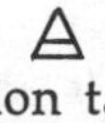 or 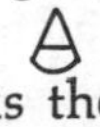 cannot be classified as *A*'s. Usually in multiple discrimination tasks there is no single feature which will allow the student to distinguish between all of the stimuli.

Below are four stimulus presentation procedures which could be used to teach a discrimination between ⊣ and ⊢. The organism sees only the material enclosed in a box at any one time. (Of course, each procedure could be continued with many more similar presentations.) Label each presentation procedure.

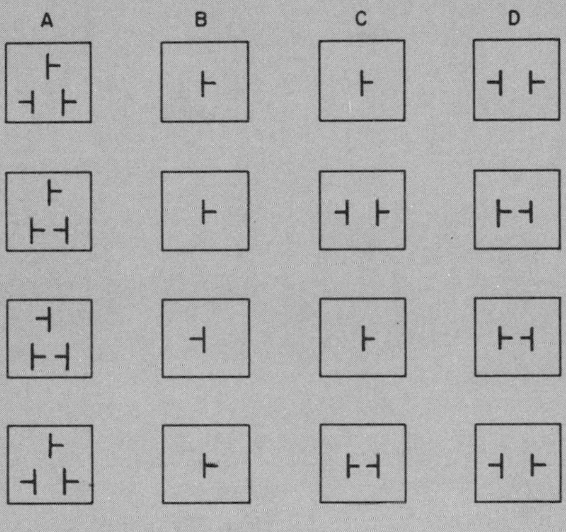

The answers appear on p. **321.**

Rather there is a combination of critical features which distinguishes each individual stimulus. The student's task in such situations is to learn the set of distinctive features that characterize each stimulus.

Borrowing from the work of linguists, Gibson (1965) has made an analysis of the distinctive features of the letters of the alphabet. Fig. 9.5 contains a *feature chart* for ten of the uppercase letters of the alphabet. The number of features which could be included in such a chart varies with the number and variety of the to-be-discriminated stimuli. Each of the features presented in Fig. 9.5 is or is not characteristic of each of the twenty-six letters of the alphabet. Regarding each letter one asks, for example, "Is there a horizontal straight segment?" and gets either a yes or a no answer. "Yes" answers are recorded as plus signs at the appropriate row and column intersection. For example, the letters *A, E, L,* and *Z* all have horizontal straight segments and this fact is indicated on the chart. To be useful, the filled-in feature chart must result in a unique pattern for each of the stimuli. By consulting such a feature chart the teacher can get an idea as to which aspects of the stimuli to draw to the

Features	A	B	C	E	K	L	N	U	X	Z
Straight segment										
Horizontal	+			+		+				+
Vertical		+		+	+	+	+			+
Oblique	+				+				+	+
Oblique	+				+		+		+	
Curve										
Closed		+								
Open vertically								+		
Open horizontally			+							
Intersection	+	+		+	+				+	
Redundancy										
Cyclic change		+		+						
Symmetry	+	+	+	+	+			+	+	
Discontinuity										
Vertical	+				+				+	
Horizontal				+		+	+			+

FIGURE 9.5 *Example of a feature chart. Whether the features chosen are actually effective for discriminating letters must be determined by experiment (from Gibson, 1965).*

attention of his students. A feature chart can be useful for simple as well as multiple discriminations. When only two stimuli must be discriminated, a chart based on an analysis of features will indicate several bases for the discrimination. The teacher may wish to emphasize all of these rather than allow students to make the discrimination on the basis of only one feature. When stimuli are discriminated on the basis of only one feature, there may be problems later when students must learn discriminations involving other stimuli.

Another value of a features analysis and accompanying chart is that it locates especially difficult-to-discriminate stimuli. Discriminations involving stimuli whose feature profiles are very similar (e.g., the letters *K* and *X*) will be learned with more difficulty than will stimuli whose feature profiles are very different (e.g., *N* and *U*). Gibson (1965) used the features presented in Fig. 9.5 to predict which letters are more likely to be confused and found a high correspondence between predicted difficulty and letter confusions among four-year-olds.

The feature chart can be an aid both in completing the task analysis and in planning the lesson itself. It indicates to the teacher the critical features of the stimuli which must be emphasized; and it indicates which stimuli will be most difficult to discriminate and, therefore, where extra practice or specific discrimination training procedures should be included in the lesson. However, the usefulness of the feature chart does not end here. We also see it as a teaching device. One good way to draw mature students' attention to the critical features of stimuli is to have them participate in the development of a feature chart. Biology students could attempt to delineate the distinctive features of the various phyla, orders, and classes of the animal kingdom, or history students could be asked to delineate the common and distinctive features of various revolutions.

Prompting and Fading

Prompting is the technique of providing information that helps a student to give correct answers. Prompting is useful for teaching new responses and can be helpful in establishing stimulus control.

Depending upon the context, a prompt may consist of a rule which can be applied to an example, a hint to help in the solution of a problem, the first letter of an answer, or a synonym for an answer. Prompting also emphasizes the S^D by making it larger, brighter, louder, or more salient in some other way, than the S^{Δ}'s.

A "prompt" is technically defined as a stimulus that already controls or partly controls a response. One of the instructional problems is to arrange a shift in stimulus control from the prompt to the S^D, which, of course, prior to instruction does not control the response. The shift in stimulus control has been accomplished when the student can make the response when the S^D alone is present.

Fading is the chief procedure for producing a shift in stimulus control. Fading means to gradually remove the prompt. Terrace's experiment with pigeons (1963a) illustrates prompting and fading. Initially the S^D (the red light) was more brightly illuminated and presented for a longer

Answers to the question on p. **319.**

A. matching-to-sample
B. successive
C. delayed matching-to-sample
D. simultaneous

period of time than the S^{Δ} (green light). Gradually differences between the S^{D} and S^{Δ} were faded, until the two stimuli were equal in level of illumination and presented for equal periods of time. At this point the S^{D} and the S^{Δ} could be discriminated only on the basis of color, whereas earlier the pigeon was helped to respond correctly if it noticed brightness or duration.

Prompting and fading can be used in conjunction with any of the stimulus presentation methods described in the previous section. Terrace presented stimuli successively. Others have used prompting and fading with matching-to-sample. One might employ matching-to-sample, for instance, and use letter size as a prompt to teach the discrimination between *b* and *d*. To begin with, make the *d* much smaller than the *b* (or vice versa). Gradually, over a number of presentations, increase the size of the *d* (or decrease the size of the *b*) until the two letters are the same size.

It is most important to withdraw the prompt gradually. Several studies have shown that when the prompt is abruptly withdrawn, students will begin to make errors and will have trouble learning the discrimination (Terrace, 1963b; Moore & Goldiamond, 1964). Hively (1962, 1965) found that once an optimal fading sequence was discovered there was serious deterioration in performance if any of the steps in the sequence were eliminated. Neither adding many similar presentations to each step remaining in the sequence nor requiring children to repeat individual problems on which errors were made resulted in any improvement. The one thing that did improve performance was to require that the children make four consecutive correct responses as a condition for advancing to the next problem. It is likely that this procedure was successful because it forced students to attend to the critical features of the stimuli, because otherwise students could advance by merely making all possible responses (pressing keys on a teaching machine) in rapid succession.

A practical application of prompting and fading. Holland and Matthews (1963) have prepared an actual lesson which employed prompting and fading with considerable success. A programmed lesson was designed to teach /S/ discrimination to children with /S/ articulation disorders, for instance, children who lisped.[6] The lesson employed a four-phase fading technique. During the first phase the student was taught to discriminate pairs of speech sounds. The child was asked to judge which of two sounds was an /S/. Early in this phase the /S/

[6] The lines around /S/ are used to indicate that we are considering the phoneme or sound of *S* rather than the grapheme or letter *S*.

sounds were longer and louder than non-/S/ sounds, and the non-/S/ sounds were phonetically quite different from /S/, for example, /S/ and /P/. As this phase progressed, the loudness and duration differences were faded and the non-/S/ sounds became phonetically more similar to /S/, for instance, /S/ and /Z/.

In the second phase of the lesson the child was taught to discriminate the /S/ phoneme (sound) in words. Pairs of words were pronounced. One contained an /S/; the other did not. Again the discriminations evolved from easy to difficult as the student progressed. Initially words containing /S/ were emphasized. Since sounds at the beginning of words are more easily recognized, the children were at first required to recognize only words which began with /S/. As the program progressed the student learned to make finer discriminations (i.e., *ship-sip*).

During the third phase of the lesson the child heard single words containing one /S/ sound. He had to judge whether the /S/ was at the beginning, in the middle, or at the end of the word. To begin with, the /S/ sounds were exaggerated and once again as training progressed discrimination ranged from easy to difficult. At the end of this phase the child was required to make discriminations with words which have within them sounds similar to /S/ as well as /S/ (i.e., *thistle*).

The fourth and final phase of the lesson required the student to discriminate correctly articulated from misarticulated /S/ sounds within words. There was a gradual progression in the misarticulations from those most audibly different from /S/ to those least different.

Two control programs used in this study were equal in length to the one discussed above. Program II was merely an extension of the first phase of the fading program; however, it sampled all the English consonants and vowels, and it gave more practice on each phoneme. Program III was a longer version of the fourth phase of the fading program. It gave the students extensive practice at discriminating words containing properly articulated and misarticulated /S/ sounds.

Children using the fading program showed substantial, significant improvement on an /S/ discrimination test (a test very similar to the task performed by students in Program III). Neither the program emphasizing "drill on fundamentals" (Program II) nor the one which provided extensive practice on the terminal behavior (Program III) resulted in much improvement. The fading program required an average of two hours and fifteen minutes per student, a much shorter time than is required to teach phoneme discriminations by traditional methods. As Holland and Matthews stated: "challenging opportunities lie in the extension of teaching machine concepts to other areas of speech. . . . It is quite possible that such programs, and extensions and modifications of them, can form the beginning in pathology and audiology of some excellent new concepts for rehabilitation of individuals with communication disorders. . . . The future should hold wide applications which go far beyond this simple start."

Magnifying the critical features. Let us suppose you want to teach an organism to discriminate two circles that differ slightly in size.

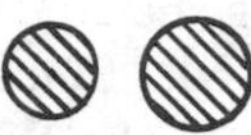

You could (if you had the necessary equipment) illuminate one of the circles more fully than the other. Over a series of presentations the prompt would gradually be removed. This technique of prompting involves juxtaposing an irrelevant feature which makes the S^D more obvious, salient, or noticeable.

Another way to prompt is to magnify the critical feature which distinguishes the S^D and the S^Δ. One of the early great American psychologists, William James (1890, pp. 505–515), recognized that "delicacy of discernment" (ability to discriminate) could be improved most easily if the initial difference between the S^D and the S^Δ were quite great and if this difference were slowly reduced. Later Pavlov (1927, p. 117) noted in his studies of conditioned salivation in dogs that discriminations between stimuli whose difference was progressively reduced were learned faster than discriminations between stimuli that were presented with a constant, small difference between them.

To teach the discrimination between two circles of slightly different sizes, one could begin with circles with markedly different areas.

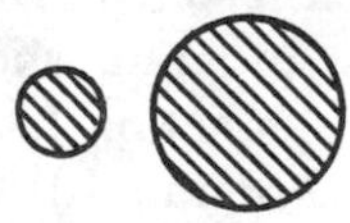

Over several presentations reduce the size differences. Research indicates that this is an effective way to teach discriminations (Schosberg & Soloman, 1943).

Exaggerating critical features is likely to be a useful way to prompt whenever the feature is continuously variable, as is the case with area, length, weight, loudness, pitch, and brightness. Unfortunately, many stimulus features are not continuously variable. Ignoring variations in handwriting and type styles, a letter is either a *b* or it is not. We might seem to be stuck with the letters of the alphabet as they are. However, even letters can be altered slightly to make the critical features more prominent. Two pairs of letters notoriously difficult for children to discriminate are *b* and *d*, and *p* and *q*. Edward Coleman[7] has suggested modifications in *b* and *q* as follows:

Coleman's alterations are especially neat since his modified lowercase *b* bears a resemblance to a capital *B*, making it easier for the child to learn this connection. His modified *q* takes advantage of the fact that *u* is the letter which most frequently follows *q*. Actually any type style which introduced variations among the two pairs of letters would make them more discriminable. The lone primary school teacher cannot very well undertake alphabet surgery by himself, because he is dependent upon prepackaged instructional materials employing traditional orthography. Publishers of basal readers could readily introduce such modifications, however. By the end of the third grade most children can discriminate left from right, and at this time they could easily make the transfer to the traditional forms of *b* and *q*.

An entirely new orthography, the Initial Teaching Alphabet (ITA), has been developed for beginning readers (see Mazurkiewicz & Tanyzer, 1966). A sample of the Initial Teaching Alphabet appears in Fig. 9.6. In addition to making letters more discriminable, the ITA deals with the even more important problem of regularizing letter-sound relationships. Many letters in English, especially vowels, are pronounced several different ways. The ITA contains a unique symbol for each sound. The early research shows that children taught with ITA read significantly better than children taught with the regular alphabet, even when the tests involve the regular alphabet (Downing, 1964). However, while ITA shows promise, the evidence at this time is incomplete.

There is reason to believe that magnifying the critical features, when this is feasible, is likely to be a better method of prompting than superimposing an irrelevant feature so as to make the S^D more salient. Any feature can provide the basis for discrimination among stimuli. When

[7] Personal communication to the senior author, February, 1969.

æbraham liŋcon'ƨ gettyƨburg address

forscor and seven yϵϵrƨ agœ our fathərƨ braut forth on thisthis continent a nue næʃhon, consϵϵvd in liberty, and dedicæted tω the proposiʃhon that aull men ɑr creæted ϵϵkwal.

nou wϵϵ ɑr engæjd in a græt sivil waur, testiŋ whether that næʃhon, or eny næʃhon sœ consϵϵvd and sœ dedicæted, can loŋ enduer. wϵϵ ɑr met on a græt battl-fϵϵld ov that waur. wϵϵ hav cum tω dedicæt a porʃhon ov that fϵϵld aƨ a fienal restiŋ-plæs for thœƨ hω gæv thær lievƨ that that næʃhon miet liv. it iƨ aultωgether fittiŋ and proper that wϵϵ ʃhωd dω this.

but in a lɑrjer sens, wϵϵ cannot dedicæt—wϵϵ cannot consecræt—wϵϵ cannot hallœ—this ground. the bræv men, liviŋ and ded, hω struggld hϵϵr, hav consecræted it fɑr abuv our pωr pouer tω add or detract. the wurld will littl nœt nor loŋ remember whot wϵϵ sæ hϵϵr, but it can never forget whot thæ did hϵϵr. it iƨ for us, the liviŋ, rather, tω bϵϵ dedicæted hϵϵr tω the unfiniʃht wurk which thæ hω faut hϵϵr hav thus fɑr sœ nœbly advanst. it iƨ rather for us tω bϵϵ hϵϵr dedicæted tω the græt task remæniŋ befor us—that from thϵϵƨ onord ded wϵϵ tæk incrϵϵst devœʃhon tω that cauƨ for which thæ gæv the last fωll meʒuer ov devœʃhon; that wϵϵ hϵϵr hiely reƨolv that thϵϵƨ ded ʃhall not hav died in væn; that this næʃhon, under god, ʃhall hav a nue birth ov frϵϵdom; and that guvernment ov the pϵϵpl, bie the pϵϵpl, for the pϵϵpl, ʃhall not periʃh from the erth.

FIGURE 9.6 *A sample of ITA (from Downing, 1966, p. 145).*

discrimination training is completed, it is hoped that the critical (distinctive, valid) features of the stimulus will control the response. Exaggerating the critical features has the virtue of drawing attention to these features from the very beginning of instruction. When an irrelevant feature is superimposed, the pupil can respond without noticing the critical feature. In fact, the irrelevant feature may even draw attention away from the critical feature.

Impressive results are sometimes obtained when the S^D is emphasized by adding an irrelevant feature. However, this technique sometimes fails.

Terrace (1963b) was unable to teach pigeons to discriminate a horizontal line from a vertical line using brightness and duration prompts.[8] Why did prompting with brightness and duration succeed in the case of the red-green discrimination but fail in the case of the horizontal-vertical discrimination? At the present time no one knows for sure.

The authors have received informal reports from several investigators describing failures to teach discriminations by superimposing an irrelevant feature. Several people have tried to teach children to discriminate difficult pairs of letters by presenting them in different colors. It is reported that the children were unable to discriminate when the color prompts were withdrawn.

A researcher will always test to see whether the students can respond when the prompts are no longer present. However, persons who develop practical teaching techniques do not always adequately test methods and materials. Prompting has received a good deal of publicity. We are afraid that curriculum developers may misapply prompting techniques. We believe that the conclusion which Anderson drew in 1967 (pp. 133–134) is still correct:

> When the prompting stimulus is of such a nature that it is possible for the subject to ignore the [critical features of] the discriminative stimulus during training, transfer of control to the discriminative stimulus may never take place, or the transfer may be a very fragile process that depends upon subtle structuring of the training environment and relationships among stimuli that are not yet well understood. . . . The type of procedure in which a prompting stimulus is superimposed on the discriminative stimulus cannot yet be warranted failsafe for nonlaboratory settings.

We, therefore, recommend that teachers employ the technique of supplementing the S^D with an irrelevant feature only as a last resort, when other methods have failed. When this technique is used, whether introduced by the teacher or embodied in prepackaged materials, it is especially important to make sure the student can make unprompted correct responses at the end of the teaching sequence. We are more enthusiastic about endorsing the technique of magnifying the critical features of the stimulus because the student must observe the valid features of the stimulus to respond correctly.

Other varieties of prompting. Speaking broadly, a prompt is simply a hint to help a student make a response. In this general sense, classroom teachers have always used prompts. However, prompting did

[8] He later succeeded in establishing this discrimination by first teaching a red-green discrimination. Then red and green were superimposed on the horizontal and vertical lines. The color was gradually faded. Pigeons taught in this manner learned the horizontal-vertical discrimination without errors.

not receive much attention from educators until the rise of programmed instruction. One of the cardinal principles of programmed instruction is to prevent student errors. Programmers have created a variety of prompting techniques to help students avoid errors.

One such technique is called the "copying frame," since all the student must do is copy into blanks one or more words which are provided. The following is an example of a copying frame from a self-instructional program on the menstrual cycle (Biological Sciences Curriculum Study, 1965, p. 11):

When an egg cell is released from the ovary, the wall of the uterus is thin.

When an egg cell is ____________ from an ovary, the wall of the uterus is ________.

While the copying frame certainly does make errors improbable, students who repeatedly encounter copying frames may begin to fill in the blanks without carefully reading all of the frame. As a consequence, the student may sometimes fail to notice the stimulus that it is hoped will control the response in the future. It should therefore be emphasized that, while self-instructional programs containing many copying frames are still being written, the leading manuals on how to prepare programs caution against their use (Markle, 1969).

Other prompting techniques used by programmers include underlining

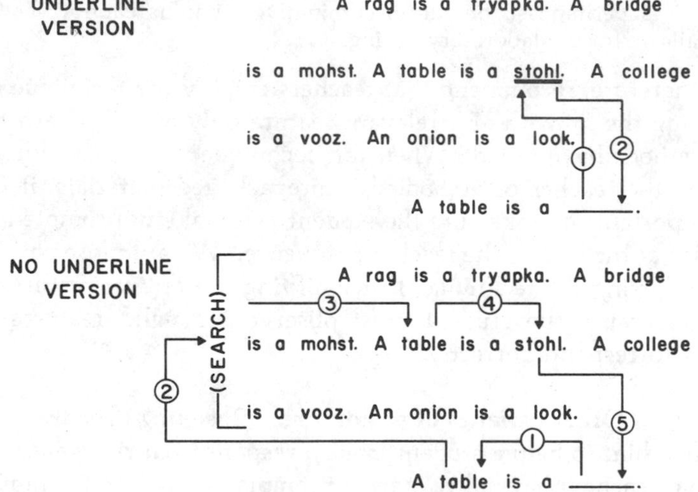

FIGURE 9.7 *Two versions of a frame from a Russian vocabulary program. The lines trace the minimal inspection of the materials required to locate the response term (from Anderson and Faust, 1967).*

or italicizing the correct answer, providing the first letter or two of the answer, or furnishing a synonym for the answer. Anderson and Faust (1967) completed a study of underlining which has implications for other prompting techniques as well. College students received a Russian vocabulary program in which each frame consisted of a paragraph of five sentences with English subjects and Russian predicate nominatives. Immediately below each paragraph one of the sentences was repeated with a blank in place of the Russian word. In a second, otherwise identical, version of the program the Russian word to be written into the blank was underlined in each frame. An example of a frame from each version of the program is presented in Fig. 9.7. On the achievement test given after the program, students had to supply the Russian words given the English equivalents.

You be the psychologist. Try to make the analysis that Anderson and Faust made when they planned their experiment.

A. Which group, the one that got the Underline program or the one that got the No Underline program, would you predict would do best on the achievement test?
B. Why?

Examine Fig. 9.7. The lines tracing the inspection of the materials required to fill the blanks correctly should prompt your responses. Convert answers will do.

The authors' analysis is presented in the following paragraph.

The Anderson and Faust experiment and others (Faust, 1967; Faust & Anderson, 1967; Royer, 1969) have all found that students who receive the No Underline program learn more Russian words than students who receive the Underline version. The reason is that the Underline version permits a short-circuiting of attention. A person can fill the blanks in the Underline program without noticing the English words (S^D's). Of course, if he just copies underlined words into blanks he won't know which Russian word goes with which English word when he takes the achievement test. The No Underline program, on the other hand, requires the student to at least notice the S^D in order to respond correctly. Some degree of stimulus control is assured.

The Underline version of the Russian vocabulary program does not prevent the student from spontaneously, or voluntarily, paying attention to the English cue words. We have repeatedly found that among those who complete the program most quickly and who, therefore, are presumably least likely to voluntarily notice the cues, the No-Underline version leads to markedly higher learning than the Underline version, while there is little difference between the two versions for subjects who complete the program slowly. Experimentally manipulating motivation, Faust (1967) found that the No Underline version was much superior to the Underline version when students were required to draw a line through each *a*, *g*, *m*, and *e* in a list of 870 words before starting the program. The advantage of the No Underline version was smallest for students who were told that performance on the program was a new test of learning ability which might relate to academic and professional success. In a concurrent experiment, Faust instructed some students that they would be judged chiefly in terms of how quickly they completed the program. Students who received the Underline version learned many fewer words than those who received the No Underline version under these conditions, presumably because voluntary attention to the cues was reduced. These results indicate that control of attention is likely to be most important when students are bored, tired, or under time pressure—conditions which sometimes prevail in classrooms despite the best efforts of the teacher.

In an "overprompted" program the student will often be able to respond correctly on the basis of prompts alone, without paying attention to the entire cue—even, for example, to the definition of a technical term. As a result the cue often will fail to become a discriminative stimulus for the response and so, for instance, the student will be unable to produce a technical term when its definition appears on the achievement test. Anderson, Faust, and Roderick (1968) altered an introductory psychology program to include additional prompts in most frames. As expected, groups that received the unaltered program scored significantly higher on the achievement test than groups that got the heavily-prompted version.

Chapter 7 presented the argument that students should be led to make relevant responses for the right reasons. This argument can now be elaborated: if stimulus control is to develop, the procedures and materials must be arranged so that the student can respond correctly if, and only if, he has noticed the discriminative stimulus. This is a principle of some importance. While the illustrations and research evidence have involved programmed instruction, the same principle undoubtedly holds for other forms of instruction—including workbooks, exercise sheets, and teacher-led classroom activities.

We do not wish to leave the impression that prompting is all bad. On the contrary, when used correctly prompts not only make the correct response probable but may also help the student to associate the S^D

and the response. Markle (1969) gives the following illustration of a prompted frame which, if you are not too particular about the order in which the colors are listed, will teach a person to name the colors of the French flag:

Like the American flag, the French flag is ______, ______, and ______.

Often prompts are used to eliminate impossible or irrelevant answers, leaving the important distinction to the student. Here is another illustration from Markle's book:

Meaningful units that go after the root are called — — — fixes.

The prompt gives the information that the response word ends in "fixes" and that the student must supply three letters; consequently many irrelevant answers are avoided. However, the student is left to make the really important distinction between *pre*fixes and *suf*fixes.

Prompting can be a useful technique, provided care is taken to insure that the student will pay attention to the S^D before he responds. This rule applies to the phase of instruction which is designed to bring behaviors under stimulus control. It does *not* apply to the response-learning phase. When new responses must be learned copying, imitating, and prompting with irrelevant features do serve a valuable function (see Chapter 6). One final word of advice regarding prompting techniques. Whatever may have gone before, test to make sure that, by the end of a teaching sequence, the student can make unprompted correct responses.

SELF-TEST ON STIMULUS CONTROL

This test is supposed to teach as well as test. Answer all of the questions on a separate sheet of paper, then grade your answers using the scoring key on p. 335. Some questions require a "brief" constructed response, meaning a sentence or two.

1. A botanist classifies some leaves as pinnate leaves and others as palmate leaves. This is an example of

a. generalization.
b. discrimination.
c. operant conditioning.
d. respondent conditioning.

2. A prompt is

   a. a neutral stimulus before learning.
   b. a stimulus which controls a response before learning.
   c. an unconditioned stimulus.
   d. a stimulus which is supposed to control a response after learning.

3. Briefly define stimulus control.

4. From which of the following presentation methods will people most easily learn a discrimination?

   a. successive
   b. simultaneous
   c. matching-to-sample

5. A neutral stimulus paired with an unconditioned stimulus will become a ______________________________.

6. Johnny refers both to *n*'s and *h*'s as "*n*'s". This is an example of

   a. generalization.
   b. discrimination.
   c. operant conditioning.
   d. respondent conditioning.

7. Give an example of a matching-to-sample problem. Label the S^D's and S^Δ's.

8. List one reason why prompting techniques sometimes fail to aid discrimination learning.

9. Give an example of an S^Δ for the response "The sum of the two numbers is 127."

10. Which of the following statements are *false*?

   a. People should get considerable practice at making the correct response to the S^D before S^Δ's are introduced.
   b. Prompts should be removed gradually.
   c. The most effective form of prompting is to superimpose a feature which makes the S^D more noticeable.
   d. People can sometimes respond correctly by paying attention to irrelevant features of a stimulus.

11. Briefly give an illustration of higher-order conditioning of word meaning. Use an example different from any of the ones used in the chapter.

12. Give an example of an S^D for the response "It's probably going to rain."

13. Briefly discuss the consequences of student errors.

14. Give a sequence of four or five problems which might appear in a successive stimulus presentation. Indicate the response(s) which is (are) required of the student.

15. A conditioned response

a. includes aspects which are not part of the unconditioned response.
b. includes some but not all aspects of the unconditioned response.
c. is usually identical to the unconditioned response.

16. A conditioned stimulus is the same as

a. a reinforcer.
b. a *UCS*.
c. an S^D.
d. an S^Δ.

17. Rachel calls bucks and large does "ponies." She calls small does and fawn "deer." This is an example of

a. prompting.
b. generalization.
c. delayed matching-to-sample.
d. discrimination.

Summary

As we grow older more of our behavior comes under stimulus control. That is, we learn what behavior is appropriate under a great variety of stimulus conditions. These stimulus conditions do not become necessary nor sufficient determinants of our behavior, but rather act as signals. Much of the teacher's day is spent trying to bring student behavior under control of the appropriate stimuli. The mathematics teacher, for instance, wants his students to be able to work word problems; in other words he wants his students to know which of a large repertoire of mathematical skills should be employed when a certain stimulus situation (the problem) is presented. Similarly, the baseball coach wants base runners to be able to recognize certain situations and respond appropriately; with two outs, base runners should know enough to run whenever the ball is hit.

If a stimulus is to control a response, the learner must be able to make the response and he must be able to discriminate the stimulus from other stimuli. Teaching the student to make new responses can be accomplished using verbal directions, or modeling and imitation as was described in Chapter 6. Or new responses can be "shaped" in the manner outlined in Chapter 7. In many situations teachers need not teach the child to make new responses. Often the desired responses are already part of the student's repertoire before instruction begins.

Before new stimuli can come to control behavior, the student must be able to discriminate between "appropriate" and "inappropriate" stimuli; in technical terms, he must discriminate S^D's and S^Δ's. This requires that the student be able to detect the critical features of the stimuli. Critical features are those which make stimuli different. Features which do not allow us to discriminate between stimuli are called "irrelevant features." In order to detect which features of stimuli are critical and which are irrelevant, the teacher may wish to construct a feature chart. A feature chart records the stimuli to be discriminated and the features which the stimuli do and do not have in common. A feature chart can be helpful in a couple of ways. It can assist in completing the task analysis or in planning the lesson since it indicates to the teacher which features of the stimuli should be drawn to the attention of the students, where difficulties in discrimination are most likely to arise and, therefore, where specific discrimination training is most needed. One way to draw critical features to the attention of mature students is to have them take part in the construction of a feature chart in class.

To *discriminate* two stimuli means to notice a difference between them and act accordingly. A person *generalizes* when he makes the same response to distinguishable stimuli. Generalization involves ignoring differences and paying attention to similarities. Whether a person will discriminate or generalize depends upon his physical capacity to detect stimulus differences, his previous experience, and the specific instruction he receives.

All too often discrimination and generalization are treated as automatic and inexorable processes which simplify the teacher's task. However, the teacher cannot rely on generalization to take the place of thorough instruction. At a minimum the teacher must test to see if generalization has taken place. Similarly, discrimination is not an automatic process. Teachers must teach the discriminations they require, or at least they must test for stimulus control to see if these discriminations are already a part of the student's behavioral repertoire.

Discriminations can be taught using both respondent and operant conditioning techniques. In respondent conditioning a neutral stimulus is paired with an unconditioned stimulus. Eventually the neutral stimulus will become a conditioned stimulus which will itself control a fractional part of the response to the unconditioned stimulus. Other neutral stimuli paired with the conditioned stimulus can also acquire control over the response. In operant discrimination training, responses in the presence of one stimulus are reinforced, whereas responses to other stimuli are not reinforced.

Procedures for presenting stimuli in discrimination training include successive, simultaneous, matching-to-sample, and delayed matching-to-sample. People learn most easily from matching-to-sample; however, the successive presentation usually resembles more closely conditions of intended use. We recommend a combination procedure which makes the discrimination easy at the start and approximates conditions of use at the end of the teaching sequence.

Research shows that organisms learn more slowly when they make errors, that organisms which make errors during training will occasionally make errors later, and that errors have undesirable emotional and motivational side effects.

Prompting involves techniques to help students avoid errors. Prompts which entail copying or imitating are valuable for teaching a student new responses; however, when it comes to the phase of instruction in which stimulus control is to be established, prompts should be of such a nature that the student will notice the discriminative stimulus. At the end of any teaching sequence employing prompting techniques, the student should be tested to assure that he can make unprompted responses.

SCORING KEY FOR THE SELF-TEST ON STIMULUS CONTROL

The standard of performance is 100 percent. It would be a good idea to review the sections of the text related to questions upon which you made mistakes.

1. b

2. b

3. A stimulus controls a response if the response almost always occurs in the presence of this stimulus and does not occur in the presence of other stimuli.

4. **c**

5. conditioned stimulus (discriminative stimulus is also correct)

6. **a**

7. In a matching-to-sample problem, an S^D (the sample) is presented and, below it, the S^D is presented again along with one or more S^Δ's (the matches). All of the stimuli are present at the same time. The subject responds by choosing the match which is the same (except, perhaps, with respect to irrelevant features) and the sample. The form is as follows:

$$\begin{matrix} & S^D & \\ S^\Delta & & S^D \end{matrix}$$

8. Sometimes prompts permit the student to respond correctly without noticing the cue, which is supposed to become an S^D.

9. Any pair of numbers which do not *add* up to 127.

10. **a** and **c** are false.

11. In higher-order conditioning of word meaning, a person learns the meaning (especially the emotional and sensory connotations) of a word which he does not know when this word is paired with one he does know. The chapter used "disgusting-sick" and "azure-blue" as illustrations. There are, of course, countless other examples.

12. Some possibilities are a weather report on TV, thunder and lightning in the distance, dark clouds in the sky.

13. Students who make errors during learning will be prone to errors later. Errors also have undesirable emotional and motivational consequences.

14. In successive presentation, one stimulus appears at a time. Previous illustrations entailed letter and form discrimination. For variety, we shall choose an example from ecology this time. A series of plants and animals is named, one at a time. After each presentation the student must say "producer," "first-order consumer," or "second-order consumer." Examples:

grass
lion
moth
snake
oak
mouse

For those not acquainted with the concepts, producers are green plants. First-order consumers eat producers. Second-order consumers eat first-order consumers. Thus grass is an S^D for producer and an S^Δ for either first- or second-order consumer. If your procedure (though not necessarily the subject matter, of course) resembled the one described here, you are correct.

15. b

16. c

17. d. While inappropriate, this is, nonetheless, an instance of discrimination. Evidently the child discriminates a pony from a deer on the basis of a partially-valid feature, size.

Selected Readings

Aiken, E. G., & Law, A. W., "Response Prompting and Response Confirmation: A Review of Recent Literature," *Psychological Bulletin* (1967), *68*, 330–341. This review covers much of the basic and applied research on prompting.

Anderson, R. C., Faust, G. W., Roderick, M. C., Cunningham, D. J., & Andre, T., eds., "Section III. Prompting, Vanishing, and Fading," *Current Research on Instruction*. Englewood Cliffs, N.J.: Prentice-Hall, 1969. Included are five chapters describing various prompting techniques and reviewing research evidence on their effectiveness.

Terrace, H. S., "Stimulus Control," in W. K. Honig, ed., *Operant Behavior: Areas of Research and Application*. New York: Appleton-Century-Crofts, 1966. Terrace's paper contains an excellent, but technical, analysis of stimulus control.

CHAPTER

10

Concepts and Principles

All three components of the teaching model—presentation, student response, and reinforcement or corrective feedback—are involved in teaching concepts and principles. From the standpoint of the student, concept and principle learning is mainly a matter of learning when and under what circumstances certain responses are appropriate. To be sure, students frequently must acquire new responses when learning concepts and principles, but stimulus control is the chief consideration. The preceding chapter emphasized narrowing the range of stimuli that control a response to include only those for which the response is appropriate. This chapter emphasizes broadening the range of stimuli that control a response so as to include all of the stimulus situations in which the response is appropriate. When you have completed this chapter you should be able to:

1. identify and design questions, test items, and problems which can be used to evaluate student learning of concepts and principles.
2. describe effective procedures for teaching concepts and principles.

When Does a Person Possess a Concept?

What it means to know a concept can be communicated most easily with an illustration. Let us suppose that you wish to decide whether an infant understands the concept "ball." The child frequently plays with a smooth, pliable, air-filled plastic ball which is orange with white polka dots. You ask the child to bring the "ball" and he does so. Does this demonstrate that he possesses the concept? Not necessarily. It may be that the child has formed an association between this particular orange ball with white polka dots and the word "ball." The association may not even be with the features of this object which make it a ball, but instead with other irrelevant features, such as its color, size, or texture. Suppose that the child finds two other balls and brings them upon request. Can it now be said that he possesses the concept "ball"? Perhaps. It is still possible, though, that the child has formed associations between each specific ball, or some irrelevant feature which they share, and the word "ball." The crucial test of the understanding of the concept is whether the child can correctly identify *new* balls rather different from those with which he has had experience. Further, if he has an adequately refined concept of "ball," he will not confuse balls with other objects such as oranges and walnuts.

The evidence of possession of a concept is the capacity to make a common response (or set of responses) to a class of objects or events. A person "knows" a concept when the class controls his behavior. Thus a person who knows the concept "ball" can make a common response (e.g., say "ball") to each thing included in the class (any ball), but will not make this response to things not in the class. In other words, understanding of a concept entails the ability to classify things as examples of the concept (called "positive instances") and nonexamples (called "negative instances"). A basketball is a positive instance of the concept "ball." A grapefruit is a negative instance.

It is usually possible, though not always easy, to state a classification rule for a concept. The rule designates the *critical features* of objects that distinguish positive from negative instances. According to *Webster's Third New International Dictionary* (1964, p. 166), a ball is "a spherical or ovoid body of any kind for throwing, hitting or kicking in games or sports."[1] There are, then, by this particular definition, two critical features of the concept "ball." An object is a ball if it is (1) spherical or ovoid in shape and (2) used in a game or sport. Any person who calls those objects which have these two features "balls," and calls only these objects "balls," possesses the concept "ball," at least as defined by Webster's.

A critical feature is an attribute which all positive instances of a particular concept share. Objects which do not display *each* critical feature required of a positive instance are negative instances of the concept. Critical features may be observable, physical properties of objects involving, for instance, size, color, form, texture, numerosity, taste, or hardness. In such cases the stimuli embodying the critical feature may control behavior directly. One discriminates red from nonred by seeing

[1] Defined here, of course, is only one sense of "ball."

color. One discriminates spheres from nonspheres by seeing or feeling shape. Often, however, the critical feature is more subtle. There is no way to tell from a simple examination of an object whether it is used "for throwing, hitting or kicking in games or sports." In a primitive society a tightly bound bunch of leather thongs might be used as a ball. An American might not recognize that the bunch of thongs was a ball, however. He would have to ask a native or wait to observe the bunch of thongs in use in order to be sure of its function.

Critical features are also called "critical attributes," "relevant dimensions," and "defining properties." By whatever name, an object must possess certain critical features in order to be an instance of a given concept. Objects will also possess other noncritical, or irrelevant, features which have no bearing on whether the objects are positive or negative instances of a concept. For example, balls may be various colors, sizes, and textures. These are irrelevant features as far as the concept "ball" is concerned.

A pervasive problem for the educator is to prevent irrelevant features from influencing the student's concepts. It often happens that positive instances share irrelevant as well as relevant features. Though size does not enter into the definition of "ball," balls are seldom greater than thirty inches in circumference. The concept of "democracy" is usually illustrated with examples showing nations friendly to one's own country, whereas "dictatorship" is most frequently illustrated with examples showing nations that are current or historic enemies of one's own country. Thus, the student may form a restricted concept when the examples in his experience have common *irrelevant* features. In technical language, the irrelevant features may control or partly control his behavior.

Sometimes critical features may be substituted for one another. In these cases the concept is said to be "disjunctive," which simply means that the thing conceptualized must possess one feature *or* another in order to be a positive instance. The legal concept of a citizen of the United States is disjunctive. A person is a citizen if he was born in the United States *or* if he was naturalized.

Not all concepts involve objects taken one at a time. Many entail relationships between two or more objects or events. One cannot, for instance, speak of an object's being "larger" without at least implying, if not directly specifying, another object which is smaller. Other examples of relational concepts include "earlier," "between," "on top of," and "equal." Like all concepts, relational concepts can be defined by one or more critical features.

That concepts can be defined by critical features is important. If this were not the case, dictionaries would be, at best, very cumbersome. The only way to define concepts would be to make exhaustive lists of positive instances. Students could be taught concepts only by being exposed to multitudes of examples.

Some educators and psychologists talk about concepts and concept learning as though concepts could not be satisfactorily defined in terms of critical features. To exaggerate slightly, they talk, for instance, as though to teach a child the concept "ball," it would be necessary to teach him to say "ball" to each and every kind of ball known to man. In this view, primitive stimulus generalization among very similar balls might provide some benefit; that is, it might be expected that if the child were taught to classify a tennis ball and a softball, he would be more likely to classify a baseball correctly. In any event, if this view were to be accepted, a very large number of instances would be required to teach the concept satisfactorily. This view is inaccurate, however. People usually do not learn concepts by learning a connection between each positive instance and the concept name. Rather, what is usually learned is the connection between the critical features which define the concept and the concept name. Technically speaking, when a person "knows a concept," behavior is under the control of the stimuli that embody the critical features which define the concept.

The Complexity of Concepts

Thus far the value of analyzing the critical features of concepts has been emphasized. Unfortunately, it is sometimes very difficult to specify those critical features. Indeed, the philosopher Wittgenstein (1958) argued that it is impossible. He used the concept of "game" to illustrate his point. Taking the game of football, the game of chess, the game of hide-and-seek, among other common games, he shows that these are difficult but perhaps not impossible to include within a single rule. However, when one also considers war games, *Games People Play* (Berne, 1964), the "selling game," and the game of life, a neat classification rule becomes impossible. A narrow rule will exclude activities which are classified as games, whereas a broad rule will include activities that are not so classified. The concept of "game" may be an extreme case, but it is not so unusual as to be misleading. Even the classification rule for a concept as apparently simple as "ball" is imperfect: both a marble and a shot put possess the two critical features listed by *Webster's Third International,* and yet neither is customarily called a "ball." And who could easily state the critical features of "justice" or "beauty"?

Over decades of use concepts become encrusted with nuances and extended meanings. New cases arise. Concepts must be stretched to accommodate them or delimited to exclude them. Thus, definition of a "concept" as a well-defined set of critical features is a simplified and idealized definition. Perhaps a more realistic one—and one in common use—is that a "concept" is a bundle of more or less distinctive features, it being the case that no single set of these features allows a perfect classification.

Scientists frequently define their own terms because they are unwilling to live with the ambiguities of concepts in ordinary, everyday language. A concept given a technical or scientific definition may bear a resemblance, sometimes a close one, to a concept in common usage. Even so, the scientist may insist on coining a new term for the concept, instead of using the common one. The practice of coining terms leads the student to complain bitterly that the concepts he is asked to learn are easily understandable and that only the jargon prevents his comprehension. In a sense, he may be right. Yet there is rarely a one-to-one correspondence between concepts in common usage and concepts in a technical specialty. For example, the common concept of "reward" is similar but not identical to the technical concept "reinforcement." The concepts defined within a discipline are intended to be more precise in meaning than those commonly employed. The use of "jargon" to name concepts helps preserve precision of definition and prevent the intrusion of unwanted meanings from common usage. Still, even within technical and scientific communities, terms have "surplus meaning" and concepts undergo change with usage.

The reason for emphasizing the complexity and mutability of concepts is to dispel excessively rationalistic ideas about the nature of concepts. Concepts are not eternal essences. They are adapted as they are used. And it may be difficult to designate the essential attributes of concepts which have an evolutionary history. Despite the foregoing problems, we do not wish to discard the definition of a concept as a classification based on a set of critical features. It is a useful simplification to define concepts by their critical features, since this is a serviceable approximation of the way concepts are typically used.

Principles

We shall define a *principle* as two or more concepts related in some manner. In his important book *The Conditions of Learning,* Gagné (1965, pp. 142–143) illustrates a principle as follows:

> A young child may be told, "Round things roll." Such a statement obviously represents two different concepts: (1) *round things* and (2) *roll.* Under what circumstances might it be expected that learning has occurred from the

making of such a statement? What are the conditions under which one can be pretty certain that the child has learned the *principle* that round things roll?

It seems fairly evident that if learning of the principle is to be expected, the child must already know the concepts *round things* and *roll.* If he has not already acquired the concept *round,* he may end up learning a more restricted principle, such as *balls roll,* and therefore be unable to show that a half-dollar will roll, or a saucer. Accordingly if he is to acquire this principle in its fullest sense, he must know the concept *round* in its full sense, as it applies to a variety of objects including round discs and cylinders as well as spherical objects like balls.

Similarly, he should have previously acquired the concept of the event *roll.* Naturally, this must be distinguished (by multiple-discrimination learning) from such events as *sliding* and *tumbling.* Such a concept as this may be considerably more difficult to learn than *round,* in fact, since the stimulus events of rotating about an axis may not be easy to discriminate from other events involving the motion of bodies. But again, if the child is to be set the task of learning the principle, and not just a partial principle, he must have acquired the concept *roll.*

The term "principle" is sometimes used to refer to the key generalizations of a discipline. The term is used here in a broader sense. As used here it may include simple and sometimes trivial facts and definitions, as well as important generalizations. For instance, in a botany class the student might learn that palmate leaves are so-called because they are approximately hand-shaped, a true but not very important fact. He might also learn in the same class that gene pools tend to remain stable from generation to generation, an important generalization. Both the fact and the generalization are principles since both entail relationships among several concepts.

From Verbal Chains to Principles

Given the word "needle" and instructions to say the first word that comes to mind, most people will say "thread." In the language that we have been using in this book, the instructions and the word "needle" are stimuli which control the response "thread." In traditional language, it would be said that "needle" and "thread" are associated.

Verbal associations may form chains. An example of a verbal chain is the one formed by the months of the year. When one recites the months of the year—January, February, March . . . and so on—each month is a stimulus which controls the name of the next month in the chain. In other words, each name is both a stimulus (S^D) and a response (R). Other examples of verbal chains are the names of the letters of the alphabet, the names of the days of the week, the Boy Scout Law, and the numerals starting with "one." Strings of words which form sentences can also be learned as chains. For instance, when a person "memorizes" a poem, the lines for a part in a play, or an oration, he typically learns a verbal chain.

A person can recite a verbal chain without knowing what he is talking about. An obvious instance is a song sung in a foreign language. Less obvious is the fact that a student can learn important sentences from his textbook as simple verbal chains. Thus, educational folklore is quite right to cast suspicion on mere rote learning. The distinction between a simple verbal chain and a principle is crucial here. The former is a chain of words involving memory with little or no understanding; the latter, a chain of concepts that have been understood. An example will help to make the distinction clear. If a person has learned the verbal chain "iron oxidizes," he has learned to say the words "iron" and "oxidizes" in the indicated order. On the other hand, if he has learned the principle "iron oxidizes," he has learned that a certain element (which he can distinguish) reacts characteristically with another element (in a manner which he can distinguish).

Concepts and principles are not limited to verbal-symbolic stimuli and responses. It is quite reasonable, for instance, to speak of motor concepts and emotional concepts. Thus, a person who consistently behaves in a deferential manner toward authority figures clearly possesses a concept. A class of stimuli (authority figures) controls a common set of responses (deferential behavior). Nor will a person necessarily be able to describe in verbal form the concepts and principles he possesses. A professional baseball player has the remarkable ability to run at the crack of the bat to the exact point where he can intercept the ball. He possesses a refined set of principles with respect to chasing down fly balls, yet his verbal descriptions of these principles might be woefully inadequate.

Since so much instruction, perhaps too much, is verbal, there is the ever present danger that the student's capacity to say the name of a concept will be confused with knowledge of the concept, or that his ability to recite a verbal chain will be mistaken for understanding of a principle.

Testing for Knowledge of Concepts and Principles

After an instructional episode designed to teach a principle, a teacher may entertain the hypothesis for each student that he now understands the principle. The hypothesis cannot be regarded as confirmed, though, until the student has successfully passed a test to demonstrate his understanding. Tests include not only formal end-of-lesson quizzes or end-of-course achievement tests but questions, tasks, or problems posed during a lesson. Probing the limits of a student's understanding is one of the chief functions of a teacher. Incidentally, while an author of a textbook or self-instructional program may build probes into his material, the teacher conducting a class in person is uniquely suited for this function. It remains to be seen whether computer-based instruction can serve as well.

A lesson may obviously fail to teach, but not all failures are obvious. Lack of understanding of a principle can easily escape detection. It is for this reason that we urge the teacher, during and after each lesson, to take the stance of a scientist with an hypothesis to test. The hypothesis is that each student has fully mastered the principle (or principles) which the lesson is designed to teach. There are at least two rivals to this hypothesis. The first is that the student has learned a verbal chain instead of a principle. The second rival hypothesis is that the student has acquired a partial or restricted form of the principle.

The next several pages contain a self-instructional program designed to review the concepts developed earlier in the chapter and to explain the types of questions which will allow a teacher to discriminate between understanding and lack of understanding of a concept or of a principle. A person who completes this program should be able to:

1. define a concept.
2. distinguish between critical and irrelevant features of a concept.
3. define a principle.
4. distinguish between a principle and a verbal chain.
5. explain the characteristics which a test item must possess if it is to probe for mastery of a concept or principle.
6. identify questions which will test mastery of a principle.

To receive full benefit from the program, read every frame completely and carefully. Fill in each blank in the way you believe makes the most sense. Then, turn the page as directed to see the answer the authors believe is best.

Please write an answer to each item *before* turning the page. Sometimes a single word is required, sometimes a phrase, or perhaps a sentence or two. Regard your answer as correct if its meaning is the same as the authors' answer.

PROGRAM II

1

Possession of a concept is marked by the capacity to make a common response to examples of a class of objects or events, also called (a) ______________ instances, and discriminate these from, nonexamples, also called (b) ______________ instances.

Turn to page **348**

ans. 18

Yes. The student who correctly answers this question may or may not understand the principle.

19

When a test item repeats the words used during instruction, the student can answer the item on the basis of a verbal chain. However, when the test item contains language *substantially different* from (but which means the same thing as) that employed during instruction, the student must answer on the basis of a ______________.

Turn to page **348**

ans. 34

We would argue that it is seldom safe to <u>assume</u> that students have fully mastered principles, least of all when a restricted variety of examples was included within instruction.

35

What is one problem with questions that duplicate the wording of instructional statements?

Turn to page **348**

ns. 9

ritical (relevant, defining)

10

When the positive instances of a concept to which a student has been exposed share common *irrelevant* features, these irrelevant features may partly ____________ the student's behavior.

Turn to page **349**

ns. 26

Yes, since the example used in the question is different from the example contained in instructional passage I (although only minimally so).

27

All positive instances of a concept or principle share ______________________________
______________________________.

Turn to page **349**

ns. 42

He is virtually certain to pass the Level III test.

43

The rule is that a person is unlikely to pass a test at a given level unless he has passed tests at ____________ levels.

Turn to page **349**

ans. 1

(a) positive
(b) negative

2

A person who knows a concept can ______________ things as positive or negative instances of the concept.

Turn to page **350**

---

ans. 19

principle (concept)

20

A test item or question which has somewhat different syntax and wording may still be answered on the basis of a verbal chain. A question tests a principle only if the wording is very unlike that used during instruction. Consider the following item in relation to instructional passage I.

> *Item B.* Resistance to extinction is
>
> A. the technical phrase for survival of the fittest.
> B. increased by partial reinforcement.
> C. a function of number of hours of deprivation during conditioning.

Does this item measure understanding of a principle?

Turn to page **350**

---

ans. 35

The student can answer such questions by repeating a verbal chain (also acceptable: because they do not test mastery of concepts or principles).

36

What would you predict would be the long-term effect on the study habits of a student if he were very frequently able to answer questions by memorizing the literal wording of instructional statements? Explain in a sentence or two *why* you answer as you do.

Turn to page **350**

ans. 10

control

11

To say that an irrelevant feature partly controls behavior is to say in common language that the student is (more) (less) likely to "think of" the concept when an instance contains the irrelevant feature than when it does not.

Turn to page **351**

---

ans. 27

In your own words:

the critical features (which define the concept or principle)

28

With what must the wording and examples in a question be compared in order to judge whether the questions test mastery of concepts and principles?

Turn to page **351**

---

ans. 43

lower (preceding, previous)

44

Consider the following records which, if the previous reasoning is correct, represent the only possible outcomes.

	Student A	*Student B*	*Student C*	*Student D*
Level I	Pass	Fail	Fail	Fail
Level II	Pass	Pass	Fail	Fail
Level III	Pass	Pass	Pass	Fail

Which student or students could be said to have learned only a verbal chain?

Turn to page **351**

ans. 2
classify (also acceptable: categorize, identify, distinguish between)

3

There are some cases in which even the ability to classify things correctly is *not* evidence that a student has mastered a concept. One such case is when the student is asked to reclassify instances that were classified for him a few moments before. In this case the student need only ________ the classification.

Turn to page **352**

---

ans. 20

In the authors' judgment the answer is "no." We feel that a person who had learned the instructional statement as a verbal chain would be able to identify the correct answer. He will probably recognize that "increases" means about the same thing as "leads to" and that "partial" is roughly equivalent to "intermittent."

Turn to page **352**

---

ans. 36

In your own words:

He would spend more of his study time memorizing the literal wording of instructional statements. Successfully answering questions leads to a variety of reinforcers—good grades, praise from the teacher, signs of respect and esteem from classmates. Study behavior that allows the pupil to answer questions correctly would undoubtedly be strengthened. Thus, the student would spend an increasing proportion of his study time committing strings of words to memory.

Turn to page **352**

ans. 11

more

12

In order to provide a valid test of a concept, an example in a question *must* possess the ______________ features of the concept.

Turn to page **353**

---

ans. 28

In your own words:

The wording and the examples of the <u>instruction</u> which was intended to teach the concepts and principles.

29

Compare the example in frame 26 (p. 364) with the example in instructional passage I (p. 361). Name at least one irrelevant way in which these examples resemble each other.

Turn to page **353**

---

ans. 44

Student C

Note: Students A and B have both learned a principle. Student D has learned nothing.

45

The contrast between students C and D (refer to frame 44) is informative. There has been a gross failure to teach student D. Perhaps he has not completed assignments nor paid attention in class. Sharpening the contingencies of reinforcement and bringing to bear the strongest reinforcers which are available is probably indicated as a first step with student D. Student C has completed assignments and he has paid attention, at least some of the time, but all he has to show for his effort is a pseudo-achievement.

Turn to page **353**

ans. 3

remember (also acceptable: recall, repeat)

4

When a person literally remembers the words to which he has been exposed, he has learned a verbal ________.

Turn to page **354**

21

> *Item* C. An organism rewarded for some but not all acceptable responses will
>
> A. be *more* highly motivated than an organism which was always rewarded.
> B. be *less* highly motivated than an organism which was always rewarded.
> C. change to another activity, when rewards are terminated, more quickly than an organism which was always rewarded.
> D. <u>persist in the original activity for a longer time, when rewards are terminated, than an organism which was always rewarded.</u>

Could this question (again, based on the instructional passage on p. 361) be answered on the basis of a verbal chain?

Turn to page **354**

37

Do you see any value in test items that duplicate or nearly duplicate the wording of instructional statements? If so, what?

Turn to page **354**

ans. 12

critical

Note: (It is, moreover, not an example of the concept unless it possesses *all* of the critical features of the concept)

13

When two or more concepts form a relationship, this is a ______________.

Turn to page **355**

---

ans. 29

Some possibilities are:

- **a. Both involve a reinforcer which is consumed.**
- **b. Both involve animals.**
- **c. Both involve an arbitrary response which would not occur in the animal's natural habitat.**

Turn to page **355**

---

ans. 45

Frame 45 is self-answering.

46

There is nothing wrong with a student's being able to repeat or recognize the literal wording of the lessons to which he has been exposed as long as he is also ______________ ______________.

Turn to page **355**

ans. 4

chain

5

The instances the student is asked to categorize in order to test mastery of a concept should be ____________ from those used to teach him the concept.

Turn to page **356**

ans. 21

Probably not. In our judgment, this item measures the student's understanding of the principle involved. We do not believe that it could be answered on the basis of a simple verbal chain.

22

How about this question?

> What is one effect of intermittent reinforcement?

Turn to page **356**

ans. 37

The question asked what value <u>you</u> saw.

38

If your answer to the preceding frame was "no," consider the fact that a coach would not begin to evaluate the high-jumping ability of junior high school students by placing the crossbar at six feet. Now, if you have not already done so, suggest a possible value to a question that repeats the words of the lesson.

Turn to page **356**

ans. 13

principle

14

A principle consists of two or more (a) _______________, whereas a verbal chain consists of several (b) _______________ in an indicated order.

Turn to page **357**

30

Name, if you can, an irrelevant way in which the example in the item below resembles the example contained in instructional passage I.

> *Item F.* It is known that a seasoned life insurance salesman will continue to make contacts in the attempt to sell even when he goes through a long period in which he sells no insurance. Which of the following is the best explanation of this behavior?
>
> A. He is highly motivated to sell.
> B. Life insurance salesmen sell to only a small proportion of the people they contact.
> C. Just contacting people has its rewards.

Turn to page **357**

---

ans. 46

able to answer questions that contain different wording (and examples)

(also acceptable: able to demonstrate that he understands concepts and principles)

47

What is the difference between the knowledge possessed by Student A and Student B? (Refer to the chart in frame 44, p. 349.)

Turn to page **357**

ans. 5

different (distinct, separate)

6

A principle consists of several related ____________.

Turn to page **358**

ans. 22

It could be answered on the basis of a verbal chain. The student could answer "resistance to extinction" without knowing what he is talking about.

23

While particular cases may be difficult to judge, the general rule for distinguishing between questions and test items which probe understanding of principles and those which require only recall or recognition of verbal chains is not complicated. Please summarize the rule in your own words.

Turn to page **358**

ans. 38

A verbatim question could help determine whether students have learned <u>anything.</u> Furthermore, concepts and principles are not the only things worth teaching. Sometimes the objective is to teach simple associations (e.g., foreign language vocabulary) and chains (e.g., counting).

Turn to page **358**

ans. 14

(a) concepts
(b) words

15

A teacher may hope that the student has learned a principle, but the student may only have learned ________________.

Turn to page **359**

---

ans. 30

This item <u>does</u> test the principle that intermittent reinforcement increases resistance to extinction, yet as far as the authors can see, it shares no irrelevant features (at least, no important ones) with the instructional passage.

31

Here is another item in which the example bears little resemblance to the instructional example.

> *Item G.* Intermittently, Mr. Jones's car fails to start when he turns the key. One day the car fails to start at all. Which of the following can be predicted?
> A. After a few attempts to start the car, Mr. Jones will call a cab.
> B. <u>Mr. Jones's attempts to start the car will extinguish slowly.</u>
> C. Mr. Jones will fly into a rage.
> D. Mr. Jones will buy a new car.

Describe, if you can, any defects in this question which would prevent it from testing the limits of a student's understanding.

Turn to page **359**

---

ans. 47

In your own words:

Student B has some understanding of the principle; however, Student A's grasp is broader and deeper.

48

This program has discussed verbal *descriptions* of examples rather than *actual* examples. There is a difference, for instance, between a description of a hamster depressing a lever and an actual live hamster pushing a lever with its paw or nose. On the basis of the concepts developed in this program, it can be concluded that a student who can successfully deal with descriptions of examples (probably would) (might not) be able to deal successfully with actual examples.

Turn to page **359**

ans. 6

concepts

7

The instances used in most questions regarding concepts should be as different as possible from the instances included within instruction, otherwise the questions may contain prompts that will help the student to correctly ______________ the instances even though he has not mastered the concept.

Turn to page **360**

ans. 23

In your own words:

When a question contains the same words, or nearly the same words as were used during instruction, the question can be answered on the basis of a verbal chain alone. When the language of a question is substantially different from the language of instruction, the question probes understanding of a principle.

Turn to page **360**

39

The questions that can be asked about a verbal subject matter form a rough hierarchy or "ladder." Classify each of the questions in frames 18, 20, 21, 22, 24, 26, 30, and 31 into one of the three levels of this hierarchy.

Level I	*Level II*	*Level III*
Questions containing examples as remote as possible from *all* instructional examples with respect to *every* irrelevant feature.	Questions that contain examples which are different from but still resemble instructional examples. Also, questions which restate principles in substantially different language.	Questions which repeat, or nearly repeat, the wording or examples employed during the lesson.

Turn to page **360**

ans. 15

a verbal chain

16

Designing questions which will discriminate between knowledge of a principle and a simple verbal chain is an important teaching skill. Whether a particular question tests understanding depends upon the wording of the question *in relation to* the wording of the lesson which taught the principle. Before proceeding, please read the following passage on intermittent reinforcement.

Turn to page **361**

---

ans. 31

While the example in this question bears almost no resemblance to the one in the instructional passage, the words "intermittently" and "extinguish" might allow the student to answer on the basis of a verbal chain. If the question were rewritten using other words, it would do a good job of testing for mastery of the principle.

Turn to page **361**

---

ans. 48

might not

49

It cannot be *assumed* that experience with verbal descriptions can substitute for experience with the real thing (though sometimes it may). Fortunately, concepts and principles based on real instances can be analyzed in the same way as concepts and principles taught and tested using only descriptions of instances. Summarize the characteristics a question must have if it is to probe complete mastery of a principle.

Turn to page **361**

ans. 7

classify

8

Which of the following are critical features and which are irrelevant features in determining whether an object is a chair?

a. color
b. material of which it is made
c. used for sitting
d. amount of padding

Turn to page **362**

24

Item D. Pigeon #1 receives food for some but not all pecking responses. Pigeon #2 receives food for every peck on the key.

A. When food is terminated pigeon #1 will peck the key a greater number of times than pigeon #2.
B. When food is terminated, pigeon #2 will peck the key a greater number of times than pigeon #1.

What is tested by this item?

Turn to page **362**

ans. 39

Level I: Frame 30
Level II: Frames 21, 26
Level III: Frames 18, 20, 22, 24
(Frame 31 is doubtful)

40

Suppose that a lesson has been taught and an examination given. The examination contains several questions at each level in the verbal subject-matter hierarchy. It is possible to give each student a "pass" or a "fail" grade at each level.

How would you predict a student would do on Level II and Level III questions, given that he has passed the Level I questions? (Refer to the chart in frame 39 when necessary.)

Turn to page **362**

16 (continued)

Instructional Passage I: One Effect of Intermittent Reinforcement

Intermittent reinforcement leads to resistance to extinction. This principle can be demonstrated in a simple experiment. For a period of time, one pigeon receives food for some but not all pecks on a key. The second pigeon receives food for every pecking response. After the food is terminated, the first pigeon will peck the key a greater number of times than the second.

Turn to page **363**

32

With respect to *irrelevant* features, text examples should be (the same as) (different from) instructional examples in order to test full mastery of a concept or principle.

Turn to page **363**

ans. 49

In your own words:

The student should be asked questions involving examples—either actual examples or descriptions of examples—different in every irrelevant way, if possible, from the examples used to teach him the concept. Of course, test examples will embody the critical features of the concept or principle. The questions should not contain "key" words from the lesson which might allow the student to answer on the basis of a verbal chain.

50

Explain why a test that contained only questions with examples very, very different from instructional examples would be unsatisfactory.

Turn to page **363**

ans. 8

critical features	irrelevant features
c. used for sitting	a. color b. material of which it is made d. amount of padding

Turn to page **364**

ans. 51

examples different (or remote) in every irrelevant way from the examples included within the lesson.

END OF PROGRAM

Turn to self-test on page **366**

ans. 24

A verbal chain. Examples can be learned as verbal chains, too. The wording of the test item is slightly different than the wording in the instructional passage on p. 361, but this item still could be answered easily on the basis of a verbal chain.

25

A student has at least some understanding of a principle when he can answer a question involving a reworded general statement of the principle. But his understanding is not necessarily broad nor deep. Especially valuable in probing the limits of a student's understanding are questions containing ______________ which were not included within instruction.

Turn to page **364**

ans. 40

He would undoubtedly pass Level II and Level III questions too.

41

What about a person who *failed* the Level I questions? How would he be expected to perform on Level II and Level III questions?

Turn to page **364**

17

Instructional passage I is supposed to teach the principle that intermittent reinforcement leads to (a) ______________________.
The example shows that a pigeon that receives food (b) (some) (all) of the time will make more pecking responses when food is no longer available than will a pigeon that previously received food (c) (some) (all) of the time.

Turn to page **365**

ans. 32

different from

33

A game some teachers like to play might be called Trap the Student. One way to play this game is to ask tricky questions which split fine hairs or employ difficult, ambiguous wording. Another way to play is to devise test examples which are very remote in every way from the instructional examples. Of course, following excellent instruction it will frequently be impossible to devise a test example which is remote in every way. The reason for this is that most teachers most of the time are trying to play another game called Teach the Student. A teacher trying to play this game will devise instruction which usually includes a wide ______________ of examples.

Turn to page **365**

ans. 50

In your own words:

Because among those who failed the test would be (a) pupils who had mastered at least a restricted form of the principle, (b) pupils who could answer questions in which the wording and examples were very much like those in the lesson, as well as (c) those who learned nothing. There would be no way to distinguish among these three groups of students.

Turn to page **365**

9

The goal of instruction on concepts and principles is to get student behavior under the control of the ______________ features of the instances of the concept.

Turn to page **347**

---

ans. 25

examples

26

> *Item E.* Hamster *J* is allowed to drink water occasionally after it depresses a lever. Hamster *M* receives water for every depression of the lever. Which hamster will depress the lever the greatest number of times when water is no longer provided?

Assuming the student has read only the instructional passage on p. 361, does this question test mastery of a principle?

Turn to page **347**

---

ans. 41

It is impossible to say. He might pass them or he might fail them.

42

Now consider a pupil who failed the Level I test, but passed the Level II test. How would he do on the Level III test?

Turn to page **347**

ans. 17

(a) **resistance to extinction**
(b) **some**
(c) **all**

18

Consider the following achievement-test item. The correct answer is underlined.

> *Item A.* Intermittent reinforcement leads to
>
> A. rapid conditioning.
> B. a decrease in rate of responding.
> C. resistance to extinction. (underlined)
> D. either a variable ratio or variable interval schedule of reinforcement.

Assume passage I (p. 361) is the only instruction students have received on the topic being tested. Could this item be answered on the basis of a verbal chain?

Turn to page **346**

ans. 33

variety (also acceptable: range)

34

When instruction includes a wide variety of examples, it may be impossible to choose test examples which differ from *all* instructional examples with respect to *every* irrelevant feature. However, satisfactory instruction does not always contain a great range of examples. The classroom teacher, or the author of a textbook, or the developer of a self-instructional program may correctly judge that students will master a principle given only, say, one example. To present more examples under these conditions would simply waste the student's time. When instruction contains just a few examples, it is probably (safe) (not safe) to assume that most students will learn the principle the instruction was designed to teach.

Turn to page **346**

51

If you can discover examples of the concept or principle which the student cannot successfully deal with, then you know that his mastery is not complete. What sort of example would a student be least likely to be able to deal with successfully?

Turn to page **362**

SELF-TEST ON KNOWLEDGE OF CONCEPTS AND PRINCIPLES

You have just completed a segment of instruction which contained a limited variety of examples. We shall now see whether this instruction has successfully taught the concepts and principles it aimed to teach.

Complete the test without looking back over the preceding pages, then check your answers against the scoring key which follows. Please write your answers on a separate sheet of paper.

1. Define a concept.

2. Distinguish between critical and irrelevant features of a concept.

3. Define a principle.

4. Distinguish between knowledge of a principle and knowledge of a verbal chain.

5. What characteristics should a question or test item possess if it is to probe mastery of a principle?

Mark with a *V* each of the items below that could be answered on the basis of a verbal chain. Mark with a *P* each of the items that tests a principle. Place a *PP* beside any question that deeply probes the limits of mastery of a principle. Mark all of the test items in one of these three ways.

Items 6 through 10 are based on instructional passage II on p. 367. Assume this passage is the only instruction the student has received on this topic. The correct alternatives are underlined.

6. Several rats learn to run down an alley and turn *right* in order to receive food. When the behavior of turning right is well established, conditions are reversed. Now the rat must turn *left* to get food. Half of the rats learn the turn to the left after being deprived of food for four hours. The remainder learn the turn to the left under twelve hours of deprivation. Which group has learned the new turn most quickly?

a. <u>the rats deprived of food for four hours</u>
b. the rats deprived of food for 12 hours
c. There should be no difference in speed of learning.

Instructional Passage II: A Prediction from Hullian Drive Theory

High drive facilitates learning when correct responses are initially dominant but inhibits learning when incorrect responses are initially nondominant. This principle has been demonstrated in research in which high anxious and low anxious subjects learn easy or hard word pairs. As the principle predicts, high anxious persons learned the easy pairs (e.g., "arctic-frigid," "crazy-insane") more quickly but learned the hard pairs (e.g., "arctic-insane," "crazy-frigid") more slowly than did the low anxious persons.

7. When correct responses are initially dominant, learning is facilitated by

- **a.** high drive.
- **b.** low drive.
- **c.** intermittent mild electric shocks.
- **d.** continuous mild electric shocks.

8. Difficult, confusing material is most easily learned

- **a.** when a person is very highly motivated.
- **b.** when a person is moderately motivated.
- **c.** just before dinner.

9. A child driven by a very strong "desire to please" would probably do best in a reading program in which

- **a.** children are punished for their mistakes.
- **b.** children are encouraged to guess freely at words.
- **c.** children are not encouraged to guess at words until it is almost certain they can respond correctly.

10. High anxious persons learn

- **a.** hard word pairs more quickly than low anxious persons.
- **b.** easy word pairs more quickly than low anxious persons.

Items 11 through 15 are based on instructional passage III.

Instructional Passage III: Reinforcers

Any thing or event which increases the likelihood of behavior that precedes it is a *reinforcer*. For example, a hungry pigeon will peck a key with increasing frequency if pecks on the key are followed by food. Food is a reinforcer for a hungry pigeon.

11. Behavior that precedes a reinforcer is

a. extinguished.
b. motivated.
c. strengthened.

12. When a thing or event following a response increases the likelihood of that response in the future, the thing or event is a

a. punisher.
b. reinforcer.
c. conditioned stimulus.

13. It is known that praise is reinforcing. Therefore

a. behavior which precedes praise will become more frequent.
b. behavior that follows praise will become more frequent.
c. behavior that follows praise will become less frequent.

14. Define a reinforcer.

15. Under some conditions, the rate at which a hamster eats food can be increased by allowing the hamster the opportunity to play on an "activity wheel" after it eats. What is the reinforcer here?

a. the opportunity to play on the activity wheel
b. food
c. rate of eating

SCORING KEY FOR THE SELF-TEST ON KNOWLEDGE OF CONCEPTS AND PRINCIPLES

Score your own test using the following guide. Your wording need not be the same, but your answer must mean the same as the authors' answer to get credit.

1. (*1 point*)

A concept is a well-defined set of critical features; a bundle of more or less distinctive features. Evidence of possession of a concept is the capacity to make a common response to a class of things or events.

2. (*2 points*)

(1) Critical features are those characteristics (properties, attributes) which an object *must* possess in order to be a positive instance (example) of a concept.
(1) Irrelevant features are characteristics that have no bearing on whether an object is a positive instance of a concept.

3. (*1 point*)

A principle consists of two or more related concepts.

4. (*2 points*)

(1) A person who "knows" a verbal chain can produce or recognize a certain string of words, usually in a fixed order.
(1) A person who knows a principle will be able to answer questions that entail new words and examples.

5. (*2 points*)

(1) Test questions should not contain the "key" words used during instruction.
(1) The test example should be different from every instructional example with respect to all irrelevant features, if possible.

6. (*2 points*) PP

(*1 point*) P

7. (*2 points*) V

8. (*2 points*) P
(*1 point*) PP

9. (*2 points*) PP
(*1 point*) V. The words "driven" and "respond correctly" may allow the student to answer on the basis of a verbal chain; the item would be improved if these words were changed.

10. (*2 points*) V

11. (*2 points*) V
(*1 point*) P

12. (*2 points*) V

13. (*2 points*) V
(*1 point*) P

14. (*2 points*) V

15. (*2 points*) PP
(*1 point*) P

A total of 28 points could be earned on the self-test. A score of 25 or better is very good. A score of 22 is passing. If you got fewer than 22 points, it would be a good idea to review all or part of the program.

The Teaching of Concepts

Psychologists have been investigating concept learning for many years; and during this time an enormous number of experiments have been completed. This research has been concerned almost exclusively with how and under what conditions people *induce* concepts from series of positive and negative instances. This approach, of course, is exactly opposed to the one usually employed in school, in which the concept is defined for the student and illustrated with one or more examples. Unfortunately little systematic research has investigated concepts learned under these conditions.

Most psychological laboratory research on inductive concept learning deals in a simplified way under simplified conditions with what educators call "discovery learning." In discovery learning the student is led to induce concepts and principles instead of being told them. Many educators, particularly science and mathematics educators, are enthusiastic about this form of learning. (Following a summary of the psychological literature on induction of concepts, the claims for discovery learning will be evaluated. Some, but not all, of the conclusions based on this laboratory research are also applicable to instruction in which the student is told about the concept.)

In a typical laboratory concept learning task the stimuli are abstract geometric designs that differ in a variety of ways. For example, Anderson (1966) used 128 distinct stimuli which represented all possible combinations of seven characteristics: (1) number—one or two figures; (2) color—red or green; (3) form—rectangle or diamond; (4) shading—solid, outline; (5) centered black bar—vertical, horizontal; (6) border—continuous, broken; (7) position of figures—horizontal, vertical. These stimuli are illustrated in Fig. 10.1. The subject saw one geometric design at a time on a small screen in front of him. His task was to classify each design as an *X* or a *Y*. As soon as he made a response, he was told whether he was right or wrong. When the subject could make fifteen consecutive correct classifications, it was assumed that he had learned the concept. (Actually, the subject had to learn a pair of related concepts. He had to learn which things were *X*'s and which things were *Y*'s.)

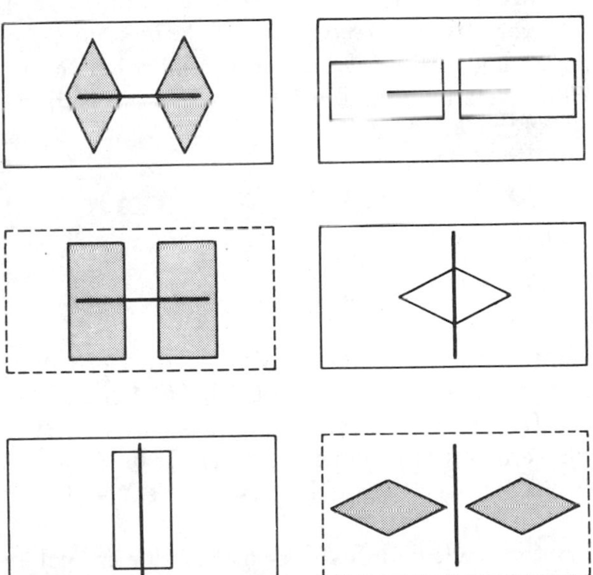

FIGURE 10.1 *Typical stimulus figures employed in research on concept learning.*

The experimenter arbitrarily chose the shape of the geometric designs as the characteristic which defined the concepts. All designs displaying a rectangular shape were *X*'s and all designs displaying a diamond shape were *Y*'s. Thus, the critical features of the concepts involved shape. All of the other features of the designs—for instance, color and number—were irrelevant. Technically speaking, when the subject learned the concepts, behavior (responding *X* or *Y*) came under control of the discriminative stimulus, shape.

From the many laboratory studies of concept learning, there is one major conclusion which has direct implications for educational practice: the speed with which a person will induce a concept (or the likelihood that he will learn it at all) is increased by any arrangement of instances or any procedure that makes the critical features of the concept more noticeable. Several ways of emphasizing critical features have been studied. We shall now consider these.

Eliminate or hold constant irrelevant features. There is a wealth of experimental evidence showing that the difficulty of learning a concept is directly proportional to the number of irrelevant features embodied in the instances (e.g., Archer, Bourne, & Brown, 1955). The more irrelevant features there are, the greater the difficulty people have in learning a concept. The simplest way, therefore, to get people to induce concepts—for instance, *rectangle-X* and *diamond-Y*—is to simplify the task, eliminating all irrelevant features. Present one or the other of the following two stimuli in an irregular order until the person always responds correctly.

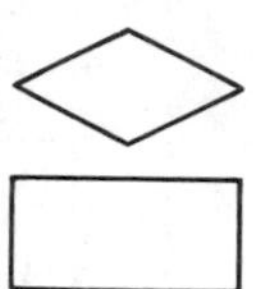

After the person can perform correctly with these "stripped down" designs, switch to designs, such as those in Fig. 10.1, which are elaborated with irrelevant features. After switching, the chances are excellent that the person will continue to respond correctly. If he does so, he will have induced the concepts that rectangular designs are *X* and diamond-shaped designs are *Y*.

Suppressing the irrelevant features makes the critical features relatively more obvious. No longer distracted by the irrelevant features, the person does not have to go through the process of checking out incorrect hypotheses about them.

However, it is not always feasible to eliminate the irrelevant features of instances. Another procedure which will have much the same effect is to hold the irrelevant features constant during the initial stages of instruction. That is, positive and negative instances are presented which share the same irrelevant features. Anderson and Guthrie (1966) presented college undergraduates with six geometric designs, one at a time. In this study the critical feature alternated from one instance to the next. For example, it was defined by color for some students. For these students the six designs alternated between red and green but in every noncritical respect—for instance, form—the six designs were the same. Another group of college students were shown six designs chosen at random, with the restriction, again, that half were red and half were green. Then both groups received a series of test trials until they made 10 consecutive correct responses. The test trials consisted of instances chosen at random from the total collection of designs, showing all possible combinations of features. On the test trials, the group for whom the irrelevant features were held constant over the first six designs required an average of 11.8 instances before they induced the concept, whereas those for whom the irrelevant features varied required an average of 28.7 instances.

Two of the key processes involved in concept learning are (1) discrimination of critical features, and (2) generalization across irrelevant features. Suppressing irrelevant features, either by eliminating them or holding them constant, reduces a concept learning task to a discrimination learning task. In other words, the technique of suppressing irrelevant features partitions concept learning into two stages. At the first stage the person discriminates the critical features. At the second stage he generalizes across the irrelevant features. At this point the person has learned the concept; his behavior is under the control of the critical features which define the concept.

Getting the student to generalize across irrelevant features is a step which cannot be neglected. To "generalize across irrelevant features" means to pay attention to and respond on the basis of the critical features no matter what combination of irrelevant features is present. As we have repeatedly emphasized, generalization is not an automatic process. Irrelevant features of a situation, even constant ones, can control or partly control behavior (House & Zeaman, 1963). Overing and Travers (1967), for instance, in a study dealing with this point, taught sixth graders the principle of refraction and then had them apply the principle by aiming at a target submerged in water. (When they enter water, light rays are bent, or "refracted," so that a submerged target is not where it appears to be. The principle of refraction allows a person to adjust his aim so that he can hit the target.) One group practiced aiming under realistic conditions, in which irrelevant visual cues were present. Another group practiced aiming under a condition in which all possible irrelevant visual cues were elminated. "The student viewing the demonstration in this training condition could see little except the light beam passing through the air and water" (Overing & Travers, 1967, p. 63). When the test presented later involved irrelevant features, the students who had practiced with irrelevant cues present applied the principle significantly better than students who had practiced with irrelevant cues eliminated. This experiment demonstrates that when the opportunity for practicing generalization across irrelevant features is provided, the student will be better able to apply a principle in new situations.

Although the view that instruction should simulate reality as closely as possible (Dale, 1959) has much common sense appeal, research shows that students learn more when instructional materials are stripped of realistic but irrelevant detail. Francis M. Dwyer (1967), for instance, compared four lessons on the anatomy of the human heart with groups of college undergraduates. While the same tape-recorded lecture was used with all groups, the groups differed with respect to the visual aids which accompanied the lecture. Group I saw no illustrations, but the names of the parts of the heart were projected on the screen as they were mentioned in the lecture. Group II viewed abstract line drawings of the form and relative locations of the parts of the heart. Group III was shown more detailed, shaded drawings representing the parts of the heart. Students in Group IV saw realistic photographs of the parts of the heart being described. Fig. 10.2 shows the results of the experiment. As you can see, presenting simple line drawings was the most effective procedure. The group that saw the realistic photographs actually learned slightly less than the group which got only the lecture.

Similar results were obtained by Barrett and Otto (1969), who investigated the ability of first, second, third, fourth, fifth, and sixth graders to induce principles—what they called "main ideas"—from paragraphs of prose. The experiment showed that performance was significantly better when the paragraph was written in short sentences using simple words and contained no irrelevant detail. Barrett and Otto (1969) concluded that "the shorter the sentences and the easier the words in a reading selection, the less energy the child has to exert in decoding words and eliciting literal meanings and the more energy he can exert in synthesizing the ideas in a selection and inferring the main idea. The implication seems clear: instructional programs designed to teach children to formulate main ideas should employ very easy materials."

In summary, the evidence from a variety of sources—involving a

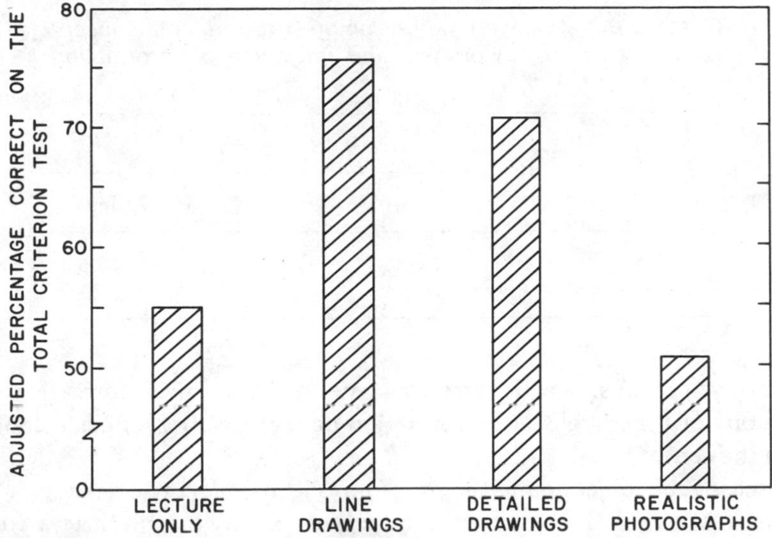

FIGURE 10.2 *Achievement as a function of the amount of realism in visual illustrations.* (*Based on Dwyer, 1967, p. 257, Table 1.*)

variety of tasks and subject matters, and various kinds of students from first graders to college undergraduates—indicates that people learn concepts and principles most readily when irrelevant features are eliminated or suppressed. In the beginning stages of instruction realism and rich detail will only distract and confuse the student. Later in instruction, when the goal is to teach the student to generalize in a broad range of situations, realism and a wide variety of examples should be employed.

Magnify the critical features. A second way to make the critical features of a concept more obvious is to magnify or exaggerate these features. The value of this technique was demonstrated in an experiment by Archer (1962; also 1965). The subjects participating in this experiment were required to induce a concept involving geometric designs that differed with respect to such dimensions as size, color, number, and form. One of the manipulated dimensions was size. Under the *low* obvious condition, the large figure was 1 inch long and the small figure was ⅞ of an inch long. Under the *high* obvious condition the large figure was still 1 inch long, but the small figure measured ¾ of an inch. The results of the experiment appear in Table 10.1. Look first at the column labeled "Relevant." Notice that the participants in the experiment induced the concept in a shorter period of time when the "relevant information" (i.e., critical feature) was obvious than when it

TABLE 10.1 *Average time (in minutes) to induce a concept as a function of obviousness and relevance of information (from Archer, 1962).*

	Relevance	
Obviousness	*Relevant*	*Irrelevant*
High	12.7	15.6
Low	16.5	11.7

was not so obvious. The reverse was true for irrelevant information; the more obvious the irrelevant information or features the longer it took to learn the concept.

A reasonable objection to the procedure of magnifying or exaggerating critical features is that the person may have to pay attention to a subtle difference between stimuli when he is actually using the concept. There is a real danger that he may not be able to handle nonobvious features if his only experience is with obvious ones. The way to get around this problem is to begin by emphasizing the critical features—making them obvious—and then later to remove the emphasis. Trabasso (1963) illustrated the value of this procedure experimentally. The instances in his experiment were geometric designs, in this case stylized flower patterns. The critical dimension was the angle at which leaf stems joined the main stem. Under the control condition the angular difference between positive and negative instances was 15°. Under a second condition the critical feature was emphasized by doubling the size of the angular difference (from 15° to 30°). College students required an average of 19.5 instances to induce the concept under the low obvious control condition, while only 8.4 instances were required under the high obvious condition. Finally, those who had learned the concept under the high obvious condition were given the low obvious instances as a test. Virtually all of the students passed the test without making a single error. The Trabasso experiment shows that magnifying the critical features of a concept makes it easier to learn the concept. The experiment further shows—and this is the important point—that once behavior has come under the control of an exaggerated critical feature, the exaggeration can be removed while still maintaining control.

Not all methods of emphasizing the critical features of a concept will work successfully. Trabasso included a condition in his experiment in which a prompt was added. The angle at which the leaf stem joined the main stem (the critical feature) was colored red in positive instances.

Students who received this condition learned the concept within an average of just 3.5 instances. However, on test trials in which positive instances were not colored red, there was no evidence of any learning at all. Behavior had come under the control color instead of the angle at which the leaves joined the stem. As was repeatedly cautioned in Chapter 9, prompts must be of such a nature that the student will notice the cue (critical feature). Otherwise there will be the appearance of learning rather than its substance. Instead of adding an extra stimulus as a prompt, the superior technique is to magnify the cues which embody the critical features of the concept.

Gradual reduction of the exaggeration of the critical features—that is, "fading"—is to be preferred to abrupt reduction. An abrupt shift was successful in the Trabasso experiment; however, a gradual fading of the emphasis on the critical features would undoubtedly work better with children (Moore & Goldiamond, 1964; Hively, 1965; Bijou, 1965). It seems likely that the gradual fading procedure would be superior for adults when they are expected to learn difficult concepts involving subtle features.

Introduce concepts using highly familiar examples. Research shows that concepts are most easily induced from "dominant" (or highly representative and familiar) examples (Underwood & Richardson, 1956). The research on which this conclusion is based involved lists of words instead of geometric designs. It was shown, for instance, that people will induce the concept *fruit* more quickly from such examples as apple, orange, banana, and peach than they will from such examples as avocado, tangerine, mango, pomegranate, and paw-paw.

In practical application it would probably be a good idea to start with highly representative, familiar, dominant examples and then, as an important second step, include examples that are not so representative or familiar. The purpose of the second step is to achieve generalized stimulus control: in common language, to teach a broad concept.

Group together examples of each concept. There is one further conclusion about inductive concept learning that has received strong support in a number of experiments, namely this: when several concepts are being taught, learning is facilitated when the examples of each concept are grouped together (Dominowski, 1965). "Grouping the examples" means to present all the examples of the first concept in immediate succession, then all the examples of the second concept, and so on. Again, we believe that grouping examples makes the critical features of the concepts more obvious. Other writers (Dominowski, 1965; Underwood, 1952, 1966) have stressed that grouping examples helps the person to remember the features of the examples, thus helping him to avoid confusing the examples of one concept with the examples of another.

Experimental research further shows that when instances of a concept are grouped together, learning is facilitated when the irrelevant features vary as greatly as possible (Anderson & Guthrie, 1966). Presumably this procedure makes the critical features more obvious by contrast, and also provides for generalization across irrelevant features.

Despite the foregoing positive evidence, we are cautious about recommending the grouping of examples as a general technique for teaching concepts in the classroom. It is possible that the value of this technique may be limited to the restricted laboratory situations in which it has been studied. Regrettably there is no research with actual lesson materials which bears on the question.

Induction of conjunctive concepts. The preceding sections describing procedures to facilitate the induction of concepts were based largely on research with concepts involving a single critical feature. (Positive instances contain this feature; negative instances do not.) A substantial proportion of the concepts (and all of the principles) taught in school entail more than one critical feature, however. Usually these concepts are conjunctive, meaning that each of two or more critical features is embodied in every positive instance. For example, an object is not a ball unless it is *both* (1) spherical or ovoid in shape *and* (2) used for hitting, kicking, or throwing in a game or sport. An example of a conjunctive concept studied in the laboratory is "green rectangle with a black border." An object or event is not an example of this concept unless it displays each of the three critical features.

It is well established that the more distinct (not overlapping or redundant) critical features there are which define a concept, the harder the concept is to learn. Unfortunately techniques for dealing with the difficulties posed by the conjunctive concept are not equally well established. Each of the procedures outlined on the preceding pages will make conjunctive concepts easier. But, none of them comes to grips with the special difficulty inherent in the conjunctive concept.

The special difficulty posed by the conjunctive concept is that behavior must come under the control of at least two critical features. To illustrate the difficulty, suppose a person is trying to induce a concept from a series of geometric designs presented one at a time. Imagine that the concept is "red circle." The first design contains a red circle. Redness attracts the person's attention so he responds, correctly as it happens, on the basis of color. The next time the design contains a red diamond.

Since he was reinforced for responding to color the first time, he does so again. Only this time he is wrong since a red diamond is a negative instance of the concept "red circle." The difficulty is that the person may now conclude that red is not part of the concept.

Despite the lack of adequate evidence, we hazard the guess that the best way to overcome the difficulty illustrated in the preceding paragraph would be to teach the critical features one at a time, presenting positive and negative instances which differ only with respect to a single critical feature. When behavior is under the control of this feature, the second feature can be introduced, by way of variation, until it too controls behavior. While teaching the second feature, occasionally review the first feature to be sure that it still exercises control. Proceed in this manner with all of the critical features. But we emphasize again that there is little research evidence to support our guess that this really is an efficient procedure for teaching conjunctive concepts (and, in fact, there is at least one study that does not support our conjecture (Naylor & Briggs, 1963).

On Learning Concepts and Principles from Being Told Them

The title of this section was suggested by the title of John B. Carroll's Presidential Address to the Division of Educational Psychology of the American Psychological Association in 1967. In his address Carroll (1968, p. 1) stated:

> By far the largest amount of teaching activity in educational settings involves telling things to students, whether orally or in print. Traditional instruction characteristically uses the lecture method, along with plentiful reading assignments. Even in more "progressive" educational settings which avoid the lecture method, much of the teacher's activity consists of asking questions and imparting information verbally. To be sure, verbal instruction is often accompanied with supplementary aids—diagrams on the blackboard, charts, pictures, film strips, motion pictures, demonstrations, field trips, and the like. But language still functions in many of these. A picture without a caption is usually meaningless, and most educational films would be unintelligible without sound track or titles. It seems obvious that meaningful verbal discourse is the primary tool of teaching. We expect our students to learn most things by being told about them.

Carroll is unquestionably right. Most formal instruction consists of telling things to students. Since this is so, how applicable to school learning is the usual sort of laboratory research on the induction of concepts? It is evident that many issues important to classroom learning have not yet been treated in laboratory research on concept learning.

When you tell a person a concept you describe its critical features—that is, you define the concept in words. Provided the person understands the words, this is often the simplest and most effective technique there is for teaching a concept. Like the techniques described on the preceding pages, telling the student about the critical features of the concept makes these features salient. Describing the critical features, however, does not merely make the critical features *more* obvious; in the case of many concepts, it often makes them *completely* obvious, provided the student understands the words.

The fact is that there are many concepts that it would be difficult, if not impossible, to teach by contrasting positive and negative instances. This is true of any concept in which the critical features are not physically embodied in examples of the concept. It is even true of such a commonplace concept as "ball." One cannot discern by looking at an object whether it is used for kicking, throwing, or hitting in a game or sport. "Uncle" (see Gagné, 1966) is another commonplace concept defined by a critical feature not physically represented in the examples of the concept. An uncle is a brother of a parent or the husband of a sister of a parent. Such characteristics cannot be ascertained by merely looking at a man. Concepts which do not have point-at-able features are difficult to learn from a series of instances, but often they can be learned quite easily from definitions.

A definition describes the to-be-learned concept in terms of other concepts. Of course, a person will not learn a concept from a definition unless he knows each of the concepts contained in the definition. For instance, a person would not learn what an uncle is from the statement, "An uncle is a brother of a parent or a husband of a sister of a parent," unless he already knew the concepts *brother, parent, husband,* and *sister.* As a general rule, mastery of concepts and principles depends upon prior mastery of the subconcepts upon which the concept or principle being taught is based. Several experiments completed by Gagné and his associates provide evidence for this rule. In one of these experiments (Gagné, 1965) sixth graders completed a programmed lesson in nonmetric geometry, arranged so that the pupil progressed from simple, prerequisite concepts to more complicated concepts and principles. The achievement test included a subtest for each of the simple concepts upon which the more complex concepts and principles were assumed to depend. The results showed that students almost never mastered the advanced concepts and principles unless they had also mastered the prerequisite concepts.

Despite the value of definitions, we cannot be absolutely certain that students will learn concepts and principles thoroughly from definitions alone, even when they understand the prerequisite concepts. A definition of a principle and nothing else may be sufficient if one's goal is merely to have the student name the principle when the definition appears in the verbatim form employed during instruction. If, on the other hand, one wants the student to be able to recognize various expressions of the principle, to discuss the principle fluently in his own words, to identify new instances of the principle, and to apply the principle to novel cases not treated during the course of instruction, then it is probably necessary to require the student to deal with a variety of forms of the principle and a variety of examples.

Johnson and Stratton (1966) have completed research showing the instructional value of defining a concept *and* presenting examples *and* using the concept in a sentence. In their study college students learned four concepts taught in one or another of several ways. One group was given practice classifying short descriptions of things and events as positive and negative instances of the concepts, a condition much like the familiar laboratory procedure for inductive concept learning. For a second group, each of the concepts was defined in terms of a synonym (e.g., "Chide means to criticize") and then practice was provided in relating the concept name to other synonyms. A third group read a short story within which the four concepts were used; the student was expected to infer the concepts. A fourth group received definitions (which did not entail synonyms) of the concepts and practiced writing definitions in their own words. The final group got a combined method; there was a paragraph provided for each concept in which (1) the concept was defined in general terms; (2) the concept was defined in terms of two synonyms; (3) the concept name was used in a sentence; (4) an example of the concept was provided; and finally (5) the student was required to write a definition in his own words. The paragraph provided this final group for the concept *chide* appears below:

> To chide someone is to talk to him to get him to correct his mistakes. Chide means to criticize or reproach. Thus a mother might chide her children for fighting with each other. An example might be a group of fellows poking fun at a boy with dirty clothes. Now write in your own words what chide means. [Johnson & Stratton, 1966, p. 51]

All of the methods in the study involved lesson materials of about the same length and under each method exactly twelve minutes was allowed to study the materials. An achievement test was given that consisted of four subtests requiring, respectively, definitions of each concept, identification of new instances of each concept, selection of (new) synonyms to match each concept name, and the use of each concept name in a meaningful sentence. The results showed, as one would expect, that every method was better than no instruction at all. The results further showed that students who received the combined procedure, illustrated above with the concept *chide,* learned significantly more than those who received any of the other four procedures.

The question, then, is *not* whether concepts can or should be taught by the direct expedient of explaining them. Rather the question is, as a practical matter, under what conditions other, less direct means should be employed.

Sometimes general definitions are not useful for instruction. Consider the definition of "triangle": a closed three-sided figure. This definition would not be helpful in teaching the concept of "triangle" to kindergarten pupils. A better technique is for the teacher to illustrate this concept with an example or two and then to give the pupil practice in identifying various examples and nonexamples of the concept. The exercise might look like this:

1. TEACHER: "This is called a triangle."

 Draws ◺

 (pause)

 "And this is a triangle."

 Draws △

2. TEACHER: Erases board.

 Draws ○ △ ▭

 "Does anyone see a triangle here?"

3. PUPIL: Identifies triangle.

4. TEACHER: Draws ○

 "Is this a triangle?"

5. PUPIL: "No" (hopefully)

6. TEACHER: Draws ◿

 "What is this called?"

7. PUPIL: "A triangle."

It will, in other words, be easier to teach some concepts using illustrations than by defining them in terms of other concepts.

Although a student may learn a concept upon being presented with its definition, it cannot be assumed that the concept he has acquired in this way alone is either broad or deep. An ever-present danger when a concept or principle is taught by definition is that all the student will learn is a verbal chain. That is, he may not actually learn the principle; he may only learn to recognize or repeat certain words in a certain order. Research suggests that the danger of "rote" learning can be guarded against by illustrating the concept with examples and providing practice both at identifying new instances of the concept and applying the concept or principle in new situations. A wide variety of instances should be employed in order to insure that behavior is not under the control of irrelevant features and is under the control of every form of the critical features. The value of a wide variety of examples was illustrated by Traub (1966), who taught sixth graders a method of adding positive and negative numbers. Following the basic instruction in which the concepts were explained and illustrated, one group received 20 problems to work which were all very similar to the examples earlier used to illustrate the concepts. Another group practiced solving 20 problems in which all irrelevant features varied as widely as possible. The latter group did significantly better on an achievement test consisting of 26 new problems.

In summary, concepts and principles often can be taught very efficiently by defining them in terms of other concepts the student already understands. Indeed, it is difficult to teach concepts which do not have point-at-able critical features by any other means. Included in this category are not only such "abstract" concepts as *energy, mass, truth, liberty, unicorn, gross national product* and *genotype* but such common concepts as *uncle*. One important condition for teaching concepts and principles by definition is that the student must understand the concepts contained in the definition. Otherwise learning cannot occur. Though little research has been done to date, the available evidence suggests that the effectiveness of lessons can be increased by including examples of concepts and using the concepts in various ways (such as in a sentence or story) in addition to defining them in general terms. A danger in teaching concepts and principles by definition is that the student may only memorize a string of words. This danger can be guarded against by requiring the student to apply what he has hopefully learned to a variety of new examples in different contexts.

On Learning Concepts and Principles by Discovering Them

Few educational innovations have been more enthusiastically advocated than *discovery learning*. The spirit of this advocacy is represented in a statement by Suchman about a project to improve problem-solving skills. Suchman has written:

The need for improvement is great. Current educational practice tends to make children less autonomous and less empirical in their search for understanding as they move up the elementary grades. The schools must have a new pedagogy with a new set of goals which subordinate retention to thinking.

It is clear that such a program should offer large amounts of practice in exploring, manipulating and searching. The children should be given a maximum of opportunity to experience autonomous discovery. New goals must be set for the children. Instead of devoting their efforts to storing information and recalling it on demand, they would be developing the cognitive functions needed to seek out and organize information in a way that would be the most productive of new concepts. Both the teacher and the pupil would have to be cast in new roles. The pupil must become more active and aggressive in his learning role. Direction of the concept formation process should be his own, and he should come to regard his environment (including the teacher) as a potential source of information which can be obtained through his own acts of inquiry. The teacher must abandon his traditionally directive mode and structure an environment that is responsive to the child's quest for information. The teacher must see to it that the child's efforts at inquiry are rewarded by success, that the child is able to obtain the information he needs, and that he *does* discover new concepts on his own. The teacher can help the child by posing problems that are reasonably structured and will lead to exciting new discoveries. The teacher can also coach him in the techniques of data collection and organization that will lend power and control to his searching. The educator should be concerned above all with the child's process of thinking, trusting that the growth of knowledge will follow in the wake of inquiry. [Cited in Wittrock, 1966, pp. 37–38.]

We must begin our discussion of discovery learning on a cautious note. As Cronbach (1966, p. 76) has indicated, "In spite of the confident endorsements of teaching through discovery that we read in semi-popular discourses on improving education, there is precious little substantiated knowledge about what conditions these advantages accrue." We are not endorsing Cronbach's conclusion in order to discredit discovery learning, however. The general claims for almost any educational innovation—for instance, team teaching or programmed instruction, as well as discovery learning—are difficult to prove or disprove. It is the nature of research that it leads to circumscribed conclusions about what specified kinds of students will learn with respect to a certain type of subject matter under specified conditions. Typically, it takes years of patient research before even circumscribed conclusions are warranted.

In the meantime, teachers must teach, curriculum developers must prepare materials, school administrators must make decisions about instructional programs, and for that matter educational researchers must judge which issues to investigate. Decisions can seldom be made on the basis of complete knowledge. They should be made on the basis of the best evidence available.

"Discovery teaching" is so named because the student is not told the concept or principle. Instead, he is expected to induce the principle from a series of examples. Discovery teaching can be contrasted with expository teaching, in which the student is told the concept or principle, which he then applies to a series of examples. Note that few real lessons are either "pure" discovery lessons or "pure" expository lessons. In most discovery lessons the student is usually told many things, and may be given hints of some sort. And even the lecturer leaves at least some small discoveries to the student. Note also that a discovery lesson can be taught using any one of several different media or combinations of media. Discovery lessons have been taught with programmed booklets (Gagné & Brown, 1961), with teachers using textbooks (Beberman, 1963), and with teachers using films (Suchman, 1964).

Not all instruction can be meaningfully classified as discovery teaching or expository teaching, or at some point in between. In the exercise teaching the concept "triangle" outlined in the previous section, the child was not told the concept nor did he discover it on his own. This exercise is typical of much instruction. While the issue of whether students should discover concepts or be told about them is currently receiving a lot of attention, we think the question, put in this way, is greatly oversimplified.

In our judgment, if the goal of a lesson is to get the student to master a *particular* principle (or a particular set of concepts and principles), an expository method usually will be superior to a discovery approach under most circumstances. By "superior" we mean that somewhat more will be learned or that the same amount will be learned in less time. When the achievement test consists of new examples of principles learned during the lesson, research generally shows that instruction in which the principle is presented is superior to instruction in which the student is expected to discover the principle (Irwin, et al., 1934; Anderson, 1949; Craig, 1956; Kittell, 1957; Haselrud & Meyers, 1958; Kersh, 1958; Gagné & Brown, 1961; Wittrock, 1963; Wittrock & Twelker, 1964; Guthrie, 1967). Moreover, in the studies in which students were required to reach a criterion of mastery (instead of simply being exposed to a fixed amount of instruction, whether or not they mastered the principle), the results invariably show that an expository method leads to quicker learning than a discovery method. For instance, Guthrie (1967) found that when students were told a principle, they needed only an average of 11 examples to master that principle, whereas when students were expected to *discover* the principle, they needed an average of 23 examples for mastery.

The main claim for discovery teaching is not that it is an efficient way to teach particular concepts and principles but rather that it makes the student a better problem-solver. Jerome S. Bruner, in an influential article entitled "The Act of Discovery" (1961, p. 26) wrote:

> I would urge now in the spirit of an hypothesis that emphasis upon discovery in learning has precisely the effect upon the learner of leading him to be a constructionist, to organize what he is encountering in manner not only designed to discover regularity and relatedness, but also to avoid the kind of information drift that fails to keep account of the uses to which information might have to be put. It is, if you will, a necessary condition for learning the variety of techniques of problem solving, of transforming information for better use, indeed for learning how to go about the very task of learning. Practice in discovering for oneself teaches one to acquire information in a way that makes that information more readily viable in problem solving. So goes the hypothesis. It is still in need of testing. But it is an hypothesis of such important human implications that we cannot afford not to test it—and testing will have to be in the schools.

The hypothesis that learning by discovery will make a person a better problem-solver is entirely reasonable, and the argument, very simple: experience at discovering concepts develops skill at discovery. After such training, it is assumed that when a person faces a problem (either in school or out of it) in which there is no teacher or book to guide him, he will be better able to induce the concept or principle needed to solve the problem.

Though this is a reasonable possibility, the evidence is inconclusive with respect to the actual effects of discovery experiences on problem-solving or concept formation. Some studies warrant one conclusion; others show the opposite; many show no difference one way or the other. Unfortunately, many of the experiments on discovery learning have been poorly conceived and poorly executed (see Wittrock, 1966; and Cronbach, 1966). One important difficulty has been an inappropriate research strategy. Premature comparisons have been made to see whether discovery teaching is better (or worse) than expository teaching—comparisons that were premature because there is insufficient knowledge about how to make either technique an effective tool for improving problem-solving skills.

Transfer of training. At this point a new concept must be introduced—*transfer of training*—defined as the influence which learning one task has on the learning or performance of a subsequent task. The following simple experimental model is frequently used to determine whether transfer of training has occurred. (In the model an *X* indicates that a given activity occurs; *O* means it does not occur.)

	Teach	Test
	Task 1	*Task 2*
Group A	X	X
Group B	O	X

Group A is taught Task 1, whereas Group B, which is called the "control group," is not.[2] Then both groups are tested on Task 2. If there is a reliable difference between the two groups on Task 2, it is reasonable to conclude that transfer of training has occurred. The greater the difference, the greater the transfer. Transfer may be either *positive* or *negative;* that is, the instruction on Task 1 may either facilitate or interfere with performance on Task 2.

There are many variations on the simple model (research plan) outlined in the preceding paragraph. Both groups may be taught Task 1, but by different methods. If there is a significant difference in performance on Task 2, the difference may be attributed to the advantage of one method over the other. Many experiments of this sort have compared expository teaching with discovery teaching.

The learning-by-discovery hypothesis is that experience at discovery with one task will transfer positively to other tasks in which the student must discover new concepts or principles. Guthrie (1967) has completed one of the best experiments to date to test this hypothesis. His task was rearranging scrambled letters to form words. Consider the following sets of letters. Try to make a word from each set.

lospeg
telvev
hiltf
dortifiem

These four sets of letters are easy to arrange into words if you know the principle, which is to exchange the first and last letter in each set. One group in Guthrie's experiment, called the Rule-Example group, was told principles for unscrambling and then practiced applying the principles to sets of letters until eight consecutive sets of letters were correctly arranged into words. Students in the Example (discovery) group were not taught the principle; they received sets of scrambled letters until they made eight words in a row, at which point it was assumed they had discovered the principle. The Example-Rule group was just like the

[2] Subjects must be randomly assigned to groups in order for this sort of experiment to yield a valid conclusion.

Example group, except that students in this group were told the principle *after* they had presumably discovered it. A final group received no training. After training all students were tested on three new tasks, each of which involved ten sets of letters, presented one at a time, which could be unscrambled according to a single principle. The results of the Guthrie experiment appear in Table 10.2.

In Guthrie's experiment students taught by the Rule-Example (expository) method learned the principle more quickly and learned it better, as evidenced by their superior performance on the test consisting of new examples of the principle. However, persons in the Example-Rule (discovery) group and, particularly, the Example (discovery) group did significantly better on the tests which required the student to discover a new principle. In fact, when the test required the student to discover a new principle very different from the principles encountered during instruction, the Example-Rule group actually did significantly worse than the group which received no training.

The Guthrie experiment seems to show that discovery teaching can develop problem-solving skills which transfer to new tasks in which the student is required to discover new principles. However, other experiments have yielded the opposite result. Wittrock (1963), for instance, found that students who received expository teaching did vastly better on every test than those who received discovery teaching—even on a test in which the student had to discover a new principle. Thus, the results of research completed to date are inconclusive. More research is needed. The hypothesis that experience at discovery improves skill at discovery is plausible—but unproven.

Discovery teaching and student motivation. A frequently expressed theme is that discovery learning is more fun than exposition learning. Students are said to enjoy the challenge of discovery, to enjoy the competition with classmates to see who will be the first to induce a principle, and to enjoy the active give and take often involved in a discovery lesson. It is argued that the fact (if it is a fact) that discovery learning is fun has important long-term implications. The student will learn, it is argued, that thinking and problem-solving are rewarding activities.

There is some evidence (though not adequate evidence) that discovery teaching can have motivational effects (Kersh, 1958, 1962). Some of the anecdotes offered (see Hendrix, 1947; Davis, 1966) to support the belief that discovery learning can be an exciting experience are not completely convincing, since the excitement may be more attributable to novelty, and the skill and enthusiasm of the instructor, than to the method.

TABLE 10.2 *Summary of Guthrie's Experiment. (Adapted from Guthrie, 1967.)*

	Teach	*Test*		
Order of groups from best to worse	*Speed of learning the first task*	*New examples of principle learned in the first task**	*Examples of new principle similar to principle learned in the first task*	*Examples of new principle different from principle learned in the first task*
Best	Rule-Example	Rule-Example	Example }	Example
Second	Example }	No Training }	Example-Rule }	Example-Rule }
Third	Example-Rule }	Example-Rule }	No Training }	No Training }
Worst		Example }	Rule-Example }	Rule-Example

NOTE: There were significant differences in performance among groups *not* bracketed together.

*Includes only letter sets that could be unscrambled on the basis of a transformational principle.

What is the chief difference in procedure between the expository method and the discovery method? A covert answer will do.

The explanation appears on p. **393.**

Conditions under which discovery teaching will be successful. In our judgment, the one condition necessary to make a discovery lesson a success is that the student must actually be able to discover the principle himself. If the student is unable to discover the principle, it is unlikely that he will develop problem-solving skills that he can apply later to discover a new principle; it is unlikely that the experience will be much fun; and, of course, there will be nothing that he can successfully apply to new examples.

Some of the experiments which have failed to show any value for a discovery method may have been expecting too much from the students, expecting a discovery which was impossible for most of them. This seems to have been true of the Wittrock (1963) experiment. In that experiment very few of the students who got the discovery lesson were able to discover the principles, so it is not surprising that they were later unable to do well at discovering new principles. On the other hand, there is some evidence to suggest that when students *are* able to discover the principle—either because the discovery expected is a small one or because the student is helped to make the discovery—a discovery technique can be quite successful.

Gagné and Brown (1961) taught ninth- and tenth-grade boys some principles for working with number series using one of three different procedures called, respectively, the Rule and Example program, the Discovery program, and the Guided Discovery program. The Rule and Example began with a general formula which the student was asked to copy, and was followed by several examples for the student to work. The Discovery program began by abruptly requesting the student to write the general formula (principle) for a number series. If the student was unable to do so, he was provided with progressively more explicit hints until he was finally able to write the general formula. The Guided Discovery group began with examples and questions designed to draw the student's attention to the critical features of the principle; he was then asked to write the general principle. All students were given a test comprised of four new number series problems which could be solved by discovering new principles similar but not identical to those involved in the lessons. The results showed that the Guided Discovery group did significantly better than the Discovery group, which in turn did significantly better than the Rule and Example group. Gagné and Brown (1961, p. 320) concluded that "discovery as a method appears to gain its effectiveness from the fact that it requires the individual learner to . . . [use] . . . the concepts he will later use in solving new problems. . . . The practice provided by the [Rule and Example] program, in contrast, did not *require* the use of these essential concepts (although it permitted it). Accordingly it led to distinctly inferior problem solving performance."

Worthen (1968) has performed a practical classroom experiment that yielded results similar to those obtained by Guthrie (1967) and Gagné and Brown (1961). Each of eight teachers taught certain concepts and principles in mathematics to one fifth- or sixth-grade class using a discovery method and taught the same concepts and principles to another class using an expository method. Unlike many other practical experiments comparing teaching methods, special pains were taken in this study to assure that teachers consistently used the two methods and that students mastered each important subskill and subconcept before moving on to the next. While there are questions about the adequacy of the statistical analysis, the results of the Worthen experiment did show that the expository method led to slightly better performance on an immediate achievement test covering the concepts actually taught. However, the children taught by the discovery method remembered the concepts slightly better when the test was repeated at a later date. Children taught by the discovery method also performed slightly better than those who received the expository method on a test requiring application of the concepts in new situations and on two tests requiring the discovery of principles to solve problems.

The experiments in which discovery teaching has shown up well and the descriptions of discovery lessons employed to illustrate the technique at its best generally seem to involve a thorough analysis of the concepts and skills the student will need to possess in order to make the discovery. The lessons seem to be designed to insure that the student has mastered each of these prerequisites before or sometimes during, the discovery episode. Discovery teaching at its best, in other words, does not seem to be a hit-and-miss procedure. Successful discovery lessons seem to be arranged so that it is highly likely that most of the students will be able to make the discovery.

There is a striking resemblance between outstanding examples of discovery lessons and the procedures that experimental psychologists have found to facilitate concept learning in the laboratory. In general, in the discovery lessons developed by such persons as Beberman (1963) and Davis (1966), examples are selected and sequenced in such a way as to

In your judgment, which method—discovery or expository—will be more generally useful to the teacher? A covert response will be satisfactory.

The authors' opinion appears on p. **394.**

make the critical features obvious. The main conclusion from research on concept and principle learning in the laboratory is that learning is facilitated when the critical features are made obvious, which can be done using one or more of several techniques.

The techniques used to make principles easy to discover are best illustrated with an example from an actual lesson. An excellent example is the UICSM (University of Illinois Committee on School Mathematics) lesson on a mathematical principle called "distributive principle for multiplication over addition" (Beberman, 1963).

After a few preliminaries, the teacher writes the following equation on the board:

$$7 \times \square + 3 \times \square = 20$$

After the students have had a chance to experiment and find a solution, the teacher asks a student for the solution and checks it:

$$7 \times \square + 3 \times \square = 20$$

$$\begin{array}{r} 7 \\ \times 2 \\ \hline 14 \end{array} \qquad \begin{array}{r} 3 \\ \times 2 \\ \hline 6 \end{array} \qquad \begin{array}{r} 14 \\ +6 \\ \hline 20 \end{array}$$

The teacher then proceeds with a sequence such as the following, each time erasing the solution from the frames and writing a new equation.

$$7 \times \square + 3 \times \square = 50$$
$$7 \times \square + 3 \times \square = 30$$
$$7 \times \square + 3 \times \square = 80$$
$$7 \times \square + 3 \times \square = 130$$
$$7 \times \square + 3 \times \square = 120$$
$$7 \times \square + 3 \times \square = 170$$
$$7 \times \square + 3 \times \square = 380$$
$$7 \times \square + 3 \times \square = 210$$
$$7 \times \square + 3 \times \square = 460$$
$$7 \times \square + 3 \times \square = 5270$$

"The correct solutions are listed in the frames each time," Beberman goes on to say, "but are checked only occasionally." Most children have now become aware of a generalization which produces correct solutions. The teacher does not ask for a statement of any such generalization. If he did, he would probably get something like "Just drop the zero." Instead he offers the following equation:

$$7 \times \square + 3 \times \square = 291$$

This is greeted with groans and cries of "not fair." One or two students will offer the right solution after just a little contemplation. The teacher can stimulate activity by asking for "approximate" solutions. In any case, once the correct answer has been exhibited *and checked* by the teacher, rapid responses are obtained for equations of the form:

$$7 \times \square + 3 \times \square = n$$

in which the n is replaced by "79," "122," "15608," etc.

As Beberman says, "The teacher may now move to equations of the form:

$$6 \times \square + 4 \times \square = n$$

or of the form:

$$78 \times \square + 22 \times \square = n$$

Each alternative either reinforces the generalization a student has been forming or causes him to modify his generalization."

"The next step is quite important," according to Beberman, "because many students have become aware of a generalization which is based on the fact that it is easy to divide by a power of 10. `Although the distributive principle for multiplication over addition does play a role in the thinking of some students at this stage, there may be a few who have not become aware of the step in which the coefficients are added. That this is the case is borne out by the answers the teacher gets for the next equation:

$$7 \times \square + 5 \times \square = 48$$

Answer to the question on p. **390.**

In an expository method the teacher or teaching material presents a rule, generalization, or principle. The student then practices applying the principle to instances or to problems. The discovery method begins with a series of instances or problems from which the student is expected to induce the rule.

"In fact the teacher should try to find a student who will say '4.8' for this equation. Many students are amazed when the check reveals that 4.8 is not a solution. When the correct solution [4] is obtained, the teacher is ready to bring the students closer to discovering the distributive principle."

A student who has discovered a generalization as a result of a search for a pattern among related problems may be able to use it only in problems which are much like those from which he formed the original pattern. He may fail to use his discovery in settings which do not preserve the symbolic arrangements of the original pattern. The teacher, therefore, must provide a variety of "transfer" situations so that the student can "rediscover" the generalization. For example, in connection with the foregoing lesson on the distributive principle, the equation-solving sequence should be followed by computational exercises like:

$$7 \times 8 + 3 \times 8 = ?$$
$$7 \times 19 + 3 \times 19 = ?$$
$$6 \times 83 + 4 \times 83 = ?$$
$$74 \times 98 + 226 \times 98 = ?$$
$$6.5 \times 7 + 2.5 \times 7 = ?$$

and with word problems like:

Mrs. A buys 7 cans of peaches at 37 cents per can and 3 cans of pears at 37 cents per can. What is the total bill for the peaches and pears?

Eventually, the pattern appears in the following form:

$$(7 \times \square) + (3 \times \square) = (7 + 3) \times \square$$

and the student learns that the name for the pattern of which this is an instance is "the distributive principle for multiplication over addition."

Authors' opinion on the question raised on p. **392.**

In our judgment, the expository method is more generally useful. Many people, it should be emphasized, probably hold the opposite opinion. But note that we are not saying that the expository method is better—only that it is more generally useful in the sense that it probably can be used successfully with a greater variety of concepts and principles than the discovery method. Students are probably not often capable of discovering from a series of instances alone many of the principles they are expected to learn in school.

In conclusion discovery lessons cannot be successful unless students are actually able to discover. Discovery can be made more probable by (1) assuring that students have mastered all of the prerequisite skills and concepts, and (2) selecting and sequencing examples in such a way that the principle is made as obvious as possible.

SELF-TEST ON THE TEACHING OF CONCEPTS AND PRINCIPLES

Answer the following questions and then check your answers against the scoring key on *p. 397.*

1. Describe at least four ways in which you can make it easier for students to discover a concept besides simply defining the concept for them.

2. As you know, learning concepts involves more than mere rote learning of rules. Consider that you are an elementary school teacher attempting to teach the concept of "freedom" to your students. What would you do to insure that students learned more than just the verbatim definition of this word?

3. Advocates of discovery teaching claim that its main advantage is that it is

- **a.** more efficient than expository teaching.
- **b.** easier to employ in the classroom than more conventional methods.
- **c.** applicable to a great variety of subjects.
- **d.** helpful in teaching students to be problem-solvers.
- **e.** helpful in eliminating negative transfer of training.

4. Assume that you are a high school art teacher. You are teaching the concept "Gothic architecture." Early in this instruction it is best to keep your visual aids

- **a.** as simple as possible, including only the dimensions which are exemplary of Gothic architecture.
- **b.** as realistic as possible, including pictures of Gothic architecture as seen in the real world.
- **c.** colorful and bright so that they appear attractive to the students.

5. List conditions which should prevail if discovery teaching is to be most successful.

Summary

Concepts can be defined by their critical features. A person knows a concept when his behavior is under the control of the critical features which define the concept—in other words, when he can respond appropriately to any positive instance of the concept. A test for mastery of a concept must entail "new" instances; that is, instances which the student did not encounter in the course of the lesson from which he learned the concept. Questions containing examples which differ in every irrelevant way from instructional examples will probe the limits of the student's understanding of a concept.

A principle consists of two or more related concepts. Principles must be sharply distinguished from verbal chains. A verbal chain consists of a string of words which the student can repeat or recognize. A question or test item which repeats the definition of a concept or expresses a principle in the same words as were used during instruction does not test mastery of the concept or principle because the student can answer on the basis of a verbal chain. Questions that entail substantially reworded definitions and general statements *do* test mastery of concepts and principles. However, the best test of understanding a principle, as well as a concept, is whether the student can apply the principle to new instances.

When teaching a concept or principle, it is useful to think of the instructional process in two stages. At the first stage, the aim is to get the student to discriminate the critical features. "Discriminate the critical features" means to notice, pay attention to, and behave in terms of the defining properties of the concept or principle. The goal of the second stage is to achieve generalization across irrelevant features. When a student "generalizes across irrelevant features," he is able to apply the concept or principle in a broad variety of circumstances regardless of what combination of irrelevant (and potentially distracting or confusing) features are present.

No matter what style, method (e.g., expository, discovery, or some other), or medium of instruction (e.g., book, film, self-instructional program, or live teacher), research indicates that learning during the initial discrimination stage will be facilitated if the critical features of the concept or principle are made more obvious. Some specific techniques for making the critical features more obvious are (1) to eliminate or hold constant irrelevant features; (2) to magnify the critical features; (3) to begin with highly familiar examples; and (4) to group together examples of each concept or principle. At the generalization stage, irrelevant features are deliberately introduced, the critical features are not exaggerated, unfamiliar examples are provided, and the student is given the opportunity to apply the concept or principle under a variety of circumstances, including realistic or lifelike circumstances if possible.

A time-honored way of teaching concepts and principles is to tell them to students, either orally or in writing. This is called the "expository method." When a teacher or book tells a student a principle, the principle is defined in terms of other concepts which, hopefully, the student already understands. Students can easily learn a concept and principles from a general definition, provided they have mastered the concepts included in the definition. It cannot be assumed that the principle a student will learn from a general definition or description will be either broad or deep, however. The student can be helped to attain a broad and deep grasp of a principle by defining it in several ways, providing a variety of examples, and requiring the student to use and apply the principle.

In "discovery teaching," on the other hand, a series of instances is provided from which the student is expected to induce the concept or principle. Available research (much of which is not adequate from a scientific point of view) indicates that discovery teaching may be less efficient than expository teaching. However, the main claim for discovery teaching is not that it is an efficient method, but rather that experience at discovery makes the student a better problem-solver. While this is a reasonable hypothesis, the evidence regarding the effects of discovery teaching on problem-solving skill is also inconclusive. One important condition for a successful discovery lesson is that the student actually be able to discover. Discovery can be made more probable by a careful analysis of the skills and concepts that are prerequisites for discovery and, therefore, assuring that the student possesses the prerequisites. As with other methods for teaching concepts and principles, discovery learning is facilitated if the critical features of the to-be-discovered concept or principle are made obvious by appropriately selecting and sequencing examples.

SCORING KEY FOR THE SELF-TEST ON THE TEACHING OF CONCEPTS AND PRINCIPLES

A satisfactory score is 9 out of 11 points. Review portions of the chapter related to questions which you miss.

1. *(4 points)*

(1) Make the problems simpler by eliminating or holding constant the irrelevant features.
(1) Magnify the critical features of the concept.
(1) Use familiar examples early in instruction.
(1) Group together examples of one concept.

2. (*2 points*)

(1) Provide students with a variety of examples or instances of the concept during teaching—don't use just a definition of "freedom" to explain what it is.
(1) Test to insure that students have learned the concept by having them explain it and apply what they have learned to new instances of the concept.

3. d

4. a

5. (*3 points*)

(1) The student must be able to discover the concept or principle.
(1) You should take steps to insure that the students have mastered all prerequisite skills and concepts.
(1) Examples should be carefully selected and sequenced so that the critical features of the concepts or principles are made obvious.

Selected Readings

Anderson, R. C., Faust, G. W., Roderick, M. C., Cunningham, D. J., & Andre, T., "Section VI. Facilitation of Concept Learning," *Current Research on Instruction*. Englewood Cliffs, N.J.: Prentice-Hall, 1969. Reprinted are six papers with implications for classroom instruction.

Gagné, R. M. *Conditions of Learning*. New York: Holt, Rinehart & Winston, 1965. Gagné describes concept and principle learning in relation to simpler kinds of learning.

Klausmeier, H. J., & Harris, C. W., eds., *Analyses of Concept Learning*. New York: Academic Press, 1966. This book contains original papers by both psychologists and educators.

Shulman, L. S., & Keislar, E. R., eds., *Learning by Discovery*. Chicago: Rand-McNally, 1966. This book contains the best collection of papers on discovery learning.

CHAPTER

11

Motivation

In the context of the classroom, "motivation" refers to such characteristics of student behavior as interest, alertness, attention, concentration, and persistence. These are motivational qualities of immediate interest to the teacher. If students will not pay attention, follow instructions, and complete assignments, it is obviously difficult to teach them. The educator is also concerned with long-term motivational characteristics. For instance, the primary school teacher wants children to learn to enjoy reading and the high school history teacher wants students to develop a continuing interest in current events. The person who completes this chapter should be able to

1. define motivation and indicate the conditions under which motivation is aroused.
2. describe the development of long-term motivation.
3. describe the conditions under which strong motivation will promote learning and the conditions under which it will interfere with learning.
4. describe procedures for coping with excessive student motivation.

Motivation in Historical Perspective

In the one hundred years since the beginning of scientific psychology, motivation has received a great deal of attention. Around the turn of the century, instinct was a preferred explanation of motivation. (The preference for regarding instinct as the well-spring of motivation can be traced to the influence of Darwin.) At that time, "instinct" was a rather vague concept, referring simply to tendencies a person is allegedly born with. Anybody could speculate about what man's instincts might be and almost everyone did. Most psychology texts of the time contained lists of instincts. The lists usually overlapped, but there was no one-to-one correspondence between them, a fact giving rise to considerable controversy and hair-splitting. Some authors seemed to list indiscriminately every activity in which a person might engage and every emotion he might be said to feel. Others purported to list only *basic* instincts, from which all other tendencies and emotions could be derived. In 1908 William McDougall published such a list of instincts (given below), the first seven of which were said always to be accompanied by a characteristic emotion, indicated in parentheses:

flight (fear)
repulsion (disgust)
curiosity (wonder)
pugnacity (anger)
self-abasement (subjection)
self-assertion (elation)
parental-care (tenderness)

reproduction
gregariousness
acquisition
construction

McDougall believed that the last four instincts did not arouse specific and well-defined emotions.

Of course not one of these psychologists could demonstrate that he was cataloging instincts. And since proof would have been extremely difficult to come by, few bothered to worry about it. Freed from the constraint to provide evidence that an alleged tendency *was* an instinct, anything at all could be called one. In 1924 Bernard reviewed the literature and found that no less than 850 separate instincts, and maybe as many as several thousand, depending upon how they were classified, had been proposed by various writers.

Beginning in about 1920, however, strong attacks were directed against the concept of "instinct" (Dunlap, 1919) and new concepts were introduced in its place. Some of these, such as "reflex" and "habit," were not motivational in nature. One popular substitute for the motivational aspect of instinct was the concept of acquired or learned "need." Today it is rather widely believed that learning plays an important, perhaps predominant, role in the development of motivation in adult humans. On the other hand, the instinct concept has recently undergone something of a renaissance, thanks to the influence of European ethologists who have made detailed studies of the behavior of animals in natural settings (e.g., Tinbergen, 1951; Hess, 1962). The ethologists have advanced rather convincing arguments that animal behavior, including human behavior, cannot be accounted for without a concept such as "instinct," although some of the claims for the overriding importance of instincts that have been made in popular articles seem extravagant.

With the increasing emphasis on the role of learning in shaping human motivation, one would imagine that there would be fewer attempts to catalog motives (or needs) since it seems reasonable to conclude that learning could produce an indefinitely large variety of motives. Indeed, each person's motives could be unique. Nonetheless, efforts to compile exhaustive lists of motives have continued almost unabated. However, in recent years writers have seldom claimed that motives are instinctive. Murray (1938) has presented a particularly influential taxonomy of needs, which appears in Table 11.1. (In this taxonomy, the lowercase *n* preceding each term stands for "need.")

TABLE 11.1 *Manifest Needs Proposed by Henry A. Murray (from Murray, et al., 1938, pp. 80–83.)*

Need	*Brief description*
n Abasement	need to submit passively to external force
n Achievement	need to accomplish something difficult
n Acquisition	need to gain possessions and property
n Affiliation	need to form friendships
n Aggression	need to attack, injure, or kill
n Autonomy	need to be independent and free
n Blameavoidance	need to avoid blame
n Cognizance	need to explore and satisfy curiosity
n Construction	need to organize and build
n Counteraction	need to overcome obstacles and weaknesses
n Deference	need to admire and support a superior person
n Defendance	need to defend the self against assault and criticism
n Dominance	need to control other people
n Exhibition	need to make an impression, to be seen and heard
n Exposition	need to give information, explain, interpret, and lecture
n Harmavoidance	need to avoid pain and physical injury
n Infavoidance	need to avoid humiliation
n Inviolacy	need to preserve a good reputation
n Nurturance	need to give sympathy to helpless persons
n Order	need to arrange, organize; to be tidy and clean
n Play	need to have fun
n Recognition	need to command respect, praise, and social prestige
n Rejection	need to exclude an inferior person
n Retention	need to hoard
n Seclusion	need to be alone
n Sentience	need to seek and enjoy sensuous impressions
n Sex	need for erotic pleasure
n Succorance	need to be nursed, supported, and indulged
n Superiority	need for superior status
n Understanding	need to analyze, theorize, and conceptualize

A list such as Murray's suffers from many of the same defects as the lists of instincts that appeared in earlier treatises. While the list does represent an important range of human concerns, there is no assurance that it contains *all* of man's important needs and no convincing argument, either, that the needs listed could not be combined into a smaller number. The fact of the matter is that the cataloging of needs is a rather speculative business, and the fruits of its labor must be interpreted with this in mind.

Deprivation and Satiation

In behavior theory, "need" (we shall use the terms *need, drive, motive,* etc., interchangeably) is a term that refers to the condition that occurs when an organism is deprived of a reinforcer. A deprived organism will show an increase in general restlessness and alertness and will act with greater vigor and speed. It will be less "distractible." There will be physiological effects such as changes in respiration and heart rate. Cotton (1953) has completed an experiment that shows the effects of various periods of food deprivation. Rats were trained to run down a ten-foot runway (a miniature tunnel with a plexiglass roof) to get food. Then the rats were tested to see how fast they would run after various periods of food deprivation. The dashed line in Fig. 11.1 represents the average speed over all trials and indicates that the greater the number of hours of deprivation, the faster the average running speed. The solid line (the bottom one) represents average running speed, including only those trials on which the rat did nothing but run. The experiment shows that *when it did run,* the rat ran equally fast under all conditions of deprivation. However, the shorter the period of deprivation, the less likely it was to run directly down the runway and the more likely it was to engage for a period of time in competing responses such as "retracing, face-washing, touching the cover of the runway, exploring the openings through which the photocell light beam passed, scratching self, and biting self" (Cotton, 1953, p. 191).

The opposite of deprivation is *satiation.* A rat will run down a runway to get food until it gets as much food as it will eat. Technically speaking, the rat stops running or runs lackadaisically when it is satiated. Of course, after it has once again been deprived of food, the rat will again run in order to get food. Food *deprivation* is necessary for food to function as a reinforcer; under conditions of food *satiation,* food no longer functions as a reinforcer.

For the most part, the concepts of deprivation and satiation were developed with reference to hunger and thirst. By analogy, it has been

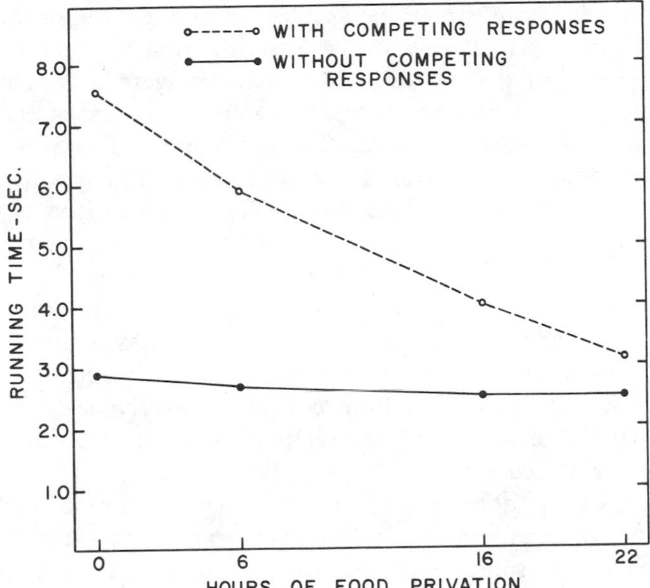

FIGURE 11.1 *Average running time as a function of hours of food deprivation (from Cotton, 1953).*

In the light of the relationship between deprivation, satiation, and the effectiveness of reinforcers, name an advantage of intermittent reinforcement as compared to continuous reinforcement. A covert response will be satisfactory.

The answer appears on p. **405.**

presumed that deprivation and satiation would function with other reinforcers in the same way as they do for food and water. One may reasonably ask how fruitful the analogy has been. Though not everyone would agree, we believe it has been quite fruitful. Research has shown, for instance, that social deprivation and satiation influence how vigorously people will work in order to receive attention and approval. To illustrate, Gewirtz and Baer (1958a; 1958b) played a marble game with first and second graders, in which the child dropped marbles into holes. Unknown to the child, dropping a marble into one of the two holes was a correct response. During the first four minutes, the adult experimenter simply observed the child without making any comments. During the next ten minutes, the experimenter praised (reinforced) the child after each correct response (without, however, specifying that his response was correct). The measure was the increase from the first four minutes to the last ten minutes in the rate at which marbles were dropped into the correct hole. Prior to playing the marble game, one-third of the children were left alone in a vacant room for twenty minutes. This was the social deprivation condition. Another one-third engaged in friendly conversation with the experimenter for twenty minutes before the experiment, during which period the experimenter tried to praise the child thirty times. This was the satiation condition. The remaining children began playing the marble game as soon as they entered the experimental room, which was the neutral condition. The results of the experiment, pictured in Fig. 11.2, demonstrated that social deprivation enhances the effectiveness of praise while social satiation reduces its effectiveness. These relationships parallel those of food deprivation and satiation on the effectiveness of food reinforcement.

A further kind of deprivation is illustrated by the loss of opportunity to see, hear, feel, and smell. When people are placed in dimly lit or unlighted, partially sound-deadened rooms and made to wear cardboard tubes over their arms, few are willing to continue beyond 48 to 72 hours, despite being paid a high wage. After a period of sleep, the typical subject becomes increasingly bored, restless, and irritable. Eventually these feelings become almost unbearable. Subjects report a craving for stimu-

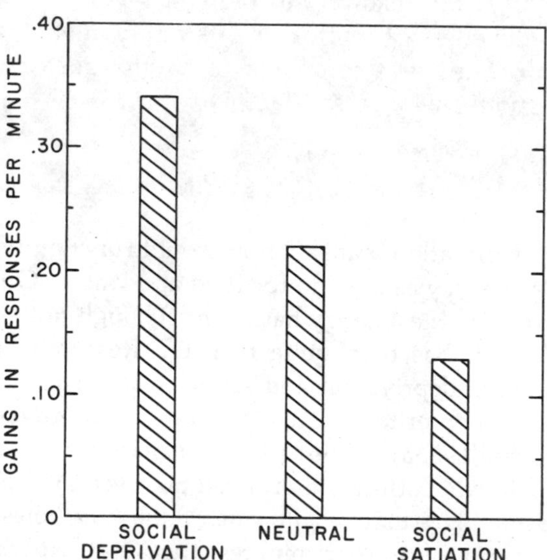

FIGURE 11.2 *Effects of social deprivation and satiation on rate of responding (from Gewirtz and Baer, 1958b).*

lation and action; and they look forward with relish to receiving tests or, in one case, to hearing an old stock market report (Bexton, Heron, & Scott, 1954). This research shows that sensory deprivation has motivational consequences. Butler (1957) demonstrated that, at least up to a point, the longer the deprivation, the harder an organism will work to get a reinforcer that consists simply of an opportunity to look briefly at the surrounding environment. Rhesus monkeys in a completely enclosed test cage were trained to push a panel that intermittently caused a small window to open for 12 seconds. When the window was open, the monkey could view the monkey colony outside the test cage. The monkeys were deprived of the opportunity to look through the window for 0, 2, 4, or 8 hours and then tested over a one-hour period to determine how frequently they would push the panel that sometimes caused the window to open. The data, which are graphed in Fig. 11.3, indicated that attempts to open the window increased sharply with up to four

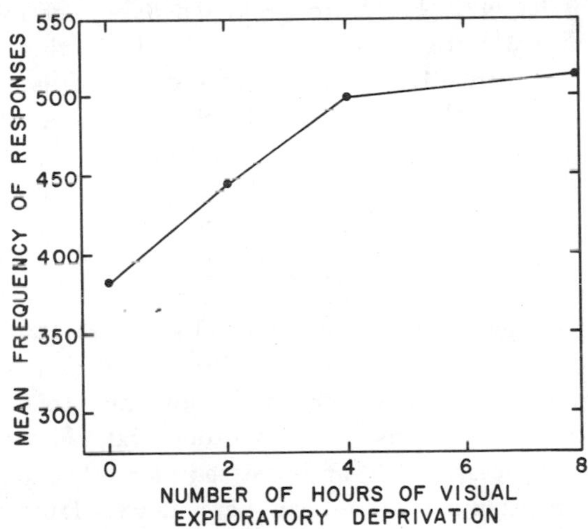

FIGURE 11.3 *Mean frequency of responses as a function of duration of deprivation (from Butler, 1957).*

Answer to the question on p. **403.**

A person will become satiated less quickly if he is reinforced intermittently. Indeed, it is sometimes possible to design a schedule of reinforcement in such a way that an organism will perform indefinitely without ever getting satiated.

hours visual deprivation. Butler interpreted this result as a demonstration of a "curiosity motive."

> Elementary school educators have seldom questioned the wisdom of decorating classrooms in an attractive manner. Assume the displays around a room are reinforcing for children (which may or may not be true). Under this assumption, consider the pros and cons of an attractively decorated classroom. A covert answer will be satisfactory.
>
> *The following paragraph contains the authors' discussion of this question.*

If the displays around the room are reinforcing, children will look at them. Looking around the room is frequently incompatible with paying attention to the lesson at hand. In other words, to the extent that displays are actually attractive, they may also be distracting. Furthermore, if the children were relatively deprived of other kinds of stimulation, this would probably enhance the reinforcing value of the stimulation arising from instruction. It is possible, therefore, to make an argument for bare, unadorned classrooms. On the other hand, it is undoubtedly reinforcing to a child to have his own work displayed in the room, and this probably outweighs the (possibly) negative effects of distraction. Also, if the displays in a room are particularly attractive, they may reinforce coming to school and help create a "liking" for school.

In summary, deprivation is the condition in which a reinforcer is denied or unavailable, or in which the opportunity to engage in some activity is restricted. Two consequences of deprivation are (1) an increase in alertness and restlessness, (2) an increase in the efficacy of appropriate reinforcers in maintaining vigor and persistence. Humans will often report a craving for the object or activity that has been denied. Up to a point, these effects increase the longer the period of deprivation. The effects of deprivation are found not only when the reinforcer withheld has an obvious biological function, as do food and water, for example; but the effects are found also with a very broad range of other events and activities. We may suppose, therefore, that deprivation enhances any reinforcer. Satiation is the absence of deprivation and is associated with a decrease in alertness and restlessness and a decrease in the efficacy of reinforcers. Satiation is complete at the point at which an organism will no longer perform in order to acquire or consume something, or in order to engage in some activity.

Arousing Stimuli

Deprivation involves *withholding* something. *Introducing* a stimulus can also have motivational consequences. The aroma of a freshly baked apple pie stimulates one's appetite more or less independently of the number of hours since one has eaten. A shapeply girl in a bikini can be a provocative stimulus for a man whether or not he has been to sea for three months. When the introduction of a stimulus invigorates behavior, it is called an *arousing stimulus*.

One important class of arousing stimuli are those which cause pain. A painful or aversive stimulus can be counted on to goad an organism into action. A stimulus that always precedes the aversive stimulus will come to serve as a warning, thus it too will instigate action. This illustrates a general characteristic of arousing stimuli: they frequently allow the organism to anticipate some future event which itself has motivational consequences.

Daniel Berlyne, in his book *Conflict, Arousal, and Curiosity* (1960), has made much of arousing stimuli. He has emphasized the importance of curiosity as a motive to explore and understand new and unusual situations. Berlyne's research suggests that stimuli which are novel, surprising, complex, or incongruous have arousal value.

With the exception of aversive stimuli, arousing stimuli have not been as thoroughly studied as have deprivation and satiation. Many arousing stimuli are themselves reinforcers, or allow the organism to anticipate reinforcement. In commonsense terms, such arousing stimuli "whet one's appetite." On the negative side, stimuli that allow the organism to anticipate an aversive (painful, unpleasant) stimulus arouse "fear" or "anxiety."

Motivation and the Direction of Behavior

It is commonly said that the motivated organism is "seeking a goal." The common belief is that one identifies the motive in order to explain why behavior was directed in one way rather than another. While there is little doubt that deprivation and arousing stimuli produce internal cues or "drive stimuli" that sensitize the organism to some reinforcers (and not others), as well as play a role in guiding behavior, this function of motives should not be overemphasized. There are many factors at work which determine the direction behavior will take. Chief among these is habit or learning. Organisms do what they have learned to do, not only what they are motivated to do.

The late Clark L. Hull, a major American psychologist, postulated that the drive instigated by deprivation or arousing stimuli is nonspecific, and serves to energize *various* forms of behavior. In other words, Hull (1943) expressly denied that motivational energy is mobilized for only a restricted goal. While the data are not entirely consistent, the evidence does seem to indicate that at least to some extent the energy released by food deprivation, for instance, will increase the vigor of a wide variety of behaviors, not just those behaviors that have led to food in the past (cf. Cofer & Appley, 1965, pp. 534–538).

According to psychological research and theory, which of the following is the most accurate statement?

A. The motivation of human adults can be traced directly to instincts.
B. Motivation is energy released by deprivation or the appearance of an arousing stimulus.
C. Motivation is energy directed toward a certain goal.

The answer appears on p. **410.**

Up to this point, the basic concepts of motivation have been introduced. Research on animals has received a good deal of attention. Hunger has been the need most discussed. We turn now to a program of research using humans as subjects and considering an exclusively human motive: the achievement motive.

An Analysis of Achievement Motivation

In 1953, David C. McClelland and his associates published an important book entitled *The Achievement Motive.* According to these writers, some people more than others are ambitious and strive to get ahead in the world. McClelland believed that because of their concern with achieving success and avoiding failure, such people would interpret even ambiguous or neutral situations as related to achievement. Clinical psychologists had long employed "projective" tests, so named because it is believed that people project their personalities into a test situation, even though they may not be conscious of this fact. The particular projective test employed by McClelland in his study is called the *Thematic Apperception Test* (abbreviated *TAT*) and was developed by Henry Murray, mentioned earlier in this chapter.

The TAT consists of a series of pictures depicting various situations.

The person taking the test is supposed to tell the stories suggested to him by the pictures. The content of the stories is then analyzed with the purpose of revealing the hopes, fears, motives, and problems of the storyteller.

In the version of the *TAT* employed by McClelland, the exercise is introduced as a test of imagination. The following four sets of questions are presented to structure the stories:

1. What is happening? Who are the persons?
2. What has led up to this situation? That is, what has happened in the past?
3. What is being thought? What is wanted? By whom?
4. What will happen? What will be done?

One *TAT* picture, for example, shows "an adolescent boy looking straight out of the picture; the barrel of a rifle is visible at one side, and in the background is the dim scene of a surgical operation" (Smith & Feld, 1958, p. 694; Smith and Feld developed the training manual for McClelland). Consider the following stories which were written by two people as they looked at this picture (Smith & Feld, 1958, p. 717). The numbered divisions of the stories refer to the four sets of questions described above.

Story D–23

1. A young boy is thinking about a medical operation on a soldier. He pictures the gory details.
2. This young boy's older brother was probably badly injured during the war, and died of his injuries despite medical attention.
3. The young fellow feels sad and lonely without his dead brother, but he is proud of him.
4. The young boy's pride in his brother will assert itself more strongly, for he has now become accustomed to living without his brother. He does not need him, now, but he is proud of him.

Story D–24

1. This young boy is dreaming of the day he will have completed his training and become a great and famous doctor. Perhaps this portrays someone already famous for research.
2. He has been asked by his father or relative what he wants to do when he grows up and he is trying to tell them the mental picture that he has in his mind of himself in thirty years.
3. The boy is thinking of the great thrill that must be experienced by a doctor when he performs a delicate operation saving someone's life.
4. The boy will go out through college and eventually become a world-famous doctor.

Obviously the second story is about achievement, while the first is not; but not all stories are so clear-cut. Rather than depend upon subjective judgments—which might be variable or subject to irrelevant considerations—specific criteria for rating stories were developed by McClelland and his associates.

First, the story is judged according to the following criteria to determine whether it shows achievement imagery (McClelland, et al., 1958, pp. 181–184): (1) One of the characters in the story is engaged in *competition with a standard of excellence.* "Winning or doing as well as or better than others is *actually stated* as the primary concern" (Ibid., p. 181), or there are words to the effect that a character wants to do a good, workmanlike job of which he can be proud. (2) One of the characters is concerned with a *unique accomplishment.* "Inventions, artistic creations, and other extraordinary accomplishments fulfill this criterion" (Ibid., p. 183). (3) One of the characters has a *long-term involvement* with an achievement goal. "Being a success in life, becoming a machinist, doctor, lawyer, successful businessman, and so forth, are all examples of career involvement which permit the inference of competition with a standard of excellence . . ." (Ibid., p. 184). The second of the stories above could be counted as showing achievement imagery in terms of either of the McClelland study's latter two criteria. (The second story is concerned with a long-term achievement goal and also with an extraordinary accomplishment; namely, becoming "a world-famous doctor.")

If a story is judged to meet one or more of the three criteria, it is then checked—according to McClelland's technique—for other specific characteristics indicative of a concern for achievement. These additional characteristics include statements that someone desires success or wants to do well; descriptions of "instrumental activity" (i.e., mental or physical action intended to reach an achievement goal); and expressions of pleasure and pride when an achievement goal is reached or expressions of disappointment at failure. The statement in the second story above that the boy imagines "the great thrill that must be experienced by a doctor when he performs a delicate operation" is an example of pride in achievement. The specific characteristics indicative of a concern for achievement are counted to yield a total "need for achievement" score. Research has shown that properly trained persons working independently can score stories with a high degree of agreement.

Answer to the question on p. **408.**

B. Motivation is energy released by deprivation or the appearance of an arousing stimulus.

Thus far we have described a fairly objective technique for measuring the amount of achievement imagery in the stories people write. But is it reasonable to conclude, as McClelland and his associates claim, that the person who writes a story containing a lot of achievement imagery has a high "need for achievement"? This conclusion does not necessarily follow. It is entirely possible that people write stories about crime, unrequited love, the pleasures of smoking pot, alienation, sports, or achievement as the whim of the moment dictates.

Some light may be thrown on this matter by considering the effects of hunger on *TAT* stories. Atkinson and McClelland (1948; also 1958) completed an experiment in which naval trainees were deprived of food for one, four, or sixteen hours before writing stories. The stories were scored for amount of food imagery which was, by hypothesis, a measure of "need for food." Fig. 11.4 pictures the amount of food imagery as a function of hours of food deprivation. As you can see, the longer the period of the food deprivation, the more food imagery appeared in the stories. In the case of hunger, evidently the content of stories does reflect motivation.

When they began to study achievement, McClelland and his associates reasoned that if there is a tendency which can be called "need for achievement," this need should affect achievement imagery in the same way that hunger affects food imagery. The question, then, is whether people will write stories that contain more achievement imagery under conditions that could reasonably be supposed to arouse the hypothesized need to achieve. McClelland, et al. (1949; also 1958) performed an experiment

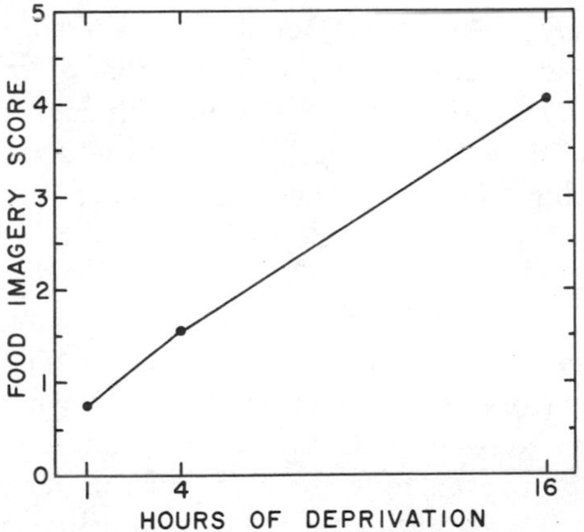

FIGURE 11.4 *Food imagery score as a function of number of hours of food deprivation. (Based on Atkinson & McClelland, 1948.)*

to answer this question. Prior to writing stories, subjects completed a series of tests. These tests were introduced casually in one group—students were told that the tests were being tried out for the purpose of revising them and that their performance as individuals would not be judged. In another group the experimenter explained:

> The tests which you are taking directly indicate a person's general level of intelligence. These tests have been taken from a group of tests which were used to select people of high administrative capacity for positions in Washington during the past war. Thus in addition to general intelligence, they bring out an individual's capacity to organize material, his ability to evaluate crucial situations quickly and accurately; in short, these tests demonstrate whether or not a person is suited to be a leader.

The experimenter then quoted fake average test scores which were so high that it made it seem that practically everyone in the group had done very poorly. At this point the *TAT* was introduced as a "test of imagination." The results of the experiment indicated that there was a great deal more achievement imagery in the stories of those who had been led to believe that they had done poorly on tests of important abilities than in the stories of those who wrote under relaxed conditions, which is the result one would expect if the content of the stories reflected achievement motivation.

Other things being equal, people with a high need for achievement should excel in competitive activities. Thus, assuming that the content of imaginative stories reflects motivation, those whose stories contain large amounts of achievement imagery would be expected to do well in competition and on tasks that entail success or failure. There is some evidence that seems to confirm this expectation. For instance, Lowell (cited in McClelland, 1961, p. 44) obtained the results pictured in Fig. 11.5. The task was decoding anagrams—that is, rearranging groups of scrambled letters to form words. Subjects with high need for achievement started out at the same level of performance as those with low need for achievement, but they improved more rapidly, presumably because they tried harder to learn how to do the task well than did those with a lower need to achieve.

Not all of the experiments of this sort have come out as expected, however. In some cases those with a high need to achieve have performed no better or even worse than those whose need was presumably low. John W. Atkinson, one of McClelland's original colleagues, has constructed a theory that seems to fit the pieces of the puzzle into a coherent pattern. Briefly, his idea is that a person with a high need for achievement is uninterested in very easy or routine tasks because they present no challenge. Extremely difficult tasks are also uninteresting to the per-

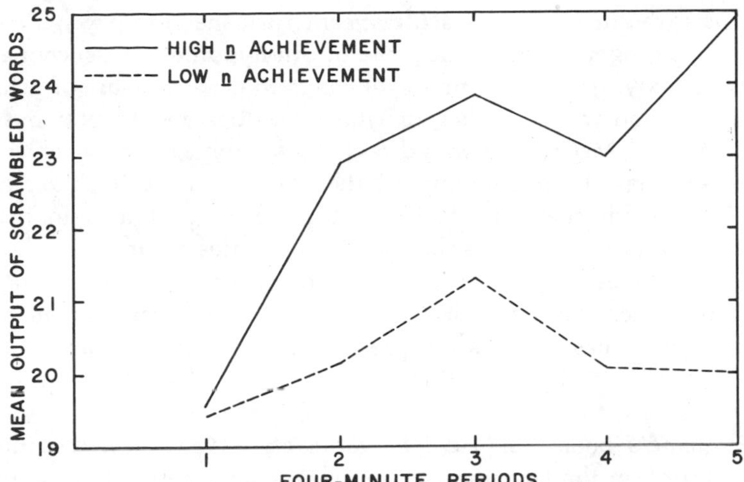

FIGURE 11.5 *Mean output of scrambled words per four-minute period for subjects with high and low need for achievement scores (from McClelland, 1961, p. 44).*

son with high need for achievement because it is no disgrace to fail at a very difficult task. According to Atkinson's theory people whose need for achievement is high should do best on tasks of moderate difficulty that entail moderate risks of failure. Most of the data seem to fit the theory (Atkinson, 1965).

The pioneering German sociologist Max Weber (1904) developed a persuasive argument that the Protestant Reformation was instrumental in the rise of modern capitalism. He maintained that the Protestant was a new personality type especially suited for the development of an industrial society. For the Protestant, according to Weber, the central satisfaction in life was "the irrational sense of having done his job well" (Weber, 1930). Money was not important for what it could buy, but rather as the visible evidence of a job well done. So the Protestant ethic was the goad that drove the early capitalist to accumulate wealth, and the same ethic caused him to plow the money back into the business rather than spend it on himself. Similarly the virtuous Protestant worker made a conscientious, hard-working employee.

Impressed with the similarities between Weber's assessment of the character of the early capitalists and his own picture of the person with a high need for achievement, McClelland was prompted to try to explain in achievement terms the economic growth of nations and the rise and fall of civilizations, topics which the psychologist is usually content to leave to the historian, economist, and sociologist. McClelland's key hypothesis was that need for achievement furnishes the psychic energy for periods of vigorous economic growth. An hypothesis on such a grand scale is not easy to test. The first problem is to get a measure of achievement motivation which applies to whole societies and to previous historical periods. McClelland found a clever solution to this problem for modern societies. He simply applied the scheme for scoring the amount of achievement imagery in stories to the stories contained in reading primers! His assumption was that children's stories accurately reflect the dominant motives and values of a culture. Moreover, the message in children's stories is usually stated in a very clear, direct manner. As Margaret Mead has said, "a culture has to get its values across to its children in such simple terms that even a behavioral scientist can understand them."

McClelland's book *The Achieving Society* (1961) describes his attempt to confirm the hypothesis that achievement motivation is an important factor in economic and technological growth. First, the period from 1925 to 1950 was studied. An adequate sample of stories from children's readers in use in 1925 could be located for 23 nations. These stories were scored for achievement motivation. Then data on economic development were assembled. (The measures of economic growth are rather complicated. The actual gain a country shows during a period is strongly determined by its starting level. A rich country is almost certain to gain substantially and a poor country, probably, to gain less. It is possible, using statistics, to estimate "expected gain" on the basis of starting level. The comparison of actual gain and expected gain is then a reasonable measure of how well or poorly a country has done.) McClelland's analysis shows that actual gains tended to exceed expected gains more often in countries in which children's stories contained large amounts of achievement imagery. This relationship was most pronounced for the growth in the production of electricity. In fact, "78 percent of the countries above the mean in [achievement motivation] were 'overachievers' so far as electrical output is concerned, as compared with only 25 percent of those below the mean" (McClelland, 1961, p. 93).

McClelland next determined the relationship between gains in the production of electricity from 1952 to 1958 and the amount of achievement imagery in children's readers in 1950. This time information was available from 39 nations. The data are summarized in Table 11.2. Once again nations high in achievement motivation tended to exceed expectations, whereas nations low in achievement motivation tended to fall short of them. Another important fact is that need-for-achievement levels in 1950 were unrelated to *previous* economic growth from 1925 to 1950. This suggests that need for achievement can be regarded as a

TABLE 11.2 *Gains in electrical output from 1952 to 1958 compared to expected gains for 39 nations. (Adapted from McClelland, 1961, p. 100.)*

Level of need for achievement based on children's stories in 1950	*Growth in electrical output per capita from 1952 to 1958*		
	Gains below *expectations*	*Gains* above *expectations*	*All nations*
High need for achievement	7	13	20
Low need for achievement	14	5	19
Both high and low need	21	18	39

cause of economic growth rather than a reflection of growth already attained.

Further research showed that the amount of achievement imagery in folk tales was related to level of technological development in 46 primitive societies (Child, Storm, & Veroff, 1958). In other fascinating applications of the technique, it has been shown that achievement imagery in literature was associated with the rise and decline of economic vigor in ancient Greece, in Spain during the Middle Ages, and in England from Tudor times to the industrial revolution (McClelland, 1961, pp. 107–149). In each case a rise in amount of achievement imagery in literature coincided with or slightly preceded the period of greatest economic growth. McClelland (Ibid., p. 105) concluded that these diverse findings "confirm our general hypothesis to a surprising extent, considering the many sources of error that could affect our measures. . . . The generalization is confirmed not only for Western, free enterprise democracies like England and the United States, but also for Communist countries like Russia, Bulgaria or Hungary, or primitive tribes that are just beginning to make contact with modern technological society. It holds in the main whether a country is developed or undeveloped, poor or rich, industrial or agricultural, free or totalitarian. In other words there is a strong suggestion here that men with high achievement motives will find a way to economic achievement given fairly wide variations in opportunity and social structure."

We have recounted some extraordinary successes based on a conception of achievement motivation and techniques for measuring it. But it should not be imagined that the need to achieve is some sort of master motive. In the first place, achievement motivation as it has been defined by McClelland and his associates and as it is reflected in imaginative stories seems to be largely, if not exclusively, related to economic achievement and vigor. It has shown little relationship to professional, scholarly, artistic, or humanistic involvement and achievement. Though repeated studies have been made, need for achievement, as defined and measured by the McClelland group, shows only weak relationships with academic performance. Generally speaking, the grades of those scored high in need for achievement are no higher than those whose need for achievement is scored low. Apparently, though they could not have predicted this in advance, McClelland and his associates have succeeded in developing a measure which is peculiarly sensitive to aspirations in the economic realm, but, unaccountably, is relatively insensitive to aspirations which lead to success in other realms.

The Psychological Origins of Achievement Motivation

Earlier it was stated that the research on the key-pecking behavior of the pigeon can be important for understanding human motivation (Chapter 7). We shall now try to see whether this statement can be justified as far as the development of achievement motivation is concerned. Let us begin by making a provisional assumption. The assumption is that there is a great deal in common between the behavior of pecking at a key at a high rate and the behavior of striving to reach an achievement goal. From the intensive laboratory studies summarized earlier, a great deal is known about the dynamics of the development of key-pecking behavior in pigeons. If key-pecking behavior and the behavior of striving to reach achievement goals really do have a great deal in common, we will be able to understand more fully the development of achievement motivation.

If you want to get a pigeon to "work hard" at the task of pecking a key, the procedure is (1) to define a standard of performance and then (2) to reinforce the pigeon only when its behavior meets the standard. To get a pigeon to peck a key at a high rate, one allows the bird to eat only when he pecks the key at a high rate for a certain period of time. This is the process of differential reinforcement. If the standard of performance is gradually raised and if reinforcement is delivered on an intermittent schedule, the bird can be made to sustain a high rate of performance indefinitely. The pigeon that has been treated in this manner could be called "hard working," "persistent," and even "inner directed" since its behavior seems to be relatively independent of external reinforcement. It will continue to peck the key during long periods without reinforcement. In short, the bird displays all of the qualities said to be characteristic of "high motivation."

Consider now how parents raise children who develop high achievement motivation. Winterbottom (1958) studied a group of eight-year-old boys from a small midwestern city. Each of the boys wrote stories suggested to them by ambiguous pictures. These stories were scored for need for achievement according to the procedure detailed in the preceding section. The mothers of the boys were interviewed to get information about child-rearing practices. Included was a list of twenty items inquiring about demands for independence and mastery in various areas. Each mother was asked to check every item she considered to be a goal she had for her child and to indicate the age by which she expected her child to have learned the behavior. The demands were as follows (Ibid., p. 455):

To stand up for his own rights with other children.
To know his way around his part of the city so that he can play where he wants without getting lost.
To go outside to play when he wants to be noisy or boisterous.
To be willing to try new things on his own without depending on his mother for help.
To be active and energetic in climbing, jumping, and sports.
To show pride in his own ability to do things well.
To take part in his parents' interest and conversations.
To try hard things for himself without asking for help.
To be able to eat alone without help in cutting and handling food.
To be able to lead other children and assert himself in children's groups.
To make his own friends among children his own age.
To hang up his own clothes and look after his own possessions.
To do well in school on his own.
To be able to undress and go to bed by himself.
To have interests and hobbies of his own. To be able to entertain himself.
To earn his own spending money.
To do some regular tasks around the house.
To be able to stay alone at home during the day.
To make decisions like choosing his clothes or deciding how to spend his money by himself.
To do well in competition with other children. To try hard to come out on top in games and sports.

The results showed that the mothers of boys with high achievement motivation made demands at a significantly earlier age than did the mothers of boys with low achievement motivation. The relationship is graphed in Fig. 11.6.

Another section of the questionnaire asked the mother what she did when her son fulfilled her expectations. Three of the alternatives provided were (Ibid., pp. 455–456):

1. Kiss or hug him to show how pleased you are.
2. Tell him what a good boy he is. Praise him for being good.
3. Give him a special treat or privilege.

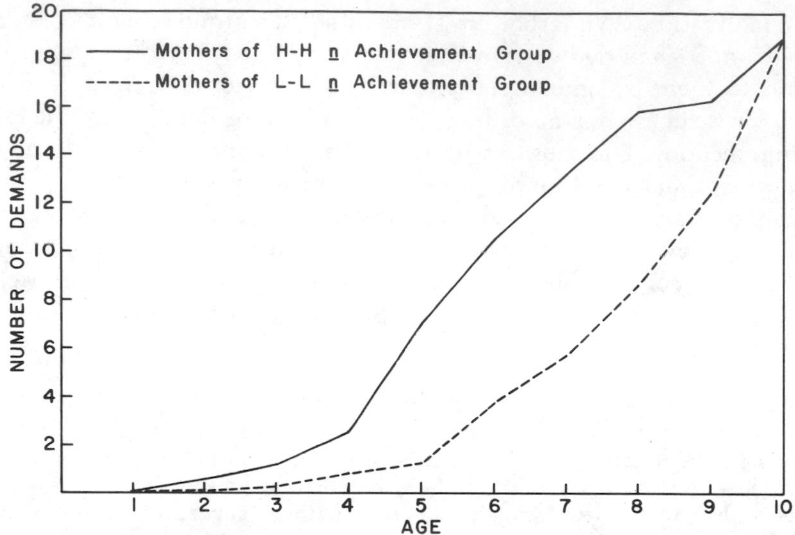

FIGURE 11.6 *Cumulative number of demands for independence and mastery by mothers of boys who were high and low on measures of need for achievement (from Winterbottom, 1958, p. 462).*

The mothers of boys who were high in need for achievement reported using physical affection, kissing, or hugging, more frequently than did mothers of boys with a low need for achievement. And, the total frequency with which a boy was reinforced when he fulfilled an expectation was reported to be higher by the mothers of boys with a high need to achieve.

To get a pigeon to peck a key at a high rate, the procedure is (1) to set a standard of performance and then (2) to reinforce the bird when its performance meets this standard. The Winterbottom study suggests that mothers who (1) make demands for independence and mastery at a relatively early age and who (2) reinforce their sons with physical signs of affection when they meet these demands will raise boys who strive to achieve. One psychologist who reviewed the Winterbottom study concluded in these words (Brown, 1965, p. 448): "It is as if the boy as a son internalizes his mother's stress on early independent achievement and generalizes it into a feeling that achievement in this world earns hugs and kisses."

Long-Term Motivation

Of special interest to educators is a motive which might be called "love of learning," "a thirst for knowledge," or a "need to understand." Our best guess is that such a motive develops in about the same way as need for achievement. If this is the case, then it is important (1) to make demands on the child to learn, know, and understand; and (2) when he meets these demands, to make sure that he receives reinforcement. At the early stages, social reinforcement from parents and teachers is probably especially important. Later, the tendency to seek knowledge and to try to acquire skills will lead naturally to reinforcing consequences. The tendency which can be called a "thirst for knowledge" is not so much a strong inner urge as it is a persistent pattern of behavior established and maintained by reinforcement. We believe that it is most useful and accurate to conceive of other higher motives in the same manner.

Consider now the question of whether there is an intrinsic motive to learn for learning's sake. There are psychologists who believe firmly in the existence of such a motive and who have written in appealing and plausible terms to justify their conviction (Allport, 1938; Maslow, 1954; White, 1959; Berlyne, 1960). Still, the fact of the matter is that intrinsic motivation has a dubious status in psychology. An illustration will help clarify the questions that arise with regard to "higher" human motives. Consider the person who is an avid reader. Could it not be said that such a person reads because of a love of reading for its own sake, in other words, a "need to read"? In order to make such a claim it would have to be shown that the person's reading was not instrumental to obtaining approval, money, sexual stimulation, vicarious release of aggression, vicarious accomplishment through identification with a hero, and so on. The point is that reading can be adequately explained as a means to gain more basic satisfactions. A similar argument can be made for other supposed higher needs.

Let us summarize. There are people who read avidly. There is satisfaction in a job well done. The discovery of a principle or the solution of a challenging problem can be a thrilling experience. And there is satisfaction in an explanation that makes sense of an otherwise disorganized array of facts. But these gratifications probably do not arise automatically. Before a consequence, such as satisfaction in a job well done, can become a generalized, conditioned reinforcer, it is probably necessary that a person be reinforced many times with more basic gratifications for doing jobs well. One of the most important tasks of education is to nurture the socially-valued behavior tendencies called "motives" by making appropriate demands and arranging for frequent reinforcement when the demands are met.

The Educator's Conception of Motivation

Probably as a heritage from the progressive education movement, motivation has generally had a much broader meaning for the educator than for the psychologist. In 1918, William H. Kilpatrick, a prominent spokesman for progressive education, published an article in the *Teachers College Record* entitled "The Project Method," which asserted that "the purposeful act" is at the heart of the educative process. Every activity of the school program was supposed to be based on the child's interests and needs, consonant with the child's own goals. Although progressive education as an organized movement came to an end in the 1950's, many of the values and theories of the movement have had a lasting influence on education. In fact, according to Cremin (1961), the progressive ideology which undoubtedly seemed radical in 1920 was part of the "conventional wisdom" of educators by 1950. And still today it seems a matter of common sense to educators that school programs should be built on the "needs of the child."

The assertion that education should be based on the needs of the learner is frequently a kind of moral imperative. The argument is that the child, like everyone else in a democracy, has a right to select his own goals and, within limits, to pursue them as he sees fit. Psychology is irrelevant to this argument, since if it is ethically right that school programs spring from the interests and motives of the student, then whether such a policy works well is irrelevant. The policy is followed because it is morally correct, not because it is effective. Though this issue is beyond the scope of a psychology text, a counterargument is that the good of society and the long-term good of the child should take precedence over the hypothetical immediate rights of the child.

Another argument for basing instruction on the needs of the learner involves a special conception of the objectives of education. Kilpatrick (quoted in Cremin, 1961, p. 218) posed the following rhetorical question illustrating this conception: "Don't you think that the teacher should often supply the plan? Take a boy planting corn for example; think of the waste of land and fertilizer and effort. Science has worked out better plans than a boy can make." Kilpatrick answered his own question in this way: "I think it depends on what you seek. If you wish corn, give the boy the plan. But if you wish boy rather than corn, that is, if you wish to educate the boy to think and plan for himself, then let him make his own plan." Kilpatrick's contention makes sense, at least within limits. The whole point of Chapter 6, "Teaching New Responses," for example, was that if instruction is to be successful, then sometime during the course of instruction the student must actually do what the instruction is intended to teach him to do. Thus "if you wish to educate the boy to think and plan for himself," the boy must during the process actually think and plan for himself, as Kilpatrick says. But this too is a proposition that is not particularly relevant to the psychology of motivation.

Finally we come to an argument to which the psychology of motivation *is* relevant: namely, the claim that students will learn better when education is based on their needs (using the term "need" here in a restricted way, to mean being deprived of a reinforcer). At the high tide of the progressive education movement, there were those who argued that you should teach a child only those specific skills, concepts, and bits of information he expresses a "felt need" for. For example, a teacher following this policy would not teach about weather until a child asks a question such as, "Why does it rain?" This policy, obviously, makes it difficult to plan. The teacher may not be prepared to teach about weather, insects, magnetism, or whatever at the time the child feels the need to learn about it. Furthermore, while children show an interest in many things and, when encouraged, ask many questions, they do not always display a "felt need" for the skills and knowledges adults believe are important. An increasing awareness of this fact led to a somewhat more conservative formulation of the progressive philosophy, in which the teacher for the most part plans what will be studied and when; however, special pains are taken to make lessons relevant to the student. The first step is always to "motivate" the student, if possible by showing him the relationship of the lesson to his interests.

The crux of the progressive philosophy is to base instruction on intrinsic motivation. Then, presumably, the things a student learns will automatically lead to intrinsic reinforcement. ("Intrinsic reinforcement," you will recall, is reinforcement that is not arranged by a teacher, but occurs instead as a natural consequence of an action.) The difficulty with this view is that a certain level of competence is required before such reinforcement can occur. For example, as we indicated in Chapter 7, it typically takes several years of hard work before most children have learned to read well enough to receive much gratification from reading. The sensible thing to do is to use extrinsic reinforcement to shape the skills of students to the point where they will get intrinsic (i.e., self-induced) reinforcement. Nothing we know indicates that extrinsic reinforcement is inferior to intrinsic reinforcement. The conclusion is that educators are quite right to be concerned with motivation, but, in the past at least, have placed too restrictive an emphasis on intrinsic motivation.

Anxiety as an Underlying Factor in Human Motivation

While no one has argued that need for achievement is a master motive, such a claim has been made for anxiety. Brown (1961, pp. 168–

176), for one, rejects the idea that there is a separate motive for money, praise, recognition, affection, and so on. The argument is that the underlying theme for all of these hypothetical needs is really fear of deprivation—fear of loss of esteem, fear of loss of status, fear of loss of affection. Recall that one operation for arousing achievement motivation is to make it seem that a person has done poorly on a test of important abilities. Perhaps achievement motivation, then, could more aptly be called "fear of failure." McClelland and his associates (1953) recognized early in their research that part, if not all, of what their measure tapped was fear of failure; and later research has confirmed that this is the case (Moulton, 1958; Anderson, 1962).

Earlier the research of Gewirtz and Baer (1958a, 1958b) was cited to show that social deprivation and satiation influence how hard people will work to receive praise. Walters and Ray (1960) have contended that social deprivation arouses anxiety and that social satiation reduces anxiety, thereby influencing the effectiveness of praise. Their research seemed to show that social deprivation does not enhance the effects of praise and attention unless it provokes anxiety. Schacter (1959) has completed a number of experiments that seem to indicate that people, especially girls, want to spend time with other people when they are made to feel anxious. Upon reporting for one of the experiments, groups of girls were greeted by a man in a white coat with a stethoscope in his pocket who introduced himself as Dr. Gregor Zilstein. He gave a talk about research with electric shock and then told the girls about the experiment in which they were to participate. "Dr. Zilstein" told one group that they would receive severe electric shocks (high anxiety condition). The other group was told that each girl would receive mild, harmless shocks that would tickle rather than hurt (low anxiety condition). After completing a questionnaire given to ascertain whether "Zilstein's" talk had created low or high anxiety as intended, it was indicated to the girls that there would be a delay before the experiment began. Each girl was asked to decide whether she would prefer to wait alone in a comfortable room containing books and magazines or whether instead she would prefer to pass the time in a classroom in the company of other girls who were also waiting to take part in the experiment. This ended the experiment, the purpose of which was then explained. The results showed that 20 of the 32 girls in the high anxiety condition, who had been threatened with severe electric shocks, chose to wait with others as compared to only 10 of the 30 girls in the low anxiety group, which had been promised only mild shock. This experiment, and others Schacter has completed, suggests that stress which could be said to produce anxiety tends to make people want to affiliate with one another.

The notion that anxiety underlies most, if not all, of human motivation is inviting because it seems to lead to a single, unified interpretation of a variety of motivational phenomena. Most psychologists today consider that human motives are largely learned. Yet it is an embarrassing fact that it has never been possible to show in the laboratory how a "positive," appetitive motive could be learned. Learned motives of a positive nature that have been produced in the laboratory just haven't proved very stable or persistent (Cofer & Appley, 1965, pp. 580–582). Fear and anxiety are another matter. Fear-based needs are very stable and persistent. So it seems reasonable to suppose that human motivation is based largely on anxiety. Brown (1961, pp. 168–176) has presented a detailed analysis of how an "acquired drive for money" could be based on anxiety. Children observe the worried looks on their parents' faces as they talk about lack of money. From time to time parents warn their children of the consequences of not having enough money. "If you lose your money, you won't be able to go to the movie." "If we run out of money by the end of the month, we may not have enough food to eat." "So you broke your bicycle. That's tough. Money doesn't grow on trees you know." Brown (Ibid., p. 173) concludes, "Now in each of these statements, and in innumerable ones like them, an anxiety-arousing warning is paired with a statement about the lack of money. Through repeated pairings, by other children as well as by parents, of these two kinds of assertions, cues denoting a lack of money might come to arouse anxiety reactions." The idea is that people learn to seek money because doing so reduces their anxiety. Brown believes that a drive to reduce anxiety also explains why people seek prestige, affection, power, and the like.

There is evidence that anxiety is a factor in much human motivation. However, the notion that human motivation is nothing but anxiety is a much stronger claim, one which would be difficult to support. As a practical matter, though, we fear that anxiety is sometimes used as a convenient catchall explanation which precludes further analysis on the part of a teacher. There is a functional value to labeling a reaction as "anxiety" only if the particular events which arouse and reduce anxiety can be identified. When every reaction to stress is called "anxiety," the actual effects of a certain kind of stress on behavior may be lost sight of. For example, in contrast to Schacter's work, which showed that people want to affiliate with one another when they are anxious, Sarnoff and Zimbardo (1961) aroused "anxiety" by leading college males to expect that they would be required to suck on things such as their thumbs, baby bottles, oversized nipples, pacifiers, breast shields, and lollipops. Under these conditions, high anxious subjects showed much *less* desire to affiliate with others during a waiting period than did low anxious subjects.

Anxiety, General Drive, and Drive Stimuli

Much of the research on anxiety has entailed questionnaires. One of these is the Manifest Anxiety Scale developed by Janet Taylor (1953), which consists of 50 items that clinical psychologists judged were indicative of chronic anxiety. A sample of the items appears in Fig. 11.7.

I work under a great deal of strain. (True)
I frequently notice my hand shakes when I try to do something. (True)
I worry quite a bit over possible troubles. (True)
I practically never blush. (False)
I am usually calm and not easily upset. (False)
I feel anxious about something or someone almost all of the time. (True)
I am very confident of myself. (False)

FIGURE 11.7 *Items from the Manifest Anxiety Scale. The response indicative of anxiety is shown in parentheses (from Taylor, 1953).*

One of the most influential traditions in behavior theory was begun by Clark L. Hull. Janet Taylor (now Janet T. Spence), and her husband, the late Kenneth W. Spence, have been among the many psychologists who have modified and extended Hullian theory. Since those who have employed the Manifest Anxiety Scale have by and large interpreted the scores on the scale in terms of Hullian conceptions of motivation, we shall take this occasion to describe these views more fully. In the Hullian tradition, the term "drive," symbolized by the letter *D*, is used for motivation. Drive entails energy mobilization and the invigoration of behavior. While it is not denied that internal cues (or drive stimuli) associated with a high level of drive may guide or steer behavior, Hull and others associated with this position stress that the energy released by a particular deprivation or arousing stimulus is not "bound" to the behavior of "seeking a certain goal." Instead, drive is "free energy" which serves to invigorate any and all behavior. In other words, according to this notion, the organism that has been deprived of food is more vigorous not only in the pursuit of food, but more vigorous in all of its behavior, whether or not the behavior is related to getting food. As indicated earlier, there is evidence that deprivation and arousing stimuli have general invigorating effects.

At any moment in its life an organism may have been deprived of various reinforcers for various periods of time and a number of different arousing stimuli may currently impinge on the organism. The energy instigated by these sources accumulates to form total drive *D*. Notice that according to this theory, it is not quite correct to speak of different drives. It is more appropriate to talk about different *sources* of drive. Drive is the sum of all motivational energy available at any one time.

The basic Hullin equation relating motivation to performance is as follows:

$$E = D \times H$$

The *D*, as already explained, stands for drive. The *H* stands for *habit*, which is the Hullian name for skill or learned sequence of responses. The *E* represents "excitatory potential," meaning, simply, the product directly underlying actual behavior. In words, the equation says that behavior is the product of drive and habit.

Now we shall see how this theory makes predictions about learning and performance which are not at all obvious and which are very unlikely to arise from a commonsense analysis. People (or animals) have a repertoire of habits that will be evoked in any given situation. Some of these are well-learned; others are weakly established. The degree to which a habit is established is referred to as *habit strength.* Available drive indiscriminately energizes all of the habits which the situation evokes. Usually only one habit can occur at a time; this is the one for which excitatory potential is the highest. Other things being equal, the responses for which the habit strength is greatest will have the highest excitatory potential and, therefore, be most likely to occur. This becomes increasingly true as drive increases. Here is the important point: high drive magnifies the likelihood that the responses with the highest habit strength will occur. Under low drive, the dominant habit may not always occur because of momentary changes in the situation and changes in habit strength due to learning and unlearning which show up more quickly in behavior under conditions of low drive.

To make this analysis clearer, let us consider an imaginary numerical example. Suppose that there are three habits—H_1, H_2, and H_3—evoked in a certain situation. Then three equations may be written as follows:

(1) $E_1 = D \times H_1$
(2) $E_2 = D \times H_2$
(3) $E_3 = D \times H_3$

Suppose further that the habits are of different strengths such that their respective values are $H_1 = 3$, $H_2 = 2$, and $H_3 = 1$. If drive is at a low level, say $D = 1$, then $E_1 = 3$, $E_2 = 2$, and $E_3 = 1$. What will happen if drive is at a high level, say, $D = 3$? Computing on the basis of the three equations, it is now the case that $E_1 = 9$, $E_2 = 6$, and $E_3 = 3$. This exercise shows that high drive levels exaggerate the differences in excitatory potential among habits of various strengths.

A number of experiments have been completed based on the rationale that in simple tasks, in which the dominant habit has a strong probability of leading to correct responses, high drive will facilitate learning and performance because it increases the likelihood that the dominant habit will occur. Many of these experiments have employed the Manifest Anxiety Scale under the assumption that those who obtain a score indicative of high anxiety are operating under a chronic high level of drive, or, at least, that they are emotionally responsive in such a way as to make them especially sensitive to arousing stimuli. The prediction that high drive (high anxious) subjects will perform better than low drive (low anxious) subjects on simple tasks has been repeatedly confirmed in studies of eye blink conditioning (e.g., Spence, 1958). In eye blink conditioning, a puff of air (unconditioned stimulus) is delivered to the eye, causing a blink. Shortly before the puff of air some other stimulus, such as the sound of a buzzer (conditioned stimulus), is presented. Conditioning is complete when the subject always blinks his eye at the sound of the buzzer. The "correct response" (blinking the eye) is certainly dominant in this case—in fact, is virtually inevitable. As predicted, high anxious subjects more quickly learn to blink at the sound of the buzzer than low anxious subjects.

A second prediction from Hullian behavior theory is that high drive will *interfere* with learning and performance on difficult tasks in which the correct habit is *not* initially dominant. This hypothesis has been investigated using paired-associate lists. Spence, Farber, and McFann (1956) prepared one easy list in which the pairs were highly associated—that is, one member of the pair suggested the other. For example, the subject had to learn to say "Arctic" when he saw "Frigid," "Crazy" when he saw "Insane," and "Evil" when he saw "Wicked." On this list the correct response is highly likely, therefore this was a case in which high anxious subjects were expected to learn more rapidly than low anxious subjects. The results confirmed this expectation. The words in the second list, however, were unrelated to the words with which they were supposed to be paired, but highly related to other words in the list. Therefore the correct associations (habits) were initially of low or zero strength and there were incorrect associations of fairly high strength. Consequently, high drive (high anxious) subjects should have performed badly because they persisted in giving incorrect answers. (Since the correct responses could not be learned until they occurred, this learning was likely to be delayed on the part of high drive subjects as the effective strength [excitatory potential] of incorrect habits or associations is magnified.) This prediction was also confirmed in this and other experiments (Spence, Taylor, & Ketchel, 1956).

A somewhat different interpretation of the relationship between anxiety and behavior has been offered by Mandler and Sarason (1952), who developed an instrument called the Text Anxiety Questionnaire. As the name suggests, this questionnaire deals with anxiety reactions during individual and group intelligence tests and course examinations. Included are items "dealing with the student's subjective experiences in the testing situation such as uneasiness, accelerated heart-beat, perspiration, emotional interference, and 'worry' before and during the testing session" (Ibid., p. 167). These investigators have emphasized the role of drive stimuli that accompany high levels of anxiety. Drive stimuli are the internal cues (subjectively, the "feelings") that may be aroused by stress. Low to moderate anxiety is conceived to produce drive stimuli that elicit adaptive responses helpful for doing well on the task. High anxiety, on the other hand, is hypothesized to produce drive stimuli that elicit interfering emotional behavior. In the words of Mandler and Sarason (Ibid., p. 166), "These responses may be manifested as feelings of inadequacy, helplessness, heightened somatic reaction, anticipations of punishment or loss of status and esteem, and implicit attempts at leaving the test situation." Research with the Test Anxiety Questionnaire has shown, among other things, that when people are led to believe that they have done poorly on a task, the subsequent performance of those with low anxiety improves whereas the subsequent performance of highly anxious persons *deteriorates*.

The two interpretations of anxiety that have been described are not inconsistent; rather, they are complementary. Those who emphasize the drive interpretation, for example, Farber (1954), have stressed that drive stimuli associated with high levels of anxiety can evoke responses incompatible with successful performance. Mandler, Sarason, and their associates, on the other hand, have assumed that anxiety represents drive, as well as furnishing a source of cues for responses incompatible with rapid learning and performance.

Practical Application of Research on Anxiety

There are some recommendations for school practice that can be made in the light of the research on anxiety. It should first be noted that these recommendations probably apply not only to anxiety but to any circumstance in which the student could be said to be "excited," "highly aroused," or "intensely motivated." Such excitement appears in schools when students take part in athletic, music, and speech contests; when students perform or appear before audiences; during examinations, achievement tests, quizzes, and aptitude tests; and from time to time during regular classroom activities. In each of these instances students are "turned on" by strong stimuli arising from the situation. Remember that less intense, less provocative situations may arouse to a high degree students who are characterized by high sensitivity to arousing stimuli, such as those who score high on anxiety questionnaires.

The basic rationale for the recommendations which follow was developed in the preceding section. To repeat, strong motivation facilitates learning and performance when the desired behavior is already established or can easily be acquired. Strong motivation interferes with learning and performance when the desired behavior is not firmly established nor easily acquired. The phrases "firmly established" and "easily acquired" are, regrettably, oversimplifications. The key factor in deciding whether a skill will be easily acquired is the presence or absence of potential competing responses—that is, similar skills, concepts, or terms which could become confused with that which is to be learned or performed. No generalizations about the multitude of different tasks which comprise school lessons is possible. Each individual task and subtask has to be analyzed in terms of the nature of the task and the previous experience of the student to determine the likelihood of competing responses. For reasons that will be detailed below, we believe it safest to assume that every task entails competing responses.

The first recommendation is to take steps before and during the period of greatest stress to insure that the desired behavior is firmly established. Herein lies a justification for the common practice of preparing students very thoroughly for contests and public performances. The football player whose skills are well established will employ them under the stress of the game. The pianist who has practiced a piece beyond the point of mastery will be likely to perform it well at a recital.

A less obvious application of the principle of insuring desired behavior is always to give directions for tests and important projects very carefully. Anxious or strongly motivated students are more likely to persist in inappropriate strategies if they become confused or happen to misunderstand what they are supposed to do. They are less flexible in adapting to the demands of the situation. A practical experiment has demonstrated the importance of clear instructions for anxious students. Gifford and Marston (1966) gave fourth-grade boys a reading speed test. When only brief directions were presented, boys whose scores on a test anxiety scale indicated high anxiety read at a substantially lower rate than boys with low anxiety. However, when given an entire practice test beforehand high anxious boys read at the same rate as low anxious boys. Presumably the practice test allowed the high anxious boys to learn the correct strategy for taking the test.

From theory we can predict that high anxious students will be helped by instruction which proceeds in a careful step-by-step fashion such that appropriate strategy and correct responses are highly probable at every point in the lesson. At least one practical study suggests that this theory is correct. Grimes and Allinsmith (1961; also 1966) located two similar schools, one of which employed what they called a "structured" approach to reading instruction and the other of which employed an "unstructured" approach. As they stated (1966, p. 488): "Structure in teaching involves the availability of cues within the whole that give certainty of meaning, definiteness of form, or clearly understood expectations. Usually this means that material is presented sequentially in such a way that when new stimuli are introduced, the learner is able to recognize familiar elements and attack each problem on the basis of prior learning of fundamental skills, facts, or principles. In structured teaching, the child is made aware of all expectations through carefully defined rules; when new situations are presented, the child is prepared to act with certainty on the basis of previously taught information."

Grimes and Allinsmith argue that the phonics method of reading instruction, in which the child learns to sound out words, is more structured than the whole-word method. In their words: "The phonics method, because of its reliance upon rules, systematic arrangement, and provision for certainty in problem-solving, appears to represent a high degree of structuring. The whole-word method, particularly in its earlier stages, can be judged as relatively unstructured because of its lack of discipline in work attack, and its encouragement of 'intelligent guessing' on the basis of loosely defined cues." The results of the experiment appear in Fig. 11.8. For third-grade children who received the structured reading program, there was no difference among those with low, medium, or high anxiety; or perhaps there was slightly greater achievement the higher the anxiety level. The effect was much different for children who received the unstructured reading program. As pictured in Fig. 11.8, the higher the anxiety, the *lower* the school achievement (see also Hill & Sarason, 1966). The conclusion is, based on the evidence now available, that anxious students (and, presumably, very strongly motivated students, no matter what the exact nature of the motivation) will do best in instructional programs allowing them to master each component skill thoroughly before proceeding and in which standards of performance are made very clear.

The analysis of the relationship of anxiety (drive) to learning and performance furnishes another argument for approaches to instruction that minimize student errors. In Chapter 9 evidence was presented to show that if the student is allowed to make mistakes he will be prone to

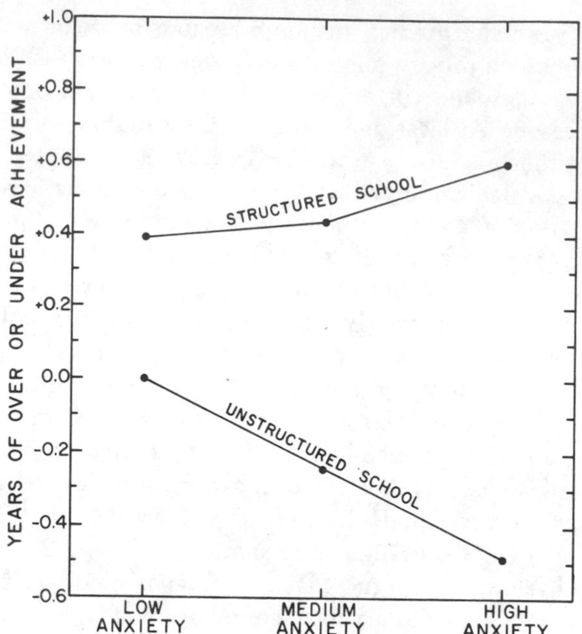

FIGURE 11.8 *School achievement by anxiety level and type of school reading program (from Grimes & Allinsmith, 1966, p. 493).*

repeat these mistakes in the future. From the evidence and reasoning developed in this chapter it is obvious that highly anxious pupils will be especially vulnerable to interference from the errors they are permitted to make. Moreover, if the already anxious student begins to make errors, this may increase his anxiety to the extent that he may get flustered and his performance may go to pieces. Thus, teaching procedures that embody thorough preparation of the student for each step he is expected to make are especially important for anxious students. In fact such procedures can be recommended for all students, those whose anxiety is low as well as those for whom it is high.[1]

It is recommended therefore that when a teacher is emphasizing problem-solving or using a discovery method, both of which necessarily entail some risk of error or blind alleys, special care should be taken to insure that the situation is not stressful and anxiety-provoking. Other-

[1] In the Grimes and Allinsmith experiment, the structured school scored higher than the unstructured school. This cannot be regarded as proof that a structured approach is generally better since the approaches were applied in two different schools. It is entirely possible that the pupils were brighter or the teachers more skilled in the structured school. However, while this particular experiment does not prove the point, other evidence does (Chall, 1967).

wise students, particularly those who are chronically anxious, may persist in using inappropriate strategies. Stress and anxiety do not promote problem-solving, creativity, or discovery of principles. Furthermore, by the same line of reasoning, the problems to be solved or the discoveries to be made should be well within the reach of the students.

A second recommendation is to try to reduce excessive drive in stressful situations. The manner in which a stressful situation is handled by the teacher can have a material effect on the amount of anxiety that is aroused. Wrightsman (1962) led one group of students to believe that performance on an intelligence test was very important, whereas another group was told that they were just helping in the tryout of the test. When the test was seen as important, anxious students scored significantly lower than nonanxious students. Under the "relaxed" condition, anxiety was unrelated to performance. W. J. McKeachie and his associates believe that many students become anxious, angry, and frustrated while taking class examinations, particularly when they encounter questions that they regard as ambiguous or unfair. For the reasons already developed in detail, these emotions—which reflect high drive—can be expected to interfere with performance. McKeachie, Pollie, and Speisman (1955) argued that if students were given the opportunity to write comments about questions they regarded as misleading, anxiety and frustration would be dissipated. This notion was tested experimentally with undergraduates taking regular class examinations in introductory psychology at the University of Michigan. Half of the students were given answer sheets with spaces for comments and half were given standard answer sheets. The students who had the opportunity to write comments made higher scores on the tests. These results held up in a series of experiments. On another occasion McKeachie (1958) gave some students tranquilizers before an exam and gave others placebos. Female students who got tranquilizers scored higher on the exam than female students who got placebos; however, there were no differences among male students. McKeachie suggested that possibly this result was arrived at because females are more anxious than males. Generally, the research indicates that performance can be improved by procedures which reduce or dissipate strong drive or prevent it from being aroused in the first place.

It should be cautioned that steps which reduce anxiety, anger, and frustration may impair the performance of pupils whose drive is low to begin with. This possibility was illustrated in an experiment by Calvin, McGuigan & Sullivan (1957), who confirmed in each of five introductory psychology classes that the opportunity to make comments improved performance on class achievement tests. However, a further analysis showed that only highly anxious students improved their performance from the first to the second half of the test. Low anxious students did better on the second half of the test if they were not permitted to write comments. The theoretical explanation of the performance of the low anxious students is that the opportunity to make comments reduced drive to the point where the students were not sufficiently vigorous, alert, and persistent to do well. Smith and Rockett (1958) have completed a similar experiment with similar results. The available data suggest that under conditions of strong motivation, procedures that reduce stress will improve learning and performance—particularly for students who are chronically anxious—but may slightly impair performance of students who come to the situation with low motivation or low chronic levels of anxiety.

For students who are crippled by anxiety in stress situations, a "desensitization" procedure may be appropriate. In this procedure, the anxious person is made to relax thoroughly by having him alternately tense and release each set of muscles in the body. Then he is asked to imagine as vividly as he can some situation long in advance of the stressful situation, but somehow related to it. Gradually, provided he does not show anxiety at the early stages, the person is asked to visualize situations which more and more closely approximate the situation of ultimate stress, and finally the situation of greatest stress itself. Illustrated below are the stages in the desensitization process employed by Paul (1966, pp. 117–118) to cure "stage fright":

(1) Reading about speeches alone in room (one to two weeks before).
(2) Discussing coming speech a week before (in class or after).
(3) In audience while another gives speech (week before presentation).
(4) Writing speech in study area (room, library).
(5) Practicing speech alone in room (or in front of roommate).
(6) Getting dressed the morning of speech.
(7) Activities just prior to leaving for speech (eating, practice).
(8) Walking over to room on day of speech.
(9) Entering room on day of speech.
(10) Waiting while another person gives speech on day of presentation.
(11) Walking up before the audience.
(12) Presenting speech before the audience (see faces, etc.).

By the time the student gets to the point where he can *imagine* giving a speech and still not feel fear, the chances are excellent that he will actually be able to give a speech in front of an audience without being troubled by anxiety. The typical teacher will have neither the skill nor the time to apply the full desensitization procedure, so it is probably best left to therapists and counselors. Nonetheless, the classroom teacher can profitably apply the general idea. For instance, a student who was nervous about an impending speech contest could be asked first to give his speech for the speech teacher alone, then for an audience composed of several friends who will also take part in the speech contest, then for one or more small classes. When the contest finally arrives, his anxiety should be under control. The same technique, involving practice tests, could be used for the student who "panics" during examinations.

In summary, in situations of great stress, excitement, or high arousal, student learning and performance can be improved by (1) preparing students thoroughly so that it is highly likely they will be able to give the correct responses or engage in the desired behavior; and (2) reducing or ameliorating stress and anxiety, though this latter procedure may slightly impair the performance of students who come to the situation with low levels of anxiety.

A Further Consideration of the Concept of Need

It may seem obvious that the reason food functions as a reinforcer for the food-deprived pigeon is that the pigeon is "hungry." Indeed many psychologists are willing to make inferences of this sort (Farber, 1954). But to B. F. Skinner, saying that the pigeon is "hungry" or that it is driven by a "need for food" goes beyond direct factual evidence. You can see a pigeon peck a key or observe a record of its responses. You cannot see a pigeon's "need for food." The existence of a need must be inferred. According to Skinner, this is precisely the kind of inference that gets the psychologist into trouble. In his view of the nature of science, the scientist's task is to discover factual laws, and the scientist who permits himself to speculate about unobservable, hypothetical events and processes is likely to be diverted from his main task. According to Skinner (1959, pp. 95–96):

> We are within reach of a science of the individual. This will be achieved, not by resorting to some special theory of knowledge in which intuition or understanding takes the place of observation and analysis, but through an increasing grasp of relevant conditions to produce order in the individual case. . . . It is the function of learning theory to create an imaginary world of law and order and thus to console us for the disorder we observe in behavior itself. . . . We argue that if learning is, as we hope, a continuous and orderly process, it must be occurring in some other system of dimensions—perhaps in the nervous system, or in the mind, or in a conceptual model of behavior. . . . When we have achieved a practical control over the organism, theories of behavior lose their point. In representing and managing relevant variables, a conceptual model is useless; we come to grips with behavior itself. When behavior shows order and consistency, we are much less likely to be concerned

with physiological or mentalistic causes. A datum emerges which takes the place of theoretical fantasy.

Skinner's position, which is called "radical behaviorism," is by no means universally accepted by experimental psychologists. Many psychologists, including the authors, believe that the task of constructing theories and experimentally testing them lies at the heart of the scientific process. In the accepted practice of the physical and biological sciences, the theories may include unobservable, hypothetical events and processes, so long as these are rigorously defined in terms of observable facts. Skinner (1959, p. 41) himself has admitted that "it would be foolhardy to deny the achievements of theories of this sort in the history of science."

What Skinner is arguing for is an emphasis on the immediate, the observable, and the practical. His is a hardheaded, no-nonsense approach which should and does appeal to the practical man. In addition to a number of experimental psychologists, enthusiastic Skinnerians are to be found in clinical psychology, where they are developing promising innovations in psychotherapy (Krasner & Ullmann, 1965; Paul, 1966), and in educational psychology, where Skinnerians have taken a leading role in the development of programmed instruction.

Is the concept of "need" or "motivation" necessary? Imagine for the moment that you are a theoretical psychologist trying to answer this question. One's first impulse is to answer, yes, the concept of "need" is necessary. After all, there are some impressive analyses of human behavior in terms of motivation; for instance, McClelland's analysis of the economic and technological growth of nations in terms of achievement motivation. But consider the question more carefully. While there is no doubt that "need" has been a useful concept, this does not mean, however, that the concept is necessary. The theorist tries to account for behavior by using the smallest possible number of basic concepts. A concept can be regarded as basic only if there is an irreducible core of facts and relationships that cannot be understood without the concept. Other concepts are entertained as a matter of convenience, but these concepts can be reduced to more basic ones. The relationship is similar to that between axioms and theorems in a mathematical system.

Rephrasing the question, is the concept of "need" or "motivation" a basic or a derivative concept? Consider the case of "achievement motivation." A convincing argument can be made that all of the facts and relationships McClelland has discovered can be explained without recourse to the concept of "need." Instead of speaking of achievement motivation, we might without loss of meaning talk about the *habit* of working hard to achieve. This behavior was established as the result of differential reinforcement of attempts at mastery early in life—attempts in which the mother played an important role as a definer of standards and as a reinforcing agent. People who try hard to achieve frequently will achieve, so the behavior involved in striving to achieve is intermittently reinforced and for this reason persists at high levels. If an inner tension accompanies achievement-related behavior, then, this tension need not be regarded as a causal force but merely as a reflection of the strength of the behavior and the controlling schedule of reinforcement. By this line of reasoning it is not necessary to regard motivation as a basic concept in order to account for need for achievement. Rather, it seems possible to do away with the notion of need and speak instead of behavior established and maintained by reinforcement.

One criterion of the value of a concept is its capacity to generate important research. Whether it will ultimately turn out that a concept can be eliminated in favor of other different or more basic concepts is difficult to predict. In the meantime, however, we should value concepts which stimulate people to discover new facts and which provide a plausible account of these facts. Motivational concepts have been very valuable in stimulating research. The research on achievement motivation is one example and there are many others. Many discoveries might not have been made if it were not for the concept of "need."

A concept can also be judged in terms of its usefulness in explaining, predicting, and controlling behavior in practical situations. Whereas the value of the concept of "need" in scientific psychology perhaps cannot be denied, it is possible to have serious doubts about its value in applied psychology. The practitioner, for instance, the school teacher who is thinking in motivational terms, may be led into misleading speculations about "inner forces"—speculations which will seldom suggest a course of action which is helpful in managing behavior. Let us consider a concrete illustration. A boy frequently disrupts class by making surreptitious wisecracks, throwing things, and playing the clown. It might be concluded that the boy's behavior results from his "insatiable need for attention." Suppose this were true. Now what? What can the teacher do about the boy's behavior? The fact is that identifying a need which causes the behavior (even when correctly identified) does not in and of itself help the teacher plan a course of action to deal with the behavior. Furthermore, it is quite possibly wrong to assume that this boy's "need for attention" is any stronger than that of his classmates. Earlier we observed that a pigeon will peck a key at a high, stable rate over long periods of time under certain conditions of food reinforcement. Such a pigeon may be no hungrier than other pigeons who peck at slower rates for shorter periods of time. This fact shows that it is not safe to infer that strong, persistent behavior is caused by a high level of need.

Now let us try another analysis of the behavior of the boy who plays the clown. We shall assume that the boy has a *habit* of engaging in disruptive behavior which was established and is maintained by certain conditions of reinforcement operating in the classroom. The reinforcers undoubtedly include the reactions of the boy's classmates. They laugh when he does something silly. They pay attention to him when he disrupts classroom routine. The reactions of the teacher—confusion, dismay, anger, attention—may be reinforcing also. The key to changing the boy's behavior is to change the contingencies of reinforcement. The boy should be reinforced for behavior incompatible with playing the clown and not reinforced for silly, disruptive behavior.

We conclude that the concept of "need" or "motivation" is probably necessary to form a logically complete and satisfying explanation of behavior, and that important psychological research has been and continues to be stimulated by the concept. Nevertheless, we believe that it should be deemphasized in the application of psychology to education. Much of what commonsense "folk" psychology ascribes to motivation is better understood as habitual behavior. It is mistaken to assume that strong, persistent behavior is always caused by a high level of need. Indeed, the teacher is seldom in a position to know very much about student needs. Such matters are perhaps best left to the clinician. Even if a student need has been correctly identified, little has been learned that is ordinarily educationally useful. Taking practical advantage of such needs as students may have usually means controlling the frequency and contingencies of reinforcement. And since having knowledge about student motivation is not essential to utilize reinforcement successfully, we suggest that teachers concern themselves with reinforcement instead of motivation.

SELF-TEST ON MOTIVATION

Answer the following questions and then check your answers against the scoring on p. 439.

1. Define "motivation" in psychological terms.

2. There are research data that have been interpreted to mean that in the United States girls have a higher need for approval from other people than boys. Which of the following is the best explanation of these data?

   a. Females have a greater instinctual tendency to affiliate with others than males.
   b. Parents, teachers, and other agents of society make fewer demands on girls than on boys.
   c. Parents and teachers tend to use positive reinforcement when dealing with girls and tend to use aversive methods when dealing with boys.
   d. Girls tend to be reinforced for showing concern for others while boys tend to be reinforced for being aggressive and competitive.

3. List three procedures to use with a student who does poorly on examinations because of nervousness.

4. Briefly describe the conditions that are likely to produce a person who is independent and takes initiative.

5. Under conditions of high stress, which teaching technique is likely to be most effective, a textbook or a self-instructional program? Briefly explain your answer.

6. List one disadvantage to a policy of basing instruction on the "felt needs" of the learner.

7. A boy who is a junior in high school has never had a date. He would like to invite a girl to a forthcoming party; however, he says he hasn't got the courage. Assume you are a guidance counselor and the boy comes to you for advice. Describe how a desensitization procedure could be used to help him. Be sure to list concrete illustrations of the stages in the process. This is an open book question. Refer to the description on p. 432 of the technique used to cure "stage fright," if you wish.

Summary

Psychologists define "motivation" as the invigoration of behavior caused when an organism is exposed to an arousing stimulus or is deprived of a reinforcer. Food and water deprivation have been studied most thoroughly, but the same effects may be observed when a person is deprived of human attention or sensory stimulation.

It is commonly believed that motives are directed toward specific goals, and to some extent this is true; however, research suggests that motivation may be thought of as "free energy" not bound to a particular goal.

One of the most exhaustively studied of human motives is the need for achievement, which is typically measured by analyzing people's imaginative stories. Need for achievement is related to the economic success of individuals; it is even possible to predict the economic and technological development of whole nations with measures of achievement motivation. People who develop a high need for achievement are likely to have parents, especially mothers, who make demands for independent achievement at an early age and who reinforce with attention, praise, privileges, and physical affection when independent achievement is displayed. It is probable that other motives—ranging from a "love of reading" to an "interest in scientific inquiry"—develop in a similar fashion, although in these cases it is obvious that teachers will have as large a role to play as parents. We believe that it is most accurate and useful to conceive of "higher human motives" and "interests" as persistent behavior patterns which have been established and are maintained by reinforcement.

Educators have urged that instruction should be based on intrinsic motivation to learn. Learning and the search for knowledge can lead to apparently spontaneous gratifications that have not been arranged by a teacher. However, a level of competence often beyond the reach of the beginner is required before a sustaining frequency of "natural" or "intrinsic" reinforcement is likely. There must be a payoff for the beginner if he is to learn. It is, therefore, important to supplement with extrinsic reinforcement whatever intrinsic reinforcement may arise from, say, learning to read. Furthermore, despite some claims, it is doubtful whether people are born ready to find satisfaction in a job well done or to find a thrill in discovery. If discovery is to become thrilling, it is probably necessary for the experience of discovery to be associated with frequent external reinforcement in various forms.

Some psychologists argue that anxiety is the pervasive factor underlying human motivation. They contend that people are driven by fear of failure more than hope for success, fear of isolation more than desire for social contact and affection, and fear of deprivation more than desire for money and the things money can buy. People who report on questionnaires that they are tense, anxious, and easily upset often do better than other people on simple tasks under relaxed circumstances. However, anxious persons tend to do relatively poorly on difficult, complex tasks under conditions of stress. Examples of stressful situations that arise in school are contests, public performances, achievement tests, and aptitude tests. There are several procedures that can be recommended for dealing with stress. The first is to deal directly with anxiety by getting the person to relax. The second is to prepare the person very carefully and make sure he understands exactly what he is supposed to do. Anxious people are not flexible in stressful situations; they often persist in inappropriate behavior. Severe anxiety, such as stage fright and panic during examinations, can often be alleviated using a desensitization procedure.

Finally, motives are not the only cause—or perhaps even the most important cause—of strong, persistent behavior. Explanations of behavior in terms of motivation are frequently misleading, if not wrong; and motivational analyses seldom suggest a useful course of action in practical situations. The most important thing a teacher can actually do with respect to motivation is to arrange for the frequency and contingencies of reinforcement.

SCORING KEY FOR THE SELF-TEST ON MOTIVATION

A satisfactory score is 9 out of the 11 possible points. Review the sections of the chapter related to questions you got wrong.

1. *(1 point)*

Motivation is the invigoration of behavior caused when an organism is exposed to an arousing stimulus or deprived of a reinforcer.

2. *(1 point)* **d**

3. *(3 points)*

(1) Make sure the student is thoroughly prepared.
(1) Take steps to relax him and put him at ease.
(1) Desensitize him.

4. *(2 points)*

(1) Encourage him to be independent and take initiative.
(1) Reinforce him whenever he displays independence and initiative.

5. *(1 point)*

The self-instructional program is likely to be more effective. People are likely to persist in ways that are nonadaptive under conditions of stress. Error is less likely with a program than with a text.

6. (*1 point*) Some possibilities are that

a. It is difficult to plan to teach things at the moment students feel the need to learn them.

b. Students do not always express the desire to learn the things that it is important for them to learn.

c. Relying on natural or intrinsic reinforcement alone is unrealistic, because beginners cannot easily acquire enough competence to receive intrinsic reinforcement automatically.

7. (*2 points*)

The first step is to talk to the boy to discover the situations involving girls that make him ill at ease and, hopefully, to discover the situations in which he does not feel ill at ease. On the basis of this conversation, prepare a series of situations that you will ask the boy to imagine.

(1) Credit one point for listing a series of concrete situations ranging from least stressful to most stressful. To earn credit, your list need not match the one below, nor be as complete and detailed.

- sitting alone in your room thinking about a girl.
- seeing a girl from a distance.
- saying "Hi" to a girl in class.
- sitting next to a girl in class.
- talking to the girl sitting next to you about a class assignment.
- sitting alone, thinking about asking a girl for a date.
- walking to school the day you're going to ask a girl for a date.
- seeing the girl you are going to ask for a date.
- saying "Hi" to her.
- listening to her say something before you ask her for a date.
- talking to her about . . . (football game, class play, assignment, etc.) before you ask her for a date.
- mentioning the party to her.
- asking her for a date.

(1) Credit one point for saying that you will get the boy to relax as thoroughly as possible, perhaps by asking him to tense and then relax each set of muscles in his body. Then you will ask him to imagine the first situation in the sequence. Provided he shows no discomfort, you will move progressively to more stressful situations.

If the boy gets to the point where he can imagine asking a girl for a date without feeling anxiety, he probably will actually succeed in doing so. One final suggestion: it might be a good idea to advise him against choosing the prettiest and most popular girl in the school for his first date. Suggest that he ask a girl he knows fairly well and likes a little.

Selected Reading

Cofer, C. N., and Appley, M. H., *Motivation: Theory and Research.* New York: Wiley, 1967. A comprehensive treatment of motivational research and theory.

CHAPTER

12

Memory

The teacher wants students to remember as much as possible of what they have learned over the longest possible period of time. Unfortunately, though, memory is seldom perfect. Even something well-learned can be forgotten. Forgetting is a ubiquitous phenomenon. It can occur within a single lesson and, of course, it can and does occur over the long term. Consequently, it is important for the teacher to understand why forgetting occurs and what can be done to reduce it. The person who completes this chapter will be able to:

1. identify the causes of forgetting
2. describe instructional procedures that will improve remembering.

"Forgetting" can be defined as the loss in capability to perform over a period of time during which there is no opportunity to practice. It takes at least two tests to demonstrate that forgetting has occurred. Suppose that on Tuesday a fifth-grade class receives an exercise to teach them to spell 20 words. On Friday a test is given. A boy gets 17 of the 20 words right on this test. Could it be said that he had forgotten three words? The answer is "no." He may have been able to spell only 17 words after the exercise on Tuesday. If there had been an immediate test on Tuesday upon which he spelled 20 words correctly, then it would be accurate to say that he had forgotten three words by Friday. The amount that he has forgotten must also be considered in the light of how much he learned on Tuesday. Suppose on a pretest given before the lesson the boy spelled none of the words correctly. After the exercise he spells 20 correctly and on Friday he spells 17 correctly. In this case it is proper to conclude that he has forgotten three words. It is very likely, however, that the boy will know at least some of the words before the lesson. Suppose that he spells 14 words correctly on the pretest before the spelling lesson Tuesday. On the test immediately after the lesson he spells all 20 words correctly. Thus he has learned six new words. On Friday he spells 17 words correctly. In this case he has remembered 3/6 or 50 percent of the words he learned to spell on Tuesday (and forgotten 3/6 or 50 percent).

Trace-Decay Versus Interference Theories of Memory

One of the oldest theories of forgetting is that memory traces automatically grow dimmer with the passage of time: they grow faint or fade away. (The term "memory trace" simply means the impression which experience makes on the nervous system.) This is a theory with a great deal of commonsense appeal. Our subjective experience of remembering and forgetting *is* one of impressions which grow faint with time. Early psychologists, too, were impressed by the notion of trace decay. In fact, Thorndike (1913, p. 4) believed that trace decay—or, as he called it, the Law of Disuse—was a fundamental fact of psychology. In the 1920's and 1930's, though, there were many experiments completed to test the trace-decay theory of memory and many objections were raised against it. John A. McGeoch, one of the pioneers in research on memory, wrote in 1932:

> Even were disuse and forgetting perfectly correlated, it would be fruitless to refer the forgetting to the disuse as such. Such reference is equivalent to the statement that the passage of time, in and of itself, produces loss, for disuse, literally interpreted, means only passivity during time. In scientific descriptions of nature time itself is not employed as a causative factor nor is passive decay with time ever found. In time iron, when unused, may rust, but oxidation, not time, is responsible. In time organisms grow old, but time enters only as a logical framework in which complex biochemical processes go their ways. In time all events occur, but to use time as an explanation would be to explain in terms so perfectly general as to be meaningless. [Cited in Adams, 1967, p. 24.]

Most psychologists since McGeoch have believed that interference is the main reason—and perhaps the sole reason—for forgetting. Interference occurs when a person confuses similar things which he has learned. For example, the simple experimental arrangement diagrammed at the top of page 444 is likely to produce interference. In the diagram the pairs of capital letters stand for the stimulus and response terms in a paired associate list. The first letter designates the stimulus terms and the sec-

	Learn first list	Learn second list	Time interval	Test first list
Experimental group	AB	AC	}	AB
Control group	AB	—	}	AB

ond letter indicates the response terms. For example, the following lists might be used in the experiment diagrammed above.

AB List	AC List
BAZ—lucky	BAZ—smaller
VEL—sad	VEL—good
MOK—faster	MOK—happy
ZUG—hopeful	ZUG—sick
JIZ—rapid	JIZ—lonely
CEH—angry	CEH—smooth

Subjects in the experimental group first learn the AB list. The pairs appear one at a time, and subjects must learn to associate them so that when the stimulus term (trigram) appears alone they will be able to give the response term (adjective). Usually the list is repeated several times in different orders. Then the experimental subjects learn the second list (AC list) which, in the design diagrammed above, involves the *same* stimuli as the first list but *different* responses. Meanwhile the control subjects engage in an irrelevant activity, such as doing arithmetic or cancelling letters. In order to equalize total amount learned, control subjects often learn an irrelevant list of paired associates involving both stimuli and responses different from those in the first list. Later, after an interval ranging from a few minutes to several weeks, both the experimental group and the control are tested on the AB list.

The typical result in experiments like the one outlined above is that the experimental group forgets significantly more than the control group. This greater forgetting is attributable to the interference generated by the second list. Notice that the results of such experiments cannot be explained by trace-decay resulting from disuse since an equal amount of time intervenes between learning and testing for both the experimental and control groups. If the simple trace-decay notion were correct, forgetting would be a function solely of the passage of time no matter what had happened during this time.

When experience *after* learning produces interference with the retention of learning, this interference is called *retroactive inhibition.* This is the traditional name for such interference because the interfering events can be thought of as acting backward to interfere with or "inhibit" that which was learned earlier. *Proactive inhibition* is the name for interference with retention produced by activities *before* learning occurs. The following experimental arrangement is frequently used to demonstrate proactive inhibition.

	Learn first list	Learn second list	Time interval	Test on second list
Experimental group	AC	AB	}	AB
Control group	—	AB	}	AB

Again, in order to equalize total amount learned, the control group is often given neutral material (here, to take the place of the first list). Typically the experimental group will do less well on the test of AB than will the control group.

It is one thing to say that interference is *a* cause of forgetting, and quite another thing to say that it is the *only* cause. Even the control groups in experiments like the one diagrammed above show a considerable amount of forgetting. How is it possible to explain such forgetting in terms of interference? One answer is that normal, everyday activities are a source of interference. A classic experiment was completed in 1924 by Jenkins and Dallenbach to test this hypothesis. At each of several sessions two people learned a list of nonsense syllables. In the time interval that followed they either slept or engaged in normal waking activity. Overall, more than twice as many nonsense syllables were recalled after periods of sleep than after periods of normal activity. Similar results have been obtained in other experiments, including experiments with meaningful prose materials (Newman, 1939; Grisom, Suedfeld, & Vernon, 1962). Jenkins and Dallenbach (1924, p. 612) concluded that "forgetting is not so much a matter of the decay of old impressions and associations as it is a matter of the interference, inhibition, or obliteration of the old by the new."

Experiments involving the effects of sleeping and normal activity on memory can be criticized on the grounds that during some of the time when they were supposedly sleeping, human subjects may actually have been rehearsing (practicing to themselves) the material previously learned. Rehearsal may be less likely to occur during normal activity.

One way to get around the inclination of human subjects to rehearse would be to use animals. Experiments in which animals were subjected to cold or given drugs to make them quiet failed to yield the expected results, but these treatments may have had physiological effects which impaired memory. Minami and Dallenbach (1946) were able to show interference from normal activities in an experiment employing cockroaches as subjects. The cockroaches were placed in an enclosure with a light and a dark end. While their natural tendency is to go to the dark end of the enclosure, they were trained to go to the light end by giving them mild electric shocks when they went to the dark end. Jenkins and Dallenbach made use of the fact that cockroaches enter a quiet, trancelike state when they are in contact with surrounding materials. During the retention interval, cockroaches in the experimental group were placed in small boxes packed with soft tissue paper where they remained immobile. Control cockroaches were allowed to run freely about their living cages during the retention interval. After intervals of 1, 2, 3, 8, and 24 hours, the cockroaches were again placed in the experimental enclosure and it was determined how long it took them to relearn the habit of going to the light end of the enclosure. As Fig. 12.1 indicates, the restricted-activity group relearned more quickly than the group allowed normal activity, a result entirely consistent with the interference theory of forgetting.

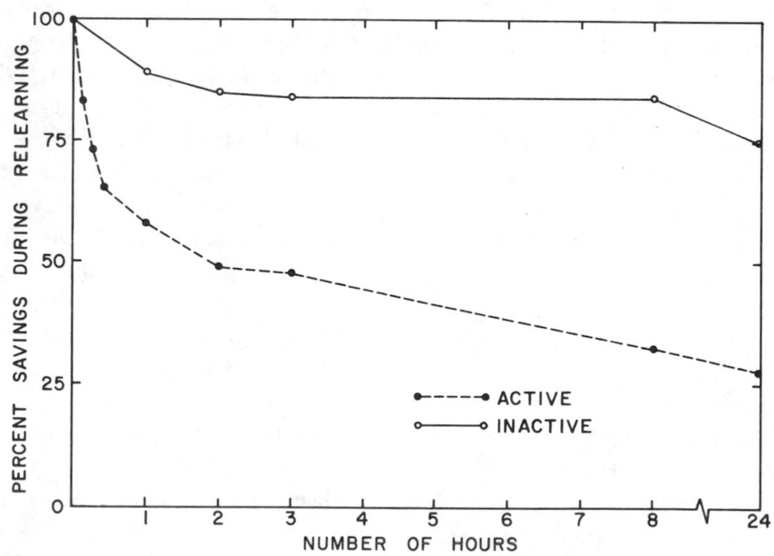

FIGURE 12.1 *Retention for active and inactive cockroaches as a function of the length of the retention interval (from Minami & Dallenbach, 1946).*

Another explanation of why forgetting almost always occurs in experiments despite the absence of any activities during the experiment which could produce interference was emphasized in an important paper by Benton Underwood (1957), one of the most influential contemporary investigators of memory processes. He argued that a lifetime of experience before a particular task is learned produces interference. If this hypothesis is correct, and no one—to the best of our knowledge—questions its logic, then there should be more forgetting when new habits are in conflict with old (preexperimental) habits than when new habits are not conflicting. Several experiments have been completed to test this hypothesis (Underwood & Postman, 1960; Underwood & Keppel, 1963). The results have been generally negative. If these findings are accepted at face value, the conclusion would have to be that interference theory is not adequate to account for all of the facts of forgetting.

Jack Adams, however, in *Human Memory* (1967, pp. 91–96), suggests that there may have been confounding factors in these experiments which prevented the expected interference from occurring. Adams and his associates (e.g., Adams & Montague, 1967) have shown that whether or not a person will be able to learn and remember a pair of items is strongly related to whether he is able to discover an association to link the two items. Adams believes that the subjects in the experiments mentioned above may have been able to discover associations for many of the pairs which were supposed to be in conflict with previous habits. In the Underwood and Keppel experiment (1963) subjects learned pairs of letters. An example of a pair not in conflict with well-learned language habits is T-H. The sequence occurs very frequently in English. On the other hand X-V is very rare, and it would be expected that memory for this pair would suffer from interference from conflicting language habits. However, Adams observes that X-V would be easy to remember if the subject views it as the Roman numeral 15.

In summary, while there are questions which cannot be answered satisfactorily at the present time in terms of interference, interference theory does provide the best explanation of memory we now have. As Adams maintains (1967, p. 307), "Trace decay theory has always been a challenger of the interference theory of forgetting, but never a serious one."

The Laws of Interference

The interference theory of forgetting says that things learned before or after a certain task cause the deterioration in performance which is called forgetting. The amount of interference and, therefore, the amount of forgetting depend upon several factors which will now be considered.

Amount of training. As common sense would suggest, the greater the strength of interfering habits, the *more* forgetting there is. Conversely, the greater the strength of the to-be-remembered habits, the *less* forgetting there is.

There is a great deal of evidence to support these generalizations. One study will be detailed for illustration. Briggs (1957) studied retroactive inhibition with lists of paired adjectives (e.g., "awful-soft"). Subjects received either 2, 5, 10, or 20 practice trials on the AB list, and then got either 0 (control), 2, 5, 10, or 20 trials with the interfering AC list. Amount of recall of the AB list was an *increasing* function of the number of trials on the AB list during original learning and a *decreasing* function of the number of trials on the AC list.

Amount of interfering material. The more interfering material there is, the greater is the forgetting. This, too, is a proposition for which there is a great deal of experimental support. For example, Underwood (1945) gave subjects 0, 2, 4, or 6 AC lists of paired adjectives before learning the AB list. Each list involved the same stimulus terms but different response terms. Twenty-five minutes after the learning of the AB list, subjects were tested for recall of AB. Recall was a decreasing function of the number of AC lists.

Similarity. Thus far, all of the discussion concerning memory has been about the single case in which interfering material involves the *same* stimuli and *dissimilar* responses. The question to be considered now concerns the effects of variations in stimulus and response similarity. In 1949, Charles E. Osgood presented a model which he claimed summarized perfectly all of the research on similarity. Osgood's model, which he called the Transfer and Retroaction Surface,[1] is diagrammed in Fig. 12.2. In this model the shaded plane represents the region of zero effect. The space above the plane signifies facilitation, (i.e., performance improves) whereas the space below the plane represents interference. The condition of greatest facilitation is represented by the point in the upper left-hand corner of the model, where both the stimuli and the responses in the second list are identical. Obviously, if a person first

[1] "Retroaction" refers to the effects of practice with a second task on the recall of a first task. As its name suggests, the Transfer and Retroaction Surface also summarizes the effects of similarity on transfer of training. "Transfer of training," you will recall from Chapter 10, refers to the effects of a first task on the learning or performance of a second task. Osgood's model indicates that retroaction and transfer of training are parallel processes. In other words, when retroactive facilitation occurs, positive transfer of training will also occur. And when retroactive inhibition occurs, negative transfer of training will occur.

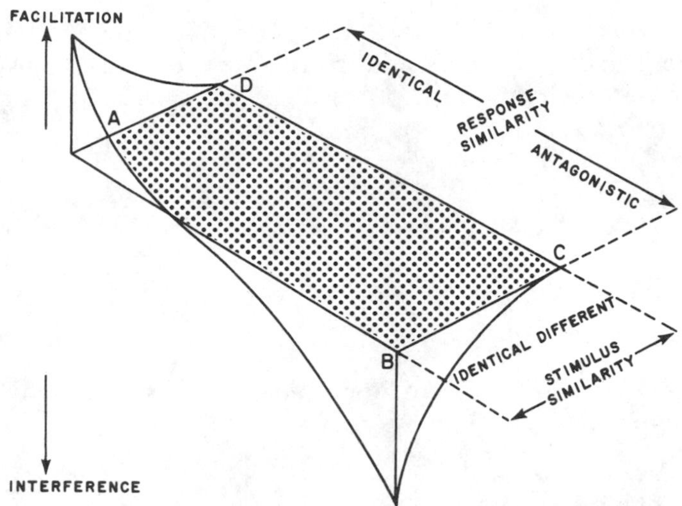

FIGURE 12.2 *Osgood's Transfer and Retroaction Surface.* (*Based on Osgood, 1949.*)

learns an AB list and then on the "second list" practices the same AB items, his recall of AB will be improved.

Just what is meant by "similarity"? With respect to trigrams, similarity has been interpreted as the number of letters two trigrams have in common. By this definition ZAP is more similar to XAP than to XEP and more similar to XEP than to KET. With respect to words, it is possible to scale "associative similarity," which means, roughly, similarity in meaning. This can be done by the simple expedient of having judges rate the similarity of words, as well as by more complicated methods. When the degree of similarity between words is known, it is possible to predict, using the Transfer and Retroaction Surface, whether facilitation or interference will occur. For example, it can be predicted that the student of French who has learned that *fille* means "girl" will have an easy time learning and remembering that *fille* means "maiden," but a harder time learning and remembering that *fille* means "horse."

The following questions pertain to the Osgood Transfer and Retroaction Surface. In answering them, examine the diagram in Fig. 12.2 whenever necessary.

The correct answers appear on the bottom of p. **453.**

1. The length of the shaded plane represents (stimulus? response?) similarity.
2. At point A the stimuli are ______________ and the responses are ______________.
3. At point B the stimuli are ______________ and the responses are ______________.
4. At point D the stimuli are ______________ and the responses are ______________.
5. Given that the stimuli are identical, what is the effect when the responses are antagonistic?
   a. facilitation
   b. interference
   c. zero effect
6. Given that the stimuli are identical, what is the effect when the responses are very similar?
   a. facilitation
   b. interference
   c. zero effect
7. Given that the stimuli are very different, what is the effect when the responses are very similar?
   a. facilitation
   b. interference
   c. zero effect
8. Given that the stimuli are very different, what is the effect when the responses are antagonistic?
   a. facilitation
   b. interference
   c. zero effect

Osgood's Transfer and Retroaction Surface can be summarized by saying that stimulus similarity determines the *magnitude* of the effect, whereas response similarity determines the *direction* of the effect. When the stimuli are very dissimilar there will be little or no effect regardless of the degree of response similarity. When the stimuli are identical or very similar there will be strong facilitation when the responses are very similar, changing to strong interference as the responses change from similar to dissimilar to antagonistic.

Osgood pieced together his model from a variety of different studies completed under a variety of different conditions, guessing at certain aspects of the model. One could have more confidence in the model if it were confined to a single major experiment designed expressly to test it. Such an experiment has been completed by Bugelski and Cadwallader (1956). In the main, the data from this experiment support Osgood's model. However, one discrepancy Bugelski and Cadwallader found was that, given identical stimuli, interference occurred even when the responses were highly similar. However, other recent experiments (Gladis & Braun, 1958; Barnes & Underwood, 1959) have found facilitation when the response terms of the first and second list are highly similar. All in all, while there are still questions about the details, the model does seem to satisfactorily summarize the effects of stimulus and response similarity.

Length of the retention interval. The retention interval is the period of time between the learning of a task and the test for recall. Typically forgetting is rapid immediately after learning and then occurs at a slower and slower rate with increasing time. The general form of the retention curve is remarkably stable. It has appeared in studies of memory employing diverse procedures and measuring techniques, and materials ranging from nonsense syllables to school subject matter. While the general form of retention curves is usually stable, the rate of forgetting at different points in time and the total amount of forgetting may vary, depending upon particular conditions.

Generality of the Laws of Memory

The laws of forgetting are based largely on research with nonsense syllables and lists of discrete words. An important question therefore is whether these laws also apply to memory for meaningful material, concepts, principles, and physical skills. Unless this is the case, the painstaking research with rote tasks is irrelevant to education. Fortunately, while the picture is incomplete and there are anomalies, the laws of forgetting that have emerged from research with rote tasks do seem to apply to school learning.

Organized, meaningful material. Norman J. Slamecka (1959, 1960, 1961, 1962) has completed a systematic series of experiments to ascertain whether the forgetting of meaningful prose obeys the same laws as the forgetting of nonsense syllables and isolated words. Slamecka had subjects learn passages like the following:

We must postulate that, from strictly semantic points of vantage, most confusions in communication revolve about inadequate stipulation of meaning.

The passages were learned by the serial anticipation method. The words in the passage appeared in the window of a memory drum (an apparatus designed to present visual material at a given rate) one at a time at a 3-second rate. As each word appeared the subject had to "anticipate"—that is, say—the next word in the passage. Learning was complete when every word in the passage could be correctly anticipated.

In one of the experiments using the materials and procedures described in the preceding paragraph—an experiment on retroactive inhibition—subjects learned a passage; then learned either 0 (control), 2, 4, or 6 additional passages; and finally, after 20 minutes, attempted to recall the first passage (Slamecka, 1962). The results of this experiment are pictured in Fig. 12.3. Slamecka's research has also shown that verbatim recall of prose passages (1) increases as the amount of practice on the to-be-remembered passage increases, (2) decreases as the amount of practice on interfering passages increases, (3) decreases as the similarity between the to-be-remembered passage and interfering passages increases, (4) decreases as the number of passages presented *before* the to-be-remembered passage increases (proactive inhibition), and (5) decreases as the length of the retention interval increases. All of these

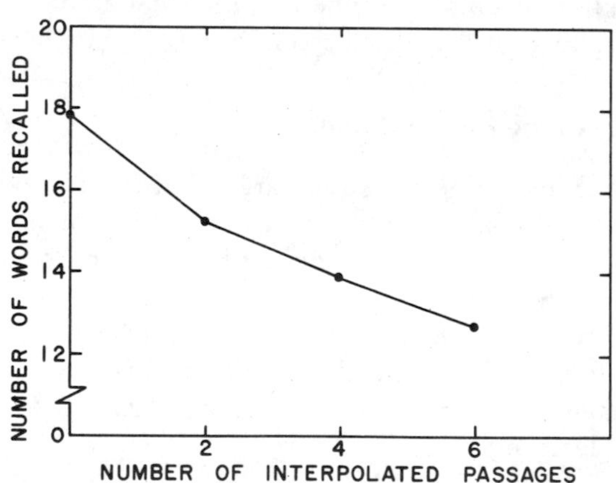

FIGURE 12.3 *Recall after 20 minutes as a function of number of interpolated passages. (Based on Slamecka, 1962.)*

findings are entirely consistent with the results obtained with nonsense syllables and discrete words. It would appear that the laws of forgetting apply to meaningful prose passages.

Slamecka's experiments do not simulate the conditions of school learning very realistically, however. For this reason, the prominent educational psychologist David P. Ausubel (1963), among others, has insisted that Slamecka's results cannot be accepted as evidence about the dynamics of memory for school subjects. It can be argued that the serial anticipation procedure conceals the meaningful relationships among the words in the sentences. Furthermore, the passages themselves were obscure; unrelated to the experience of the learner; and contained difficult, unfamiliar vocabulary. The style of exposition was quite different from the style used in textbooks and lectures. Finally, verbatim recall was demanded. It was not enough that the subject learn the sense of the passage, not enough that he say words with the same meanings as the words in the passage. Literal word-by-word repetition of the passage was required.

Ausubel and his associates have completed experiments under conditions which more realistically approximate the conditions of school learning. Ausubel, Robbins, and Blake (1957), for example, gave college undergraduates a 1700-word passage dealing with Buddhist concepts of God, immortality, soul, faith, salvation, morality, and responsibility. On the same day a Buddhism test was given. On the second day one subgroup studied a 1700-word passage on Christianity, whereas another subgroup received no interpolated material. Eight days after studying the Buddhism passage, the entire group was again given the Buddhism test. On the basis of interference theory, it would be expected that the subgroup that studied the Christianity passage would perform less well than the subgroup which got no interpolated passage; however, in fact, the former group retained 82 percent of what they had learned while the latter group retained 83 percent. In an experiment several years later, Ausubel, Stager, and Gaite (1968) actually found that a "similar but con-

Answers to questions on p. **450.**

1. response
2. identical, identical
3. identical, antagonistic
4. very different, identical
5. b
6. a
7. c
8. c

flicting" passage facilitated memory for a passage studied earlier. Students in Grade 13 of two suburban high schools studied a 2200-word passage on Zen Buddhism, then either a 2100-word passage on Buddhism or a 1500-word, irrelevant passage on drug addiction. Finally, a Zen Buddhism test was given. Students who had received the Buddhism passage did significantly *better* on this test than those who had received the drug addiction passage. Gaite (1968) replicated this experiment, finding that the group that got the Buddhism passage did slightly but not significantly better than the control group on the retention test.

Anderson and Myrow (1971) argue that there is a simple explanation for the confusing results from previous research on retroactive inhibition of textbook-style passages: the previous studies probably included test questions which could be answered correctly on the basis of both passages. Marked interference would be expected only on questions which would be answered differently on the basis of the two "similar but confusing" passages. Thus, answers to these two types of questions, in the final tally, would balance each other—leaving a net effect of no retroaction. In their experiment Anderson and Myrow asked high school students to read two 2,000-word pamphlets, each describing a fictitious primitive tribe. Control groups read the pamphlet describing the first tribe and then an irrelevant passage. A week later a test was given. A third of the questions tested information which was the same for both tribes. These can be called "response-same" questions. For example, the religious practices of both tribes allowed only a deceased tribesman's clan to prepare the tribesman's body for cremation. Reading about the second tribe was expected to facilitate performance on response-same questions. Another third of the test consisted of "neutral" questions, so called because the information tested was unrelated to anything described in the second passage. The final third of the test consisted of "response-different" questions, based on conflicting information about the two tribes. For example, both tribes had a complex clan system, but the Himoots' system was based on occupation, while the Gruandas' was based on the stars. On these questions retroactive inhibition was predicted. The results of the experiment are graphed in Fig. 12.4. Clearly, the findings are in close agreement with interference theory.

Anderson and Myrow (1971) completed a second experiment using the Zen Buddhism passage, the Buddhism passage, and the Zen Buddhism test employed by Ausubel, Stager and Gaite (1968). However, unlike these investigators, Anderson and Myrow divided the test into response-same items, neutral items, and response-different items. Once again, interference theory was confirmed. On the test given after an interval of a week, the groups that studied both the Zen Buddhism and Buddhism

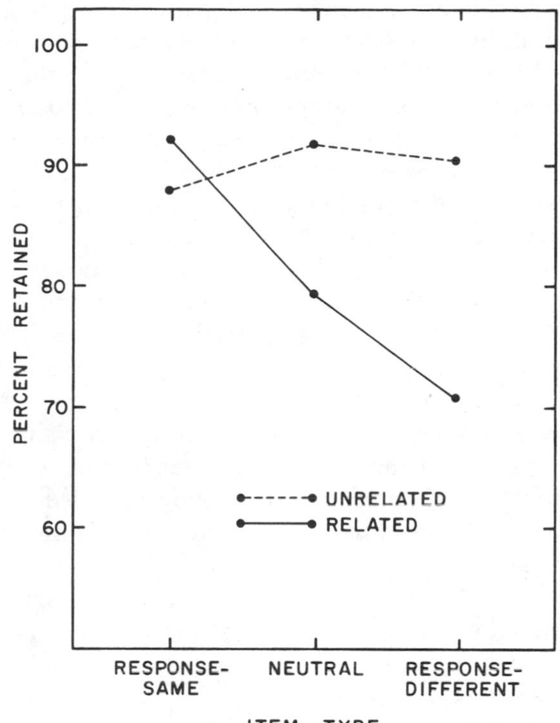

FIGURE 12.4 *Percent retained for students who received the related or the unrelated second passage as a function of the item type. (Adapted from Anderson & Myrow, 1971, p. 87.)*

passages did better than the control groups on response-same items, but worse on response-different items. This study is persuasive since it used the materials employed in a previous study which had raised doubts about whether interference theory applies to the forgetting of meaningful prose.

Entwisle and Huggins (1964) have performed two experiments on forgetting in the context of an introductory college course in electrical engineering. After lectures covering prerequisite concepts, 80 students taking the course were randomly assigned to an experimental group and a control group, with the restriction that each group contain equal numbers of students from each of four levels of mathematical aptitude. Both groups spent 15 minutes studying voltage principles. Then the experimental group spent 15 minutes studying current principles, which are similar to, but conflict with, voltage principles. Meanwhile the control group studied irrelevant material on computer programming. On the test of voltage principles given immediately thereafter, the control group performed significantly better than the experimental group. After three more lectures, a second experiment was completed. Students matched for mathematical aptitude were randomly reassigned to an experimental group or a control group. Both groups spent 15 minutes studying "node-pair solutions." Then the experimental group studied potentially interfering material on "loop solutions," while the control group studied irrelevant material on matrix theory. The control group scored significantly higher on the test on node-pair solutions than the experimental group. The findings of both of these experiments are in accord with interference theory. They provide especially important evidence about the generality of the laws of forgetting because they were completed as part of an ongoing instructional program.

In conclusion, the available evidence suggests that the forgetting of organized, meaningful material obeys the same laws as the forgetting of lists of nonsense syllables and isolated words. While a good deal more research will be required before any firm conclusions are warranted, it does seem at the present time that the studies giving rise to apparent exceptions to interference theory can be discounted because of such factors as the nature of the testing procedure.

Concepts and principles. A generally accepted conclusion among psychologists and educators is that concepts are not as readily forgotten as rote material. The classic experiment which supports this generalization was completed by Reed (1946). Subjects in Reed's experiment learned concepts by the anticipation method. The stimuli consisted of strings of four words and the responses consisted of nonsense syllables. Each string of stimulus words contained one key word which determined the concept. For example, the correct response for "horn-leaf-monkey-debt" was KUN. KUN was also the correct response for "uncle-fried-sheep-pear." The critical feature defining the concept is the presence of an animal word. There were six different concepts defined in this manner. The subjects went through the instances again and again until they completed one errorless trial. After intervals of one, three, or six weeks, the instances were presented again to test for retention. An independent group of subjects was tested at each interval. This means, for example, that the group that was tested after six weeks had not received earlier tests. This is a good experimental procedure since it is known that repeated testing reduces forgetting (see Chapter 6) and thus leads to inflated estimates of retention. Reed's results are graphed in Fig. 12.5. There was virtually no forgetting of concepts over the six-week period. For comparison and to show the striking contrast

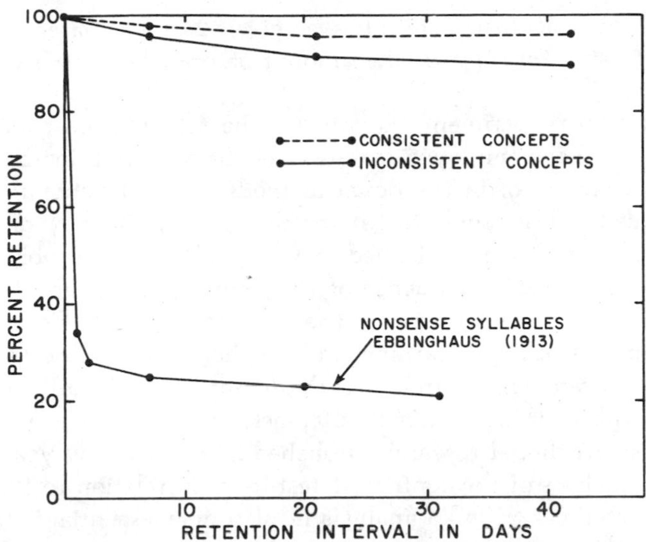

FIGURE 12.5 *Retention of concepts as compared with the retention of a serial list of nonsense syllables (from Reed, 1946).*

between retention of concepts and rote materials, Reed reproduced Ebbinghaus' (1913) retention curve for a serial list of nonsense syllables (see Fig. 12.5).

The Reed experiment and others (Oseas and Underwood, 1952; Lloyd, 1960) appear to show that concepts are remembered better than rote-learned materials. Adams (1967, pp. 201–206), however, has raised some searching questions about the validity of this conclusion. He points out that the so-called "inconsistent concepts" in Reed's experiment were not really concepts at all. Since the inconsistent concepts were retained almost as well as the actual concepts, there must have been other factors operating in the experiment to facilitate retention. Adams goes on to discuss aspects of procedure and scoring which could also have led to inflated estimates of retention.

Whether or not concepts are better remembered than isolated associations, it does appear that the forgetting of concepts follows the laws of interference. Richardson (1956), for instance, employed 16 stimulus words which defined four concepts. The subject was expected to learn to say the correct concept name for each stimulus word. After practice with this task, a second task was given which involved the same 16 stimulus words but different concepts. The word "pot," for example, was an instance of the concept "black" during the first task and an instance of the concept "round" during the second task. Finally, a test for the recall of the first-learned concepts was given 24 hours later. Retention was a decreasing function of the amount of practice on the interfering second task.

There are few experimental studies of the retention of concepts and principles that have employed materials of the sort used in schools. No doubt many studies of instructional methods and instructional variables have included at least some test items that probed mastery of concepts and principles in the sense defined in Chapter 10. The problem is that despite the considerable influence of Benjamin S. Bloom and his associates (1956), who have emphasized the importance of the distinction between simple associative learning and "higher mental processes," contemporary educational research workers do not systematically distinguish between varieties of instructional outcomes. It is a sad fact but true that reports of instructional research published in the last few years seldom contain an analysis of the content of test items in relation to the content of lesson materials. Such an analysis is, of course, essential if the learning and retention of concepts and principles are to be distinguished from other outcomes.

An earlier generation of educational researcher sometimes did distinguish between kinds of instructional outcomes. During the decade from 1930 to 1940, and to a lesser extent before and after this period, there were many investigations of the retention of school subjects. Especially notable were several studies completed under the leadership of the influential educator, Ralph W. Tyler. In one study (Tyler, 1933), students in an introductory college zoology course were given the course examination before the course and immediately after it. Fifteen months later the examination was again given to the 82 students who had not subsequently taken another zoology course. The pretest, posttest, and delayed test scores of these 82 students were analyzed to determine the amount of forgetting. What interested Tyler, and what concerns us here, was whether some course outcomes would be better remembered than others. Table 12.1 contains the results. The striking finding was that the students retained 100 percent on the subtest called "Applying principles to new situations" and actually improved over the retention interval on the one entitled "Interpreting new experiments." Wert (1937) repeated Tyler's study with a new group of zoology students and got exactly the same pattern of results. McDougall (1958) has completed a similar study involving an educational psychology course. On the delayed test four months after the completion of the course, retention was 72.6 percent for knowledge of facts and 79.2 percent on a subtest called "Interpretation and extrapolation." This difference is not significant, though the trend was in the direction of the results obtained in the earlier studies.

TABLE 12.1 *Retention of Information and Concepts Learned in a Zoology Course (from Tyler, 1933)*

Type of test	Average examination score: Pretest	Posttest	Fifteen months later	Percent retention*
1. Naming animal structures pictured in diagrams	22%	62%	31%	22.5%
2. Identifying technical terms	20	83	67	74.6
3. Recalling information				
a. Function for given structures	13	39	34	80.7
b. Other facts	21	63	54	78.6
4. Applying principles to new situations	35	65	65	100.0
5. Interpreting new experiments	30	57	64	125.9

$$* = \frac{\text{15 month} - \text{Pre}}{\text{Post} - \text{Pre}} \times 100$$

These studies suggest that concepts, principles, and reasoning skills are remembered better than "facts" and technical terminology, and indeed they may be. There are, however, explanations other than this generalization. It may well be that in the zoology courses studied by Tyler and Wert, more class time was devoted to application of principles and interpretation of experiments than to the explication of "facts." Therefore, there could have been differences in the level or strength of learning which led to differences in retention. Activities during the retention interval could also have had an influence. While none of the students had a subsequent course in zoology, many of them may have taken courses in botany, physiology, psychology, chemistry, physics, mathematics, or logic which helped them to apply zoological principles in new situations and interpret new experiments. Tyler himself proposed this explanation.

The results of a number of studies are consistent with the conclusion that concepts, principles, and reasoning skills are better remembered than discrete associations. But it would be premature to conclude that such learnings are inherently more "memorable." Quite possibly there has been better long-term performance with concepts, principles, and the like because they were more thoroughly learned to begin with or because they were reviewed and used during the retention interval.

Motor skills. Motor skills or physical skills, as they are commonly called, involve bodily movements. Following Adams (1967, pp. 217–220), two types of motor skills can be distinguished. *Discrete* motor skills entail independent, distinctive responses. Two examples are pushing buttons or pulling levers. *Continuous* motor skills involve finely graded sequences of responses. Handwriting and bicycle riding are examples of continuous motor skills.

Memory for discrete motor responses seems to follow exactly the same pattern as memory for discrete verbal responses. The picture is different for continuous motor skills. Common observation suggests that skill at riding a bicycle, ice skating, or driving a car is rarely forgotten. Experimental studies of continuous motor skills leads to the same conclusion. Such experiments, typically involving a task much like the task of a pilot flying a plane, show extremely little forgetting after intervals as long as two years (Fleishman & Parker, 1962).

Why are continuous motor skills remembered better than verbal skills? One likely explanation is that motor skills are usually overlearned (i.e., practiced beyond the point at which the task is first mastered), even in laboratory studies. Another possibility is that normal activities seldom interfere with motor skills. A person uses language every day in ways that interfere with particular to-be-remembered verbal habits. But how often do people engage in physical activities which are in conflict with, say, balancing a bicycle?

Retroactive inhibition has been demonstrated with continuous motor skills (e.g., Lewis, 1947). Thus it does seem that, while the amount of forgetting of continuous motor skills is small, it can be accounted for in terms of interference.

Conditions Which Improve Retention

The preceding section considered the generality of the laws of forgetting. Typically there seems to be less forgetting of organized, meaningful material, of concepts, principles, and continuous motor skills than of discrete verbal associations. Nonetheless, it does seem that the laws of forgetting, which were developed primarily in research with lists of nonsense syllables and unrelated words, apply generally to the forgetting of all kinds of materials and skills.

The next question is what sorts of features can be incorporated into lesson materials and teaching procedures in order to reduce forgetting.

Level of learning. The main determiner of level of remembering is level of learning. The more thoroughly something is learned, the more likely it is to be remembered. Other things being equal, the level of learning is a function of the amount of practice. Repetition, further explanation, continued practice, more examples, and review will all lead to increased mastery of a task, and will decrease the amount of forgetting. There is considerable value to overlearning or continued practice beyond the point at which a student first masters a task. Many experimental studies, dating back forty years or more (e.g., Krueger, 1929), show that overlearning improves retention.

Repetition improves memory for organized meaningful material as well as rote tasks. For instance, Ausubel and Youssef (1965) had college undergraduates study a 1400-word passage on the endocrinology of pubescence for 25 minutes on each of two days. A control group studied the passage only once, on the second day. Both groups completed a multiple-choice test 48 hours later. The group that studied the passage twice scored 67.4 percent, while the group that studied the passage once scored 54.5 percent, a highly significant difference. Similar results have been obtained in many other experiments (Ausubel, Robbins & Blake, 1957; Ausubel, Stager & Gaite, 1968; Gilbert, 1957; McTavish, 1949; Slamecka, 1960).

Getting a student literally to repeat a lesson may be difficult. The student may not pay close attention the second time. Lengthening the original lesson to include more explanation, more examples, and review will have much the same effect as repetition. In 1948, Mary G. Wilson (cited in Chall, 1958, pp. 12–14) reported an experiment showing the effects of adding further explanation and examples to passages from elementary school social studies textbooks. Each of three 300-word passages was expanded into a 600- and a 1200-word version. The statements in the 300-word versions were retained in the 600-word versions. The 600-word versions also contained additional illustrations. Likewise, the 1200-word versions contained all of the 600-word versions plus more details and examples. Significantly higher achievement was found with every long version as compared with the 300-word versions. However, the 1200-word versions were only slightly superior to the 600-word versions.

Many other experiments also show the value of expanding the amount of explanation and increasing the number of examples and illustrations. For instance, Lumsdaine, Sulzer, and Kopstein (1961; also 1969) included either 3, 6, or 12 examples in versions of an instructional film designed to teach Air Force trainees to use the micrometer. The results of a large experiment involving over a thousand men showed that the larger the number of examples, the greater the achievement.

Spaced review. Repetition, further explanation, additional practice, and review have a greater impact if these activities are spaced over a period of time instead of massed at one time and place. Using a paired associate task, Greeno (1964) found that there were fewer errors during training when items were repeated in close succession. However, spaced repetition led to consistently better recall on test trials. In fact, Greeno reported that "In some cases there was no evidence that any learning occurred when an item was repeated very soon after a previous presentation (1964, p. 294)." Rothkopf and Coke (1963) have obtained comparable results with organized, meaningful material. Subjects saw two presentations of eight sentences describing the food sacrifices which a fictitious primitive tribe gave to their gods. For example, one of the sentences was, "The Kirbys are given melons." The percentage of correct responses on the test was an increasing function of the interval between the two repetitions of a sentence. Twice as great a proportion of correct responses was given at the largest interval than was given when the two presentations occurred in immediate succession.

Spaced review also produces improved retention of actual school lessons. Reynolds and Glaser (1964) conducted two experiments investigating the effects of spaced review in which a 1280-frame self-instructional program covering ten topics in biology was presented to junior high school students. For the groups which received the massed condition, all of the frames dealing with the topic of mitosis appeared in one place in the program. Under the spaced condition, the same material was split into three sections. Two short sequences of frames on mitosis appeared at widely-spaced intervals after the main section on this topic. In each experiment, the spaced-review condition resulted in significantly better performance than the massed condition on both immediate and delayed posttests.

Similarity of conditions of learning and conditions of recall. The greater the similarity between the situation in which a person learns something and the situation in which he is expected to recall it, the better will be the recall. This conclusion follows from the laws of similarity described earlier in this chapter. Given that the same responses are required, the greater the similarity of the stimuli in the first task (learning) to the stimuli of the second task (test), the greater the facilitation. Nonessential and even apparently trivial differences between the learning situation and the testing situation can impair retention. This fact was demonstrated in an experiment by Bilodeau and Schlosberg (1951), who had subjects learn lists of paired adjectives (e.g., "generous-small"). For some subjects, the lists were learned in one situation and the test for recall was presented in another. The situations differed with respect to the room in which the session was conducted, whether the subject was standing or sitting, and the method of presentation of the materials. The experiment showed that those who were instructed and tested in different situations recalled less than those who were instructed and tested in the same situation. Greenspoon and Ranyard (1957) have obtained similar results.

One especially effective way to increase long-term retention is to give a test immediately after instruction. Students who receive the immediate test will perform better when the test is presented again later than will students who did not take the immediate test. Some evidence to support this generalization was reviewed in Chapter 6. Roderick and Anderson (1968) recently completed an experiment which illustrates the same point. Groups of high school and college students completed either a 3400-word programmed introduction to respondent conditioning involving 140 written responses or, instead, studied an 1800-word textbook-style summary of the material contained in the program. As soon as they finished the lesson half of the students took a test covering the material that consisted of 19 short-answer items and 19 equivalent multiple-choice items. One week later all of the students completed the same test. The results are graphed in Fig. 12.6. Students who took the immediate test did

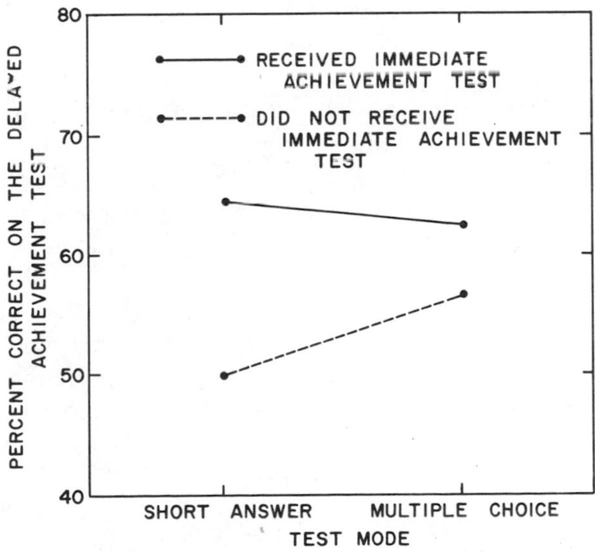

FIGURE 12.6 *Percent correct on the delayed achievement test for groups that did or did not receive the immediate achievement test as a function of test mode (from Roderick & Anderson, 1968).*

significantly better on the delayed second test than those who did not have the first test. The figure also shows that taking the immediate test was relatively more beneficial for responses to short-answer items.

Critics of programmed instruction often voice the complaint that programs present material in steps that are unnecessarily small and that they involve too much repetition. The Roderick and Anderson (1968) experiment illustrates the value of considerable redundancy. Especially interesting were the results obtained with the college students in that experiment. On the immediate test undergraduates who completed the program averaged 83.9% correct, whereas those who read the summary averaged 84.2%—actually a slight advantage for the summary. However, on the delayed test (considering only those who did not also take the immediate test) college students who used the program averaged 75.5%, but those who studied the summary averaged only 64.6%. This experiment illustrates the point made earlier that the painstaking, repetitious development of concepts and principles, which may not be necessary for immediate comprehension of the material, can improve retention over the long haul. Of course, the advantages of redundancy are not limited to self-instructional programs. Additional explanation, examples, practice, and review should lead to better long-term memory, no matter what the form of instruction.

Returning now to the effects of giving an immediate test, why is it that this practice so consistently improves retention? We believe that the answer can be found in the fact that when testing immediately follows instruction, it serves as an extension of the instructional episode. The immediate test helps the student to transform what he has learned into exactly the form which will be required later when the test is given again. In other words, considering the immediate test as part of the instruction, the provision for an immediate test increases the similarity between the conditions of learning and the conditions of recall (see Gillooly & Furakawa, 1969).

Teachers want students to remember and use what they have learned not only on tests, but on other occasions as well. Herein lies the importance of the rule that the conditions of learning—at the end of the instructional episode, at least—should resemble the conditions of intended use as closely as possible. Otherwise, the student may fail to remember; he may not "think of" using that which he has previously learned.

Distinctive features of similar materials. Forgetting is caused by interference. The potential for interference is greatest when the student must learn similar materials. Consider, for instance, the electrical engineering students studied by Entwisle and Huggins (1964). Interference occurred because these students had to learn similar sets of principles. It stands to reason that interference would be reduced if the distinctive features of similar materials were emphasized. Emphasizing distinctive features and deliberately comparing and contrasting similar materials should help the student avoid confusion. There is some evidence from research employing actual instructional passages that interference can be avoided in this manner (Ausubel & Blake, 1958).

Meaningfulness. The most time-honored exhortation to prospective teachers is "Make your lessons meaningful to the student." Unfortunately "meaningfulness," as the term is used by educators, has many vague connotations but no agreed-upon denotation. It is not at all clear how one makes a lesson "meaningful."

"Meaningfulness" does, however, have a distinct technical meaning in the verbal-learning laboratory. As was indicated in Chapter 6, even nonsense syllables differ in meaningfulness. The meaningfulness of nonsense syllables can be scaled by asking people to rate how easy it is to think up an association for each syllable. Syllables with high association-values are learned much more quickly than syllables with low association-values (Underwood & Schultz, 1960). The meaningfulness of individual words can be determined by counting the frequency of usage, by having people rate them, and by other methods both simple (e.g., number of syllables) and complex (e.g., associative overlap). Still, the best way to explain meaningfulness is to say that it represents word difficulty. There is ample evidence that the meaningfulness of words is strongly related to the speed and ease with which they are learned. It also seems to be true, though there is less evidence on this point, that the more meaningful materials are the better they are remembered (McGeoch & Irion, 1952, p. 383; Underwood & Richardson, 1956; Dowling & Braun, 1957).

For the past fifty years educators and psychologists have tried to determine what makes prose "readable." Their goal has been to discover the characteristics of written materials (and oral discourse, too) which make them easy or difficult to understand. "Readability" is actually a misleading label for this research; it suggests a superficial level of analysis. It would be better to say that this is research on what makes prose meaningful.

The main users of information about readability are elementary school educators, librarians, publishers, journalists, and editors of popular magazines. Each has a somewhat different purpose. The educator wants to prepare or select reading material which the pupil will understand.

The librarian wants to be able to recommend books of an appropriate level of difficulty to people of different ages and educational attainment. The publisher, journalist, and editor want to increase the impact and appeal of their books, newspapers, and magazines. Although readability research has uncovered some concepts which are potentially of great importance for learning and instruction, unfortunately these concepts are not widely appreciated by teachers and instructional researchers. Part of the reason for the lack of wide appreciation and understanding is to be found in the fact that the research has had only a very immediate practical aim: to find a simple formula to predict readability. The deeper logic which makes a formula successful has seldom been made clear.

The techniques for investigating readability are very simple. A number of passages—varying in difficulty from beginning reading primers to advanced technical literature—are given to people to read. Test questions are devised for each passage. The proportion of questions answered correctly is the index of difficulty. An alternative way to measure difficulty, called the "cloze procedure," is to delete a random 20 percent (usually) of the words in the passage. When the cloze procedure is used, the index of difficulty is the proportion of blanks filled correctly with the missing words.

The next step in research on readability is to find the characteristics of the prose that are related to the difficulty of the passages. All manner of characteristics have been investigated. One which shows a strong relationship to the difficulty of the passage as a whole is the meaningfulness (or difficulty) of the individual words. Here is where the painstaking research on isolated words has its application.

Not surprisingly, passages which contain mostly common words tend to be easy to understand, while passages containing large numbers of infrequently used words are difficult to understand. Coleman (1970) reports a correlation of .85 between the average frequency-of-usage of the "content" words (all words not including articles, prepositions, conjunctions, and the like) in a passage and passage difficulty. This is a very strong relationship. It means that over 70 percent of the variations in difficulty among the passages Coleman used could be accounted for in terms of the meaningfulness of the individual words contained in the passages.

All readability formulas give heavy weight to word difficulty. For example the Dale-Chall (1948) formula involves counting the proportion of words in a passage which fall outside of the 3,000 words known by most fourth graders. Other formulas get at the difficulty of words indirectly. One technique is to compute the average number of syllables per word. Polysyllabic words tend to be used less frequently and tend to be less meaningful in every respect than shorter words. Furthermore,

Coleman's data indicates that number of syllables per word is actually a better predictor of readability than frequency of usage.

Common sense suggests that there is more to the meaningfulness of prose than the meaningfulness of individual words. And research too indicates that this is the case. First of all, pairs of words are much easier to learn when they are included in a phrase or sentence than when they are presented in isolation. Rohwer (1966), for example, had groups of sixth graders learn to associate pairs of common nouns. Some pupils saw only the noun pairs (e.g., "cow-ball"). For others the nouns were presented in a simple sentence, for instance, "The cow chases the ball." Under all conditions the test consisted of showing the first word (*cow*) in each pair. The child had to say the second word (*ball*). Children who saw the nouns in sentences did much better on the test. Further research (Rohwer, 1967) has not yet revealed exactly why learning is easier when paired associates are embedded in sentences. However, research has shown that prepositional phrases ("the cow behind the ball") increase learning almost as much as sentences. On the other hand, phrases containing a conjunction ("the cow and the ball") cause no improvement, nor does adding modifiers; thus, "The running cow chases the bouncing ball" is no better than "The cow chases the ball." A final conclusion from Rohwer's research is that the sentence must make sense if learning is to be improved. The sentence "Roses like rain" will help a person associate *roses* and *rain*. The sentence "Roses kill rain" will not.

It is not surprising that including words which are to be associated in a sentence makes learning easier. There probably is no such thing as true rote learning, even for lists of nonsense syllables. Associations are not "stamped in" by repetition. Rather, the process is one of finding meaningful links between the terms. Montague and Adams and their associates (e.g., Montague, Adams, & Kiess, 1966) call these meaningful links "natural language mediators." The nature of natural language mediators can be indicated with an illustration. Suppose a person was required to learn to say "door" when he sees GAR. One meaningful link, or mediator, is to note that both terms end in *r*. Another is to observe that GAR comprises the first three letters of "garage" and that garages have doors. Still another is to recall the name of the famous sportsman, Gar Wood, and notice that doors are (often) made of wood. In such ways as these a subject makes even rote tasks meaningful.

Montague and Adams have interviewed people during and after completion of paired associate tasks. Their finding is that people seldom learn a pair unless they use a natural language mediator. What is more, there is less forgetting of mediated pairs than unmediated pairs (at least when the mediators can be recalled).

Of course, including the words to be associated in a sentence, as

Rohwer did, *provides* the person with a mediator. This is why the sentence makes learning easier. Asking the person to create a sentence of his own in which he uses the words is also facilitative (Jensen & Rohwer, 1963), indeed, in the case of college students, more facilitative than providing the sentence.

The complexity of sentences affects meaningfulness. The basic unit of understanding is probably the simple, active declarative sentence (e.g., "He saw the tiger"). There is evidence that when he reads or hears a sentence a person "transforms" it into a simple declarative sentence (or sentences). A transformation is a mental operation which presumably makes the sentence understandable. There is, for instance, the transformation from passive to active. "The dog was run over by the truck" transforms to "The truck ran over the dog." The prominent psychologist, George A. Miller (1962), reasoned that transformations take time. If, in comprehending sentences, people mentally transform them into active, affirmative declarative sentences, then the more transformations that are required, the longer it should take to deal with a sentence. His data were in close agreement with the theory. Mehler (1963), in completing an experiment based on the same logic as Miller's, found that active, declarative sentences are easier to learn and better remembered than the same sentences to which one or more transformations had been applied.

Readability research also shows that complexity interferes with understanding. For instance, nominalized verbs decrease meaningfulness. Consider the sentence, "The reaction of the audience was immediate." This sentence could be understood more easily if it were written, "The audience reacted immediately." Coleman (1971) found a strong negative correlation (−.75) between the proportion of nominalized verbs in passages and comprehensibility.

Information density is a final factor determining the comprehensibility of printed and oral discourse. A passage in which many ideas are expressed in few words is hard to understand. On the other hand, the same ideas are easier to comprehend when they are expressed with more words in more sentences. The density notion is not new. But until recently not much has been done with it. The problem was that "idea" is a vague concept. Thanks to modern linguistics, it is now possible to replace the vague concept "idea" with a better-defined concept, the "kernel." The kernel is the simple, active, declarative sentence we have been talking about. Coleman (1971) presents the following example of a "dense" sentence:

John's explanation of her singing was misunderstood.

This sentence can be decomposed into three kernels:

She sang. John explained the singing. The explanation was misunderstood.

Coleman found that the number of kernels in passages of a given length has a strong, negative relationship (−.77) with comprehensibility.

Thus, the ways to make written and oral instruction more meaningful can be summarized simply. Use easy words. Use simple, active, declarative sentences.

Meaningful processing. Using easy words and simple sentences will make a lesson *potentially* meaningful. But whether the lesson is *actually* meaningful depends critically upon what the student does with it. There is now good reason to believe that there are at least two stages, or levels, of processing which must occur if a person is to learn from a communication. Probably the first thing a person does with written sentences is translate them into speech. If he is reading silently the speech is implicit, or internal, but speech nonetheless. This process can be called "phonological encoding." Next a person *may* bring to mind the meanings of the words he is saying. This process has been called "semantic encoding" (Anderson, 1970).

It is a common observation that a person can read aloud or recite the Gettysburg Address or the Preamble to the Constitution without bringing to mind the meaning of the words he is speaking. Probably more often than we recognize or would care to admit, we "read" or "listen" without comprehending, even when we are perfectly capable of understanding the message. A good working assumption is that people tend to follow the law of least effort (cf., Underwood, 1963). We tend to do no more processing than the task requires—particularly when we are tired, bored, the assignment is lengthy or difficult, or we are under pressure to work quickly.

There is rather dramatic evidence that the mere pronunciation of words is ineffective in producing learning. Anderson and Hidde (1971) asked college undergraduates to help evaluate a list of thirty sentences, which the students were told were to be used in a future experiment. Half of the students were asked to evaluate the pronunciability of the sentences. As each sentence was exposed the student read it aloud again and again, then rated the pronunciability. The remaining students were asked to evaluate "image-evoking value." The student attempted to form an image of the event described in each sentence and then rated the vividness of that image. On a surprise test, students who rated imagery recalled three times as many sentences as students who rated pronunciability. The explanation is that to form images the student had to understand the sentences.

Bobrow and Bower (1969) have done several experiments which demonstrate that procedures which cause subjects to comprehend the meaning of sentences strongly facilitate learning. In one experiment, college students were instructed to compose a sentence which was a sensible continuation of each sentence that was presented. For example, if he saw the sentence "The farmer discovered a diamond," a student might give, "He sold it to a jeweler and used the money to buy a tractor." The continuation group recalled twice as much as the group required to read each sentence aloud three times.

In a related study, Anderson, Goldberg, and Hidde (1971) constructed sentences in which the last word was determined by the rest of the sentence. By "determined," they meant that when the sentence was incomplete almost anyone would complete it with the same word, and do so quickly and easily. An example is, "Mothers bake delicious apple ______." Sentences, or incomplete sentences, were presented rapidly (at a 4-second rate) one at a time. Students were instructed to read each sentence aloud as it appeared, supplying as they read the last word if it was missing. In two experiments, college students who filled blanks as they read recalled significantly more than students who read aloud whole sentences. Another of the incomplete statements was, "Elevators stop at every ______." The argument is that to complete the sentence with the word "floor" required a person to bring to mind a meaningful representation of the rest of the sentence. "Floor" is semantically rather than acoustically related to the other words. Simply translating the printed words into speech would not allow a person to fill the blank correctly, because the mere sound of the rest of the sentence could not evoke "floor."

There is a point with enormous practical implications in the studies just reviewed: when people learn from sentences, ordinarily they acquire meanings rather than strings of speech sounds. Learning by "rote"—that is, by memorizing a string of words in a more or less meaningless way—seems to be a peculiar, special case (Bobrow, 1970; Anderson, 1971). The implication for education is clear: students will learn more when they are required to understand.

As was detailed in Chapter 6, research has shown that students learn more from textbook passages when they are occasionally required to answer questions inserted within the text (Rothkopf, 1966; Rothkopf & Bisbicos, 1967; Frase, 1967). Typically in this research the questions and answers have been lifted verbatim from the instructional materials and have usually involved names, dates, technical terms, and quantities. Most important educational goals, however, do not entail verbatim recall. Therefore Watts and Anderson (1971) contended that questions which required students to apply concepts and principles to new examples would be more educationally relevant. And they argued that such questions would force meaningful processing of the instructional materials.

For each of five 450-word passages explaining a psychological principle, Watts and Anderson prepared a set of questions according to a single plan: given the name of the principle, the student had to select an example of it from among a list of four possible examples. In half the questions the correct alternative repeated an example from the text. The remaining questions included a new example of the principle, different from any described in the text. A third type of question, comparable to the questions employed in the previous research, required the student to select the name of the psychologist associated with a given principle. After each of the five passages, high school students answered one question of *one* of the types. Then everyone took a criterion test containing all the questions. The group of students which answered questions that required them to apply principles to new examples averaged significantly higher on the criterion test than all other groups, including the group which had received otherwise identical questions repeating examples described in the text. The group which answered name questions while reading performed worst on the criterion test, worse even than the reading-only control group. Anderson and Watts concluded that asking application questions during reading induces students to process the text in a meaningful fashion.

In summary, teachers (as well as textbook authors, developers of self-instructional programs, and so on) have the obligation to devise instruction which will get students to engage in meaningful processing. One good way to do this is to include within lessons problems and questions which the student can solve or answer only if he understands the main points of the preceding instruction.

Organization. It is often said that organization is the hallmark of good instruction. As a matter of fact, the organization of a lesson does seem to influence how much a student will learn and remember.

In 1953, Bousfield reported an interesting discovery. Subjects were shown sixty nouns, one word at a time. There were fifteen words in each of four categories: animals, names, professions, and vegetables. However, the words were presented in a random order. Immediately after seeing the list the subject attempted to recall as many words as he could. A "free recall" technique was used, meaning that the subject was free to recall the words in any order he wished. While the order of presentation of the words was random, the order of recall was definitely not random. Instead, subjects tended to cluster their responses within the four categories. In other words they tended to give several animal words in succession, several vegetable names in succession, and so on. A second experiment (Bousfield & Cohen, 1953) investigated the effects of increasing the number of trials. Each trial consisted of a presentation of all of the words (in a different random order each time) and a free-recall test. Not only did the total number of words recalled increase from trial to trial, but the amount of clustering increased. There was about twice as much clustering at the fifth trial as there was at the first one. These experiments show that people try to use organization to learn and remember verbal materials.

Several experiments show that highly organized lists of words are easier to learn than lists with less organization. For instance, Watts and Anderson (1969) composed the two 20-word lists that appear in Table 12.2. The high organization list consists of four words in each of five categories, whereas there is no evident overall organization in the low organization list. One hundred and twenty university students alternately studied and attempted to recall the words. Those who received the high organization list averaged 6.4 trials to recall all 20 words. Persons who received the low organization lists required an average of 11.4

TABLE 12.2 *Lists employed in a free-recall experiment (from Watts & Anderson, 1969).*

Organized List	*Unorganized List*
Bulgaria	adobe
Denmark	canyon
Chile	debtor
Israel	filter
	gill
heron	hawser
thrush	idyl
raven	jester
penguin	kennel
	latch
taffeta	necklace
brocade	octave
serge	paraffin
denim	query
	rabble
chipmunk	sandal
panther	tallow
weasel	veneer
gazelle	yeast
	zephyr
drunkenness	
homicide	
fraud	
blackmail	

trials. Since the words in the two lists were matched for frequency of usage, the advantage of the high organization list must be attributed to its organization.

Procedures and arrangements of material which make organization more obvious facilitate learning. One way to make organization more obvious is to use highly representative familiar examples (see Chapter 10; Bousfield, Cohen, & Whitmarsh, 1958). To illustrate, Watts and Anderson could have made the animal category more obvious by using *dog, cat, cow,* and *pig* instead of *chipmunk, panther, weasel,* and *gazelle.* Another way to emphasize organization is to present the items in each category together. This increases clustering and improves recall (Cofer, Bruce, & Reicher, 1966).

Ausubel (1963) argues that learning from meaningful prose can be facilitated by providing "advance organizers." These "organizers" are previews or introductions (usually brief written passages) which the student reads before he studies the main body of the new material. The organizer compares and contrasts the new material with what the student already knows or outlines the new material in general terms. Ausubel says that the organizers improve learning and remembering by providing "ideational scaffolding." He believes that the student is more likely to remember detailed information when this information is subsumed under organizing concepts. This theory is consistent with the results of research on the free recall of lists of words.

There is evidence that organizers increase learning from meaningful lesson material. Ausubel and Youssef (1963), for instance, prepared a 2500-word passage on Buddhism. Before studying the Buddhism passage, one group (of college undergradutes) read a 500-word "comparative organizer" which pointed out the principal similarities and differences between Buddhist and Christian doctrines. The control group read an historical introduction to Buddhism which contained no organizing concepts. The group that received the comparative organizer scored significantly higher on the achievement test. Other experiments involving material on Buddhism (Ausubel & Fitzgerald, 1961), the endocrinology of pubescence (Ausubel & Fitzgerald, 1962), and interpretations of the Civil War (Fitzgerald & Ausubel, 1963) have also shown that organizers improve learning and retention; however, in no case has the improvement been very large.

Lee (1965) has completed two experiments concerned with the organization of instructional prose. One group of naval officer candidates read the standard, unaltered pamphlet on disciplinary problems in the Navy. A second group received the same material modified in such a way as to make the organization more explicit. An introduction previewing the topics that would be covered and a summary reviewing the main points which had been covered were added. Also included were detailed headings and subheadings within the passage itself. A final group studied a version of the material in which the organization existing in the standard version was destroyed by removing headings and transitional phrases and rearranging the paragraphs into a random order. An essay test was given which required the officer candidates to summarize the main ideas presented in the pamphlet. The group that received the organized version averaged 67% on this test. The figures for the groups that got the standard version and the disorganized version were 47% and 44%, respectively. Comparable results were obtained in the second experiment.

Lee has a very simple explanation for the advantages of organization: the people were better able to reproduce the main ideas after receiving the organized passage because the main ideas were repeated more often in this passage. As we have already seen, Ausubel has a more elaborate argument about the advantages of organization. He says organization provides ideational scaffolding which helps the student learn and remember the details of the lesson. In any event—no matter exactly what their function is—previews, outlines, and summaries do improve learning and retention.

SELF-TEST ON MEMORY

Answer the following questions and then check your answers against the scoring key on p. 477.

1. Which of the following would be the worst way to study for a world history quiz?

- **a.** Study for the world history quiz immediately after studying for a math quiz.
- **b.** Study for the world history quiz using pictures to make the major battles vivid.
- **c.** Study world history dates before studying American history dates.
- **d.** Do not study anything during the day before studying for the world history quiz.

2. Name two characteristics of language that would help make a lecture meaningful to students.

3. Forgetting is caused by

   a. confusion between whatever it is you are trying to remember and similar things you have learned.
   b. the inability of the human mind to retain lots of different material at the same time.
   c. combination of the new with the old material forming a new whole, recalled as an entity.
   d. a slow weakening of memory over time, a gradual decay.

4. Which of the following would be the best procedure for getting students to remember the concepts and principles in a lesson?

   a. review the same concepts and principles immediately after the lesson.
   b. review the same concepts and principles after a period of time.
   c. review concepts and principles that are similar but not identical immediately after the lesson.
   d. review concepts and principles that are similar but not identical after a period of time.

5. Ralph and Jane took part in an experiment in which they were required to learn and remember XEG, YIV, WFH, LIT, QUI, and MAV. Before attempting to recall the syllables, Jane completed a series of arithmetic problems while Ralph rearranged odd sets of letters into groups of three. Who would recall the most syllables and why?

   a. Ralph would do better because his two tasks could be remembered together in units.
   b. Jane would do better because she could keep the numbers and letters straight in her mind.
   c. There would be no difference in recall because both situations are equally detrimental to memory.
   d. Ralph would do better because he had further practice with odd combinations of letters after learning the list of nonsense syllables.

6. List as many instructional procedures as you can which will improve memory. (We were able to think of seven.)

Summary

Forgetting occurs when a person confuses the thing he is trying to remember with other things he knows. This confusion is called interference, and this explanation of forgetting is known as the interference theory. The theory was developed mainly in research using rote verbal tasks. Research shows that while there is marked forgetting of rote verbal material, there seems to be less forgetting of organized, meaningful material, of concepts and principles, and of continuous motor skills. Although the amount of forgetting does vary, depending upon the task, the laws of forgetting seem to apply generally to all kinds of tasks.

The most important factor that determines how much will be remembered is level of learning. Poorly learned materials will be forgotten quickly. On the other hand, there is ample evidence with all kinds of materials and skills that repetition, further explanation, more illustrations, more practice, and review improve learning and remembering. Practice and review are more valuable if spaced over a long period of time instead of massed at a single time and place.

The closer the resemblance between the conditions of learning and the conditions of use, the more likely it is that the student will be able to remember and use what he has learned. Taking a test immediately after a lesson usually improves performance when the test is given again later. The immediate test is then an extension of the lesson. Taking the immediate test probably improves later recall because it increases the similarity between the learning situation and the later testing situation.

When responses differ, interference, and therefore forgetting, is greatest for highly similar materials and skills. Thus, when the student must learn potentially conflicting materials, the distinctive features of the two sets of material should be emphasized.

Meaningfulness is related to learning and retention. The meaningfulness of verbal instruction depends upon the difficulty of individual words, the complexity of sentences, and the density of ideas in the lecture or text passage. Students learn and remember more when easy words are used and when active, declarative sentences are employed.

Students who are "reading" may do no more than translate the words into speech. Meaningful processing, or comprehension, is necessary for learning and remembering. Therefore, procedures that induce students to bring to mind and think about the meaning of passages strongly facilitate learning and remembering. One such technique is asking questions that require the student to apply the concepts and principles he is reading about to new and different examples.

Clear organization facilitates learning, perhaps because the organizing concepts help the student to consolidate detailed information. Previews, outlines, and summaries have all been demonstrated to increase learning and remembering.

SCORING KEY FOR THE SELF-TEST ON MEMORY

A satisfactory score is 11 out of the 13 possible points. Review the sections of the text dealing with questions that gave you trouble.

1. (*1 point*) **c**

2. (*2 points*)

(1) Use easy words.
(1) Use short, simple sentences.

3. (*1 point*) **a**

4. (*1 point*) **b**

5. (*1 point*) **b**

6. (*7 points*)

(1) Provide for overlearning using repetition, further explanation, and more examples.
(1) Provide for spaced review.
(1) Make the conditions of learning resemble the conditions of intended use as closely as possible.
(1) Make lessons meaningful by using easy words and short, simple sentences.
(1) Organize lessons clearly using previews, outlines, and summaries.
(1) Emphasize the distinctive features of similar and potentially interfering subject matters.
(1) Use procedures to insure that students will process the text or lecture in a meaningful fashion, such as asking questions which require the student to apply concepts and principles in new and different situations.

Selected Readings

Adams, J. A., *Human Memory.* New York: McGraw-Hill, 1966. A readable summary of memory research and theory.

Kintch, W., *Learning, Memory, and Conceptual Processes.* New York: Wiley, 1970. The chapters on memory are excellent and up to date.

Klare, G. C., *The Measurement of Readability.* Ames: Iowa University Press, 1963. Research on the factors that make prose readable is summarized.

Bibliography

Ackerman, M. D., & Williams, J. P., "Simultaneous and Successive Discrimination Learning as a Function of Stimulus Similarity." Paper read at the annual meeting of the American Educational Research Association, February, 1969.

Adams, J. A., *Human Memory*. New York: McGraw-Hill, 1967.

Adams, J. A., & Montague, W. E., "Retroactive Interference and Natural Language Mediation," *Journal of Verbal Learning and Verbal Behavior* (1967), *66*, 528–535.

Addison, R. M., & Homme, L. E., "The Reinforcing Event Menu," *National Society for Programed Instruction Journal* (1966), *5*, 8–9.

Allport, G. W., *Personality—A Psychological Interpretation*. New York: Holt, 1937.

Alter, M., & Silverman, R. E., "The Response in Programed Instruction," *Journal of Programed Instruction* (1962), *1*, 55–78.

Anderson, G. L., "Quantitative Thinking as Developed Under Connectionist and Field Theories of Learning," in E. Swenson, et al., eds., *Learning Theory in School Situations*. Minneapolis: University of Minnesota Press, 1949.

Anderson, R. C., "Learning in Discussions: A Resumé of the Authoritarian-Democratic Studies," *Harvard Educational Review* (1959), *29*, 201–215.

———, "Failure Imagery in the Fantasy of Eighth Graders as a Function of Three Conditions of Induced Arousal," *Journal of Educational Psychology* (1962), *53*, 293–298.

———, "Can First Graders Learn an Advanced Problem-Solving Skill?" *Journal of Educational Psychology* (1965), *56*, 283–294.

———, "Sequence Constraints and Concept Identification," *Psychological Reports* (1966), *19*, 1295–1302.

———, "Educational Psychology," *Annual Review of Psychology* (1967), *18*, 129–164.

———, "The Comparative Field Experiment: An Illustration from High School Biology," *Proceedings of the 1968 Invitational Conference on Testing Problems*. Princeton, N.J.: Educational Testing Service, 1969.

———, "Control of Student Mediating Processes During Verbal Learning and Instruction," *Review of Educational Research* (1970), *40*, 349–639.

———, "Encoding Processes in the Storage and Retrieval of Sentences," *Journal of Experimenal Psychology* (1971), *91*, 338–340.

Anderson, R. C., & Faust, G. W., "The Effects of Strong Formal Prompts in Programed Instruction," *American Educational Research Journal* (1967), *4,* 345–352.

Anderson, R. C., Faust, G. W., & Roderick, M. C., " 'Overprompting' in Programed Instruction," *Journal of Educational Psychology* (1968), *59,* 88–93.

Anderson, R. C., Goldberg, S., & Hidde, J. L., "Meaningful Processing of Sentences," *Journal of Educational Psychology* (1971), *62,* 395–399.

Anderson, R. C., & Guthrie, J. T., "Effects of Some Sequential Manipulations of Relevant and Irrelevant Stimulus Dimensions on Concept Learning," *Journal of Experimental Psychology* (1966), *72,* 501–504.

Anderson, R. C., & Hidde, J. L., "Imagery and Sentence Learning," *Journal of Educational Psychology* (1971), *62,* 526–530.

Anderson, R. C., & Myrow, D. L., "Retroactive Inhibition of Meaningful Discourse," *Journal of Educational Psychology Monograph* (1971), *62,* 81–94.

Anrep, G. V., "Pitch Discrimination in the Dog," *Journal of Psychology* (1920), *53,* 367–385.

Archer, E. J., "Re-evaluation of the Meaningfulness of All Possible CVC Trigrams," *Psychological Monographs* (1960), *74,* 1–23.

———, "Concept Identification as a Function of the Obviousness of Relevant and Irrelevant Information," *Journal of Experimental Psychology* (1962), *63,* 616–620. Also in R. C. Anderson and D. P. Ausubel, eds., *Readings in the Psychology of Cognition.* New York: Holt, Rinehart & Winston, 1965.

Archer, E. J., Bourne, L. E., & Brown, F. G., "Concept Identification as a Function of Irrelevant Information and Instructions," *Journal of Experimental Psychology* (1955), *49,* 153–164.

Atkin, J. M., "Some Evaluation Problems in a Course Content Improvement Project," *Journal of Research in Science Teaching* (1963), *1,* 129–132.

Atkinson, J. W., "The Mainsprings of Achievement-Oriented Activity," in J. D. Krumboltz, ed., *Learning and the Educational Process.* Chicago: Rand-McNally, 1965.

Atkinson, J. W., & McClelland, D. C., The Projective Expression of Needs, *Journal of Experimental Psychology* (1948), *38,* 643–658. Also in J. W. Atkinson, ed., *Motives in Fantasy, Action, and Society.* Princeton, N.J.: Van Nostrand, 1958.

Ausubel, D. P., *The Psychology of Meaningful Verbal Learning.* New York: Grune and Stratton, 1963.

———, *Educational Psychology: A Cognitive View.* New York: Holt, Rinehart & Winston, 1968.

Ausubel, D. P., & Blake, E., "Proactive Inhibition in the Forgetting of Meaningful School Materials," *Journal of Educational Research* (1958), *52,* 145–149.

Ausubel, D. P., & Fitzgerald, D., "The Role of Discriminability in Meaningful Verbal Learning and Retention," *Journal of Educational Psychology* (1961), *52,* 266–274.

———, "Organizer, General Background, and Antecedent Learning Variables in Sequential Verbal Learning," *Journal of Educational Psychology* (1962), *53,* 243–249.

Ausubel, D. P., Robbins, L. C., & Blake, E., "Retroactive Inhibition and Facilitation in the Learning of School Materials," *Journal of Educational Psychology* (1957), *48,* 334–343.

Ausubel, D. P., Stager, M., & Gaite, A. J. H., "Retroactive Facilitation in Meaningful Verbal Learning," *Journal of Educational Psychology* (1968), *59,* 250–255.

Ausubel, D. P., & Youssef, M., "Role of Discriminability in Meaningful Parallel Learning," *Journal of Educational Psychology* (1963), *54,* 331–336.

———, "The Effects of Spaced Repetition on Meaningful Retention," *Journal of General Psychology* (1965), *73,* 147–150.

Azrin, N. H., & Holz, W. C., "Punishment," in W. K. Honig, ed., *Operant Behavior: Areas of Research and Application.* New York: Appleton-Century-Crofts, 1966.

Baldwin, A. L., *Theories of Child Development.* New York: John Wiley & Sons, 1967.

Bandura, A., Ross, D., & Ross, S. A., "Imitation of Film-Mediated Aggressive Models," *Journal of Abnormal and Social Psychology* (1963), *66,* 3–11.

Bandura, A., & Walters, R. H., *Social Learning and Personality Development.* New York: Holt, Rinehart & Winston, 1963.

Barber, T. X., Calverley, D. S., Forgione, A., McPeake, J. D., Chaves, J. F., & Bowen, B., "Five Attempts to Replicate the Experimenter Bias Effect," *Journal of Consulting and Clinical Psychology* (1969), *33,* 1–14.

Barnes, J. M., & Underwood, B. J., " 'Fate' of First-List Associations in Transfer Theory," *Journal of Experimental Psychology* (1959), *58,* 97–105.

Barrett, T., & Otto, W., "Elementary Pupil's Ability to Conceptualize the Main Idea in Reading," in R. C. Anderson, et al., eds., *Current Research on Instruction.* Englewood Cliffs, N.J.: Prentice-Hall, 1969.

Beberman, M., "Searching for Patterns," in H. Fehr, ed., *Mathematics Today.* Paris: Organization for Economic Cooperation and Development, 1963.

Becker, W. C., Madsen, C. H., Jr., Arnold, C. R., & Thomas, D. R., "The Contingent Use of Teacher Attention and Praise in Reducing Classroom Behavior Problems," *Journal of Special Education* (1967), *1,* 287–301.

Bereiter, C., & Engelmann, S., *Teaching Disadvantaged Children in the Preschool.* Englewood Cliffs, N.J.: Prentice-Hall, 1966.

Berlyne, D., *Conflict, Arousal, and Curiosity.* New York: McGraw-Hill, 1960.

Bernard, L. L., *Instinct: A Study in Social Psychology.* New York: Holt, 1924.

Berne, E., *Games People Play.* New York: Grove Press, 1964.

Bernstein, A. L., "Temporal Factors in the Formation of Conditioned Eyelid Reactions in Human Subjects," *Journal of Genetic Psychology* (1934), *10,* 173–197.

Bexton, W. H., Heron, W., & Scott, T. H., "Effects of Decreased Variation in the Sensory Environment," *Canadian Journal of Psychology* (1954), *8,* 70–76.

Bijou, S. W., "Systematic Instruction in the Attainment of Right-Left Form Concepts in Young and Retarded Children," in J. G. Holland and B. F. Skinner, eds., *An Analysis of the Behavioral Processes Involved in Self-Instruction.* Final Report, USOE, NDEA, Title VII, Project No. 191, 1965.

Bilodeau, I. M., & Schlosberg, H., "Similarity in Stimulating Conditions as a Variable in Retroactive Inhibition," *Journal of Experimental Psychology* (1951), *41,* 199–204.

Biological Sciences Curriculum Study, *Hormone Control of the Menstrual Cycle in the Human Female.* Boulder, Col.: BSCS, 1965.

———, *Cell Energy Processes Unit Test, Form B.* Boulder, Col.: BSCS, 1968.

———, *Ecology Unit Test, Form B.* Boulder, Col.: BSCS, 1968.

Birnbrauer, J. S., Wolf, M. M., Kidder, J. D., & Tague, C. E., "Classroom Behavior of Retarded Pupils with Token Reinforcement," *Journal of Experimental Child Psychology* (1965), *2,* 219–235.

Bisbicos, E. E., "A Test of a Simplified Technique for Implementing Looping Programs," *Journal of Programed Instruction* (1965), *3,* 15–20.

Bivens, L. W., "Feedback Complexity and Self-Direction in Programmed Instruction," *Psychological Reports* (1964), *14,* 155–160.

Bloom, B. S., *Taxonomy of Educational Objectives.* New York: Longmans, Green, 1956.

Bobrow, S. A., "Memory for Words in Sentences," *Journal of Verbal Learning and Verbal Behavior* (1970), *9,* 363–372.

Bobrow, S. A., & Bower, G. H., "Comprehension and Recall of Sentences," *Journal of Educational Psychology* (1969), *80,* 455–461.

Bousfield, W. A., "The Occurrence of Clustering in the Recall of Randomly Arranged Associates," *Journal of General Psychology* (1953), *49,* 229–240.

Bousfield, W. A., & Cohen, B. H., "The Occurrence of Clustering in the Recall of Randomly Arranged Words of Different Frequencies-of-Usage," *Journal of General Psychology* (1955), *52,* 83–95.

Bousfield, W. A., Cohen, B. H., & Whitmarsh, G. A., "Associative Clustering in the Recall of Words of Different Taxonomic Frequencies of Occurrence," *Psychological Reports* (1958), *4,* 39–44.

Briggs, G. E., "Retroactive Inhibition as a Function of the Degree of Original and Interpolated Learning," *Journal of Experimental Psychology* (1957), *53,* 60–67.

Brown, J. S., *The Motivation of Behavior.* New York: McGraw-Hill, 1961.

Brown, R. W., *Social Psychology.* New York: Free Press, 1965.

———, "Format Location of Programed Instruction Confirmations," *Journal of Programed Instruction* (1966), *3,* 1–4.

Bruner, J. S., *The Process of Education.* Cambridge: Harvard University Press, 1960.

———, "The Act of Discovery," *Harvard Educational Review* (1961), *31,* 21–32.

Bugelski, B. R., & Cadwallader, T. C., "A Reappraisal of the Transfer and Retroaction Surface," *Journal of Experimental Psychology* (1956), *52,* 360–366.

Bulfinch, T., *Mythology: The Age of Fable.* Garden City, N.Y.: Doubleday, 1948.

Buss, A. H., Braden, W., Orgel, A., & Buss, E., "Acquisition and Extinction with Different Verbal Reinforcement Combinations," *Journal of Experimental Psychology* (1956), *52,* 288–295.

Butler, R. A., "The Effect of Deprivation of Visual Incentives on Visual-Exploration Motivation," *Journal of Comparative and Physiological Psychology* (1957), *50,* 177–179.

Butler, R. A., & Harlow, H. F., "Persistence of Visual Exploration in Monkeys," *Journal of Comparative and Physiological Psychology* (1954), *47,* 258–263.

Calvin, A. D., McGuigan, F. J., & Sullivan, M. W., "A Further Investigation of the Relationship Between Anxiety and Classroom Examination Performance," *Journal of Educational Psychology* (1957), *48,* 240–244.

Campbell, V. N., "Bypassing as a Way of Adapting Self-Instruction Programs to Individual Differences," *Journal of Educational Psychology* (1963), *54,* 337–345.

Carmichael, L., & Dearborn, W. F., *Reading and Visual Fatigue.* Boston: Houghton Mifflin Company, 1947.

Carroll, J. B., "On Learning from Being Told," *Educational Psychologist* (March, 1968), *5,* 1, et passim.

Carson, R. L., *The Sea Around Us,* rev. ed. New York: Oxford University Press, 1961.

Cason, H., "Backward Conditioned Eyelid Reactions," *Journal of Experimental Psychology* (1935), *18,* 599–611.

Chall, J. S., *Readability: An Appraisal of Research and Application.* Columbus: Bureau of Educational Research, Ohio State University, 1958.

———, *Learning to Read: The Great Debate.* New York: McGraw-Hill, 1967.

Child, I. L., Storm, T., & Veroff, J., "Achievement Themes in Folk Tales Related to Socialization Practice," in J. W. Atkinson, ed., *Motives in Fantasy, Action, and Society.* Princeton, N.J.: Van Nostrand, 1958.

Cofer, C. N., & Appley, M. H., *Motivation: Theory and Research.* New York: Wiley, 1964.

Cofer, C. N., Bruce, D. R., & Reicher, G. M., "Clustering in Free Recall as a Function of Certain Methodological Variations," *Journal of Experimental Psychology* (1966), *71,* 858–866.

Coleman, E. B., "Developing a Technology of Written Instruction: Some Determiners of the Complexity of Prose," in E. Rothkopf & P. Johnson, eds., *Verbal Learning Research and the Technology of Written Instruction.* New York: Columbia University Teacher's College Press, 1971.

Conant, J. B., *Modern Science and Modern Man.* New York: Columbia University Press, 1952.

Cotton, J. W., "Running Time as a Function of Amount of Food Deprivation," *Journal of Experimental Psychology* (1953), *46,* 188–198.

Coulson, J. E., Estavan, D. P., Melaragno, R. J., & Silberman, H. F., "Effects of Branching in a Computer-Controlled Autoinstructional Device," *Journal of Applied Psychology* (1962), *46,* 389–392.

Craig, R. C., "Directed Versus Independent Discovery of Established Relations," *Journal of Educational Psychology* (1956), *47,* 223–234.

Cremin, L. A., *The Transformation of the School.* New York: Alfred Knopf, 1961.

Crist, R. L., "Overt Versus Covert Responding and Retention by Sixth-Grade Students," *Journal of Educational Psychology* (1966), *57,* 99–101.

Cronbach, L. J., "Processes Affecting Scores on 'Understanding of Others' and 'Assumed Similarity,'" *Psychological Bulletin* (1955), *52,* 177–194.

———, "Evaluation for Course Improvement," *Teachers College Record* (1963), *64,* 672–683.

———, "The Logic of Experiments on Discovery," in L. S. Shulman and E. R. Keislar, eds., *Learning by Discovery: A Critical Appraisal.* Chicago: Rand-McNally, 1966.

———, "How Can Instruction be Adapted to Individual Differences?" in R. M. Gagné, ed., *Learning and Individual Differences.* Columbus, Ohio: Charles E. Merrill Books, 1967.

Crow, J. F., "Genetic Theories and Influences: Comments on the Value of Diversity," in *Environment, Heredity, and Intelligence.* Cambridge, Mass.: *Harvard Educational Review,* 1969.

Dale, E., *Audio-Visual Methods in Teaching.* New York: Henry Holt & Co., 1959.

Dale, E., & Chall, J. S., "A Formula for Predicting Readability," *Educational Research Bulletin* (1948), *27*, 11–20.

Davis, R. B., "Discovery in the Teaching of Mathematics," in L. S. Shulman and E. R. Keislar, eds., *Learning by Discovery: A Critical Appraisal.* Chicago: Rand-McNally, 1966.

Della-Piana, G., "An Experimental Evaluation of Programmed Learning," *Journal of Educational Research* (1962), *55*, 495–501.

DeMott, B., "The Math Wars," in R. W. Heath, ed., *New Curricula.* New York: Harper & Row, 1964.

Dominowski, R. L., "Role of Memory in Concept Learning," *Psychological Bulletin* (1965), *63*, 271–280.

Dowling, R., & Braun, H., "Retention and Meaningfulness of Material," *Journal of Experimental Psychology* (1957), *54*, 213–217.

Downing, J. A., "The i.t.a. (Initial Teaching Alphabet) Reading Experiment," *The Reading Teacher* (1964), *18*, 105–109.

———, *The Initial Teaching Alphabet Explained and Illustrated,* 5th ed. New York: MacMillan, 1966.

Dressel, P. L., ed., *Evaluation in General Education.* Dubuque, Iowa: William C. Brown Co., 1954.

Duell, O. K., & Anderson, R. C., "Pitch Discrimination Among Primary School Children," *Journal of Educational Psychology* (1967), *58*, 315–318.

Dunlap, K., "Are There Any Instincts?" *Journal of Abnormal Psychology* (1919), *14*, 35–50.

Dwyer, F. M., "Adapting Visual Illustrations for Effective Learning," *Harvard Educational Review* (1967), *37*, 250–263.

Ebbinghaus, H., *Memory: A Contribution to Experimental Psychology,* tr. H. A. Ruger and C. E. Bussenius. New York: Teachers College, Columbia University, 1913.

Ebel, R. L., "Behavioral Objectives: A Close Look," *Educational Technology* (November, 1970), *10*, 171–173.

Eigen, L. D., & Margulies, S., "Response Characteristics as a Function of Information Level," *Journal of Programed Instruction* (1963), *2*, 45–54.

Entwisle, D. R., & Huggins, W. H., "Interference in Meaningful Learning," *Journal of Educational Psychology* (1964), *55*, 75–78.

Farber, I. E., "Anxiety as a Drive State," in M. R. Jones, ed., *Nebraska Symposium on Motivation, 1954.* Lincoln: University of Nebraska Press.

Faust, G. W., "The Effects of Prompting in Programed Instruction as a Function of Motivation and Instructions." Unpublished doctoral dissertation. University of Illinois, 1967.

Faust, G. W., & Anderson, R. C., "Effects of Incidental Material in a Programmed Russian Vocabulary Lesson," *Journal of Educational Psychology* (1967), *58*, 3–10.

Ferster, C. B., & Skinner, B. F., *Schedules of Reinforcement.* New York: Appleton-Century-Crofts, 1957.

Fitzgerald, D., & Ausubel, D. P., "Cognitive Versus Affective Factors in the Learning and Retention of Controversial Material," *Journal of Educational Psychology* (1963), *54*, 73–84.

Fleishman, E. A., & Parker, J. F., Jr., "Factors in the Retention and Relearning of Perceptual-Motor Skills," *Journal of Experimental Psychology* (1962), *64*, 215–226.

Frase, L. T., "Learning from Prose: Length of Passage, Knowledge of Results, and Position of Questions," *Journal of Educational Psychology* (1967), *58*, 266–272.

Fries, C. C., *Linguistics and Reading.* New York: Holt, Rinehart & Winston, 1963.

Gagné, R. M., "The Acquisition of Knowledge," *Psychological Review* (1962), *69*, 355–365.

———, *The Conditions of Learning.* New York: Holt, Rinehart & Winston, 1965.

———, "Some Factors in Learning Nonmetric Geometry," *Monographs of the Society for Research in Child Development* (1965), *30*, 42–49.

———, "The Learning of Principles," in H. J. Klausmeier and C. W. Harris, eds., *Analyses of Concept Learning.* New York: Academic Press, 1966.

Gagné, R. M., & Brown, L. T., "Some Factors in the Programming of Conceptual Learning," *Journal of Experimental Psychology* (1961), *62*, 313–321.

Gagné, R. M., Maynor, J. R., Garstens, H. L., & Paradise, N. E., "Factors in Acquiring Knowledge of a Mathematical Task," *Psychological Monograph* (1962), *76* (Whole No. 526).

Gagné, R. M., & Paradise, N. E., "Abilities and Learning Sets in Knowledge Acquisition," *Psychological Monograph* (1961), *75* (Whole No. 518).

Gaite, A. J. H., "A Study of Retroactive Inhibition and Facilitation in Meaningful Verbal Learning." Unpublished doctoral thesis. University of Toronto, 1968.

Ganz, L., & Riesen, A. H., "Stimulus Generalization to Hue in the Dark-Reared Macaque," *Journal of Comparative and Physiological Psychology* (1962), *55*, 92–99.

Gates, A. I., "Recitation as a Factor in Memorizing," *Archives of Psychology* (1917), *26* (Whole No. 40).

Geis, G. L., & Knapp, S., "A Note on Nonfunctional Branching in a Linear Program," *Journal of Programed Instruction* (1963), *2*, 15–17.

Gephart, W. J., & Antonoplos, D. P., "The Effects of Expectancy and Other Research-Biasing Factors," *Phi Delta Kappan* (1969), *10*, 579–583.

Gewirtz, J. L., & Baer, D. M., "The Effect of Brief Social Deprivation on Behaviors for a Social Reinforcer," *Journal of Abnormal and Social Psychology* (1958), *56*, 49–56. (a)

———, "Deprivation and Satiation of Social Reinforcers as Drive Conditions," *Journal of Abnormal and Social Psychology* (1958), *57*, 165–172. (b)

Gibson, E. J., "Learning to Read," *Science* (1965), *148*, 1066–1072.

Gifford, E. M., & Marston, A. R., "Text Anxiety, Reading Rate, and Task Experience," *Journal of Educational Research* (1966), *59*, 303–306.

Gilbert, T. F., "Mathetics: The Technology of Education," *Journal of Mathetics* (1962), *1*, 7–73.

Gilbert, T. H., "Overlearning and the Retention of Meaningful Prose," *Journal of General Psychology* (1957), *56*, 281–289.

Gillooly, W. B., & Furakawa, J., "The Effect of Familiarization and Response Mode on the Programed Learning of Foreign Language Vocabulary." Paper read at the annual meeting of the American Educational Research Association, February, 1968.

Gladis, M., & Braun, H. W., "Age Difference and Retroaction as a Function of Intertask Similarity," *Journal of Experimental Psychology* (1958), *55*, 25–30.

Glaser, R., "Implications of Training Research for Education," in E. R. Hilgard, ed., *Theories of Learning and Instruction.* The 63rd Yearbook of the National Society for the Study of Education. Chicago: University of Chicago Press, 1964.

———, "Adapting the Elementary School Curriculum to Individual Performance." Address delivered at the 1967 Invitational Conference on Testing Problems, New York, October, 1967.

Glaze, J. A., "The Association Value of Nonsense Syllables," *Journal of Genetic Psychology* (1928), *35,* 255–269.

Greeno, J. G., "Paired-Associate Learning with Massed and Distributed Repetitions of Items," *Journal of Experimental Psychology* (1964), *67,* 286–295.

Greenspoon, J., "The Reinforcing Effect of Two Spoken Sounds on the Frequency of Two Responses," *American Journal of Psychology* (1955), *68,* 409–416.

Greenspoon, J., & Ranyard, R., "Stimulus Conditions and Retroactive Inhibition," *Journal of Experimental Psychology* (1957), *53,* 55–59.

Grimes, J. W., & Allinsmith, W., "Compulsivity, Anxiety and School Achievement," *Merrill-Palmer Quarterly* (1961), *7,* 247–271. Also in J. F. Rosenblith and W. Allinsmith, eds., *The Causes of Behavior, II.* Boston: Allyn and Bacon, 1966.

Grisom, R. J., Suedfeld, P., & Vernon, J., "Memory for Verbal Material: Effects of Sensory Deprivation," *Science* (1962), *138,* 429–430.

Gronlund, N. E., *Measurement and Evaluation in Teaching.* New York: The MacMillan Company, 1965.

———, *Constructing Achievement Tests.* Englewood Cliffs, N.J.: Prentice-Hall, 1968.

Guthrie, J. T., "Expository Instruction Versus a Discovery Method," *Journal of Educational Psychology* (1967), *58,* 45–49.

Hall, J. F., "Retroactive Inhibition in Meaningful Material," *Journal of Educational Psychology* (1955), *46,* 47–52.

Harlow, H. F., "Learning and Satiation of Response in Intrinsically Motivated Complex Puzzle Performance by Monkeys," *Journal of Comparative and Physiological Psychology* (1950), *43,* 289–294.

Harris, F. B., Johnston, M. K., Kelley, C. S., & Wolf, M. M., "Effects of Positive Social Reinforcement on Regressed Crawling of a Nursery School Child," *Journal of Educational Psychology* (1964), *55,* 35–41.

Hartman, T. F., Morrison, B. A., & Carlson, M. E., "Active Responding in Programed Learning Materials," *Journal of Applied Psychology* (1963), *47,* 343–347.

Haselrud, G. M., & Meyers, S., "The Transfer Value of Given and Individually Derived Principles," *Journal of Educational Psychology* (1958), *49,* 293–298.

Havighurst, R. J., & Breese, F. H., "Relation Between Ability and Social Status in a Mid-western Community. III. Primary Mental Abilities," *Journal of Educational Psychology* (1947), *38,* 241–247.

Havighurst, R. J., & Janke, L. L., "Relations Between Ability and Social Status in a Mid-western Community. I. Ten-Year-Old Children," *Journal of Educational Psychology* (1944), *35,* 357–368.

Hawkins, R. P., Peterson, R. F., Schweid, E., & Bijou, S. W., "Behavior Therapy in the Home: Amelioration of Problem Parent-Child Relations with the Parent in a Therapeutic Role," *Journal of Experimental Child Psychology* (1966), *4*, 99–107.

Hendrix, G., "A New Clue to Transfer of Training," *Elementary School Journal* (1947), *48*, 197–208.

Hess, E. H., "Ethology: An Approach Toward the Complete Analysis of Behavior," in R. Brown, E. Galanter, E. H. Hess, and G. Mandler, eds., *New Directions in Psychology.* New York: Holt, Rinehart & Winston, 1962.

Hill, K. T., & Sarason, S. B., "The Relation of Test Anxiety and Defensiveness to Test and School Performance Over the Elementary Years: A Further Longitudinal Study," *Monographs of the Society of Research in Child Development* (1966), *31*, Serial No. 104.

Hively, W., "Programming Stimuli in Matching-to-Sample," *Journal of the Experimental Analysis of Behavior* (1962), *5*, 279–298.

———, "Parametric Experiments with a Matching-to-Sample Program," in J. G. Holland and B. F. Skinner, eds., *An Analysis of the Behavioral Processes Involved in Self Instruction with Teaching Machines.* Final Report, USOE, NDEA, Title VII, Project No. 191, 1965.

Hoffman, A. C., "Eye-Movements During Prolonged Reading," *Journal of Experimental Psychology* (1946), *36*, 95–118.

Holland, A. L., & Matthews, J., "Application of Teaching Machine Concepts to Speech Pathology and Audiology," *Asha* (1963), *5*, 474–482.

Holland J. G., "Response Contingencies in Teaching-Machine Programs," *Journal of Programed Instruction* (1965), *3*, 1–8.

Holland, J. G., & Kemp, F. D., "A Measure of Programing in Teaching-Machine Material," *Journal of Educational Psychology* (1965), *56*, 264–269.

Holland, J. G., & Porter, D., "The Influence of Repetition of Incorrectly Answered Items in a Teaching Machine Program," *Journal of the Experimental Analysis of Behavior* (1961), *4*, 305–307.

Holland, J. G., & Skinner, B. F., *The Analysis of Behavior.* New York: McGraw-Hill, 1961.

Homme, L. E., C. de Baca, P. C., Devine, J. V., Steinhorst, R., & Rickert, E. J., "Use of the Premack Principle in Controlling the Behavior of Nursery School Children," *Journal of the Experimental Analysis of Behavior* (1963), *6*, 544.

Honzik, M. P., MacFarlane, J. W., & Allen, L., "The Stability of Mental Test Performance Between Two and Eighteen Years," *Journal of Experimental Education* (1948), *17*, 309–324.

House, B. J., & Zeaman, D., "Miniature Experiments in the Discrimination Learning of Retardates," in L. P. Lipsitt and C. C. Spiker, eds., *Advances in Child Development and Behavior,* Vol. I. New York: Academic Press, 1963.

Hull, C. L., *Principles of Behavior.* New York: Appleton-Century-Crofts, 1943.

Irwin, F., Kaufman, K., Prior, G., & Weaver, H. B., "On Learning Without Awareness of What is Being Learned," *Journal of Experimental Psychology* (1934), *17*, 823–827.

James, W., *Principles of Psychology.* New York: Henry Holt & Co., 1890.

Jenkins, J. G., & Dallenbach, K. M., "Oblivescence During Sleep and Waking," *American Journal of Psychology* (1924), *35*, 605–612.

Jenkins, W. O., & Stanley, J. C., "Partial Reinforcement: A Review and Critique," *Psychological Bulletin* (1950), *47*, 193–234.

Jensen, A. R., "How Much Can We Boost IQ and Scholastic-Achievement," in *Environment, Heredity, and Intelligence.* Cambridge, Mass.: *Harvard Educational Review*, 1969.

Jensen, A. R., & Rohwer, W. P., Jr., "Verbal Mediation in Paired-Associate and Serial Learning," *Journal of Verbal Learning and Verbal Behavior* (1963), *1*, 346–352.

Johnson, D. M., & Stratton, R. P. "Evaluation of Five Methods of Teaching Concepts," *Journal of Educational Psychology* (1966), *57*, 48–53.

Kaess, W., & Zeaman, D., "Positive and Negative Knowledge of Results on a Pressey-Type Punchboard," *Journal of Experimental Psychology* (1960), *60*, 12–17.

Kahn, M., "A Polygraph Study of the Catharsis of Aggression." Unpublished doctoral dissertation. Harvard University, 1960.

Kapfer, P. G., "Behavioral Objectives and the Curriculum Process," *Educational Technology*, (May, 1970), *5*, 14–17.

Kemp, F. D., & Holland, J. G., "Blackout Ratio and Overt Responses in Programed Instruction: Resolution of Disparate Results," *Journal of Educational Psychology* (1966), *57*, 109–114.

Kendler, H. H., "Reflections on the Conference," in L. S. Shulman and E. R. Keislar, eds., *Learning by Discovery: A Critical Appraisal.* Chicago: Rand-McNally, 1966.

Kersh, B. Y., "The Adequacy of 'Meaning' as an Explanation for Superiority of Learning by Independent Discovery," *Journal of Educational Psychology* (1958), *49*, 282–292.

———, "The Motivating Effect of Learning by Directed Discovery," *Journal of Educational Psychology* (1962), *53*, 65–71.

Kilpatrick, W. H., "The Project Method," *Teachers College Record* (1918), *19*, 319–335.

Kimble, G. A., "Conditioning as a Function of the Time Between Conditioned and Unconditioned Stimuli," *Journal of Experimental Psychology* (1947), *37*, 1–15.

Kimble, G. A., Mann, L. I., & Dufort, R. H., "Classical and Instrumental Eyelid Conditioning," *Journal of Experimental Psychology* (1955), *49*, 407–417.

Kittell, J. E., "An Experimental Study of the Effect of External Direction During Learning on Transfer and Retention of Principles," *Journal of Educational Psychology* (1957), *48*, 391–405.

Klausmeier, H. J., & Goodwin, W., *Learning and Human Abilities*, 2nd ed. New York: Harper & Row, 1966.

Krasner, L., "Studies of the Conditioning of Verbal Behavior," *Psychological Bulletin* (1958), *55*, 148–170.

Krasner, L., & Ullmann, L. P., *Research in Behavior Modification.* New York: Holt, Rinehart & Winston, 1965.

Krueger, W. C. F., "The Effect of Overlearning on Retention," *Journal of Experimental Psychology* (1929), *12*, 71–78.

Krumboltz, J. D., "The Nature and Importance of the Required Response in Programed Instruction," *American Educational Research Journal* (1964), *1*, 203–209.

Krumboltz, J. D., & Weisman, R. G., "The Effect of Intermittent Confirmation in Programed Instruction," *Journal of Educational Psychology* (1962), *53*, 250–253.

Lambert, P., Miller, D. M., & Wiley, D. E., "Experimental Folklore and Experimentation: The Study of Programmed Learning in the Wauwatosa Public Schools," *Journal of Educational Research* (1962), *55,* 485–494.

Lee, W., "Supra-Paragraph Prose Structure: Its Specification, Perception, and Effects on Learning," *Psychological Reports* (1965), *17,* 135–144.

Lewis, D., "Positive and Negative Transfer in Motor Learning," *American Psychologist* (1947), *2,* 423. (abstract)

Lloyd, K. E., "Retention of Responses to Stimulus Classes and Specific Stimuli," *Journal of Experimental Psychology* (1960), *59,* 54–59.

Loess, H. B., & Duncan, C. P., "Human Discrimination Learning with Simultaneous and Successive Presentation of Stimuli," *Journal of Experimental Psychology* (1952), *44,* 215–221.

Lublin, S. C., "Reinforcement Schedules, Scholastic Aptitude, Autonomy Need, and Achievement in a Programed Course," *Journal of Educational Psychology* (1965), *56,* 295–302.

Luh, C. W., "The Conditions of Retention," *Psychological Monographs* (1922), *31* (Whole No. 142).

Lumsdaine, A. A., "Assessing the Effectiveness of Instructional Programs," in R. Glaser, ed., *Teaching Machines and Programed Learning, II.* Washington, D.C.: National Education Association, 1965.

Lumsdaine, A. A., Sulzer, R. L., & Kopstein, F. F., "The Effect of Animation Cues and Repetition of Examples on Learning from an Instructional Film," in A. A. Lumsdaine, ed., *Student Response in Programmed Instruction.* Washington, D.C.: National Academy of Sciences—National Research Council, 1961.

Maccoby, N., Michael, D. N., & Levine, S., "Further Studies of Student Participation Procedures in Film Instruction: Review and Preview Covert Practice, and Motivational Interactions," in A. A. Lumsdaine, ed., *Student Response in Programmed Instruction.* Washington, D.C.: National Academy of Sciences—National Research Council, 1961.

Mager, R. F., *Preparing Objectives for Programmed Instruction.* San Francisco: Fearon, 1962.

Mager, R. F., & McCann, J., *Learner-Controlled Instruction.* Palo Alto, Calif.: Varian Associates, 1961.

Mandler, G., & Sarason, S. B., "A Study of Anxiety and Learning," *Journal of Abnormal and Social Psychology* (1952), *47,* 166–173.

Margolius, G. J., & Sheffield, F. D., "Optimum Methods of Combining Practice with Filmed Demonstrations in Teaching Complex Response Sequences: Serial Learning of a Mechanical-Assembly Task," in A. A. Lumsdaine, ed., *Student Response in Programed Instruction.* Washington, D.C.: National Academy of Sciences—National Research Council, 1961.

Markle, S. M., *Good Frames and Bad.* New York: John Wiley & Sons, 1969.

Maslow, A. H., *Motivation and Personality.* New York: Harper, 1954.

McClelland, D. C., *The Achieving Society.* Princeton, N.J.: Van Nostrand, 1961.

McClelland, D. C., Atkinson, J. W., Clark, R. A., & Lowell, E. L., *The Achievement Motive.* New York: Appleton-Century-Crofts, 1953.

———, A Scoring Manual for the Achievement Motive, in J. W. Atkinson, ed., *Motives in Fantasy, Action, and Society.* Princeton, N.J.: Van Nostrand, 1958.

McClelland, D. C., Clark, R. A., Roby, T. B., & Atkinson, J. W., "The Projective

Expression of Needs. IV. The Effect of Need for Achievement on Thematic Apperception," *Journal of Experimental Psychology* (1949), *39,* 242–255. Also in J. W. Atkinson, ed., *Motives in Fantasy, Action, and Society.* Princeton, N.J.: Van Nostrand, 1958.

McDougall, W., *An Introduction to Social Psychology.* London: Methuen, 1908.

McDougall, W. P., "Differential Retention of Course Outcomes in Educational Psychology," *Journal of Educational Psychology* (1958), *49,* 53–60.

McGeoch, J. A. "Forgetting and the Law of Disuse," *Psychological Review* (1932), *39,* 352–370.

McGeoch, J. A., & Irion, A. L., *The Psychology of Human Learning.* New York: Longmans, Green, 1952.

McGeoch, J. A., & McKinney, F., "The Susceptibility of Prose to Retroactive Inhibition," *American Journal of Psychology* (1934), *46,* 429–436.

McKeachie, W. J., "Students, Groups, and Teaching Methods," *American Psychologist* (1958), *13,* 580–584.

———, "Research on Teaching at the College and University Level," in N. L. Gage, ed., *Handbook of Research on Teaching.* Chicago: Rand-McNally, 1963.

McKeachie, W. J., Pollie, D., & Speisman, J., "Relieving Anxiety in Classroom Examinations," *Journal of Abnormal and Social Psychology* (1955), *50,* 93–98.

McKinney, F., "Retroactive Inhibition and Recognition Memory," *Journal of Experimental Psychology* (1935), *18,* 585–598.

McNeil, J. D., "Concomitants of Using Behavioral Objectives in the Assessment of Teacher Effectiveness," *Journal of Experimental Education* (1967), *36,* 69–74.

McTavish, C. L., "*Effect of Repetitive Film Showings on Learning,*" Port Washington, N.Y.: Office of Naval Research, Special Devices Center, 1949.

Mazurkiewicz, A. J., & Tanyzer, H. J., *Early-to-Read i/t/a Program.* New York: i/t/a Publications, 1966.

Mehler, J., "Some Effects of Grammatical Transformation on the Recall of English Sentences," *Journal of Verbal Learning and Verbal Behavior* (1963), *2,* 346–351.

Melaragno, R. J., "Effect of Negative Reinforcement in an Automated Teaching Setting," *Psychological Reports* (1960), *7,* 381–384.

Michael, D. N., & Maccoby, N., "Factors Influencing the Effects of Student Participation on Verbal Learning from Films: Motivating Versus Practice Effects, 'Feedback,' and Overt Versus Covert Responding," in A. A. Lumsdaine, ed., *Student Response in Programed Instruction.* Washington, D.C.: National Academy of Sciences—National Research Council, 1961.

Miller, G. A., "Some Psychological Studies of Grammar," *American Psychologist* (1962), *17,* 748–762.

Minami, H., & Dallenbach, K. M., "The Effect of Activity Upon Learning and Retention in the Cockroach," *American Journal of Psychology* (1946), *59,* 1–58.

Moeller, G., "The CS-UCS Interval in GST Conditioning," *Journal of Experimental Psychology* (1954), *48,* 162–166.

Montague, W. E., Adams, J. A., & Kiess, H. O., "Forgetting and Natural Language Mediation," *Journal of Experimental Psychology* (1966), *72,* 829–833.

Moore, R., & Goldiamond, I., "Errorless Establishment of Visual Discrimination Using Fading Procedures," *Journal of the Experimental Analysis of Behavior* (1964), *7*, 269–272.

Moore, W. J., & Smith, W. I., "Role of Knowledge of Results in Programed Instruction," *Psychological Reports* (1964), *14*, 407–423.

Morgan, Clifford T., & King, Richard A., *Introduction to Psychology.* New York: McGraw-Hill, 1966.

Moulton, R. W., "Notes for a Projective Measure of Fear of Failure," in J. W. Atkinson, ed., *Motives in Fantasy, Action, and Society.* Princeton, N.J.: Van Nostrand, 1958.

Murray, H. A., et al., *Explorations in Personality.* New York: Oxford University Press, 1938.

Mussen, P. H., Conger, J. J., & Kagan, J., *Child Development and Personality.* New York: Harper & Row, 1963.

Naylor, J. C., & Briggs, G. E., "Effects of Task Complexity and Task Organization on the Relative Efficiency of Part and Whole Training Methods," *Journal of Experimental Psychology* (1963), *65*, 217–224.

Newman, E. B., "Forgetting of Meaningful Material During Sleep and Waking," *American Journal of Psychology* (1939), *52*, 65–71.

O'Leary, K. D., & Becker, W. C., "Behavior Modification of an Adjustment Class: A Token Reinforcement Program," *Exceptional Children* (1967), *33*, 637–642.

Oliver, D. W., & Shaver, J. P., *Teaching Public Issues in the High School.* Boston: Houghton Mifflin, 1966.

Oseas, L., & Underwood, B. J., "Studies of Distributed Practice: V. Learning and Retention of Concepts," *Journal of Experimental Psychology* (1952), *43*, 143–148.

Osgood, C. E., "The Similarity Paradox in Human Learning," *Psychological Review* (1949), *56*, 132–143.

Overing, R. L. R., & Travers, R. M. W., "Variation in the Amount of Irrelevant Cues in Training and Test Conditions and the Effect upon Transfer," *Journal of Educational Psychology* (1967), *58*, 62–68.

Paul, G. L., *Insight vs. Desensitization in Psychotherapy.* Stanford, Calif.: Stanford University Press, 1966.

Pavlov, I. P., *Conditioned Reflexes.* (Translated by G. V. Anrep). London: Oxford University Press, 1927.

Perry, H. M., "The Relative Efficiency of Actual and 'Imaginary' Practice in Five Selected Tasks," *Archives of Psychology* (1939), *34* (Whole No. 243).

Peterson, N., "Effect of Monochromatic Rearing on the Control of Responding by Wavelength," *Science* (1962), *136*, 774–775.

Piaget, J., "How Children Form Mathematical Concepts," in R. C. Anderson and D. P. Ausubel, eds., *Readings in the Psychology of Cognition.* New York: Holt, Rinehart & Winston, 1965.

Pierce-Jones, J., "Socio-Economic Status and Adolescents' Interests," *Psychological Reports* (1959), *5*, 683.

Popham, W. J., "The Instructional Objectives Exchange: New Support for Criterion-Referenced Instruction," *Educational Technology* (November, 1970), *10*, 174–175.

Porter, J. M., Jr., "Backward Conditioning of the Eyelid Response," *Journal of Experimental Psychology* (1938), *23*, 403–410.

Postman, L., "Choice Behavior and Recognition," *American Journal of Psychology* (1950), *63,* 576–583.

Postman, L., & Rau, L., "Retention as a Function of the Method of Measurement," *University of California Publications in Psychology* (1957), *8,* 217–270.

Premack, D., "Reinforcement Theory," in D. Levine, ed., *1965 Nebraska Symposium on Motivation.* Lincoln: University of Nebraska Press, 1965.

Reed, H. B., "Factors Influencing the Learning and Retention of Concepts: I. The Influence of Set," *Journal of Experimental Psychology* (1946), *36,* 71–87.

Reynolds, J. H., & Glaser, R., "Effects of Repetition and Spaced Review Upon Retention of a Complex Learning Task," *Journal of Educational Psychology* (1964), *55,* 297–308.

Richardson, J., "Retention of Concepts as a Function of the Degree of Original and Interpolated Learning," *Journal of Experimental Psychology* (1956), *51,* 358–364.

Roderick, M. C., & Anderson, R. C., "A Programed Introduction to Psychology Versus a Textbook-Style Summary of the Same Lesson," *Journal of Educational Psychology* (1968), *59,* 381–387.

Rohwer, W. D., Jr., "Constraint, Syntax and Meaning in Paired-Associate Learning," *Journal of Verbal Learning and Verbal Behavior* (1966), *5,* 541–547.

———, "Social Class Differences in the Role of Linguistic Structures in Paired Associate Learning: Elaboration and Learning Proficiency." Final report, USOE Project No. 5–0605, Contract No. OE6–10–273. November, 1967.

Rosenstock, E. H., Moore, J. W., & Smith, W. I., "Effects of Several Schedules of Knowledge of Results on Mathematical Achievement," *Psychological Reports* (1965), *17,* 535–541.

Rosenthal, R., & Jacobson, L., *Pygmalian in the Classroom.* New York: Holt, Rinehart & Winston, 1968.

Roshal, S. M., "Film-Mediated Learning with Varying Representation of the Task: Viewing Angle, Portrayal of Demonstration, Motion, and Student Participation," in A. A. Lumsdaine, ed., *The Student Response in Programed Instruction.* Washington, D.C.: National Academy of Sciences—National Research Council, 1961.

Rothkopf, E. Z., "Learning from Written Instructive Material: An Exploration of the Control of Inspection Behavior by Test-Like Events," *American Educational Research Journal* (1966), *3,* 241-249.

Rothkopf, E. Z., & Bisbicos, E. E., "Selective Facilitative Effects of Interspersed Questions on Learning from Written Materials," *Journal of Educational Psychology* (1967), *58,* 56–61.

Rothkopf, E. Z., & Coke, E. U., "Repetition Interval and Rehearsal Method in Learning Equivalences from Written Sentences," *Journal of Verbal Learning and Verbal Behavior* (1963), *2,* 406–416.

Royer, J. M., "Inspection Behavior During Verbal Learning." Unpublished MA thesis. University of Illinois, 1969.

Ryans, D. G., *Characteristics of Teachers, Their Description, Comparison, and Appraisal.* Washington, D.C.: American Council on Education, 1960.

Samuels, S. J., "Effects of Simultaneous Versus Successive Discrimination Training on Paired Associate Learning," *Journal of Educational Psychology* (1969), *60,* 46–48.

Sarnoff, I., & Zimbardo, P. G., "Anxiety, Fear and Social Affiliation," *Journal of Abnormal and Social Psychology* (1961), *62*, 356–363.

Sassenrath, J. M., & Garverick, C. M., "Effects of Differential Feedback from Examinations on Retention and Transfer," *Journal of Educational Psychology* (1965), *56*, 259–263.

Sax, G., & Reade, M., "Achievement as a Function of Test Difficulty Level," *American Educational Research Journal* (1964), *1*, 22–25.

Schachter, S., *The Psychology of Affiliation: Experimental Studies of the Sources of Gregariousness.* Stanford: Stanford University Press, 1959.

Schlosberg, H., & Solomon, R. L., "Latency of Response in a Choice Discrimination," *Journal of Experimental Psychology* (1943), *33*, 22–39.

Scriven, M., "The Methodology of Evaluation," in R. Stake, ed., *Perspectives of Curriculum Evaluation.* Chicago: Rand-McNally, 1967.

Sheffield, F. D. "Theoretical Considerations in the Learning of Complex Sequential Tasks from Demonstration and Practice," in A. A. Lumsdaine, ed., *Student Response in Programed Instruction.* Washington, D.C.: National Academy of Sciences—National Research Council, 1961.

Silberman, H. F., *Experimental Analysis of a Beginning Reading Skill.* Santa Monica, Calif.: Systems Development Corporation, 1964.

Skinner, B. F., "The Science of Learning and the Art of Teaching," *Harvard Educational Review* (1954), *24*, 86–97.

———, *Verbal Behavior.* New York: Appleton-Century-Crofts, 1957.

———, *Cumulative Record.* New York: Appleton-Century-Crofts, 1959.

Slamecka, N. J., "Studies of Retention of Connected Discourse," *American Journal of Psychology* (1959), *72*, 409–416.

———, "Retroactive Inhibition of Connected Discourse as a Function of Practice Level," *Journal of Experimental Psychology* (1960), *59*, 104–108.

———, "Proactive Inhibition of Connected Discourse," *Journal of Experimental Psychology* (1961), *62*, 295–301.

———, "Retention of Connected Discourse as a Function of Duration of Interpolated Learning," *Journal of Experimental Psychology* (1962), *63*, 480–486.

Smith, C. P., & Feld, S. "How to Learn the Method of Content Analysis for *n* Achievement, *n* Affiliation, and *n* Power," in J. W. Atkinson, ed., *Motives in Fantasy, Action, and Society.* Princeton, N.J.: Van Nostrand, 1958.

Smith, L. M., & Hudgins, B. B., *Educational Psychology.* New York: Alfred A. Knopf, 1965.

Smith, W. F., & Rockett, F. C., "Test Performance as a Function of Anxiety, Instructor, and Instructions," *Journal of Educational Research* (1958), *52*, 138–141.

Solomon, R. L., "Punishment," *American Psychologist* (1964), *19*, 239–253.

Spence, K. W., "A Theory of Emotionally Based Drive (D) and Its Relation to Performance in Simple Learning Situations," *American Psychologist* (1958), *13*, 131–141.

Spence, K. W., Farber, I. E., & McFann, H. H., "The Relation of Anxiety (Drive) Level to Performance in Competitional and Non-competitional Paired-Associate Learning," *Journal of Experimental Psychology* (1956), *52*, 296–305.

Spence, K. W., Taylor, J., & Ketchel, R., "Anxiety (Drive) Level and Degree of Competition in Paired Associate Learning," *Journal of Experimental Psychology* (1956), *52*, 306–310.

Spielberger, C. D., & DeNike, L. D., "Descriptive Behaviorism Versus Cognitive Theory in Verbal Operant Conditioning," *Psychological Review* (1966), *73*, 306–326.

Sptizer, H. F., "Studies in Retention," *Journal of Educational Psychology* (1939), *30*, 641–656.

Staats, A. W., "A Case In and a Strategy For the Extension of Learning Principles to Problems of Human Behavior," in L. Krasner and L. P. Ullmann, eds., *Research in Behavior Modification.* New York: Holt, Rinehart & Winston, 1965.

———, *Learning, Language, and Cognition.* New York: Holt, Rinehart & Winston, 1968.

Staats, A. W., & Butterfield, W. H., "Treatment of Nonreading in a Culturally Deprived Juvenile Delinquent: An Application of Reinforcement Principles," *Child Development* (1965), *36*, 925–942.

Stake, R. E., "The Countenance of Educational Evaluation," *Teachers College Record* (1967), *68*, 523–540.

Stanley, J. C., *Measurement in Today's Schools.* Englewood Cliffs, N.J.: Prentice-Hall, 1964.

Stephens, J. M., *Psychology of Classroom Learning.* New York: Holt, Rinehart & Winston, 1965.

Stolurow, L. M., & Walker, C. C., "A Comparison of Overt and Covert Response in Programmed Learning," *Journal of Educational Research* (1962), *55*, 421–429.

Suchman, J. R., "The Child and the Inquiry Process," in A. H. Passow, ed., *Intellectual Development: Another Look.* Washington, D.C.: Association for Supervision and Curriculum Development, 1964.

Sullivan, H. J., Baker, R. L., & Schutz, R. E., "Effect of Intrinsic and Extrinsic Reinforcement Contingencies on Learner Performance," *Journal of Educational Psychology* (1967), *58*, 165–169.

Suppes, P., & Ginsberg, R., "Application of a Stimulus Sampling Model to Children's Concept Formation With and Without Overt Correction Responses," *Journal of Experimental Psychology* (1962), *63*, 330–336.

Taylor, J. A., "A Personality Scale of Manifest Anxiety," *Journal of Abnormal and Social Psychology* (1953), *48*, 285–290.

Terrace, H. S., "Discrimination Learning With and Without 'Errors,'" *Journal of the Experimental Analysis of Behavior* (1963), *6*, 1–27. (a)

———, "Errorless Transfer of a Discrimination Across Two Continua." *Journal of the Experimental Analysis of Behavior* (1963), *6*, 223–232. (b)

Thorndike, E. L., *Educational Psychology.* Vol. II.: *The Psychology of Learning.* New York: Teachers College, Columbia University, 1913.

Thorndike, E. L., & Lorge, I., *The Teacher's Word Book of 30,000 Words.* New York: Bureau of Publications, Teachers College, Columbia University, 1944.

Tiemann, P. W., "Student Use of Behaviorally-Stated Objectives to Augment Conventional and Programed Revisions of Televised College Economics Lectures." Paper read at the annual meeting of the American Educational Research Association, Chicago, 1968.

Tiemann, P. W., Paden, D. W., & McIntyre, C. J., *An Application of the Principles of Programed Instruction to a Televised Course in College Economics.* Urbana: University of Illinois, 1966.

Tinbergen, N., *The Study of Instinct.* Oxford: Oxford University Press, 1951.

Tobias, S., & Weiner, M., "Effect of Response Mode on Immediate and Delayed Recall from Programed Materials," *Journal of Programed Instruction* (1963), *2*, 9–13.

Trabasso, T. R., "Stimulus Emphasis and All-or-None Learning in Concept Identification," *Journal of Experimental Psychology* (1963), *65*, 398–406.

Traub, R. E., "Importance of Problem Heterogeneity to Programed Instruction," *Journal of Educational Psychology* (1966), *57*, 54–60.

Travers, R. M. W., *Essentials of Learning,* 2nd ed. New York: MacMillan, 1967.

Travers, R. M. W., Van Wagenen, R. K., Haygood, D. H., & McCormick, M., "Learning as a Consequence of the Learner's Task Involvement under Different Conditions of Feedback," *Journal of Educational Psychology* (1964), *55*, 167–173.

Tyler, R. W., "Permanence of Learning," *Journal of Higher Education* (1933), *4*, 203–204.

Underwood, B. J., "The Effect of Successive Interpolations on Retroactive and Proactive Inhibition," *Psychological Monographs* (1945), *59* (Whole No. 273).

———, "An Orientation for Research on Thinking," *Psychological Review* (1952), *59*, 209–220.

———, "Interference and Forgetting," *Psychological Review* (1957), *64*, 49–60.

———, "Stimulus Selection in Verbal Learning," in C. N. Cofer and B. S. Musgrave, eds., *Verbal Behavior and Learning.* New York: McGraw-Hill, 1963.

———, "Some Relationships Between Concept Learning and Verbal Learning," in H. J. Klausmeier and C. W. Harris, eds., *Analyses of Concept Learning.* New York: Academic Press, 1966.

Underwood, B. J., Ham, M., & Ekstrand, B., "Cue Selection in Paired-Associate Learning," *Journal of Experimental Psychology* (1962), *64*, 405–409.

Underwood, B. J., & Keppel, G., "Retention as a Function of Degree of Learning and Letter-Sequence Interference," *Psychological Monographs* (1963), *77* (Whole No. 567).

Underwood, B. J., & Postman, L., "Extraexperimental Sources of Interference in Forgetting," *Psychological Review* (1960), *67*, 73–95.

Underwood, B. J., & Richardson, J., "Verbal Concept Learning as a Function of Instructions and Dominance Level," *Journal of Experimental Psychology* (1956), *51*, 229–238.

———, "The Influence of Meaningfulness, Intralist Similarity, and Serial Position on Retention," *Journal of Experimental Psychology* (1956), *52*, 119–126.

Underwood, B. J., & Schultz, R. W., *Meaningfulness and Verbal Learning.* Chicago: Lippincott, 1960.

Verplanck, W. S., "The Control of the Content of Conversation: Reinforcement of Statements of Opinion," *Journal of Abnormal and Social Psychology* (1955), *51*, 668–676.

Wallen, N. E., & Travers, R. M. W., "Analysis and Investigation of Teaching Methods," in N. L. Gage, ed., *Handbook of Research on Teaching.* Chicago: Rand-McNally, 1963.

Walters, R. H., & Ray, E., "Anxiety, Social Isolation and Reinforcer Effectiveness," *Journal of Personality* (1960), *28*, 358–367.

Watts, G. H., & Anderson, R. C., "Retroactive Inhibition in Free Recall as a

Function of First- and Second-List Organization," *Journal of Experimental Psychology* (1969), *81*, 595–597.

———, "Effects of Three Types of Inserted Questions on Learning from Prose," *Journal of Educational Psychology* (1971), *62*, 387–394.

Webb, W. B., & Schwartz, M., "Measurement Characteristics of Recall in Relation to the Presentation of Increasingly Large Amounts of Material," *Journal of Educational Psychology* (1959), *50*, 63–65.

Weber, M., *The Protestant Ethic and the Rise of Capitalism* (1904), tr. T. Parsons. New York: Charles Scribners Sons, 1930.

Webster's Third New International Dictionary. Springfield, Mass.: Merriam, 1964.

Wert, J. E., "Twin Examination Assumptions," *Journal of Higher Education* (1937), *8*, 136–140.

Wertheimer, M., *Productive Thinking*. New York: Harper, 1945.

White, C. T., & Schlosberg, H., "Degree of Conditioning of the GSR as a Function of the Period of Delay," *Journal of Experimental Psychology* (1952), *56*, 339–343.

White, R. W., "Motivation Reconsidered: The Concept of Competence," *Psychological Review* (1959), *66*, 297–333.

Williams, J. P., "Comparison of Several Response Modes in a Review Program," *Journal of Educational Psychology* (1963), *54*, 253–260.

———, "Effectiveness of Constructed-Response and Multiple-Choice Programing Modes as a Function of Test Mode," *Journal of Educational Psychology* (1965), *56*, 111–117.

Wilson, A. B., "Social Stratification and Academic Achievement," in A. H. Passow (Ed.), *Education in Depressed Areas*. New York: Teachers College Press, Columbia University, 1963.

Wilson, M. C., "The Effect of Amplifying Material Upon Comprehension," *Journal of Experimental Education* (1948), *13*, 5–8.

Winterbottom, M. R., "The Relation of Need for Achievement to Learning Experiences in Independence and Mastery," in J. W. Atkinson, ed., *Motives in Fantasy, Action, and Society*. Princeton, N.J.: Van Nostrand, 1958.

Witmer, H. L., "Children and Poverty Children," *Children* (1964), *2*, 207–213.

Wittgenstein, L., *Philosophical Investigations*. Oxford: B. Blackwell, 1958.

Wittrock, M. C., "Verbal Stimuli in Concept Formation: Learning by Discovery," *Journal of Educational Psychology* (1963), *54*, 183–190.

———, "The Learning by Discovery Hypothesis," in L. S. Shulman and E. R. Keislar, eds., *Learning by Discovery: A Critical Appraisal*. Chicago: Rand-McNally, 1966.

Wittrock, M. C., & Twelker, P. A., "Prompting and Feedback in the Learning, Retention and Transfer of Concepts," *British Journal of Educational Psychology* (1964), *34*, 10–18.

Worthen, B. R., "Discovery and Expository Task Presentation in Elementary Mathematics," *Journal of Educational Psychology Monograph Supplement* (1968), *59*, No. 1, Part 2.

Wrightsman, L. S., Jr., "The Effects of Anxiety, Achievement Motivation, and Task Importance upon Performance on an Intelligence Test," *Journal of Educational Psychology* (1962), *53*, 150–156.

Yerkes, R. M., & Margulis, S., "The Method of Pavlov in Animal Psychology," *Psychological Bulletin* (1909), *6*, 257–273.

Zacharias, J. R., & White, S., "The Requirements for Major Curriculum Revision," in R. W. Heath, ed., *New Curricula.* New York: Harper & Row, 1964.

Zimmerman, J., & Ferster, C. B., "Intermittent Punishment of S^{Δ} Responding in Matching to Sample," *Journal of the Experimental Analysis of Behavior* (1963), *6,* 349–356.

Author Index

Subject Index

ans. 10

definition

11

A complete behavioral definition states (a) ______________________________, under specified (b) ______________, according to a certain (c)______________________________.

Turn to page **25**

---

ans. 30

condition (proviso, restriction)

31

The principal verb in a behavioral objective should

____.

Turn to page **25**

---

ans. 49

The statement tells what the teacher will do ("acquaint . . . participants") rather than what the students should be able to do. The statement is really a course description, and not a very clear one at that, since it leaves the reader in the dark about the nature of the "principles" and "theories" to be presented.

Turn to page **25**

ans. 1

In your own words:

be able to read the paragraph.

2

The test for deciding whether a person "knows" how to do something is whether under the proper conditions he ______ the appropriate something.

Turn to page **26**

ans. 21

(b)

22

The key word in a behavioral objective is the main verb, which should specify some active, observable ______________ on the part of the student.

Turn to page **26**

ans. 41

objectives

42

"This course covers topics such as atomic and molecular structure, properties and thermodynamics of gases, liquids, crystals, phase equilibria, surface chemistry, and chemical kinetics."

The preceding statement is a

______________________________.

Turn to page **26**

ans. 11

(a) what the person is to do or say (behavior, actions)
(b) conditions
(c) (minimum) standard (of performance)

12

When an educational objective is defined in terms of what the student should be able to ______, the statement is called a *behavioral objective.*

Turn to page **27**

ans. 31

In your own words:

specify a kind of active, observable behavior on the part of the student.

32

Typewriting performance can be described in specific numerical terms, such as words typed per minute, number of errors per page. In many other areas, such as the fluency with which a child reads out loud, it is (a) __________ (more, less) difficult to be specific about characteristics of performance. In the preceding statement, (b) __________ refers to reading (or speaking) at an appropriate rate of speed with an acceptably small number of hesitations and misarticulations.

Turn to page **27**

50

How do the following three objectives differ from one another?

(a) "The student should be able to solve quadratic equations."
(b) "The student should be able to solve quadratic equations containing one unknown."
(c) "The student should be able to solve quadratic equations containing one unknown, when the equations are presented in canonical form, without consulting the teacher or a reference book. The student should solve equations involving small integer roots ($X < 10$) with paper and pencil only. A slide rule or tables may be employed otherwise."

Turn to page **27**

ans. 2

does (or says)

3

Taking a philosophy examination without hidden notes or other aids is one of the *conditions* that a professor of philosophy would insist upon before agreeing that the results of the test show that a student ____________ philosophy.

Turn to page **28**

---

ans. 22

behavior (action)

23

"... the child should be able to read correctly any printed material, provided its difficulty level does not exceed that of a third-grade primer."

Underline the phrase that describes a *condition* of the child's reading performance.

Turn to page **28**

---

ans. 42

course description

Note: It is *not* a behavioral objective since it describes what topics the course covers and not what the desired behavioral outcomes of the course are.

43

____

____

specify desired terminal behavior.

Turn to page **28**